The China Journals

The China Journals

Ideology and Intrigue in the 1960s

Hugh Trevor-Roper

edited by
Richard Davenport-Hines

BLOOMSBURY ACADEMIC
LONDON · NEW YORK · OXFORD · NEW DELHI · SYDNEY

BLOOMSBURY ACADEMIC
Bloomsbury Publishing Plc
50 Bedford Square, London, WC1B 3DP, UK
1385 Broadway, New York, NY 10018, USA
29 Earlsfort Terrace, Dublin 2, Ireland

BLOOMSBURY, BLOOMSBURY ACADEMIC and the Diana logo
are trademarks of Bloomsbury Publishing Plc

First published in Great Britain 2020
Reprinted 2020, 2021

Cover design: Terry Woodley
Cover images: Parade of youth during the National Day in Beijing, China on
October 5, 1965. (Photo by Keystone-France \ Gamma-Rapho via Getty Images)
and Shutterstock

A catalogue record for this book is available from the British Library.

ISBN: HB: 978-1-3501-3605-2
         ePDF: 978-1-3501-3604-5
         eBook: 978-1-3501-3603-8

Typeset by Integra Software Services Pvt. Ltd.
Printed and bound in Great Britain

To find out more about our authors and books visit www.bloomsbury.com
and sign up for our newsletters.

This collection of writings by Hugh Trevor-Roper
1914–2003
Fellow of Oriel College, Oxford 1957–80
is dedicated to the memory of

Jeremy Catto   Mark Whittow
1939–2018   1957–2017
Fellow of Oriel 1970–2006   Provost-Elect of Oriel 2017

Contents

List of Illustrations   viii

Acknowledgements   x

A Note on the Text   xii

List of Abbreviations   xiii

Introduction   1

Part 1 China, 1965   57

Part 2 London and Oxford, 1965   133

Part 3 History of a Front-Organisation, 1966: The Suppressed
Encounter Article   151

Part 4 Taiwan and Cambodia, 1967   177

Appendix A In Others' Words: Peking and London   233

Appendix B Trevor-Roper's Companions in China   243

Bibliography   253

Index   257

Illustrations

1   Hugh Trevor-Roper at the time of his election as Regius Professor of Modern History at Oxford, 1957 (Godfrey Argent, © National Portrait Gallery, London)

2   Mary Adams at BBC television centre at Alexandra Palace, 1949 (Photo by Bert Hardy/Hulton Archive/Getty Images)

3   Robert Bolt at the time of his sell-out play, *A Man For All Seasons*, 1960 (Photo by Jeremy Grayson/*Radio Times*/Getty Images)

4   Ernie Roberts at the wheel of his car (Working Class Movement Library, Salford)

5   Lady Alexandra Haig (afterwards Trevor-Roper), 1939 (Bassano; © National Portrait Gallery, London)

6   Joseph Needham, chairman of the British-China Friendship Association, which was proscribed by the Labour Party, and then of the Society for Anglo-Chinese Understanding, 1949 (Walter Stoneman, © National Portrait Gallery, London)

7   Joan Robinson, a delegate at the Moscow Trade Conference, and a zealous supporter of Maoist economic planning and social engineering, 1959 (Walter Bird; © National Portrait Gallery, London)

8   Lord Boyd-Orr, President of the communist front organization called the British Council for the Promotion of International Trade, 1942 (© National Portrait Gallery, London)

9   The Oxford physicist Nicholas Kurti, Trevor-Roper's ally and confidante in SACU intrigues, 1989 (© Godfrey Argent Studio/Royal Society)

10 Imperial Palace, Peking (Public domain)

11 Chinese garage, Beckenham, which Ernie Roberts likened to the Imperial Palace (Public domain)

Acknowledgements

Judith Curthoys is the archivist nonpareil who enabled me to consult the Dacre papers at Christ Church, Oxford. I also thank the staff of the Bodleian Library, Oxford; Cambridge University Library; the Hoover Institution, Stanford University; King's College, Cambridge; the National Archives, Kew; the School of Oriental and African Studies, London; the State Library of New South Wales; and the Working-Class Movement Library, Salford. The amenities of the London Library were once again indispensable to my work. My work on various collections of private papers held in the Bodleian was undertaken when I was the beneficiary of the Visiting Fellowship scheme at All Souls College, Oxford.

I am grateful for material or advice furnished by Tom Buchanan, of Kellogg College, Oxford; Youssef Cassis, of the European University Institute, Florence; Patric Dickinson, Clarenceux King of Arms; Simon Ertz, of the University of Stanford at Berkeley; Henry Hardy, of Wolfson College, Oxford; Mike Luft, of Oldham United Against Racism and of the Anti-Nazi League; Jeffrey Hackney, of Wadham College, Oxford; James Howard-Johnston, of Corpus Christi College, Oxford; Simon Malloch, of the University of Nottingham; Rana Mitter, of St Cross College, Oxford; Francis Pike; Frederic Raphael; Adam Sisman; Tom Stacey; John Tallon, QC, of Pump Court Tax Chambers; Hugo Vickers, Captain of the Lay Stewards of St George's Chapel, Windsor; Peter Wellby; and Edward Wilson, of Worcester College, Oxford. Above all I am grateful to Graham Perry, for a long, candid interview in January 2019.

I thank Nicholas Garland for his consent to my use of a letter written by his mother Peggy Garland; Sara Holdsworth for permission to quote from the letters of her mother Valerie Pearl; and Jane Reilly, who has once again allowed me to quote from the unpublished memoirs of her father Sir Patrick Reilly. Extracts from the unpublished correspondence of Sir Isaiah Berlin are published with the agreement of the trustees of the Isaiah Berlin Literary Trust.

This is the fourth collection of Trevor-Roper's letters and journals that I have edited or co-edited. It has been enriched and honed by the patient criticism of Trevor-Roper's literary executor Blair Worden. I thank him for trusting me with this work, and for improving it by his careful reading, reflection and reasoning. His temperance has restrained my tendencies to excess. My admiring gratitude to my three friends who have been trustees of the Lord Dacre of Glanton Charitable Trust, †Jeremy Catto, James Howard-Johnston and Sir Noel Malcolm, is hefty, fathomless and the utmost pleasure to acknowledge.

Le Meygris, 15 January 2019

A Note on the Text

Trevor-Roper used the Wade-Giles system of transliteration to spell the names of Chinese people and places. This was the system devised in the nineteenth century, and used throughout the English-speaking world for most of the twentieth. The *pinyin* system of transliteration was adopted by China in 1958, but did not become prevalent in the international community for twenty years. Trevor-Roper's usage was neither a mannerism nor an intentional act of cultural aggression. I have tried to maintain consistency with it.

In my editorial introduction and annotations, I prefer to use names that are entrenched in English usage, such as Taoism, Confucius, Peking, Kuomintang, rather than their *pinyin* versions. Similarly, Mao Zedong, Zhou Enlai and other *pinyin* names of individuals were unknown to Trevor-Roper when he kept these journals. It is as unthinkable to change them as to try to improve his punctuation.

I have, however, silently corrected a few misspellings of proper names: it seemed pedantic to gloss insignificant aural slips. I have modified two adjectives and one noun that might be libellous. And I have cut from Part 4 some mundanities about travel arrangements.

Abbreviations

AEU	Amalgamated Engineering Union
BBC	British Broadcasting Corporation
BCFA	British-China Friendship Association
BCPIT	British Council for the Promotion of Foreign Trade
CIA	Central Intelligence Agency, USA
CND	Campaign for Nuclear Disarmament
CPA	Chinese People's Association for Cultural Relations with Foreign Countries
CPGB	Communist Party of Great Britain
CPGBML	Communist Party of Great Britain (Marxist-Leninist)
FBA	Fellow of the British Academy
FBI	Federal Bureau of Investigation, USA
FCO	Foreign & Commonwealth Office
FO	Foreign Office
FRS	Fellow of the Royal Society
IRD	Information Research Department

JIC	Joint Intelligence Committee
KMT	Kuomintang (Chinese nationalist party)
LSE	London School of Economics
MI	Military Intelligence
NATO	North Atlantic Treaty Organisation
NKVD	People's Commissariat for Internal Affairs, Russia
OSS	Office of Strategic Studies, USA
SACU	Society for Anglo-Chinese Understanding
PPE	politics, philosophy and economics (Oxford)
PRC	People's Republic of China (mainland China)
RAB	Radio Analysis Bureau
ROC	Republic of China (Taiwan)
SIGINT	signals intelligence
SIS	Secret Intelligence Service
SOAS	School of African and Oriental Studies, London
SS	Schutzstaffel, Germany
UNESCO	United Nations Scientific, Educational & Cultural Organisation
UNRRA	United Nations Relief & Rehabilitation Administration

INTRODUCTION

Most of Hugh Trevor-Roper's writings were on European subjects. His command of languages, although formidable, was restricted to European tongues and their classical antecedents. Yet his historical enquiries, which recognized no boundaries of time, likewise acknowledged no limits of geography. Interested in non-European civilizations for themselves, he was also drawn to them by his instinct for historical comparison and by his belief that the distinctiveness of European history can be grasped only by enlarged perspectives. Thus he encouraged his friends to read Edward Evans-Pritchard's pioneering work of African anthropology, *Witchcraft, Oracles and Magic among the Azande* (1937), which showed a system of rational consistency and coherence totally different from that of Christian Europe; and relished Robin Zaehner's *The Dawn and Twilight of Zoroastrianism* (1961), which led him to think comparatively about the great monotheisms, Judaism, Christianity and Islam.[1]

Of non-European civilizations it was the Chinese that interested him most. He was captivated by the successive volumes of *Science and Civilisation in China* by the biochemist and historian Joseph Needham, which began publication in 1954. During an otherwise hostile review of R. H. Tawney's collection of essays *The Attack*, he praised 'a happy essay on China, in whose "medieval" unchanging peasant society Professor Tawney is emotionally at home'.[2] In 1959, in a long and admiring review of Arthur Waley's *The Opium War through Chinese Eyes*, he explored the conflicts of power and mentalities between the nineteenth-century British and Chinese worlds.[3] In 1965, the

---

1 *One Hundred Letters of Hugh Trevor-Roper*, ed. Davenport-Hines and Sisman (Oxford: Oxford University Press, 2014), pp. 205, 325, 358–9; Trevor-Roper, 'An Old Religion's Fire Burns Low', *Sunday Times*, 3 September 1961.

2 Trevor-Roper, 'Fifty Years of Change', *Books of the Month*, February 1953.

3 Trevor-Roper, 'Through Eastern Eyes', *Reporter*, 2 April 1959.

year of his visit to the People's Republic of China (PRC) which is recorded in the diary reproduced as Part One of this book, his *The Rise of Christian Europe* carried an excursus on the contacts and differences between Europe and China in Europe's later middle ages.[4] During the visit he asked historians at the University of Peking for their views of the Hungarian-French historian Étienne Balázs, whose studies of Chinese bureaucracy and civilization he admired and who had placed the 'Great Leap Forward', the abruptly transformative initiative of Mao's state in 1958–62, within a conspectus of Chinese history from the early imperial dynasties. In 1976 he returned to these themes in essay-reviews of the letters of an Australian who had been *The Times* correspondent in Peking until 1912, and of an Ulsterman who headed the Chinese maritime customs until 1906.[5] His interest in these runs of correspondence was aroused by the work for his biography, published in the same year, of the remittance man, forger and fantasist Sir Edmund Backhouse, who lived in Peking from 1899 until his death in 1944.[6] In 1977, in a course that he taught at Boulder, Colorado, on European intellectual traditions since Herodotus, Trevor-Roper included, by way of instructive comparison, a lecture on Chinese political thought and historiography.[7] In 1983 he steeped himself in the account left by the nineteenth-century missionary the abbé Huc of his daring incognito travels across China and of his encounter with the Chinese presence in Tibet.[8] In 1985 he wrote about Matteo Ricci, the Jesuit who had begun his missionary work in China four hundred years earlier.[9]

Trevor-Roper, who continuously meditated on modern global politics, was interested in China's present as well as its past. To his mind it was a public duty of historians to illuminate the present by bringing a historical dimension to the interpretation of it. In an essay of 1960 he placed recent upheavals in China and Cuba alongside a succession of revolutions, in Savonarola's Florence, in

---

4 Trevor-Roper, *The Rise of Christian Europe* (London: Thames & Hudson, 1965), pp. 23–4, 177–82.

5 Trevor-Roper, 'An Imperialist's Progress', *New York Review of Books*, 10 June 1976, and 'The Customs of the Country', 14 October 1976.

6 Trevor-Roper, *A Hidden Life: the enigma of Sir Edmund Backhouse* (London: Macmillan, 1976); *Hermit of Peking: the hidden life of Sir Edmund Backhouse* (New York: Knopf, 1977).

7 Christ Church, Oxford, Dacre papers 2/6.

8 Trevor-Roper, *One Hundred Letters*, pp. 271–2.

9 Trevor-Roper, 'A Spiritual Conquest?', *New York Review of Books*, 13 June 1985, reprinted in Trevor-Roper, *From Counter-Reformation to Glorious Revolution* (London: Martin Secker & Warburg, 1992), pp. 1–14.

Calvin's Geneva, and subsequently in France, America and Russia.[10] In the two years after his visit to China in 1965 he wrote two articles on the Maoist regime, which he set in the perspective of the nation's past.[11] He regretted the West's indifference to the history and present condition of 'the oldest and greatest civilization of Asia', which since 1949 had undergone a transformation that he found 'staggering' in its completeness. Communist China presented him with a puzzle. As a rule, he believed that the continuities of history survive, even if only below the surface, the most radical ruptures. Yet in China 'the breach with the past is, or seems, absolute'. 'In Russia a tradition of tyranny links the Bolsheviks with the Tsars. In Germany a tradition of militarism linked Hitler with Prussia.' China by contrast had renounced its inheritance, with all its complexity and sophistication. The profundity of the change was reflected in the arts. The culture of previous ages had displayed 'a gentle self-ridicule, a humorous recognition of the insignificance of man and the absurdity of his pretensions. When we look at classical Chinese paintings we see the giant, immutable, unconquerable forms of nature towering upwards, while puny human figures scurry to and fro at the bottom of the canvas.' Now a 'totalitarian megalithic' architecture surrendered ancient scepticism to confident doctrinal slogans, and 'athletic Chinese workers' were shown 'defiantly carrying red flags to the tops of conquered mountain-peaks'.[12]

During Trevor-Roper's visit to the PRC every impulse of his mind and temperament rebelled against the drab uniformity and unrelieved indoctrination of Mao's state. The moments of delight and wonder which the diary records are prompted by his glimpses of the historic China: of social and artistic legacies which could only be viewed, as through a curtain, on the constricting terms of a regime that was determined to misrepresent or forget them. Yet revulsion was not his only response. He could not but admire the scale and energy of the communist achievement. Admittedly it had been won through the suppression of free thought, which offended the core of his beliefs. But whereas the class revolution in Russia had required reigns of terror for its continuance, the Maoist revolution seemed at the time of Trevor-Roper's visit in October–November 1965 to have won broad national support (the outbreak of the Great

---

10 Trevor-Roper, 'Puritans – from Calvin to Castro', *New York Times Magazine*, 20 March 1960.

11 Trevor-Roper, 'The Sick Mind of China', *Sunday Times*, 31 October 1965; 'China, The Revolution Devours its Children', *Illustrated London News*, 21 January 1967 (reprinted as 'Understanding Mao: or, Look Back to Stalin', *New York Times Magazine*, 12 February 1967).

12 Trevor-Roper, 'The Sick Mind of China'.

Proletarian Cultural Revolution was some months in the future). Previously China had for two centuries been supine prey to European economic exploitation. After the revolution of 1911–12, which dethroned the imperial dynasty and created a republic, the nation succumbed to civil dissension and to the humiliations of the war against Japan in 1937–42. By contrast the revolution of 1949 had been triumphant. As Trevor-Roper acknowledged, the communist regime reorganized the whole basis of Chinese society and created 'a new nation, a great power of the future, 700 million strong'. He wanted to know how it had been done. He also wondered whether it could last. The Maoist doctrine of 'permanent revolution' seemed impossible to him, for humanity cannot always live 'at white heat'. He saw Mao's achievement as the product of a generation which had been formed by its own experiences and would yield to another, formed by different ones. During his visit to China, and afterwards, he looked for the cracks.

In the essay of 1960 which included reflections on China he qualified them with the admission that he had not visited the country and was dependent on the impressions of others. Always he valued the evidence of one's eyes for historical and political understanding. Since 1947, as a special correspondent for the *Observer* and then *The Sunday Times*, he had visited France, Italy, Czechoslovakia, Germany, Israel, Morocco, Iran, the Soviet Union and Mexico. After 1965 he would make similar visits to Portugal and Pakistan. Even when he was not travelling on behalf of newspapers, he liked to record his experiences either in letters to his intimates or in journals which served as a hoard of his impressions. Thus, during his visits to communist Romania and Bulgaria in 1967–73, he kept diaries which resemble those in the present volume (and which are to be published as *The Balkan Journals*). All the writings produced by his travels were imbued with historical perspectives.

Yet travel to China was impossible without official blessing. The obtaining of visas became harder after 1957, when, in reaction against the '100 Flowers' liberalization movement, the muzzling of heresy at home was matched by the ever more frequent refusal of travel visas, even to people who had been allowed them previously. People likely to write about China were especially vulnerable to exclusion. Visas for journalists were mostly given to 'fellow-travellers' who could be trusted to reproduce without critical assessment the statements of PRC officials that Maoist policies were bringing bounty and health to hundreds of millions of people. The PRC liked visitors to be ignorant and gullible. The less they knew about Maoist China the freer they were to project utopian fantasies onto it. Thus favour was given to the Italian who presented the PRC as 'the incarnation of a new world civilization', making 'an unprecedented leap into history', under the leadership of the 'anti-dogmatic and anti-authoritarian Mao'.[13]

After 1949 most foreign residents were forced to leave mainland China. The few remaining outsiders were Maoists who spread misinformation. Perhaps the most notorious were the anti-Western journalists Wilfred Burchett and Alan Winnington.[14] David Crook, who had spied for the Soviet secret police (NKVD) on Trotskyites during the Spanish Civil War and afterwards in Shanghai, taught English at the Peking First Foreign Languages Institute from 1949, and reported the PRC's agricultural communes in idealized terms.[15] Israel Epstein, the editor of the Peking-based *China Today* and also probably a former NKVD spy,[16] and the New Zealander Rewi Alley, sometime inspector of sweat-shops in the International Settlement at Shanghai, were two other devotees.[17] For those residents nothing important could be amiss under Maoism. 'Can you, who knew something of the early struggle of the Chinese people to "stand up" after centuries of exploitation and aggression, really imagine China as an aggressor?' Alley demanded in 1952 of an Englishman, Michael Lindsay, who had worked with communist troops behind Japanese lines and been fêted by Mao but who, Alley thought, was backsliding from his Maoist sympathies. 'If only you could see it all as I have. It is China reborn in the old religious sense, and strange as it may seem … it is the Godless communist party which has led the way to this rebirth.'[18]

*

13 Richard Wolin, *The Wind from the East: French intellectuals, the Cultural Revolution and the legacy of the 1960s* (Oxford: Princeton University Press, 2010), p. 124.

14 Alan Winnington, *Breakfast with Mao: memoirs of a foreign correspondent* (London: Lawrence & Wishart, 1986).

15 See Crook's *Revolution in a Chinese Village: Ten Mile Inn* (London: Routledge & Kegan Paul, 1959), and *The First Years of Yangyi Commune* (London: Routledge & Kegan Paul, 1966). He was a friend of two SACU officials, Roland Berger and Derek Bryan.

16 See Epstein's *From Opium War to Liberation* (Peking: New World Press, 1956), pp. 129–30, and *The Unfinished Revolution in China* (Bombay: People's Publishing, 1947).

17 SACU's chairman Joseph Needham counted Alley 'among my half-dozen immortals' (Stuart and Roma Gelder, *Long March to Freedom* (London: Hutchinson, 1962), p. 196).

18 Michael Lindsay, *China and the Cold War* (Melbourne: Melbourne University Press, 1955), pp. xi–xii.

In March 1965 Trevor-Roper agreed to be a sponsor of a newly formed Society for Anglo-Chinese Understanding (SACU). In May he was nominated to its council of management, but, overcommitted as always, gave scant attention to the body. He was therefore surprised to be telephoned in September by Derek Bryan, SACU's secretary, with an invitation to replace Sir Maurice Bowra in a small group that was being mustered to visit China with Peking's approval. He forthwith dropped his existing commitments and took the chance. SACU's leadership soon came to rue their ill-considered choice of him as Bowra's substitute: he was disappointed by the sequel. As he recounted in a long article for *The Sunday Times* after his return:

> It takes some time to recover from a visit to China. The immediate frustrations are overwhelming, and any man who agrees, as I did, to go on a 'delegation' invited by a Chinese government agency should take care to protect himself before starting. We were well looked after materially. We were transported, housed, fed in comfort. But to be beset, for three weeks, by ignorant 'guides'; to be severed, apparently on purpose, from all intelligent contact; to be drenched daily with identical tabloid propaganda adapted to the minds of peasant children – this is a terrible fate, hardly compensated even by the most generous hospitality.[19]

Trevor-Roper, to whom Anglo-Chinese understanding was a laudable, indeed necessary principle, found it thwarted on both sides. The trouble began within the English delegation. He knew one of his three companions already: he and the playwright Robert Bolt, the author of *A Man for All Seasons*, had first met on 11 June 1963, when they appeared together on a television discussion programme, *Dinner Party*, chaired by Malcolm Muggeridge. In Peking, Bolt and Trevor-Roper were bonded by their irritation with their other English companions, Mary Adams (a vice-chairman of SACU, and one of the non-communists whose presence made it effective as a communist front organization) and the trade unionist Ernie Roberts, who had been expelled from the CPGB but still hankered for proletarian revolution. Both Adams and Roberts, despite being stalwarts of SACU, seemed indifferent to Chinese society and culture and projected parochial English values onto it. His diary's depiction of their responses has an aspect of social comedy, though in fairness to them

---

19 Trevor-Roper, 'The Sick Mind of China'.

it should be said that they in turn cannot have found him easy. He had no small talk. His personality, so ebullient when he was socially and intellectually at ease, would freeze in the presence of people he found unsympathetic. Biographical sketches of his three companions can be found in Appendix B.

On the Chinese side Trevor-Roper found understanding impermeably refused. Everywhere he encountered the assumption that Western thought, being the product of a corrupt social system, was inevitably and incorrigibly stuck in ideological error. The Chinese, he noted, were interested in using the English language and Western technology (which is why scientists were disproportionately well-represented among the foreigners permitted to visit), but discounted English and European thought and culture and were sure that while they had nothing to learn from their visitors, they had everything to teach them. Trevor-Roper's experience was a common one among foreign guests in China. On excursions to farm collectives and factories, visitors were subjected to commentaries of mind-numbing monotony. First there would be a preamble about the 'feudal' conditions under the previous regime of the Nationalist People's Party (Kuomintang; KMT) which Mao had overthrown. The next section would hail the 'Liberation' of 1949 and the obstacles the workers had overcome. Finally came the peroration: a deluge of triumphalist statistics, with production figures tripling, quadrupling, rising tenfold. If the distinguished French journalist Lucien Bodard stopped recording the figures in his *carnets*, his Chinese interpreter-guide, looking over his shoulder, would nag him to resume. The reproduction of voluminous statistics became a staple component of visitors' records. In 1955 Simone de Beauvoir accumulated 501 pages of notes about dams, bridges and other symbols of the PRC's modernity. In 1977 Roland Barthes kept notebooks registering exact statistics about machine-tools output, apple crops, maize yields, breast-feeding, the number of spindles in a textile factory, the total of seats in a volley-ball stadium. One cannot imagine even the most persistent of guides cajoling Trevor-Roper into noting statistical tallies.

To the Belgian sinologist Pierre Ryckmans, who wrote of his visits to the PRC under the alias Simon Leys, the experiences of political-cultural tourists were akin to indentured labour. 'Anything that might be unpredictable, unexpected, spontaneous, or improvised is ruthlessly eliminated,' he wrote. 'The visitors' programs are arranged to keep them on the go from dawn to late at night.' The Maoist authorities shrank China, 'that immense and varied universe, for the exploration of which, however superficial, a lifetime is inadequate', to a constricted area. Only a dozen or so of China's hundreds of cities were open to visitors, as were under a dozen villages selected from tens of thousands across the country: 'always the same ones' and only 'interesting in the limited way of agricultural pavilions at an international fair'. As with districts, so with the population. About sixty individuals out of eight hundred million Chinese were permitted to meet foreign visitors. 'The literary world is represented by two or three writers, always the same, who take care of the visiting men of letters; the same is true of scientists, scholars and so on,' Leys found. Requests by visitors to meet some artist, writer or scholar were parried, unless the desired acquaintance were, as he put it, among 'those few pathetic mummies who have been cleared to be full-time public relations men'.[20]

Foreign delegations were kept isolated from world news. When Michael Croft, founder of the National Youth Theatre, visited the PRC in 1956, at the time of Soviet military action in Hungary and of the Anglo-French military expedition into Egypt, he found that in every Peace Hotel where his group stayed, the radio-set was out of order or had been removed. Hotel staff discouraged guests from fraternizing with members of other foreign delegations, and patrolled corridors to deter peripatetic guests. After Croft and a Spaniard visited the bedroom of some Hungarians for political conversations, they were peremptorily moved to another hotel.[21]

Chinese intellectual life was imprisoned by Marxist formulae. The shut minds of Maoists disillusioned Michael Lindsay (son of the Master of Balliol College, Oxford, and inheritor of his barony). Their formulaic responses were typified by the party theorist who, hearing him criticize the ongoing Soviet Russian blockade of Berlin in 1949, replied: 'But, Mr Lindsay, if you had read Marx, Engels and Lenin, you would know that these stories cannot be true as it is theoretically impossible for the representatives of a socialist power to behave in such a way.'[22] In 1956 Étienne Balazs noted the 'inescapable duty' imposed on Chinese historians 'to quote a few verses from the Old or the New Testament – I mean, Marx and Lenin, or Stalin and Mao'. Sometimes, Balázs observed, the invocation of Marxist language provided outward protection for less slavish interpretation, but only at the cost of 'often childish contradictions'. State doctrine bestowed the adjective 'feudal' on 'everything that happened between a postulated slave society (the dating of which varies widely)

20 Simon Leys, *Chinese Shadows* (New York: Viking Press, 1977), pp. 2–4.

21 Michael Croft, *Red Carpet to China* (London: Longmans Green, 1958), pp. 26, 28, 263–6.

22 Lindsay, *China and the Cold War*, pp. 21, 27.

and the year of grace 1949.' So a historian might 'give a conscientious and accurate description of a period or social stratum which have nothing feudal about them at all, but in order to get his paper published, he is obliged to paste the label "feudal" on them'.[23]

Marxist indoctrination was not the only cause of the hostility encountered by Westerners. The antagonism was rooted in the century before the Communist victory of 1949, when, as Trevor-Roper put it, 'China, though nominally independent, was in fact a colony of the "imperialist" powers. Its taxes, its ports, its greatest industrial cities were leased out to foreign concessionaires. Its peripheral provinces were detached by foreign powers.'[24] His officially appointed guides bemoaned the Anglo-Chinese war of 1839–42, which ensued from Chinese attempts to suppress the British trade in opium. The guides harped on its sequel, the Treaty of Nanking, which created extraterritoriality in five treaty ports (Shanghai, Canton, Ningpo, Fuchow, Amoy), where British traders could own homes and businesses in areas ruled by British officials and laws, and which also ceded the island of Hong Kong to the British Empire. For a century after the treaty, observed Trevor-Roper, the victors regarded the vanquished 'with complacency and contempt'.[25] Extraterritoriality brought public health measures and public utilities to the Chinese inhabitants, but subjected them to treaty-port brutes. 'The English gentries of Shanghai,' remarked a concession-hunter in 1898, 'are cocktailing, kicking coolies, riding ponies (and American ladies), deploring exile from a mother country which does not miss them, and generally living on the fat of the land, with a new crisis or bogey every morning all fresh and hot.'[26] Lin Yutang, with whom Trevor-Roper was to dine in Taiwan in 1967, resented the Old China Hands who claimed local expertise without being able to speak three syllables of Chinese: men who never were invited to Chinese homes, who shunned Chinese restaurants, who got in such 'a blue funk' when 'heathen eyes' stared at them in the streets that

---

23 Étienne Balázs, *Chinese Civilization and Bureaucracy: variations on a theme* (New Haven: Yale University Press, 1964), pp. 7–8, 20, 38–9.

24 Trevor-Roper, 'The Sick Mind of China'. In this view T-R differed from his predecessor in the Regius chair, Frederick York Powell, who wrote: 'The Chinese government, faithless, ignorant, obstinate, short-sighted, and antagonistic as ever, was steadily set on destroying all trade with England, a course that was bound to end in our armed interference on behalf of our injured and legitimate interests' (Oliver Elton, *Frederick York Powell*, vol. 2 (Oxford: Clarendon Press, 1906), p. 177).

25 Trevor-Roper, 'Through Eastern Eyes'.

26 Mitchell Library, Sydney, Australia, papers of George Ernest Morrison, volume 42, Patrick Chance (formerly MP for South Kilkenny) to Morrison, 22 November 1898.

they would hide their faces by noisily blowing into disgusting handkerchiefs. The average Englishman in China, Lin wrote, 'walks as if the whole lot of them did not exist for him, and does not say "sorry" even in English when he steps on a fellow passenger's toes. He has not even learned the Chinese equivalents of *"danke sehr"* and *"bitte schön"* and *"verzeihen Sie"*, the minimum moral obligations of even a passing tourist, complains of anti-foreignism and despairs because even the pillaging of the Pekin palaces after the Boxer Uprising has not taught the Chinese a lesson.'[27]

The literary critic William Empson, who taught English at Peking University in the last years of KMT rule, spoke no Chinese, took little interest in the local arts and disdained passers-by. The Chinese whom he saw in the streets in 1948, 'though they have the great merit of not looking fussed or hurried, look pretty sordid from concentration on some half dishonest employment'. The atheist Empson did, however, like the unchristian nature of the Chinese who had, he thought, 'no sense of sin and no feeling that it is a duty to worry'. Sexual opportunities were accordingly less complicated or risky than in Europe: 'Considering the high proportion of buggers among the foreigners who genuinely "love China" it seems to be the chief thing the country has to offer.'[28]

There were hefty reassertions of national pride (as well as of prudery) under the Maoists. Albert Franklin, a diplomat with long expertise in China, observed in 1949 that to the Chinese 'at best the foreigner is a necessary evil. To show him that he is not allowed to boss anybody about, you concentrate on humiliating him and making him lose face. The charm of this process is that by so doing you yourself gain face and the common man of China will undoubtedly think the more of you.'[29] In 1954 Étienne Balázs noted that the traditional xenophobia had mutated into a 'prickly, touchy, demanding kind of nationalism' under the PRC.[30] Alain Peyrefitte, the diplomat turned *député* who became de Gaulle's Boswell and was serving as Minister of Information in Paris at the time of Trevor-Roper's visit to the PRC, remarked that the Chinese

---

27 Lin Yutang, *My Country and My People* (London: Heinemann, 1939), pp. 8–10; cf. Harold Acton, *Memoirs of an Aesthete* (London: Methuen, 1948), p. 291.

28 John Haffenden, ed., *Selected Letters of William Empson* (Oxford: Oxford University Press, 2006), p. 162. Harold Acton, Rewi Alley and Edmund Backhouse match Empson's view of foreigners who loved China.

29 NA FO 371/75914, F17349/1261/10, A. E. E. Franklin's minute of 23 November 1949; *Documents on British Policy Overseas*, series 1, volume 8, ed. Stephen Ashton and Gill Bennett (London: Whitehall History Publishing, 2002), p. 407.

30 Balázs, *Chinese Civilization and Bureaucracy*, pp. 160–1.

found the scrutiny of European intellectuals and Cold War commentators an offensive renewal of the previous 'breaking-and-entering' into sacrosanct places.[31] The Cambridge economist and SACU activist Joan Robinson, whose name recurs in the Trevor-Roper documents, wrote: 'The Chinese are sometimes accused of xenophobia, by which is presumably meant that they have a sense of superiority (damaged during the semi-colonial period) equal to that of the English.'[32] Hostile images of the Chinese indeed remained commonplace in the British Isles. Raymond Dawson, Spalding Lecturer in Chinese at Oxford, observed in 1967 that 'slant eyes, yellow skin, pigtails, bound feet, chopsticks, bird's-nest soup, and the like have been the things which the man in the street has mainly associated with China'.[33]

Some foreign visitors, exasperated by their experiences, were none the less diffident about voicing criticism. The Dutchman Hans Koningsberger had to wait four years before he was granted a visa in 1965, and was then denied most of his requested meetings. The relentless propaganda from officials, guides and interpreters proved counter-productive by provoking his resistance. A typical cadre worker in a rural commune was, he found, 'obnoxious in his self-righteousness, his lecturing attitude, and his dogmatism'. Yet Koningsberger asked himself what right had citizens of North Atlantic Treaty Organisation (NATO) countries, after plundering the world for four centuries, and now 'fat and rich and worried about calories', to fuss 'whether these people, whose former drowning or starving by the millions didn't make our front pages, have enough democratic rights?'[34] In *China Now*, published in 1969, Kurt Mendelssohn, a German-born Oxford physicist, strove to see beyond his European perspective. Western press coverage of the PRC was, he judged, 'pathetic' in its inadequacy. He extenuated Maoist methods of forming national opinion:

> The Chinese masses are only beginning to emerge from the feudal age, and information is passed on to them by the time-honoured

---

31 Alain Peyrefitte, *La Chine s'est éveillée: Carnets de route d l'ère Deng Xiaoping* (Paris: Fayard, 1996), pp. 34–5.

32 Joan Robinson, *The Cultural Revolution in China* (London: Penguin, 1969), p. 40. On Robinson, see Harry Johnson, 'Cambridge in the 1950s', *Encounter*, January 1974, pp. 30, 32, and Bodleian, Ms Berlin 241, f 53, Noël Annan to Isaiah Berlin, n.d. [1957] ('Her line is High & Dry Cambridge').

33 Raymond Dawson, *The Chinese Chameleon: an analysis of European conceptions of Chinese civilization* (Oxford: Oxford University Press, 1967), p. 164.

34 Hans Koningsberger, *Love and Hate in China* (London: Jonathan Cape, 1967), pp. 24–5.

method of repeating simple slogans over and over again. Our own idea that they might resent this method is, of course, equally misplaced. The concept of common thought for the common good has quite generally a stronger appeal in Asian civilizations than the prize which Westerners set on individuality.

Yet he admitted that the 'deeply ingrained' insularity of the Chinese prevented the meeting of minds:

> What happens in China is always to the Chinese very much more important than what happens in the outer world. The widespread ignorance, shared by many highly educated Chinese, of conditions abroad is part of this legacy. Foreigners travelling in modern China are often surprised by the kind of propaganda to which they are subjected. It seems to them unnecessarily repetitive, strangely ineffectual and sometimes even childish. In fact, they are simply told the same things that the Chinese masses are told, and it would never enter the mind of the Chinese that foreigners might respond differently from their own people.[35]

Mendelssohn, one of the low-temperature physicists brought to Oxford by Trevor-Roper's Christ Church colleague Lord Cherwell in 1933, deplored the repression of scientific and scholarly thought by a totalitarian regime in China as in Nazi Germany. Trevor-Roper, who shared that dismay, encountered Mendelssohn in his own struggles with the SACU leadership after his return, when he formed an alliance with Mendelssohn's colleague Nicholas Kurti.

*

Derek Bryan enticed Trevor-Roper to join SACU's delegation with assurances of access to Maoist leaders (Chou En-lai was mentioned) and of meetings with two veteran Marxist historians, Hou Wai-lu and Chien Po-tsan. He did meet Hou, but was unimpressed by his mechanical doctrinal orthodoxy. Chien, who preserved some independence of mind, was kept from him. It was one of many

---

35 Kurt Mendelssohn, *In China Now* (London: Paul Hamlyn, 1969), pp. 13–14. See also Bodleian, Ms Eng misc b 382, Mendelssohn papers F25, for the text of Mendelssohn's BBC talk on China, November 1971, which was never broadcast, and Mendelssohn, 'China from Inside', *Observer*, 31 November 1971.

unpleasant surprises awaiting Trevor-Roper, who went to China assuming he would have informative conversations with eminent and interesting people. Instead he was submitted, and mostly confined, to the boorish doctrinal ideological incantations of interpreter-guides.

Here too, had he but known it, his was a common experience. From 1954 the foreign businessmen, pundits, academics and journalists who visited the PRC under the auspices of the Chinese People's Association for Cultural Relations with Foreign Countries had been categorized by political labels (comrades, progressives, bourgeoisie, imperialists and revisionists) rather than by their nationality. All were allotted official liaisons, who acted as translators and guides. Lucien Bodard was allocated a translator named Li, freshly graduated from the foreign languages department of Peking University. Party officials had chosen Li to become 'a technician' in the French language: he had studied ten hours a day, living in ascetic deprivation; by the end of his training, he had mastered both vocabulary and diction; but Li knew nothing of France. With his instilled mistrust of foreigners, he showed no interest in the visitors who were put in his charge. He never once, during the course of many weeks, asked Bodard about France, which was supposed to be his speciality. Life in a bourgeois state, free of communist regulations, was incomprehensible and irrelevant to him. When Bodard offered him a cigarette he pretended not to smoke; but shortly afterwards lit one of his own. He rebuffed every civil question about himself. All that he would admit to Bodard was that he originated from Nanking – in his own words, 'the former capital of the imperialist counter-revolutionary Chiang Kai-shek'.[36]

Bodard remembered how a line of Czech-made cars would arrive every morning at Peking's hotel Hsin Chiao, where visitors admiring of China would be housed, to carry them to view the wonders of the modern state. The guests, wrote Bodard, were the international upper-crust (*le gratin international*) who flirted with communism, 'affluent comrades well placed in their own country', *penseurs*, society women, and roving opportunists ready to snatch any chances. Their interpreter-guides, dressed in their blue drab, seemed to Bodard to disdain their charges. They could not repress a contemptuous smile whenever a foreigner broke into indiscriminate raptures at the sight of a people's commune or a feat of engineering. Yet, by a 'a very oriental contradiction', the same guides foamed with rage if insufficient appreciation were expressed. Bodard himself displeased the Chinese authorities by the fair-minded, sceptical tone

36 Bodard, *La Chine de la douceur* (Paris: Gallimard, 1957), pp. 41–2.

of his book *La Chine de la douceur* (1957). A subtle and frustrating humilia-
tion was meted out to him two years later. He was granted a visa in 1959, but
when he reached Peking every request for an interview or visit was stonewalled
as retribution for his previous lack of respectful gullibility. For months he
could only walk Peking's streets, feeling disempowered beyond hope, and so
obviously shadowed by watchers that passers-by would not meet his eye or
talk to him.[37]

In the years following the revolution of 1949, the escorts for foreign visitors
had bourgeois backgrounds, and some familiarity with European culture and
customs, but from 1957 the management of foreign visitors was increasingly
given to proletarians and peasants (rather than educated bourgeois), who were
held to be uncorrupted by the pre-Liberation mentality of China's 'feudal',
'semi-colonial' past, and whose guidance was still more unfriendly. The novelist Jules Roy, who visited the PRC shortly before Trevor-Roper, was aghast, like
him, at the table-manners, conversational banality and meal-time speechifying
of his escort of interpreter-guides.

> Our companions scorned the capitalist practice of treating a meal
> as a ceremony rather than just an opportunity to slake the appetite.
> They crouched over their plates, the better to wolf down their food,
> splattered sauces over the table, and belched. When they needed a
> breather, they stood up, spoke a few words at one of us, and made
> a toast.

After the last course had been served at the first dinner, one of the escort
wiped his spectacles, replaced them portentously and delivered an edifying
speech. His associates listened with fervent looks as he recalled the state of
China before Liberation, and extolled the achievements of the Communist
Party. The condescension and complacence of Roy's escort of party members –
'*les mandarins de petite classe qui m'entourent*', as he called them – enraged
him. In the lobby of his hotel, and in every corridor on every floor, there were
displays of Chinese booklets translated into many languages. After reading
them, Roy found that it was hard to think clearly about global politics or
notions of freedom if one's mind was sodden by an outpouring of polemics,
insults and obfuscating jargon. Visiting the University of Peking in the hope
of meeting intellectuals who would share confidences, equivocate or show

---

37 Lucien Bodard, *La Chine du cauchemar* (Paris: Gallimard, 1961), pp. 32, 34, 37.

scepticism, he met only 'clerics of the new religion' preaching 'the universal truth of Marxism-Leninism'. It was less like a modern university, he decided, than like 'a seminary where obtuse Knights Templar were drilled to defend the state religion'. At a cocktail party in the French Embassy the president of the People's Association for Cultural Relations read a long speech, glutted with obligatory official banalities. He clinked glasses with Roy and said that he hoped the Frenchman was enjoying his visit to the PRC. The translator was aghast when, in response, Roy said that he was 'disgusted' by being held under tight supervision, sent on otiose sight-seeing trips, kept from meeting the people he wished, and made to waste time.[38]

Possibly the interpreter-guides who exasperated Trevor-Roper had personal spurs to incivility. No less than the Western powers, China used secret police-men, watchers, informers, agents provocateurs, penetration agents, postal and telephonic intercepts, and experts in rifling papers. Only months after its formation in 1949, the PRC had agents monitoring local communities, public spaces, bars, restaurants and overseas visitors in hotels. In 1961 the director of public security in Shanghai advised cadets and officers to read Conan Doyle: 'whereas we cannot put our faith in Holmes's repertoire of feudal, bourgeois, and fascist tricks, but must come up with our own proletarian and revolution-ary Holmes, some of that old stuff may still prove to be useful here and there'.[39] On his excursions Trevor-Roper presumably left his diary, which shows no sign of having been bent or folded into a pocket, in his hotel room, where it would have been a normal practice of Communist espionage to have it photographed. What he took to be an act of petty deception by them when he left Peking is explicable as revenge if they knew what he was writing about them.

*

The Chinese Communist Party had had tiny beginnings in 1921. By 1924 it was treating with the KMT on terms approaching parity. But in 1927 the KMT general, Chiang Kai-shek, turned against his communist companions-in-arms, decimated them and proscribed the Communist Party. Cut back to the roots, the party could flourish only underground. Its nature was thereafter generally

38 Jules Roy, *Le voyage en Chine* (Paris: René Juillard, 1965), pp. 38, 40, 76–7, 78, 87–9, 150.

39 Michael Schoenhals, *Spying for the People: Mao's secrets agents, 1949–1967* (Cambridge: Cambridge University Press, 2013), p. 179.

misprized by Westerners. Thus, a few months after the defeat of Japan in 1945, the Joint Intelligence Staff concluded that 'The Chinese Communists are not a political party in the usual sense nor are they what is usually understood by the word Communists.'[40]

On 1 October 1949, the People's Liberation Army hoisted its victorious red flag over Tiananmen, the Gate of Heavenly Peace in Peking, and thus ended a civil war that had lasted nearly thirty years. In January 1950 Clement Attlee's Labour administration became the first non-communist government to recognize the PRC. Although the outbreak of the Korean war a few months later ranged the United States against both the Soviet Union and the PRC, the Foreign Office in London focused on Moscow's ambition to control the entire Eurasian land mass, 'to turn Asiatic races against the Western democracies and to pose as the champion of oppressed colonial peoples'.[41] The bogey of communism, from which the British Labour Party anxiously distanced itself, was primarily associated with Russia and its Eastern European satellites.

In the early decades of Maoist rule Chinese communism was evaluated and understood by very few Oxford academics.[42] Outstanding among these was Geoffrey Hudson, a fellow of All Souls until 1954, when he became the first director of the Centre for Far Eastern Studies at St Antony's College. 'Marxist doctrine,' he explained in a pioneering study of Mao's thought in 1951, 'has to be at once so rigid that it will serve for the uncompromising condemnation of the unbeliever and the heretic by the touchstone of absolute truth, and so flexible that it can be adapted to whatever the party leadership wants to do.' When Trevor-Roper became involved in the conflict with SACU's leadership that is the story of this book, he consulted Hudson, a former Labour Party activist,[43] whose unassailable independence of mind and resistance to the interpretative tools of Marxism made him persona non grata to communist front organizations. Hudson was early in recognizing that the communists' expulsion of the nationalists from mainland China had provided a new Marxist revolutionary

40 *Documents on British Policy Overseas*, series 1, volume 8 (London: Whitehall History Publishing, 2002), p. 33.

41 Steve Tsang, *The Cold War's Odd Couple: the unintended partnership between the Republic of China and the UK, 1950–1958* (London: I.B.Tauris, 2016), p. 12.

42 Archie Brown and Stephen Whitefield, 'The study of Communist and post-Communist Politics', in Christopher Hood, Desmond King and Gillian Peele, eds, *Forging a Discipline: a critical assessment of Oxford's development of the study of politics and international relations in comparative perspective* (Oxford: Oxford University Press, 2014), 250–1.

43 Churchill College archives, Cambridge, GNWR 2/1/1, G. F. Hudson to Patrick Gordon Walker, 13 October 1938.

model in which the peasantry rather than the urban proletariat was the driving force. He predicted in 1951 that henceforth the strongest appeal of communism would be in 'backward and "under-developed" countries, exploiting no longer the aspirations of the factory worker in Sheffield or in Detroit so much as the agrarian ... discontents of Indonesia or Nigeria'.[44] In the ensuing decade Maoist example succoured anti-colonial uprisings and wars of liberation in Asia, Africa and South America.[45]

Maoism was moreover using new methods of agitation and propaganda to bring politics into the daily life of the masses. As Balázs noted in 1954:

> innumerable demonstrations, reunions, marches, committees, meetings, and public trials; theatrical performances, dances, public rejoicings; notices, pamphlets, journals – by every possible means official slogans are constantly drilled into every brain. In this way, what was formerly a sluggish, lethargic, undifferentiated mass of people has been shaken up, wakened up, enlivened, turned topsy-turvy, thus releasing an elemental force that will have incalculable consequences.[46]

The volatility of Mao's leadership, with the countermanding of his liberalizing '100 Flowers' initiative of 1956–57 and then the 'Great Leap Forward' campaign from 1958, made the PRC seem, in Whitehall's assessment, 'unstable and dangerous'.[47] On 16 October 1964, almost exactly a year before Trevor-Roper landed in Peking, the PRC exploded its first nuclear test bomb. On that same day Harold Wilson kissed hands with the Queen and became prime minister. Wilson trusted Soviet Russia far above the PRC. China's support for the Viet Cong produced strident propaganda from Peking against US bombing in Vietnam and against the Washington administration's allies in London. Antipathy was to be heightened in the years immediately following Trevor-Roper's visit, when Mao's Cultural Revolution, and the attack on the British Legation in Peking in August 1967, confirmed the sinophobia of Wilson's government.

---

44 G. F. Hudson, *Questions of East and West: studies in current history* (London: Odhams, 1953), pp. 189–90.

45 Julia Lovell, *Maoism: a global history* (London: Bodley Head, 2019).

46 Balázs, *Chinese Civilization and Bureaucracy*, p. 169.

47 Geraint Hughes, *Harold Wilson's Cold War: the Labour government and east–west politics, 1964–1970* (Woodbridge: Royal Historical Society, 2009), p. 165.

*

Through the post-war decades there were Britons and other Europeans who opposed Western policies antagonistic towards either Russia or China. There were businessmen who wanted to trade with those countries, and politicians and intellectuals who sympathized with them. The degree of sympathy varied. There were hard-core admirers. There were left-leaning liberals who would not have called themselves Marxists but whose thought was informed by Marxist premises. This group overlapped with anti-capitalists and anti-Americans who were ready to admire anti-capitalist or anti-American regimes. There were people in the habit of signing round-robin letters to newspapers, circulating petitions, giving their names in support of good causes, volunteering to run progressive societies, and feeling no sacrifice in spending their evenings sitting dutifully at public meetings. There were, in Alain Peyrefitte's phrase, '*chrétiens de gauche*' who found, as so many Westerners did in Marxism, the doctrinal certainties of a religion, a taste heightened by the resemblance of Maoist precepts to the vows of a monastic community: constant indoctrination, enforced group piety, obedience, poverty, abstinence, ostensible equality at work, devotion to community, heedlessness of personal profit.[48] And there were what William ('Bill') Ash, one of the founding-figures of SACU, would call in his autobiography 'radical young people politically window-shopping'.[49] During Trevor-Roper's controversy with SACU, the winds that by 1968 would produce a huge movement of student protest were beginning to stir. The mass participatory politics of the PRC inspired revolutionary theoreticians in Europe and across America and were imitated by student activists in France, Germany and England. The thoughts of Mao himself, whose *Little Red Book* was published in English in 1966, became a gospel for some students. The most violent and disruptive protests in Britain were at the London School of Economics (LSE), where a speech by Trevor-Roper in 1968 engaged him in another contest with Marxist sloganeers.

One often-quoted statement of Mao was that a revolution is not a dinner party: it requires purges, mass detentions, scapegoats, deaths. He contemplated the deaths of half the human race as a way of eliminating imperialism. 'Let us

---

48 Peyrefitte, *La Chine s'est éveillée*, p. 35. At the time of Richard Nixon's détente with the PRC, Henry Kissinger likened Mao and his core supporters to 'monks' preserving 'their revolutionary purity' (Paul Hollander, *From Benito Mussolini to Hugo Chavez: intellectuals and a century of political hero-worship* (Cambridge: Cambridge University Press, 2016), p. 199).

49 William Ash, *Red Square: the autobiography of an unconventional revolutionary* (London: Howard Baker, 1978), pp. 229–30.

imagine how many people would die if war breaks out,' he declared in a speech of 18 November 1957, during a visit to Moscow. 'There are 2.7 billion people in the world, and a third could be lost ... if the worst came to the worst, and one-half dies, there will still be one-half left, but imperialism would be erased and the whole world become socialist. After a few years there would be 2.7 billion people again.'[50] Mao's English admirers airbrushed inconvenient facts. When SACU's Secretary Derek Bryan published an educational book on modern China in 1964, for example, he extolled 'the enthusiasm of that intoxicating year of 1958 (the year of the "Great Leap Forward")', and claimed that 'No one had ever seen such plenty.' It was true that 'the worst floods and droughts in a hundred years sharply cut down the harvests', but 'what food was available was shared out fairly; there was no hoarding or black market'. Bryan denied that 'in the lean years 1959–61' there were 'millions of deaths from starvation'.[51] In truth, perhaps 30 million people died in the famine of 1958–61 caused by the 'Great Leap Forward'. Dying villagers resorted to cannibalism of their own families.[52]

Bryan diverted attention from Maoist errors and crimes by attacks on the record of the KMT. So when grave ecological and safety problems were caused by the Three Gate Gorge dam project on the Yellow River, which Mao in pharaonic mode had insisted should proceed apace despite the misgivings of hydraulic engineers, Bryan eulogized the project, and contrasted it with the great flood of 1938: 'a man-made disaster, caused when Chiang Kai-shek ordered the dikes to be broken for military reasons: the waters poured south ... drowning 890,000 people and making 12½ million homeless.' In the year of Bryan's comments, foreigners were banned from visiting the dam or its vicinity for fear of what they might see. Bryan drew cosy analogies between the Chinese communes and the Rural District Councils in England: 'all the farming, local industry, shops and trading, schools, amusements and a local militia (Home Guard) are run by an elected council'.[53]

---

50 Frank Dikötter, *Mao's Great Famine: the history of China's most devastating catastrophe, 1958–62* (London: Bloomsbury, 2010), pp. 13–14.

51 CUL, Needham papers K199, Derek Bryan to Joseph Needham, 9 July 1967.

52 Jasper Becker, *Hungry Ghosts: China's secret famine* (London: John Murray, 1996).

53 Admiration for Mao was not confined to the left. Trevor-Roper's Oxford antagonist the historian A. L. Rowse found it 'endearing' of Mao that, despite his 'superhuman' achievements, he declined the tribute 'superman'. 'His moral qualities are of a very high order'; his leadership 'points to an immensely creative future'; by his humanity, pragmatism and willingness to compromise, 'Mao is by far the greatest man in the world today – probably the greatest of this century.' See C. P. Fitzgerald, *Mao Tse-Tung and China* (London: Hodder & Stoughton, 1976), pp. v–vi.

Another enthusiast was Joan Robinson, who first visited China in 1954 and was overjoyed: 'New China is anti-posh and anti-philistine to my heart's desire.' She saw the beauties of its capital in the insular terms of Attlee's Britain: 'The palaces of Peking are like an enormous permanent Festival of Britain, with glories from the past instead of fancies for the future.' She liked the way that when workers were praised at communal meetings in factories or co-operatives, they always joined in clapping themselves, so as to show that they did not take applause personally, though even she wilted at 'slogan bores, who could not go beyond saying the correct thing, refusing to admit any drawbacks, and they seemed to me precisely people who lack inner conviction, who were resolved to be on the safe side when speaking to a foreigner'.[54] Thirteen years later Robinson revisited the PRC and, drawing on material supplied by Derek Bryan, wrote *The Cultural Revolution in China*. At a time when the Red Guards were waging state-instituted proletarian terror, beating people to death because they were educated, hounding others to suicide, and going on rampages of destruction of books and artworks, she wrote: 'When the *young things* are singing of Mao Tse-tung as the leader of all the peoples of the world, it does not occur to them that their neighbours, who have national leaders of their own, might think them arrogant or fanatical ... Thus they make enemies for themselves out of *pure goodwill*.' Robinson wrote of the 'humour' of Chen Yi, the Foreign Minister, being forced by mobs to wear a dunce's hat. She gave implicit endorsement to the cultural revolutionary programme for universities and academies: 'the intellectuals are to *serve the people*'; 'students have completely lost their old awe of professors'; 'book work should be cut down'; students should 'be imbued with a new proletarian spirit, to overcome the bourgeois prejudices in which they had been infected in the past'; examinees should be allowed to consult reference books, 'so as to prevent an examination from being a mere test of memory', or to discuss the questions together and present a joint answer: 'in this way examinations would cease to be, as Mao put it, a surprise attack by the teachers on the students'.[55]

Among SACU's activists was Bryan's friend Stuart Gelder, who for twenty years was on the staff of the liberal-inclined *News Chronicle*. He and his wife Roma had visited the PRC in 1960, and in 1962 enthused at a dozen years of Maoist progress in *The Long March to Freedom* (1962). In *The Timely Rain:*

54 Joan Robinson, *Letters from a Visitor to China* (Cambridge: Students' Bookshop, 1954), pp. 4, 6, 13, 18.

55 Robinson, *Cultural Revolution*, pp. 40, 143–4, 146. Emphasis added.

travels in new Tibet (1964), they had sniped at the Dalai Lama, deplored pre-annexation Tibet as 'a feudal society', and dismissed accusations of communist military violence after the Tibetan revolt of 1959 as unbelievable because 'the Chinese People's Army is one of the best disciplined and behaved in the world'.[56] It was in this mode that Stuart Gelder declared at the inaugural meeting of the SACU branch in Barnet in 1966 that he was 'bowled over' by the progress in the PRC, where 'there is no press censorship and correspondents can file what stories they like'.[57]

Innumerable cases belied such condonation of the Maoist regime. To take one case, in 1960 a group of Chinese students published essays and documents revealing the unfolding catastrophe of Mao's 'Great Leap Forward'. Their single-issue magazine included a poem by Lin Zhao, who was arrested along with all those involved with the journal. She spent most of the rest of her short life in prison: she was subjected to solitary confinement, beatings, and had her hair pulled out by guards; she was often handcuffed, with her hands pulled tightly behind her back, with the cuffs so tight that shoulders would be injured and flesh on the wrists would rot. Rendered manually helpless, inmates like Lin were unable to eat normally or adjust their clothing: they had no choices but to lick food from the floor and soil their trousers. During her confinement she sharpened the end of her toothbrush by scraping it on the cell floor, pricked her finger, collected the blood in a spoon, and used it to write messages to the outside world with bamboo or a reed. In 1968, during the Cultural Revolution, she was sentenced to death. After the capital sentence was passed, she was forced to wear a rubber hood with a slit cut for the eyes and a hole for the nose. The hood was only removed at mealtimes, as it had no orifice for her mouth. By then her weight had shrivelled to seventy pounds, and her mental health had correspondingly deteriorated. At the end, she was taken in a hospital gown to the prison auditorium, gagged with a rubber ball and shot. Her mother only learnt of Lin Zhao's death when an official came to her door demanding five cents to cover the cost of the bullet.[58]

*

56 Stuart and Roma Gelder, *The Timely Rain: travels in New Tibet* (London: Hutchinson, 1962), pp. 208–9.

57 CC, Dacre 13/3, 'Bid to Promote Anglo-Chinese Understanding', *Barnet Press*, 4 March 1966.

58 Lian Xi, *Blood Letters: the untold story of Lin Zhao, a martyr in Mao's China* (New York: Basic Books, 2018).

When Trevor-Roper became involved in SACU in 1965, it was the newest offshoot from a deep-rooted tangle of organizations and initiatives amicably disposed towards the PRC. These bodies originated in a conference of officials, economists and businessmen, drawn from both capitalist and communist states, which assembled in Moscow in April 1952 with the aim of inducing European governments to abate or end the economic restrictions that had been imposed, under pressure from the United States, on trade with the Soviet Union, its satellite states in Eastern Europe and the PRC. The British delegation was led by Lord Boyd-Orr, who since 1949 had become a leading proponent of Anglo-Chinese friendship. A practical idealist, Boyd-Orr believed that the only hope for world peace lay in eradicating hunger. If people must choose between freedom and sandwiches, he once said, they will take sandwiches. A doughty campaigner against malnutrition and famine, he was awarded the Nobel Peace Prize in 1949 after the Western powers rejected his world food plan. He disliked arrogant Americans and Europeans who spoke of 'gooks' or 'Chinks', and deplored caricatures of China as a place 'where habits are topsy-turvy, white is the colour of mourning, and you read a book by starting at the wrong end; a Fu Manchu land of inscrutable and mysterious beings where a life is worth only a handful of silver, and a bribe (provided it is diplomatically given), is an open sesame to gun-running or any other vice'.[59] He judged the PRC by the good intentions of its leaders and kept himself oblivious to the unintended consequences of their policies. Returning from a visit to China in 1959, he reported that Chinese food production had risen by 50–100 per cent over 1955–58, and discounted fears of famine. He had no truck with those who wished to apply Western-style democracy in 'a country where illiteracy and superstition are so widespread, and where reconstruction depends on a strong centralised administration'. He thought of Mao, 'the Great Helmsman', as an Asian equivalent of Gladstone: 'Mao Tse-tung is sufficient of a liberal to see that there must be independent thinking and criticism if initiative is to be encouraged.'[60]

Joan Robinson was Boyd-Orr's deputy in Moscow. Recommending her for appointment to the Order of Merit in 1976, Noël Annan ranked her as 'by far the greatest woman academic and intellectual in our country' – ahead even of the scientist Dorothy Hodgkin. Whispers that her papers and books, which

---

59 Lord Boyd-Orr, *What's Happening in China?* (London: Macdonald, 1959), p. 15.

60 Boyd-Orr, *What's Happening?*, pp. 17, 142; Jung Chang and Jon Halliday, *Mao: the unknown story* (London: Cape, 2005), p. 480.

coined the new economic concept of imperfect competition, had been written by her fellow SACU member Richard Kahn, were misogynistic. 'Her work has been extraordinarily original and for an economist staggeringly well written,' Annan continued.

> She is of course slightly mad, but the fact that she is very far to the Left seems to me not to matter. She has never liked Russian communism and now happily finds her ideal in China. But while being friendly towards Marxists, she has never ceased to argue how wrong Marx was about economics and how right Keynes is. She is very fierce, very pure, totally unworldly.[61]

Boyd-Orr's delegation also included four Labour MPs: Harold Davies, a left-winger who was later sent by Harold Wilson on a secret peace mission to Hanoi; Emrys Hughes and Sydney Silverman, who both had the whip withdrawn in 1963 after voting in support of unilateral nuclear disarmament; and Henry Usborne, who was managing director of the Nu-Way Heating Plants Company of Droitwich, which hoped to sell its burners in Warsaw bloc countries. Also in the party were the economists Alec Cairncross (Glasgow), Maurice Dobb (Cambridge) and Peter Wiles (Oxford), together with Charles Madge, who had renounced both poetry-writing and communism after his appointment as Professor of Sociology at Birmingham University in 1950. Several businessmen who joined the delegation to Moscow would feature in Trevor-Roper's journals: the textile merchants Bernard Buckman and Jack Perry, Alec Horsley of Northern Food, and Adolphe Silver of the Waste Trade Federation.

Foremost among these was Jack Perry. Perry was son of an East End tailor, and left school at the age of fourteen to work as a textiles warehouseman. His schooling had been much interrupted by asthma: during long spells at home, his mother brought him relays of library books; he devoured writers like Dickens, learnt to think for himself and developed a broad outlook. At a conference at Harvard in the period of Nixon's détente with China, when he appeared on a platform with a US ambassador and a Wall Street banker, he said by way of self-introduction: 'If you want to know what makes me work – I'm a Jew from Lithuania!'[62] When Oswald Mosley's Blackshirts began their

---

61 King's College, Cambridge, NGA 5/1/79/2, Noël Annan to Isaiah Berlin, 8 April 1976.
62 Information from his son Graham Perry, January 2019.

anti-Semitic demonstrations in East London, neither the Labour Party nor local rabbis encouraged resistance; but the CPGB answered the call to action. Perry attended the Battle of Cable Street in 1936, when a march by the British Union of Fascists was repulsed by local residents led by the local communist leader Phil Piratin. Perry became a committed follower of Piratin, who was elected communist councillor for Spitalfields ward of Stepney in 1937–49. By this time, in partnership with Leonard Winkleman, Perry had started a business making gowns and mantles called Leonard Perry. Originally working from East End premises (where Piratin was employed as a stock-keeper in 1941), the firm later opened showrooms in Grosvenor Street, Mayfair and in Manchester. The Security Service interest in Perry, which began in 1942, resulted from his connections with Piratin. Their assessment was that he was a briefly a party member in the 1940s, but by his own convincing account to his family, he never had a party card, as it was judged that he could be more useful outside party membership. He made no secret of his political sympathies, and was a leader of the campaign team that secured Piratin's election as communist MP for Mile End in 1945. At least one telephone call (in 1949) from Piratin to Jack Perry was recorded by MI5.[63]

In the 1950s the Perry family were amused rather than inhibited by the clicks on their telephone. CPGB leaders, including the party's general secretaries Harry Pollitt and John Gollan, were regularly entertained at the Perry house in Hampstead Garden Suburb. For nearly twenty years Perry was denied a visa to visit the United States because of his part in trading with the PRC. The fact that he was alert, astute and intelligent was presented with unmistakeable anti-Semitic undertones in official reports. 'PERRY is a sharp, unscrupulous and successful businessman, who first came to notice in a Communist organisation in 1942, and became prominent in the Communist business world around 1948', the Security Service reported to the US Embassy in 1961.[64] (The Americans relented in their travel ban in 1972, when Perry was semi-officially brought to Washington and New York to advise on Chinese business relations at the time of the Nixon administration's détente with Peking).

Overall Perry visited China 76 times, and was made an honorary Red Guard. He and other members of the Boyd-Orr delegation in Moscow were leaders of the Progressive Businessmen's Forum, which had been formed in

---

63 NA KV 2/2033, serial 252b, intercepted telephone call transcript, 24 May 1949, Temple Bar 2151 to Mayfair 4192.

64 NA KV 2/4247, serial 640a, P. F. Stewart to U.S. Embassy, 23 January 1961.

1943 under the aegis of the commercial group of the CPGB. Peter Tennant, a former fellow of the Queen's College, Oxford and wartime intelligence officer who became overseas director of the Federation of British Industries, advised the Board of Trade in 1954 that the Forum was 'a commercial Communist front organisation', which hid the purposes and influence of those who controlled it: its membership had 'earthy names such as Horowitz, Grunbaum and so forth' and seemed 'centred around the clothing trade'. Joan Robinson was among their lunchtime speakers, Tennant continued: 'they have gone progressively upwards in the venues for their lunch, which began first in modest Soho restaurants and have now graduated to the Savoy'. Other officials endorsed Tennant's view of Progressive Businessmen in more sober language: 'Special Branch,' noted the Home Office, 'are definite that the Forum is a front organisation.'[65]

In Moscow a team led by Perry discussed the reopening of Anglo-Chinese trade with PRC officials. As a result of these talks, the China National Import and Export Corporation appointed as their purchasing agents the London Export Corporation run by Perry and Buckman. In May 1952, a month after the Moscow conference, the British Council for the Promotion of International Trade (BCPIT) was established under Boyd-Orr's presidency with Robinson again his deputy. Perry and his friends sat on its executive committee. As a sequel to these developments, four Labour MPs challenged Britain's trade embargo on communist states in the Commons: Joseph Needham's friend Tom Driberg, who had been a CPGB member and MI5 informant codenamed M/8 until 1941, acted as a KGB informant (codenamed 'Lepage') in 1956–68 and as a paid informant (codenamed 'Crocodile') for Czechoslovak State Security;[66] Ian Mikardo, who was later reported by the prized defector Oleg Gordievsky to have been a Soviet agent before 1967;[67] the anti-colonialist Leslie Hale; and Geoffrey Bing, a crony of Ghana's socialist-nationalist life-president

---

65 NA HO 45/25583, Peter Tennant of FBI to C. H. Baylis, Board of Trade, 20 March 1954, and N. Critchley, Home Office, to R. F. Wood, 2 June 1954. This file has been lost in the National Archives, and I rely on photocopies which were given me by Professor Buchanan. See Tom Buchanan, *East Wind: China and the British Left, 1925–1976* (Oxford: Oxford University Press, 2012), p. 157.

66 Christopher Andrew and Vasili Mitrokhin, *The Mitrokhin Archive: the KGB in Europe and the West* (London: Allen Lane, 1999), pp. 522–6; Henry Hemming, *M: Maxwell Knight, MI5's greatest spymaster* (London: Preface, 2017), pp. 70, 109–10, 230, 314.

67 Ian Mikardo, 'British Trade with the Chinese', *Observer*, 30 December 1956; Christopher Andrew, *The Defence of the Realm: the authorized history of MI5* (London: Allen Lane, 2009), p. 758.

Kwame Nkrumah, who imitated *The Thoughts of Chairman Mao* by producing the trite *Axioms of Kwame Nkrumah* and advocated 'an All-African People's Revolutionary armed struggle'.[68]

From the outset the British government opposed BCPIT, which was twice described during the mid-1950s as a 'front' in the House of Commons by government spokesmen. Anthony Eden, as Foreign Secretary, called Perry to the Foreign Office to rebuke him for BCPIT's activities in China, but then quizzed him closely about his assessment of Peking's intentions. Eden also warned the sales manager of Rubery Owen, the great Midlands manufacturers of automotive components, against becoming involved with the 'commies' of BCPIT: 'you can't touch pitch without being defiled'.[69] Some manufacturers accordingly shunned BCPIT, among them Austin Motors, which had the distinction of publishing the first advertisement ever taken by the *Peking Daily News* (a full-page spread in the issue of 20 April 1957). Just two years before Trevor-Roper visited the PRC, in response to a parliamentary question, the Secretary of State for Industry and Trade, Edward Heath, dismissed BCPIT as 'a Communist-controlled organisation, and the advice given to business firms by Her Majesty's Government is that they should consider very carefully whether to become associated, directly or indirectly, with it'.[70]

BCPIT's operations were managed by another zestful admirer of Mao's regime, Roland ('Ro') Berger (1904–1991), whom Trevor-Roper came to regard as a malign force. Berger was a clerk in the statistical department of County Hall, Westminster when he first came to MI5's attention by visiting Soviet Russia in 1933. After the outbreak of war in 1939, he fomented communist ideas in the Home Guard. He joined the London office of the United Nations Relief and Rehabilitation Administration (UNRRA) around 1943. During 1944–45 he ran a secret research group for the CPGB preparing for the post-war general election. Despite a warning by Roger Hollis of MI5 to UNRRA about Berger's allegiance in 1944, he went to Poland in 1946 as its welfare officer. He was repatriation officer at UNRRA's Warsaw headquarters in 1947–48, social affairs officer in the United Nations Social Security section in 1950, and a member of the Office of Technical Assistance in the United Nations secretariat some months after the outbreak of the Korean war. As

68 Rita Hinden, 'Ghana's February Revolution: Sandhurst v. the L. S. E.', *Encounter* (May 1967), p. 43.

69 Percy Timberlake, *The Story of the Icebreakers in China* (London: 48 Group, 1994), p. 13.

70 House of Commons debates, vol. 685, 5 December 1963.

American communist purges intensified, he returned to England as secretary of BCPIT in 1952. Thereafter he was busy in the Progressive Businessmen's Forum, and a London mouthpiece of the Peking authorities. On a visit to China in 1958 he was exhilarated, from his vantage point in the hotel Hsin Chiao, by 'the verve and dynamism of the people'. The PRC's achievements and ambitions, he wrote to Joan Robinson, were 'absolutely breathtaking'. 'All around the place one hears the foreigners remarking "fantastic", "incredible", "astounding", but the simple fact is that words are completely inadequate to convey the sudden bursting out of a great activity which cannot have its parallel in history.'[71] In a Security Service briefing of 1961, he and his wife Nancy were described as 'both undercover members of the CPGB, with a long record of underground activity'. [72] In 1966, Trevor-Roper's wartime intelligence associate Patrick Reilly, then serving as British Ambassador in Paris, arranged for the Foreign Office to send him a précis of its material on Berger and BCPIT.[73]

*

SACU was the lineal descendant of the British-China Friendship Association (BCFA), which had been launched in 1949 soon after the formation of the PRC. The BCFA, which was swiftly proscribed as a communist front organization by the Labour Party, had Joseph Needham of Cambridge University as its chairman. It was perhaps as a reward for helping the BCFA that Needham became the first English sinologist to visit the PRC for scholarly purposes. In order to encourage his continuing compliance, he received privileged treatment on this and later research trips. Exceptionally he was permitted cross-country journeys, '12,000 miles or more', with access to whatever and whomever he wanted. His treatment marked him as 'a very special case' vis-à-vis other scholars.[74]

In the view of recent scholars, 'from the point of view of the Chinese, Needham is the most important Briton of the twentieth century'.[75] He was a

71 King's College, Cambridge, papers of Joan Robinson, JVR 7/61/13–14, Roland Berger to Joan Robinson, 9 March 1958.

72 NA KV 2/4247, serial 640z, Secret A2A briefing sheet, 20 January 1961.

73 Dacre 1/2/10, Sir Patrick Reilly to Trevor-Roper, 30 March 1966.

74 Herbert Passin, *China's Cultural Diplomacy* (New York: Frederick Praeger, 1962), pp. 112–3, 114.

75 John Forrester and Laura Cameron, *Freud in Cambridge* (Cambridge: Cambridge University Press, 2017), p. 5. This section follows Gregory Blue, 'Joseph Needham', in Peter Harman and Simon Mitton, eds, *Cambridge Scientific Minds* (Cambridge: Cambridge University Press, 2002), pp. 299–311.

man of earnest convictions and almost manic energy. He judged the Stalinist regime of the USSR in the 1930s 'a great democracy'. To him the Red Flag, with its hammer and sickle, 'was quite clearly numinous, one with the cross of our salvation and … conspicuous in the vanguard of humanity moving from the captivity of necessity into the glorious liberty of the children of God'.[76] Following the Japanese invasion of China in 1937 he became a spokesman of the Free China campaign. He went to China as representative of the Royal Society in 1942. This led to his appointment as Scientific Counsellor at the British Embassy, and then as Director of the Sino-British Scientific Cooperation Office in 1943. These were transformative years. 'Chinese civilization,' he told a London lecture hall after returning from China, 'has the overpowering beauty of the wholly other, and only the wholly other can inspire the deepest love and the profoundest desire to learn.'[77] Impelled by his sense that Chinese inventiveness had been unmatched by other ancient civilizations, he began work on *Science and Civilisation in China*, of which seventeen volumes had been published by his death in 1995. They were hailed as prodigious feats of historical synthesis.[78]

In a bugged conversation of 1951 between CPGB leaders about the BCFA's development, Jack Woddis, the secretary of the party's international department, was recorded complaining that Needham was 'a man with a terrific sense of his own importance and very ambitious': indeed 'motivated by personal ambition' rather than party interests.[79] The SACU sponsor Jacquetta Hawkes, daughter of the Nobel prize-winning biochemist Frederick Gowland Hopkins who had been Needham's surrogate father-figure, confided to Trevor-Roper: 'I have known him since I was a girl and cannot help having an affection for him – although he was always liable to be tiresome and sometimes rather worse. To know his preposterous and finally mad mother was to forgive, or at least to understand, most things. I think he really is naïf and easily deluded.'[80] Perhaps the naïveté is illustrated by Needham's readiness first to invite Trevor-Roper to become a sponsor of SACU in March 1965, and then to join the council of

---

76 Joseph Needham, *Time: the refreshing river* (London: George Allen & Unwin, 1943), p. 67.

77 Joseph Needham, *Science and Society in Ancient China* (London: Watts, 1947), p. 21.

78 Dacre 1/2/6, Sir Maurice Bowra to Trevor-Roper, 6 January 1962.

79 NA KV 2/3055, serial 72b, 24 January 1951. The merchant seaman Hillel Chayim ('Jack') Woddis (1914–1980), who used the aliases Bill Keats and Jack Knife, was the first avowed CPGB member on the council of the Movement for Colonial Freedom.

80 CC, Dacre 13/3, Jacquetta Hawkes (Mrs. J. B. Priestley) to Trevor-Roper, 15 June 1966.

management, as he did two months later. Needham also probably originated the invitation to Trevor-Roper in September to join the delegation to the PRC. A shrewder mind might have anticipated both Trevor-Roper's adverse reaction to the PRC and the likelihood of his dispute with SACU's leadership. Trevor-Roper himself seems to have been curiously unmindful of the company that he was joining, even though, in the month of his appointment to the council of management, *The Sunday Times* carried an article suggesting what his own researches the following year would confirm, that SACU was a communist front organization. It was only after his return from China that he began to explore the running of SACU.

It was Trevor-Roper's admiration for *Science and Civilisation in China* that attracted him to SACU. Needham met his ideal of the bravely pioneering historian who was ready to risk error and criticism in mapping new intellectual territory. He knew that Needham's politics were remote from his own. He acknowledged that Needham was 'no great stylist', and 'may be wrong in some matters – but the work is exciting to read'.[81] As a sign of his respect, Trevor-Roper in 1964 sent Needham a copy of his essay 'Religion, the Reformation and Social Change', which 'enthralled' its recipient during a voyage from Harwich to Denmark. The essay was 'most instructive and valuable', Needham told Trevor-Roper, 'to anyone like myself who continually studies bureaucratic feudalism ... in China', and set him thinking of parallels under Islam.[82] The two men took conspicuous pains, when first their interests in SACU clashed, never to say a disobliging word about one another. They exchanged friendly letters on Needham's pre-election as Master of Caius in January 1966, although one phrase of Needham's showed his self-deception: 'my temperament is definitely a non-dominating one and my own image of myself is much more that of the chairman of some Feast rather than that of mastering anybody or anything'.[83] Trevor-Roper, wrote a member of the Oxford branch of SACU three months later, 'is an *ardent* admirer of Joseph Needham and manages never to speak a word or give a hint of anything but affection and trust in him'.[84] Only a month later the guarded friendship between the two men was abruptly ended.

---

81 Blair Worden, ed., *Hugh Trevor-Roper: the historian* (London: I.B.Tauris, 2016), p. 278.

82 Dacre 1/2/8, Joseph Needham to Trevor-Roper, 5 April 1964.

83 Dacre 1/2/10, Joseph Needham to T-R, 18 January 1966. The formal but convivial college banquets which are known in Oxford as Gaudies are called Feasts in Cambridge.

84 SOAS, Bryan papers 99/13, Peggy Garland to Derek Bryan, 26 April 1966.

Vice-presidents of the BCFA, under Needham's leadership, included Boyd-Orr; Rajani Palme Dutt, 'a leading theoretician of British communists, whose immense talents were grotesquely squandered by the advent of Stalinism';[85] the Stalinist-minded barrister D. N. Pritt, who received a congratulatory telegram from Mao Tse-tung on his election in 1945 as MP for North Hammersmith; and Hewlett Johnson, the 'Red' Dean of Canterbury and author of *China's New Creative Age* (1953). The BCFA sponsored a quarterly magazine, *Arts and Sciences in China*, which, under the editorship of Derek Bryan, pandered to Peking's feelings. The Oxford physicist Kurt Mendelssohn, who contributed one authoritative piece, resented such instructions from Bryan as 'P. 2, last para., line 1, delete *Communist Government*, and amend to read either *new Government* or *People's Government*. (Although it may seem illogical, the Chinese object to the term. It is premature as far as they are concerned, and abusive as far as the West is concerned!)'.[86]

Bryan, the son of a Norwich dentist, had been appointed as a student interpreter in the Chinese consular service in 1932. Between 1935 and 1941 he held various posts across China as vice-consul or acting consul. As a gifted linguist he was second secretary at the British Embassy in Chungking (1941–42), and private secretary to the British ambassador, Sir Archie Clark Kerr, afterwards Lord Inverchapel. In 1943 he married Liao Hong-ying, who had read chemistry at Somerville College, Oxford and was then working for the British Council in China: the couple were introduced by Needham. Bryan served in the Foreign Office during 1944–46. Despite the rule that diplomats should not be posted to countries of which their foreign wives were nationals, he was appointed Chinese secretary at Nanking in 1946. His avowed sympathy with Chinese communist revolutionaries and his wife's anti-Americanism resulted in his being offered the post of commercial attaché in Lima, Peru in 1951. Instead, he resigned from the Foreign Service, and found work with the magazine *Far East Trade* and teaching Chinese at Holborn College of Law and Languages.

The BCFA worked almost as a London-based subsidiary of the Chinese People's Association for Cultural Relations with Foreign Countries (CPA; *Zhongguo renmin duiwai wenhua xiehui*). This Peking body was formed in

---

85 Tariq Ali, *Street Fighting Years: an autobiography of the sixties* (London: Verso, 2005), p. 75.

86 Bodleian, Ms Eng misc b 381, Kurt Mendelssohn papers F4, Bryan to Mendelssohn 4 February 1963, Mendelssohn to Bryan, 5 February 1963.

1954 to bring foreigners to the PRC and to impress them with the achievements of the Maoist state. Visitors with political influence, economic power,
social prestige or intellectual distinction were cultivated. In an orchestrated
response to the formation of the CPA, a letter was circulated by the BCFA
expressing good will towards the Chinese people. 'Though presumably drafted
by Communists, its contents were of an innocuous character,' recalled Trevor-
Roper's friend, the Oxford philosopher A. J. ('Freddie') Ayer. Some seven
hundred people of note in the arts and sciences signed it, 'many of them,' he
continued, 'those eminent persons who always do sign things'. BCFA then
sent the letter, with its impressive superscriptions, to the CPA. 'Not knowing,
perhaps, how easily such signatures were obtained in England, and possibly
also over-estimating the political influence of the kind of persons who supplied
them, the Chinese authorities offered to pay for five of the signatories to come
to Peking.'[87] The gallimaufry of Ayer, the architect-designer Hugh Casson, the
geologist Leonard Hawkes, the painter Stanley Spencer, and the poet-novelist
Rex Warner were the CPA's first English guests in 1954.

*

The BCFA began to sunder after Khrushchev's denunciation of Stalin in 1956.
The Chinese were shocked that this doctrinal somersault had been undertaken
without consultation with other communist parties. Thereafter Moscow's
escalating revisionism alarmed and outraged Peking. In the view of Roland
Berger, the Russian betrayal was threefold: 'the introduction of the profit
motive and dependence on greater material incentives in industry; the denial
of the dictatorship of the proletariat and its replacement by "the state of the
whole people"; on the international front, the pursuit of a policy based on the
domination of the world by the two powers, the U.S.A. and the U.S.S.R.'[88] As
the Sino-Soviet breach widened into a yawning gap after 1959, the dominant
CPGB cadre in the BCFA whipped it into supporting Moscow's line against
Peking's. The CPGB packed the Association's annual general meeting of 1964
with 200 new members so as to vote down all pro-Peking resolutions. The
PRC's legation in London accordingly withdrew its patronage of BCFA and
encouraged the formation of a breakaway organization.

87 A. J. Ayer, *More of My Life* (London: Collins, 1984), pp. 99–100.
88 King's, papers of Joan Robinson JVR 7/61/18, Roland Berger's memorandum for
Robinson, c. 1968.

The working committee that during the winter of 1964–65 planned and launched the new pro-Peking Society for Anglo-Chinese Understanding comprised Needham, Robinson, Bill Ash, Roland Berger, Derek Bryan, Jack Perry and Perry's business partner Bernard Buckman. Needham assured SACU'S potential supporters that the new body would not become just another communist front organization, and adduced as proof that its secretariat had no clandestine connections or intentions. Joan Robinson similarly dismissed as nonsensical any suggestion that this secretariat, comprising Berger, Perry and Percy Timberlake, was communistic. Trevor-Roper's discoveries about the workings of SACU indicate otherwise. So do Security Services dossiers.

A memorandum circulated in the Foreign Office in July 1965, prepared by the Information Research Department (IRD) and doubtless using Security Service (MI5) material and analysis, described SACU as 'a pro-Chinese Communist front organisation'. Citing a report in *The Sunday Times* of 16 May, the memorandum concluded: 'the daily business of the new organisation is in the hands of a group which controls another Communist front, the British Council for the Promotion of International Trade'.[89] The challenge for Needham and SACU, one which Derek Bryan had the plausibility and adroitness to surmount, was to combine communist purposes and management with an appeal to people who had a general interest in learning more about China, or whose liberal or progressive outlooks predisposed them to look sympathetically on the ideals of PRC without looking too closely into its practices. Needham's solution was to recruit 200 'sponsors' of SACU from the arts, business, medicine, science and universities who would vouchsafe the society's credibility by lending their names to a brochure that was circulated to attract members. Needham's influence on the brochure's wording is audible:

> In ancient and medieval times China was often in the forefront of discovery and invention, with a standard of life – as Marco Polo found – higher than anything that Europe could then show. But with the coming of the Renaissance, while modern science and technology arose in the West, generating powerful nations and communities which took their people into the era of worldwide commerce,

---

89 NA FO 1110/1994, PR 1411/20, Unsigned memorandum, 'Society for Anglo-Chinese Understanding', July 1965; John Barry and Cal McCrystal, 'All-party group for Anglo-Chinese understanding', *Sunday Times*, 16 May 1965. On the IRD, see Paul Lashmar and James Oliver, *Britain's Secret Propaganda War 1948–77* (Stroud: Sutton, 1998).

industrialisation, mass production – all the achievements of the modern age, Chinese culture continued to follow for a long time the slow growth of her age-old ways, isolated from these great upthrusts of the 19th and 20th centuries. Now, in the latter half of the 20th century, the Chinese people have thrown off the cramping features of their past society. They are emerging once again to recreate their former greatness and to take their place as a nation with an immense contribution to the striving of the human race towards abundance and peace.

Reflecting this, SACU will seek to convey to the British people something of the richness and grandeur of the old China as well as the individual initiative and united energy of the new.

Today in China, a great aggregate of peoples, more than one-fifth of the human race, is engaged in an unprecedented struggle to break out of the deprivations, poverty and backwardness of its pre-industrial society and create a new, bustling, dynamic nation-hood. This tremendous endeavour must be seen and understood by the watching world.[90]

It was after meeting Trevor-Roper at a lunch in March 1965 that Needham suggested that he become a sponsor of SACU.[91] The list of sponsors represented diverse political opinions. There were irreproachable heads of Cambridge colleges: Sir Eric Ashby, of Clare; Ruth Cohen, of Newnham; Sir Gordon Sutherland, of Emmanuel. Oxford college heads were Sir Maurice Bowra of Wadham and Dame Janet Vaughan of Somerville. There were scientists: Sir Ernst Chain, co-recipient of the Nobel Prize for Medicine for his work on penicillin, the future Nobel laureate Dorothy Hodgkin, and the epidemiologist Sir Richard Doll, later Regius Professor of Medicine at Oxford. Cyril Offord, the first professor of mathematics at LSE, and Sir Robert Macintosh, the first professor of anaesthetics at Oxford, were also sponsors, as was Freddie Ayer. So too were left-wing hereditary peers: Lords Amulree, Faringdon, Kennet and Russell. There were radical priests, such as Canon John Collins, founder of Christian Action and of War on Want, Hewlett Johnson, and Mervyn Stockwood, Bishop of Southwark. The creative artists included Michael

90 Dacre 6/14, SACU promotional pamphlet, May 1965.
91 Bodleian, papers of Nicolaus Kurti H96, Needham to T-R, 2 March 1965.

Ayrton, Benjamin Britten, Barbara Hepworth, Marie Rambert, Ruskin Spear and Basil Spence. Other representatives of the great and the good included the publisher Victor Gollancz, and the Cambridge economist Richard Kahn.[92] Among Labour MPs there were Leo Abse, who had served the interests of the Soviet bloc (perhaps unwittingly) by campaigning against German member-ship of NATO, and Will Owen, who all too wittingly served the same interests from 1957 in return for a retainer of £500 a month paid by Czechoslovak State Security. When, in 1970, Owen confessed his misdoings to MI5 in return for a guarantee of immunity from prosecution, it was Abse whom he chose to act as a sort of 'McKenzie friend' attending his interrogation.[93]

*

Trevor-Roper's diary of his visit to China, which began as a private store of impressions, acquired another function after a week or so. *The Sunday Times*, on learning of his impending journey, had asked him to write a report for it on his return. At the time he prevaricated, but his experiences of the Maoist state of mind persuaded him to accept. The diary served the purpose of an *aide-mémoire*. The article in *The Sunday Times* proved an incendiary docu-ment, appearing as it did shortly before he and his fellow delegates appeared at a meeting of SACU to report on their visit. Its effect was exacerbated by the headline given it, to Trevor-Roper's dismay, by a sub-editor, 'The Sick Mind of China', a title foreign to the spirit of a piece concerned to understand, not to denounce. By the time the article appeared he was involved in one of the pub-lic contests that recur in his career. In this case he entered the lists to champion his conviction that civic health depends on vigilant attention to the workings of power and opinion, on the uncovering of falsehood, and on the willingness of thinking people to enter controversial engagement in those causes.

It was while he was writing his *Sunday Times* article that Trevor-Roper resolved to investigate SACU's funding, management and aims. Part Two of this book, written in December 1965, describes that endeavour. Part Three is an account of SACU, and of his relations with it, written in June 1966. It is

92 Bodleian, papers of Dorothy Hodgkin, Ms Eng c 5688/G110, SACU Sponsors list, 16 March 1965.

93 Christopher Andrew and Oleg Gordievsky, *KGB: the inside story of its foreign operations from Lenin to Gorbachev* (London: Hodder & Stoughton, 1990), pp. 432–3; Leo Abse, 'The Judas syndrome', *Spectator*, 20 March 1982.

a sequel to Part Two. Although there is overlap between the documents, there is divergent material as well. There is also a difference of purpose. Whereas the text of December was written as a private record, the one composed seven months later was intended for publication. It was meant for the monthly magazine *Encounter*, but was stifled by the English legal tradition of protecting reputations at the cost of truth. The magazine's libel lawyers submitted a report, which was described as 'six pages of snorts'.[94] In consequence the document has remained unseen for more than half a century.

Trevor-Roper would have liked to overturn SACU's leadership and to make the institution what it purported to be and what a large proportion of those who had been recruited to it supposed and wanted it to be, a body devoted to the broad purpose of understanding China, past and present. He was not optimistic, and his defeat was no surprise. But at least he could expose the communist front. In the midst of a host of professional obligations and literary commitments he devoted great time and energy to the examination of the finances, personnel and management of SACU and to the penetration of the shroud which concealed its communist control. Why? The suggestion in a circular of May 1966, signed by Needham, Robinson and Adams, that he was a McCarthyite persecutor of communists is no answer. Trevor-Roper loathed 'the panic fear of communism' which swept the United States in the 1950s with Senator Joseph McCarthy as witch-hunter general.[95] At the Congress for Cultural Freedom, funded by the CIA, in West Berlin in 1950 he contested against ex-Marxists, led by Arthur Koestler and Franz Borkenau, who excited a vengeful and illiberal anti-communist atmosphere which, with his fellow delegate Freddie Ayer, Trevor-Roper found 'frightening' and 'hysterical'.[96] The memory of the conference spurred him to use a *New Statesman* review of Dorothy Vaughan's diplomatic narrative *Europe and the Turk, 1350–1700* (1954)

94 CC, Dacre papers 13/3, Bryan Healing to Trevor-Roper, 5 August 1966. When in 1985 Tariq Ali wrote his memoir of the 1960s, *Street Fighting Years*, covering some of the events in Trevor-Roper's journals, his publishers received a libel report from the solicitor Peter Carter-Ruck presenting a battery of objections to publication. These are some of Carter-Ruck's highlights: 'The assertion that Kim Il Sung liquidated political refugees is defamatory of Sung'; 'It is defamatory to say of British Labour leaders that they told "untruths"'; apropos the murder of Patrice Lumumba, 'the allegation of "sadism, systematic torture and mass murders" perpetrated by the Belgian regime and attributable to leaders of the Colonial Government of the time, is defamatory'; 'the reference to the "terror" of the Suharto regime is defamatory'.
95 Trevor-Roper, 'The bitter lessons of the great McCarthy terror', *Sunday Times*, 10 September 1978.
96 Trevor-Roper, 'Ex-Communist v. Communist', *Manchester Guardian*, 10 July 1950.

to deny the Cold-War warriors' theory 'that a frontal struggle between opposing systems is sooner or later inevitable and might as well be hastened by an ideological crusade'. He preferred the historical precedents for the wary 'coexistence' of rival empires.[97]

In the scholarly world he resisted prescription. Although in 1955 he had a fierce clash about Marx with the historian Eric Hobsbawm in the correspondence pages of the *New Statesman*, five years later he helped Hobsbawm (a long-standing CPGB member) to obtain a visa for the United States.[98] In the same year he battled for two hours at a Christ Church governing body meeting to get the Marxist historian of the ancient world Moses Finley, who had been put on McCarthyite blacklists at US universities, appointed as Student and Tutor in classics. He did so despite the volcanic fury that this aroused in his two closest college allies, Robert Blake and Charles Stuart, who were entrenched, last-ditch anti-Marxists.[99] He opposed the suppression of dissent whether of the right or of the left, and on both sides of the Cold War. He knew the power and the dangers of intellectual conformity, whether or not it was enforced. Two months after his return from the PRC he reviewed the memoirs of the editor of the *New Statesman*, Kingsley Martin. Although 'the egotism, the smugness, sometimes the double-think of professional dissenters repels me', he wrote, 'how I agree with Mr Martin about the necessity of dissent! Heresy is the only guarantee of continuing thought'. He approvingly quoted Martin's remark that 'When a great many very important people say something over and over again, very solemnly, you can be pretty sure they are wrong.'[100]

But if he was opposed to the suppression of Marxist non-conformity he had no time for Marxist theory. There were, he reckoned, fertile Marxist historians, but only because their findings took them beyond their Marxist premises. The descriptive vocabulary of Marxism seemed to him ill-fitted to the societies it affected to describe. 'As a historian,' he wrote, he could not find a single instance in which the Marxist interpretation of history survived 'the test of research'. If Marxist history were, as it claimed to be, scientific, and if the

---

97 Trevor-Roper, 'Europe and the Turk', *New Statesman*, 14 May 1955, reprinted in his *Historical Essays* (London: Macmillan, 1957), p. 177.

98 CC Dacre 1/1/H, T-R to Hobsbawm, 8 February 1960; Richard Evans, *Eric Hobsbawm: a life in history* (London: Little, Brown, 2019), pp. 384–5.

99 Dacre 17/1/3, Hugh Trevor Roper to Lady Alexandra Trevor-Roper, 27 May 1955; Adam Sisman, *Hugh Trevor-Roper: the biography* (London: Weidenfeld & Nicolson, 2010), pp. 264–5.

100 Trevor-Roper, 'The essential heretic', *Sunday Times*, 9 January 1966.

progress of society moved along predetermined Marxist lines, then the future ought to be predictable, and yet Marxists had a hopeless record of prediction. Marx had not predicted the rise of fascism. 'Marxist tipster[s] ... dismissed Hitler and Mussolini as ephemeral phenomena': as 'bubbles which would surface only to burst and be dissolved again into the majestic stream of history, rolling onward in its predetermined course.' It was above all against Marxist determinism that he reacted. The theory of dialectical materialism, 'which will triumph whether we like it or not', could not only justify tyranny but, even in free societies, sap the sense of individual responsibility.[101] Doctrines of political irresistibility themselves needed to be resisted. Determinism, in Trevor-Roper's thinking, misses the role not only of events and of 'the contingent and the unforeseen' but of free choice and its consequences.[102]

In the post-war decades, Marxist assumptions permeated the writings of historians who would not have called themselves Marxists. In the years before his visit to China, Trevor-Roper had been engaged in an intensive study of the English civil wars of the mid-seventeenth century. His rival interpreters treated the parliamentarian cause as the herald of a predestined and progressive future, as if the events and choices on which the outcome of the struggle depended were a mere surface beneath which inexorable social and economic forces, beyond human control, were at work. Few professional historians would now endorse those notions, but in the post-war decades they became a virtual orthodoxy, carrying their own conformist appeal. Trevor-Roper's at times almost solitary resistance to it rested on a belief in the efficacy of political engagement, a principle he applied to past and present alike. In a free society, those who did not engage could not complain if they were disempowered by those who did.

Communism too, a doctrine so 'intellectually false', in its consequences so 'humanly brutal', and in its implications so threatening to civil and mental liberty, must be resisted. He took membership of the Communist Party, with its obligatory surrender of thought to dogma, to be a treason of the mind.[103] The publicizing of purges and show-trials, the killings, the gulag, the scientific frauds and the surrender of individual judgement was a necessary response

---

101 Trevor-Roper, 'History and Imagination', in Hugh Lloyd-Jones, Valerie Pearl and Blair Worden, eds, *History and Imagination: essays in honour of H. R. Trevor-Roper* (London: Duckworth, 1981), p. 359.

102 Trevor-Roper, 'E. H. Carr's Success Story', *Encounter*, May 1962, p. 72.

103 Sisman, *Trevor-Roper*, p. 262.

to communist rule, but not a sufficient one: 'to destroy it, it is not enough to expose its falsity and its brutality: we must also seek to provide a better answer which will render its false appeal less tempting'.[104]

In the light of those attitudes it is no surprise to find Trevor-Roper devoting so much time and trouble to the exposure of a communist front organization which he had himself sponsored. The success of front organizations substantiated another of the convictions that he applied to past and present alike. Often, he believed, the distribution of political power is not a reflection of the opinions and values of those qualified to exercise it, but the victory of activity over passivity: of determination and decisiveness and manipulation, generally by a small minority, over the irresolution and woolliness and inertia of the mass. As he explained in an essay on the political management of seventeenth-century parliaments, the piece where that view is most forthrightly elucidated, 'over the unprepared the prepared always have an advantage', at least if they are skilful, for 'able men can work any system'.[105] The system worked by the leadership of SACU was based on the flagrant and yet, until Trevor-Roper got to work, uncontested abuse of the society's rules by a small group.

His campaign gave exercise to the forensic investigative gifts which repeatedly surface in his writing: in *The Last Days of Hitler*; in his biography of Backhouse; in his writings on wartime intelligence, which have been brought together by Edward Harrison; in his monitoring of the confidence trickster who called himself the Reverend Robert Peters.[106] He conducted his own research into SACU's papers. He received information from allies within SACU's membership, notably two Oxford intellectuals: Valerie Pearl, his friend and fellow historian of the English civil wars, who afterwards was principal of a Cambridge college; and the low-temperature physicist Nicholas Kurti.

---

104 *Why I oppose communism* (London: Phoenix House, 1956), pp. 8–10.

105 Trevor-Roper, *Religion, The Reformation and Social Change: and other essays* (London: Macmillan, 1967), pp. 363, 375.

106 Trevor-Roper, *The Last Days of Hitler* (London: Macmillan, 1947); Trevor-Roper, *The Secret World: behind the curtain of British Intelligence in World War II and the Cold War*, ed. Edward Harrison (London: I.B. Tauris, 2014); Adam Sisman, *The Professor and the Parson: a story of desire, deceit and defrocking* (London: Profile, 2019).

Kurti – a fellow of Brasenose since 1947 and vice-president of the Royal Society in 1965–67 – proved a splendid ally and abettor.[107] He had been schooled at the *Minta Gimnázium* [model gymnasium] in Budapest where Edward Teller, Thomas Balogh and Nicholas Kaldor had also been pupils. His early ambition to be a concert pianist was discarded after he failed an audition taken by Béla Bartók for the Budapest Academy of Music. He began studying physics at the Sorbonne in 1926, continued his work at Berlin University from 1928, and was inspired there by his contacts with Erwin Schrödinger. As technical assistant to Franz Simon at the Technische Hochshule in Breslau [Wroclaw], he was one of the quintet of physicists brought to the Clarendon Laboratory by Professor Frederick Lindemann, afterwards Lord Cherwell, in 1933. He recalled his first sunny morning in Oxford, riding pillion on Mendelssohn's motorcycle, from Headington to Lindemann's laboratory: 'as we crossed Magdalen bridge I thought "This is fairyland – why should I ever leave it?"' Kurti worked on the UK atomic bomb project in 1940–45: his wife was a wartime secretary in the Security Service. In the 1950s he ran a notably productive research team in cryogenics (low-temperature physics) that was for its time unusually multidisciplinary. The coldest place on earth, from 1956 until 1974, was in Parks Road, Oxford, where Kurti's nuclear cooling experiments obtained a temperature of between one and two millionths of a degree kelvin.

In Oxford, as well as nationally and internationally, Kurti sat on numerous committees. The verve and zest of his thinking, and his realism in measuring probable outcomes of decisions, made him a formidable committee man. Although he could be irksome, his spry and playful charm made him easy to forgive. Like Isaiah Berlin, he spoke of himself as 'a genuine charlatan'. For years he organized an annual workshop, held in Sicily, on molecular gastronomy and the application of experimental physics to cooking. 'It is a sad reflection on our civilisation,' he mused, 'that while we can and do measure the temperature in the atmosphere of Venus, we do not know what goes on inside our soufflés.' His book of cookery recipes contributed by fellows of the Royal Society was a characteristic piece of fun. Raymond Blanc and Heston Blumenthal both acknowledged their culinary debts to him.[108] Among other sidelines Kurti arranged the publication in *Nature* of the transcripts made in

---

107 The following two paragraphs follow J. H. Sanders, 'Nicholas Kurti CBE', *Biographical Memoirs of Fellows of the Royal Society*, vol. 46 (2000), pp. 300–15; Ralph Scurlock, 'Nicholas Kurti', *Physics Today* (June 1999), pp. 77–8.

108 Nicholas Kurti, 'Guest Cook', *The Times*, 8 August 1981; Heston Blumenthal, 'How do you make roast chicken extra moist?', *The Times*, 17 June 2010.

1945 of secretly recorded conversations of interned German nuclear scientists after they heard of the bombing of Hiroshima. In the 1970s and 1980s he attended International Conferences on the Unity of Sciences, which were held under the auspices of the Unification Church ('the Moonies') in such hot-spots as Miami Beach. He became both a defender of participation in these meetings and a quizzical critic of their begetter, the entrepreneurial Korean evangelist Sun Myung Moon.[109]

Trevor-Roper had another source too. There is no sign that when he went to China he knew of the recent conclusion of the Security Service and the Foreign Office that SACU was a front organization. On his return, however, he contacted Richard ('Dick') Thistlethwaite of the Service and also lunched with his old friend Sir Dick White, director-general of the Secret Intelligence Service (SIS; MI6), who had been responsible, at the end of the war, for Trevor-Roper's appointment to conduct the research that would produce *The Last Days of Hitler*. Trevor-Roper and Thistlethwaite would meet at the Athenaeum, a club of which they were both members, and corresponded regularly. When Trevor-Roper sought information about individuals and organizations, it was supplied from Security Service sources, although Thistlethwaite had (he said) to write 'guardedly' in his letters.[110] These were typed on the headed notepaper of the Athenaeum, which he used as a handy and discreet mail-box. In a letter to Thistlethwaite, written after a public meeting at which Trevor-Roper was assailed by Maoist devotees, he wryly described himself as 'your reliable but, alas, blown V-man': V-man standing for the word used by German wartime intelligence to indicate a 'trusted man' or agent, *Vertrauensmann*.[111] Thistlethwaite, who used several sources to monitor the doings of SACU, often sought meetings. 'We should very much like to discuss with you what you feel you should do now,' he wrote on one occasion. Security Service officers would 'be available … for discussion whenever you are in Town'. He never neglected to encourage his self-styled V-man:

> My own opinion, for what it is worth, is that you have had consider-
> able success and that you have support [within SACU], not just on
> personal grounds but on the issues of principle which you have done
> so much to bring into the open. This being so I should have thought

109 Nicholas Kurti, 'Should scientists attend the ICUS?', *Nature*, vol. 276, 16 November 1978.

110 Dacre 13/3, Thistlethwaite to Trevor-Roper, 31 March 1966.

111 CC, Dacre papers 13/3, Trevor-Roper to Thistlethwaite, 18 May 1966. This document is serial 45a in the Security Service file on SACU, to which I have not had access.

that all men of good will, inside and outside S.A.C.U., would welcome your continued presence in its deliberations. Moreover, the more that these issues can be debated on a national plane and not just between Oxford and Cambridge the better it would be.[112]

In March 1966, when it became clear that Trevor-Roper's membership of SACU was becoming untenable, Thistlethwaite advised him: 'we have to face the fact that you [will] have to go, but let it be with a bang'.[113] Trevor-Roper's 10,000-word article written three months later – Part Three of this book – was the detonation.

In his later form as Lord Dacre of Glanton, Trevor-Roper told the House of Lords in 1986 that he was the only member of the second parliamentary chamber who had worked in both MI5 and MI6.[114] The mark of his wartime intelligence work, of its attentiveness, its analytical rigour, of his awareness of the practical consequences of right or wrong conclusions, never left his mind. Donald McLachlan, another wartime practitioner, wrote that high-grade intelligence work requires 'the patience of a rock climber; the scholar's application to dull detail; the cold objectivity of a research scientist; the intuition of the archaeologist handling fragmentary fact; the discretion of a doctor; the showmanship of a journalist; and the forensic talent of a barrister'.[115] Trevor-Roper maintained intelligence contacts after his return to Oxford and to historical scholarship. He was regularly used as a source by officers of the Security Service inquiring about Oxford men in whom they were interested (the future Cabinet minister Edmund Dell being one such case). In turn he made reciprocal inquiries of intelligence agencies. After first meeting the Czech-born publisher and parliamentary candidate Robert Maxwell in 1962, his suspicions were enough aroused for him, almost by reflex, to write to Dick White of SIS asking about Maxwell's background and doings. White had Maxwell 'looked at', reported that he was unscrupulous and asked Trevor-Roper: 'Had you any particular reason for thinking I should instigate rather thorough inquiries? [116]

Numerous historians and philosophers in Oxford had worked in wartime for the Security Service, SIS, military intelligence or cognate agencies, among

---

112 Dacre 13/3, Thistlethwaite to Trevor-Roper, 28 April 1966.

113 CC, Dacre papers 13/3, Thistlethwaite to Trevor-Roper, 31 March 1966.

114 House of Lords debates, 17 December 1986, vol. 483, col. 179.

115 Donald McLachlan, *Room 39: Naval Intelligence in action, 1939–45* (London: Weidenfeld & Nicolson, 1968), p. 338.

116 Dacre 1/2/6, Dick White to Trevor-Roper, 5 December 1962.

them his friends Freddie Ayer, Robert Blake, Stuart Hampshire, Hugh Lloyd-Jones, Gilbert Ryle and Charles Stuart. Of the eight Regius professorships at Oxford in the early 1960s, three were held by men with wartime intelligence careers (Sir Godfrey Driver, Hebrew; Lloyd-Jones, Greek; Trevor-Roper himself, Modern History). Trevor-Roper's career held the pursuits of scholarship and public service – in classical terms, the spheres of contemplation and action – together.

*

It was with a view to action that he collected information on SACU. On 14 November 1965, two weeks after his *Sunday Times* article had appeared, he had a meeting with Derek Bryan. Trevor-Roper was by now well primed with awkward questions. 'I am quite satisfied that the budget, as cooked up in the office, is a completely fraudulent document,' he told Kurti after the meeting.

> I have quite enough evidence to blow up the whole of S.A.C.U., but I feel we should make at least an apparent effort to put the thing straight. I say 'at least an apparent effort' because I hardly think we will succeed in straightening it. However, if we go out of it, I feel that we should all go out together, in which case it will collapse.[117]

Two days later, on 16 November, there was an open meeting of SACU, held at Church House, Westminster, which Parts Two and Three of this book graphically describe. On 13 December Trevor-Roper attended a closed meeting of SACU's council of management, for which he was again well prepared. He succeeded in getting a discussion of the resignation as treasurer of Sir Gordon Sutherland, which Bryan and his allies had kept quiet. The cautious and honest Sutherland had quit after being presented with SACU's implausible accounts. Trevor-Roper's ally Kurti now was appointed in Sutherland's place. At the same meeting Trevor-Roper won agreement that henceforth an accurate record of donations must be kept (a stipulation that curbed SACU's fundraising from sources who shrank from being identified). He also challenged the practice of appointing the members to the General Purposes Committee by co-option for indefinite periods. The device had produced a committee whose members, with the exception of Mary Adams, were all *communisant*.

---

117 Bodleian, Kurti papers H936, Trevor-Roper to Kurti, 18 November 1965.

All the others, Roland Berger, his wife 'Nan', Ash, Percy Timberlake, Ernie Roberts and Joan Robinson, so Trevor-Roper briefed Kurti, 'are all of the faithful, and I have no doubt they support Bryan in his flouting of the Council of Management'. As a result of Trevor-Roper's protests, future members of the General Purposes Committee had to be nominated by the SACU Council. 'I now have a *deep* distrust of Bryan,' Trevor-Roper continued to Kurti. 'Some of his tactics and evasions seem to me positively crooked.'[118]

In 1965 a local branch of SACU was started in Oxford: further branches opened in north London and Cambridge early in the new year. The Cambridge branch, with Jack Perry's son Graham as its organizing secretary, had large attendances at its meetings during 1966–68: curiosity about Mao's *Red Book*, excitement at the Cultural Revolution, and opposition to the Vietnam War made Cambridge SACU thrive almost independently of anything SACU headquarters said or did. The Oxford and Cambridge branches differed in their operations from the suburban London branches. At a meeting at Hendon Town Hall on 24 February 1966 to launch the Barnet branch – the occasion on which Stuart Gelder extolled the freedom of the press in China – Joan Robinson declared that 'What is going on in China today is one of the most interesting social experiments of our time,' though 'because of political discrimination, we are not allowed to know the truth about China.'[119] Valerie Pearl became a Barnet member. 'The more I see of our local branch,' she told Trevor-Roper in May 1966, 'the more I feel it resembles the American Communist party, in consisting of no-one but agents and counter-agents! As for the rest of SACU, I have never met an organisation with so many committees and so little democracy. The rank and file is *never* consulted at any level.'[120]

Trevor-Roper's account of SACU's Oxford branch, given in Parts Two and Three, can be amplified. To the dismay of SACU's leadership, the Oxford branch, being predominantly composed of academics whose interests in China were scholarly or artistic rather than political, maintained a sturdy independence. It was chaired by the mild and scrupulous orientalist Raymond Dawson, a fellow of Wadham College since 1963 and author of works of accessible scholarship on Chinese culture and history. The membership included

---

118 Bodleian, Kurti papers H936, Trevor-Roper to Kurti, 25 December 1965.

119 'Bid to Promote Anglo-Chinese Understanding', *Barnet Press*, 4 March 1966.

120 Dacre 13/3, Valerie Pearl to Trevor-Roper, 18 May 1966. At an earlier branch meeting, 'My mild criticism of China brought first a shocked silence, then a tumultuous onslaught from the faithful' (Dacre 1/2/10, Pearl to Trevor-Roper, 14 April 1966).

grandees who were not going to be shunted into ideological sidings, such as the political economist Sir Noel Hall, then principal of Brasenose College,[121] who had been the Ministry of Information's representative in Washington during the war, the quantum chemist Charles Coulson, who held an Oxford chair in applied mathematics and was chairman of Oxfam, and an eminent professor of chemistry, Sir Harold Thompson, who had been a member of the first Royal Society delegation to Academia Sinica in 1962. The physicists and friends Nicholas Kurti and Kurt Mendelssohn also attended Oxford branch meetings. But the inner group at SACU headquarters bridled at the autonomous spirit of the Oxonians. As Trevor-Roper noted, the branch found its arrangements 'criticised, its choice of speakers condemned, its subjects of discussion declared unsuitable; and this condemnation has been expressed, in the language of authority (but also of crass factual ignorance), not by the Council or any member of it, but by a Mr Roland Berger who at the time, had no public responsibility whatever within the Society'.[122]

The Oxford membership had a sizeable left-wing component. The traditional left included Annie ('Bet') Dodds, a familiar elderly eccentric in the Bodleian reading rooms whose classicist husband was admired by Trevor-Roper;[123] the New Zealander Margaret ('Peggy') Garland, who had been an admiring visitor to China in 1952; and the crystallographer and SACU sponsor Dorothy Hodgkin, who had first visited China with Derek Bryan in 1959. Garland too had long known Bryan. The new left was represented by the Trotskyite student activist Tariq Ali, afterwards editor of *Red Mole* and then *Black Dwarf*, who would organize the mass demonstration in London on 27 October 1968, an event, in Trevor-Roper's words, 'designed to begin the revolution and usher in the new society. It failed to do either.'[124] And there was Nicholas Bateson, who in the United States in 1963 had repeatedly invoked the fifth amendment when subpoenaed and interrogated by the House Unamerican Activities Committee about propaganda on behalf of Fidel Castro's Cuba. In 1969 Bateson, by then working in the social psychology department of the London School of Economics (LSE), was dismissed with his colleague Robin Blackburn after supporting students who tore down internal security gates in

121 Isaiah Berlin considered Hall 'a really absurd Principal' for Brasenose (letter to Noël Annan, 31 October 1960; King's College archives, NGA 5/1/79/1).

122 Dacre 13/3, Trevor-Roper circular letter to SACU sponsors, c. 21 May 1966.

123 Trevor-Roper, 'The scholar's private world', *Sunday Times*, 11 December 1977.

124 Trevor-Roper, *The Letters of Mercurius* (London: John Murray, 1970), p. 1.

violent scenes which led to the school's closure for several weeks. The destroy-ers of the gates, Bateson said, acted 'in solidarity with the heroic liberation fighters of Viet Nam and Zimbabwe'. They were 'portents of a glorious future', in which students would 'smash monopoly capitalism control of education'.[125] It was perhaps through Bateson's influence that Bill Ash spoke at the Oxford branch of SACU in praise of the Cultural Revolution and showed the film *Chairman Mao is the Red Sun in our Hearts* (3 October 1967), and that Reg Birch reported on his recent visit to China (19 October 1967). Ash and Birch had first met at a Chinese Legation party, and in 1967–68 formed a new fac-tion, the Communist Party of Britain (Marxist-Leninist). Reportedly Bateson was among its members.

A committee meeting of the Oxford branch was held on the evening of 25 April 1966. Trevor-Roper attended and (in response to questions) spoke at length. Next day, in a letter to Derek Bryan which he circulated to his SACU allies, Peggy Garland reported that Trevor-Roper had given

> a quite accurate account of the birth and lineage of SACU not omit-ting to underline the fact that the old China Friendship Society was quite definitely a C'ist front – and that SACU was exactly the same – only pro-China as against pro-Russia. Well one knows the truth of this and to you I need hardly pretend. The whole question is how to run SACU. You can't dictate to this branch at Oxford policy over choice of speakers. That simply is not your function, however much it is your concern. You must allow autonomous and unilateral freedom of choice. I promise you the Cttee is not all on the side of T-R ideologically ... You will never get, and ought not to try to get, a C'ist-orientated SACU at Oxford. You may get an academic SACU on the democratic, perhaps rather cool scholarly lines of the University ... Above all, don't try to bully and dictate to them – you, Derek, use *your* brand of persuasion, and *don't* fid-dle the books. For heaven's sake don't give T-R all this excellent ammunition to use against you ... people like these at Oxford ... are far too intelligent to be fooled ... The day is past when C'ists could, under cover of respectability and non-political organisation, put over their dogmas and win converts.

---

125 Michael Beloff, 'The L.S.E. Story', *Encounter*, May 1969, p. 72; 'LSE man awaits ver-dict', *Guardian*, 23 February 1969.

Garland warned Bryan that although a few younger members had mauled the Regius Professor at the meeting, 'T-R. can do the hell of a lot of harm. Handle him – don't try to pull any wool over his eyes at all – he knows and anticipates all the moves you could make. Honesty is your only policy with a man like this one. You have either to drop the close affiliation with Peking [or make it a] lot more plausible.'[126]

Also on 26 April, as Trevor-Roper learnt from what he considered an unimpeachable source, Bateson telephoned Needham and gave what Trevor-Roper alleged was a 'grotesquely false' oral account of the previous day's meeting. Prompted by his talk with Needham, Bateson sent Bryan a letter dated 28 April, which, as Kurti and Mendelssohn would confirm, likewise gave a misleading version of the speech. In it Bateson urged Bryan to expel Trevor-Roper, with Kurti, from SACU as soon as possible. On reading Bateson's letter, as Trevor-Roper told Valerie Pearl, 'Needham and co. – who took no steps at all to check the account – decided to get rid of me.' They saw their chance eighteen days later, when a well-informed article appeared in *The Sunday Times* of 15 May, alleging that 'a powerful group in SACU' was 'trying to run it wholly as a pro-Communist organisation' by 'using standard Communist-style committeemanship'.[127] Needham and his allies, Trevor-Roper told Pearl, had decided to 'fix' the article 'on me; and they evidently decided to do it publicly at the AGM' to be held on 21 May. In fact, it was written by a pertinacious investigative journalist John Barry, who had co-authored the article which a year earlier had linked SACU to 'communist front' organizations. Trevor-Roper had declined Barry's request to make a statement and had referred him to Derek Bryan. Wanting a document to read out at the AGM on 21 May, accusing Trevor-Roper of responsibility for the *Sunday Times* article, the leadership applied to Bateson, who on 18 May sent a long letter to Needham noting that the charges made against SACU's General Purposes Committee in Barry's article were suspiciously alike to those brought by Trevor-Roper at the Oxford SACU meeting on 25 April. Bateson's renewed denunciation enabled Berger to argue that Trevor-Roper was a fanatic hell-bent on launching an anti-communist witch-hunt and on destroying SACU.[128]

On 19 May, two days before the second annual general meeting of SACU, a stencilled letter, signed by Needham, Robinson and Mary Adams, was sent to all the sponsors of SACU: Trevor-Roper's copy seems to have been posted

---

126 SOAS, Derek Bryan papers, Peggy Garland to Derek Bryan, 26 April 1966.

127 John Barry, 'Battle to Control China Society', *Sunday Times*, 15 May 1966.

128 Dacre 13/3, Trevor-Roper to Pearl, 24 June 1966.

a day later than the others, and thus did not reach him before the annual general meeting. The circular deplored Barry's article as 'obvious sensationalism', with an intention to divide and harm SACU. 'This article follows one published by Professor Trevor-Roper in the same newspaper on his return from China – which caused great indignation among SACU members – and repeats statements which we understand he has been making in Oxford.' The circular warned that the article portended 'the introduction of McCarthyism into the Society's affairs'.[129] As Trevor-Roper reported to Thistlethwaite, 'I was naturally taken aback by this document, which I suspect to be libellous and legally actionable. But I soon recovered my equipoise and buzzed off identical letters to all three writers stating that I was amazed at their action in publishing such a libel without any effort to check the facts, which were untruly stated.'[130] His icy letter to Needham ended their friendship:

> Since you, Mrs Robinson and Mrs Adams have signed a document accusing me of McCarthyism, and have circulated it without checking the facts, and have said nothing to me about it, although I spent most of last Saturday in your company, you will not expect me to feel any further sympathy with a Society of which you are the President and they are, respectively, Deputy-Chairman and Vice-Chairman.[131]

Although the attempt to secure Trevor-Roper's expulsion failed, he was removed from the council of management. Having spent the morning of 21 May at a meeting of the council, where no one mentioned the stencilled letter identifying him with 'McCarthyism', he was voted off it at the annual general meeting in the afternoon. In the same election, Bill Ash and Roland Berger, who had hitherto operated in the murky General Purposes Committee, were elected to the open authority of council of management. This resolved Trevor-Roper to resign as a sponsor of SACU. As he explained to Kurti, 'the circular letter sent out by Needham, Robinson and Adams precipitated my action. I suspect that Robinson's was the master hand: the rough, rude, graceless

129 Dacre 13/3, Needham, Robinson and Adams to Sponsors of SACU, 19 May 1966.
130 Dacre 13/3, Trevor-Roper to Thistlethwaite, 23 May 1966.
131 SOAS, Derek Bryan papers, MS 99/1/5/4 and Dacre 13/3, Trevor-Roper to Needham, 27 May 1966.

manner is hers; but Needham is the Chairman and has signed.'[132] He had no remaining hope of keeping SACU to its avowed purpose of sincere mutual understanding.

> The essential fact is the election of Berger and Ash. I have always considered that their emergence from the shadows of the General Purposes Cttee to the open authority of the Council would be the sign of the take-over; and this has now happened. I regard Robinson, Bryan, Roberts, Ash and Berger as a secret society within a society. They have consistently concealed the true machinery of SACU from the Council. Now that they are all on the Council, it will no longer be possible to outvote them ... They will never let potential critics know exactly how the Society is financed or what its true relations with the Chinese govt are; and as long as these two subjects are cloaked in mystery, I cannot regard the Society as independent, or even honest. So out I go![133]

Trevor-Roper sent to all SACU sponsors an explanation of his resignation from their ranks. His long mimeographed letter gave a mordant account of the society's management and bias, and of its inner cadre's treatment of independent thinking. He had hopes, so he told Thistlethwaite, that his indictment letter would lead 'to the ruin of our Society'.[134] It did not do so. Only a few SACU sponsors resigned after reading it. Foremost among these was Freddie Ayer, who wrote: 'I am more inclined to believe what you say than what Needham says, and I strongly disapprove of them calling you a McCarthyite.'[135] Other sponsors who resigned in early June included the sculptor Elisabeth Frink, Dame Janet Vaughan of Somerville and the political theorist Leonard Woolf. Trevor-Roper received messages of support for his stand from sponsors as varied as Edmund Blunden, Benjamin Britten, Sir Herbert Read, Sir John Cockcroft and the Nobel prize-winning physicist Sir Nevill Mott. Not all of them were moved to resign.

---

132 Bodleian, Kurti H938, Trevor-Roper to Kurti, 26 May 1966. Noël Annan, who knew Robinson well, considered her 'ferocious', 'perfectly terrifying' and 'remorseless' when pursuing her opponents (Bodleian, Ms Berlin 241, letter to Isaiah Berlin, 12 November 1953).

133 Bodleian, Kurti H938, Trevor-Roper to Kurti, 26 May 1966.

134 Dacre 13/3, Trevor-Roper to Thistlethwaite, 23 May 1966.

135 Dacre 13/3, Ayer to Trevor-Roper, 6 June 1966.

Trevor-Roper's involvement in the affairs of SACU had, however, not ended yet. His ally Kurti, who remained as SACU's joint treasurer, reproached the society's leaders for attempting to expel and then provoking the resignation of Trevor-Roper. Kurti and Raymond Dawson considered disaffiliating the Oxford branch from SACU and thus retaining the Regius Professor of Modern History as an Oxford member, even though he had repudiated the London office. Bateson determined to obviate this possibility, and proposed an anti-Trevor-Roper motion for discussion at the annual general meeting of the Oxford branch, which was held on 18 June. First Bateson telephoned Garland to ask that she would second his motion. Garland not only declined but turned from being Bryan's informant to becoming an outlier among Trevor-Roper's supporters. After Garland's refusal, Bateson persuaded Heather Spooner, who was reading for a degree in Politics, Philosophy and Economics at St Hilda's College, to second him.[136] Bateson's motion was the first item on the agenda of 18 June.

Before Bateson could speak to his motion, Mendelssohn raised Bateson's April letter to Needham, which had reported and even denounced Trevor-Roper's speech at the Oxford branch committee meeting. Dawson asked Bateson to read the letter, which after prevarication he did. Trevor-Roper, who witnessed the sparring between Mendelssohn, Bateson and Dawson, described the denouement to Pearl: 'It was a dreadful letter and the audience, hostile at the start, were even more hostile when it had finished. The language was intemperate and irresponsible, the whole committee was described as "hysterical" in its anti-communism, and at the end Bateson advised Needham that there was "no point in appeasing Trevor-Roper": he must be pushed out.' Having compared the letter with the content of Bateman's telephone conversation with Needham on 26 April, Trevor-Roper found it clear that it had been written to be read at SACU's annual general meeting of 21 May as a justification for expelling him. 'The reading of the letter,' Trevor-Roper told Pearl, 'was quite fatal to Bateson. The St Hilda's girl, called upon to second the motion, feebly ran out. She knew nothing, she said: it was merely because Mr Bateson needed

---

136 A year later Heather Spooner (b. 1946) was awarded a first in PPE before taking a second degree in economics at St Antony's. This involved a visit to Algeria to investigate conditions in a fertilizer factory, but she was mistrusted as an industrial spy and refused any information. She acquired the surname of Joshi by her first marriage in 1969. After working in the Government Economic Service, and at the London School of Hygiene and Tropical Medicine, she became a Professor of Economic and Developmental Demography in London University; and was elected FBA.

a seconder that she had been persuaded to help.'[137] Bateson's motion was not put to a vote because it had no other seconder.

The revelation that the April meeting had been informed on, and the sense that he was under surveillance, was insupportable to Raymond Dawson, who resigned the chair of the Oxford branch. He did not yet resign from SACU itself. That came a year later, among a batch of resignations, including Kurti's, after the PRC exploded its first hydrogen bomb on 17 June 1967 and SACU's leadership sent a congratulatory message to Peking, in which, according to Kurti, they hailed Mao as effectively 'a great scientist'.[138] Next day a press statement was issued over Needham's name:

> The Society for Anglo-Chinese Understanding warmly congratulates the Chinese people on China's successful testing of a hydrogen bomb. This brilliant technical achievement, less than three years after China's first nuclear test, goes a long way to defeat the policy of nuclear blackmail directed against China by her enemies. It is a great encouragement to people throughout the world who are struggling for freedom against the determination of others to impose on them the Western capitalist way of life, and particularly to the people of Vietnam.
>
> China's development of nuclear weapons for the purpose of defence is coupled with her reiterated assurance, which no other nuclear power has given, that she will never be the first to use such weapons. It brings nearer the day when they will be abolished throughout the world, and is thus an outstanding contribution to world stability.[139]

Needham's reply to Kurti's letter of resignation upbraided him as 'one who deserts his friends after engaging with them in a great and noble cause'.[140]

The challenge for SACU was that, in order to exert influence, it had to retain its liberal following while abetting an illiberal regime. In welcoming

---

137 Dacre 13/3, Trevor-Roper to Valerie Pearl, 24 June 1966. The texts of Bateson's letters are preserved in Derek Bryan's papers in the SOAS archives.

138 CC, Dacre 13/3, Kurti to Trevor-Roper, 10 September 1967.

139 SOAS, Derek Bryan papers, box 14, SACU Press Statement, 18 June 1967.

140 Bodleian, Ms Eng c 5688, Hodgkin G111, Kurti to Betty Paterson, 30 September 1967; Kurti H942, Needham to Kurti, 4 October 1967. See also 'China society loses fourth Oxford man', *The Times*, 4 October 1967, and 'Professor quits China society', *Guardian*, 4 October 1967.

the Cultural Revolution, it also had to downplay the activities of Red Guards. Needham, who under the name Henry Holorenshaw had written a book on the Levellers of the English civil wars, proposed in a lecture of 1967 that the Cultural Revolution had an honourable precedent in 'the reign of saints in Commonwealth England, when Puritans were in full control'. He likened Red Guards' vandalism to the defacing and decapitation of statues and shrines in Ely Cathedral, which had in fact been perpetrated by Reformation iconoclasts in the 1540s.[141] But a difficulty arose when SACU's fellow sympathizers were arrested by the Red Guards or other PRC agencies and accused of spying: the detainees included David Crook (a friend of both Berger and Bryan), Elsie Fairfax-Cholmeley with her husband Israel Epstein, Michael Shapiro (communist member of Stepney borough council, 1945–50, and thereafter an adviser to the state news agency in Peking, where he was a SACU contact), Eric and Marie Gordon,[142] and the Reuter's correspondent Anthony Grey.[143]

SACU's studied neutrality over the detentions offended even the faithful. Stuart and Roma Gelder, who were friends of Epstein and Fairfax-Cholmeley, were among those troubled. 'SACU,' the Gelders wrote in 1967, 'is sometimes more anxious to convince us that the Chinese are always right than to explain how the Peking Government sometimes does its best to ensure that we will be wrong about them.' In order to please Peking, SACU was ignoring the execution or suicide of individuals targeted in the Cultural Revolution: its conduct 'belies its name and defeats its purpose'.[144] Bryan's successor as secretary, Betty Paterson, regarded the agitation on behalf of the detainees as a time-wasting distraction from the aims of the society.[145] Needham agreed, but felt forced to prepare a standard letter which he sent to SACU members and interested parties who had urged the society to intervene on the detainees' behalf:

---

141 CUL, Needham papers K 197, Notes by Needham for a lecture on the Cultural Revolution, 1967.

142 CUL, Needham papers K 199, Bill Luckin to Needham, 1 & 28 April 1968, refers to the detention of Crook, Epstein and Shapiro. Crook was imprisoned 1967–73; Epstein and Shapiro, 1968–73. The Crooks' three young sons stayed for a time with the family of Jack Perry in north London.

143 Grey's memoir *Hostage in Peking* (London: Michael Joseph, 1970) and that of Eric and Marie Gordon, *Freedom is a Word* (London: Hodder & Stoughton, 1970), contain interesting material, which is however beyond the scope of this book. Grey and the Gordons were detained, 1967–69.

144 Stuart and Roma Gelder, *Memories for a Chinese Grand-daughter* (London: Hutchinson, 1967), p. 209.

145 CUL, Needham papers K 199, Betty Paterson to Needham, 21 November 1968.

Here is a nation of seven hundred million human beings which since 1946 has gone through a revolution paralleling the English, French and Russian revolutions all rolled into one; and not only that, but after stability seemed to have been achieved, has been passing through a further phase of profound upheaval, the cultural revolution. Anyone who throws in his or her lot with a people living through a revolutionary era has to expect some ups and downs, of which house arrest or worse might easily be one; anyone who even visits such a country on business or pleasure is necessarily taking a certain risk – and this is to say nothing of individuals who might really be engaged in espionage in one form or another. Presumably no one will suggest that the secret services of the capitalist powers are doing nothing about China; the Chinese therefore are right to safeguard their security, even if it means tedious investigations of some perfectly innocent people.[146]

*

Trevor-Roper had hoped that his letter-writing and his *Encounter* essay would achieve the collapse of SACU and the formation of a new organization which was not a communist front. In these hopes he was disappointed. According to the SACU website in 2019, the escalation of the Vietnam War and the outbreak of the Cultural Revolution put the society under high stress. (It mentions that Trevor-Roper 'resigned in June 1966 after he was criticised by members for launching an attack on the Cultural Revolution in *The Sunday Times* head-lined "The sick mind of China"'. His article of course made no mention of the Cultural Revolution, which had not yet begun in October 1965: his resignation was a response to being accused of 'McCarthyism' and to the emergent strength of Bill Ash and Roland Berger in SACU.) The SACU website history continues:

> With Britain's relations with China reaching a low ebb and suspi-
> cion and hostility towards China very widespread, SACU shifted
> in 1967 towards a more committed political position to 'champion
> China's case openly' and to 'counter propaganda, distortion and
> misrepresentation in the press aimed at conditioning people's minds
> to an image of China as a global menace'. Many of the organisation's

---

146 CUL, Needham papers K 199, undated circular letter from Needham, December 1968.

high-profile sponsors fell away but membership grew as SACU attracted young people opposed to the Vietnam War and with an interest in China's 'social road' and Mao Zedong thought.[147]

Scores of sponsors either resigned or withdrew from any contact during 1967–68. In 1970, however, SACU Tours was launched with the help of SACU's longstanding contacts with the Chinese People's Association for Friendship with Foreign Countries: for some years it had a near monopoly of enabling British tourists to visit the PRC; and the society's position, to the continuing concern of British government departments, was accordingly strengthened. During the 1970s, with the diminution of the hostility to Peking of Washington and London, the PRC outgrew the need for SACU. The acronym, as younger sinologists began to joke, stood for the Society for Accepting China Uncritically.

In 1972 Sir Harold Thompson, who had been one of the scientists in the Oxford branch of SACU, became the driving force in the formation of the Great Britain–China Committee. This alternative to SACU worked with quiet efficacy to improve Anglo-Chinese understanding, and especially in developing cultural, scientific, political, economic, social and sporting contacts. Exchange visits by librarians, orchestras, scientists and soccer players were arranged. Thompson's leverage in Peking was increased by his life vice-presidency of the Football Association, and by his avowed wish to bring the PRC into world soccer and to oust Taiwan. The Far Eastern Section of the IRD supported the Committee's work firmly but discreetly. The Committee's vice-chairman, Sir Humphrey Trevelyan, who had twenty years earlier been *chargé d'affaires* in Peking, was crucial in arranging for the acclaimed Genius of China archaeological exhibition to be held in London under the sponsorship of *The Times*. The newspaper's owners, doubtless instigated by the IRD, Thompson and Trevelyan, donated the exhibition's profits to the Foreign and Commonwealth Office, which used the money to transmogrify Thompson's Committee into the Great Britain–China Centre (GBCC). SACU was excluded from the Centre's executive committee: nor were any SACU representatives invited to the Centre's inaugural meeting.[148] A new phase of Anglo-Chinese contacts got underway.

---

147 https://sacu.org/history.html accessed 9 January 2019.

148 See papers in NA FCO 95/1734, notably Joe Ford, 'Great Britain-China Centre: Preliminary Stage', [May 1974] and in NA FCO 34/237, especially Sir Harold Thompson, address at opening ceremony, 16 July 1974.

*

The fourth document reproduced as an annexe to this book differs from the others. It is Trevor-Roper's diary of his journey in 1967 to Taiwan, the 'Republic of China' (ROC), and afterwards briefly to Hong Kong, Thailand and Cambodia. He had declined earlier state-sponsored invitations, which would have debarred him from obtaining a visa to the PRC under SACU's or any other auspices. 'But,' he reasoned to his wartime intelligence colleague Patrick Reilly, 'now I have been to Red China and there is no prospect of my ever being readmitted; so why not go to Formosa?' In his Taiwan journal, Trevor-Roper neither spun a daily thread of argumentative political commentary nor elaborated any unifying political theme. He learned what he could about the Taiwanese regime, pondered its character, speculated on its future. He favoured the cultural leaders whom he met, lauded to Reilly 'the deliberate preservation of the best features of the Kuomintang regime and the defence of them against Americanisation', but attempted no close dissection.[149]

In contrast to the frustrations of his SACU sponsors' visit to the mainland, Trevor-Roper's hosts in Taiwan proved civil and considerate. There were some uncomfortable journeys and ill-timings, but the abiding impression is of welcome amenities, including some sophisticated and intelligent conversation. There is nothing of the siege mentality of the diary of 1965. Even so, Trevor-Roper had no illusions about Taiwan. As the *Observer*'s Far East correspondent reminded readers in 1967, the enmity between the KMT-led ROC and the Maoist PRC hid undeniable similarities: 'The Nationalist Kuomintang in Taipeh [*sic*] is a revolutionary party, and has a cellular structure not unlike that of the Communist Party in Peking. In Formosa as in China there is a one-party system only slightly confused by the existence of other minor political groups that simply go to show how democratic everything is.' Foreign visitors in both places, if they were not assertive, 'can find themselves spending from morning until midnight tramping around model factories, model schools, model hospitals and model models, on a crowded pre-arranged schedule'.[150]

Taiwan had a far smaller population (an estimated 12 million in 1963) as well as higher living standards than the mainland. Privation and famine were not endemic problems. Demographic changes were, however, troublesome.

149 Bodleian, Mss Eng c 6888, Trevor-Roper to Reilly, 28 December 1967.
150 Dennis Bloodworth, *Chinese Looking Glass* (London: Secker & Warburg, 1967), pp. 310–11.

Some 1.2 million mainland Chinese (of whom about half were soldiers) retreated to Taiwan with the nationalist leaders in 1949. These incomers behaved like a conquering army. After 1949 all senior government posts were taken by mainlanders who had accompanied Chiang Kai-shek. Native-born Taiwanese 'had no say in political, economic or security policy decisions,' wrote David Dean, the political counsellor at the US Embassy with whom Trevor-Roper once dined.[151] The hold on power of the KMT was strengthened by its international status: at US insistence, the ROC and not the PRC had a permanent seat at the UN Security Council until 1971.

The outbreak of the Korean War, and the globalization of the Cold War, with the United States and the Soviet Union in tense confrontation, probably saved the ROC from an early invasion by the PRC. In the epoch known as the White Terror, the nationalists ruled with the backing of martial law, censored newspapers and magazines, forbad the use of Taiwanese dialect in schools, sent political police on night-time raids, and detained dissidents and suspected communists. The military bureaucracy ran print works, art groups, radio stations and publishers. It was enshrined in law that there could be no constitutional reform until the recovery of the mainland. No new political parties could be formed. Strikes and demonstrations were impermissible. So too were students joining in electioneering for any politician. *Lèse-majesté* was swiftly punished: a cartoonist who depicted Popeye marooned on a desert island and striking dictatorial poses was imprisoned for years for this satire on the Generalissimo. The requisite two years of national service for young people included citizenship training and anti-communist indoctrination. The KMT propaganda dinned into the young was no subtler than its Maoist counterpart. The communist bombardment of Quemoy and Matsu in 1958 ratcheted up the nationalists' siege mentality. A chant for the soldiery declared that defectors and traitors shamed their ancestors, that the whole mainland was drenched in blood, that the 'red bandits' were eager to slaughter the Taiwanese like sheep on a chopping-block.[152]

One reason for this trip was to give a free holiday to Trevor-Roper's wife. Her presence left him with less time for solitary reflection and for writing than he had found in the PRC two years earlier. Of the four texts in this book, the

---

151 David Dean, *Unofficial Diplomacy: the American Institute in Taiwan* (Afton, VA: Mary Dean Trust, 2014), pp. 55–6.

152 Francis Pike, *Empires at War: a short history of modern Asia since World War II* (London: I.B.Tauris, 2010), pp. 277–84.

Taiwan journal most resembles a conventional diary: it orders and distils experience, and preserves memories of places and people. The diary begins, though, with an account of his meeting, on the eve of his departure from England, with his friend Dick White, the former head both of the Security Service and the Secret Intelligence Service. They discussed SIS and in particular the Soviet spy Kim Philby, Trevor-Roper's wartime colleague in intelligence and the subject of his book *The Philby Affair* (1969). The conversation has its own interest for historians of the secret world, but no bearing on the ensuing subject matter of the diary. The text contains a digression on George Eliot's *Middlemarch*, which Trevor-Roper began reading in Taiwan and finished in Cambodia. This, too, does not relate to anything he saw or felt as a visitor. The ending of the document does not betoken, as the conclusions of the other travel-journals do, the end of a coherent episode. Having met the public, combative Trevor-Roper in the central parts of this book, we here find the private, ruminative side of him to the fore.

PART ONE

CHINA, 1965

Monday, 20 September

We left Moscow on Saturday night 18 Sept, about 11.0 p.m. We were to fly to Pekin. But after about two hours we landed, at Sverdlovsk.[1] We were told that we were held up by bad weather. It was raining at Sverdlovsk. We sat in the plane at Sverdlovsk for nearly two hours, waiting (we had to assume) for the weather to improve. Then it was announced that we would still have to wait for 'several hours', so we were taken into the airport and distributed among beds. I slept soundly for two hours, till 5.0 a.m. Then we were awakened and told to board the plane at once, as we were to leave. Once on board we waited, again for nearly two hours. At 7.0 a.m. the crew boarded the plane, and soon afterwards we resumed our flight to Pekin.

After about three hours' flying we landed at Irkutsk in Siberia.[2] Having landed, we were told that we could go no further that day on account of the weather. The weather at Irkutsk was perfect: not a cloud in the sky. We were, by this time, a little sceptical about 'the weather', which seemed a standard excuse for delay; but we had no means of knowing anything.[3] At Irkutsk we were

---

1 This was the name (1924–91) of the city founded in 1723 to the east of the Ural mountains. It is better known as Ekaterinburg.

2 During the nineteenth century dissident intellectuals and noblemen were exiled to Irkutsk, which was accordingly called the Paris of Siberia. The city was industrialized under Stalin.

3 The Soviet-built Tupolev aircraft, on which SACU delegates were passengers, was unable to land on the short runways in Peking except in daylight. To reach Peking in daylight it was necessary to leave Irkutsk at dawn. But Tupolevs could not take off unless the sky was clear, and Irkustk was often shrouded in early morning mist from Lake Baikal.

confined to the airport,[4] and we could see nothing of the place except what was visible from the airport, or while landing and, next day, taking off. It seems a large city, with many factories, set in a featureless plain sprinkled with forests of birch and poplar. We were told that it had four theatres. The airport is no different from any other airport. We were fed and distributed among beds. The distribution was conducted by rules of art not at first apparent. By these rules there was no bed for me. We were kept in national groups. There was a large French party on the plane, apparently tourists, and a French girl who gave us her life history. She was fleeing from the reactionary gloom of France in general and Cherbourg in particular, to teach French in Nanking. The illiberal French government had ruled that even journalists had no natural right to live in Paris, her illegitimate son had gone to Africa and no longer wrote to her, so what else, she asked, could she do? There were some English business men from I.C.I.,[5] and a bulky English clergyman who was imprisoned in the airport because, having visited Ulaan Baattor in Outer Mongolia, he had apparently invalidated his travel visa.[6] He was chaplain at the British embassy in Moscow. There was an Italian who was going to organise an international sporting meeting in Pekin. And there was a Czech couple, gloomy as anyone must be who had the misfortune to be Czech. There were also Russians and Chinese. As I could not be fitted into the beds assigned to the English party, and it was apparently contrary to Nature for me to be put among any other group, I was odd man out. However, by exercising my arts on the Russian lady who organised the distribution, I finally got a camp-bed put up in the private office of the Chinese representative, who was happily not there. I thus had the only single room, in which I slept soundly and read *Wuthering Heights*, happily undisturbed by the smoking of Robert Bolt[7] and the snoring of the huge person next door.

---

4 'Since Irkurtsk was in a fortified zone, we were not allowed to leave the airport. We were amazed to read in the visitors' book an entry by Hewlett Johnson, the Red Dean of Canterbury, beginning "I have spent three useful days in Irkurtsk"; we wondered what a useless day in the Deanery could be like' (A. J. Ayer, *More of My Life* (London: Collins, 1984), p. 106).

5 Imperial Chemical Industries was created by the merger of four large chemical companies in 1926. It was bought by a Dutch paint manufacturer in 2008, and its constituent businesses sold.

6 William Masters (1898–1978) had been British embassy chaplain in Vienna 1949–55, and as such ministered to the Anglican communities in Prague, Budapest, Bucharest and Sofia. In 1962–66, as Anglican chaplain of St Nicholas, Helsinki and Rural Dean of Scandinavia, he met the spiritual needs of the embassy in Moscow.

7 See Appendix B, pp. 245–8.

Next morning, Monday 20 Sept, we were up at 5.30 and were able to leave soon after 7.0. We flew over Lake Baikal and then the view below us changed. Instead of the flat steppes of Siberia we saw mountains; then the trees gradually disappeared and we were flying above a grim, brown desert. It was Mongolia, and soon we were flying over the Gobi desert. The weather was fine, and the clouds thin: whenever they parted, we could see only that grim, brown, empty, desolate waste. Then the desert turned from brown to reddish-brown, and, peering closer, I saw that there was cultivated land. This, I supposed, was the beginning of China: the peopled land from which the Northern Barbarians pressed upon it. Before long we were weaving over, if not through, formidable, sharp mountain-peaks, a great range of forbidding pinnacles, the ramparts of the Chinese plain: natural ramparts strengthened by the Great Wall. Then, suddenly, we were descending to the plain: a flat plain that lies as open at the feet of the mountains as the plain of Lombardy at the feet of the Alps. There seemed, at least from the air, no gradations: at one moment we were threading our way through those frightening peaks: at the next, we were skating over level fields; and at a third we were landing on the airfield of Pekin.

We were met by a delegation bearing bouquets of flowers. It was a delegation from the Foreign Cultural Association which has invited us.[8] There was the secretary, Jen Ying lun, a sinister little man with a dry face, half-shut politician's eyes and a nose like the beak of a parakeet: a man, we soon decided, not to be trusted an inch.[9] There were two young men who, we quickly realised, were professional party men employed by the Association. And there were two girl interpreters. The young men who are to be our guides, but who speak no English, and the interpreters, took us to our hotel, the Chien Men Hotel. Even on that journey, the position became clear. The interpreters had no function except to interpret and any direct conversation between us and them had to be communicated to the party men, who had a duty of complete control. The party men are To Chi-lou and Tsao Kue-bing. To Chi-Lou is tall and very lean, with expressionless clean-cut features and an aloof, toneless voice. He smokes cigarettes incessantly. Tsao Kue-bing is shorter, uglier and

---

8 The Chinese People's Association for Cultural Relations with Foreign Countries was founded in 1954. Since 1969 it has been known as the Chinese People's Association for Friendship with Foreign Countries.

9 Jen Ying-lun had risen in the Communist Party apparatus by writing articles decrying the Kuomintang as corrupt and dictatorial oppressors of the proletariat.

a little (but very little) more human.[10] In our hotel we rested and prepared ourselves for the next stage.

Meanwhile I get to know my companions. There is Mrs Mary Adams,[11] widow of Vyvyan Adams, the tory MP who was drowned before the war.[12] She is an official of SACU and, that being so – and also because of her sex – we have designated her as our spokesman. She has been active in the BBC; is a member of the Independent Television board;[13] is on the Council of Industrial Design;[14] and is a great believer in women's rights; also (I believe) in Basic English.[15] She has selected, as our present to our Chinese hosts, a glass bowl which has been approved by the Council of Industrial Design and has received an award from Prince Philip.[16] It seems to me very boring. Mrs. Adams is very useful: she chatters away to the Chinese about women's right, crèches, etc. She is rather apt to criticise the décor at airports, etc, from the high level of the Council for Industrial Design, which she clearly regards as the ultimate *arbiter elegantiarum*.[17] I'm afraid I always think of that boring glass bowl, and

---

10 Identification of these two men has proved impossible. 'Interpreter-guides from the Chinese travel agency are hybrids: half way between the common people and the officials, they are half-human, half-bureaucrat. Depending on which element is dominant, they can be pleasant and instructive company, or they can poison your existence' (Simon Leys, *Chinese Shadows*, pp. 194–5).

11 See Appendix B, pp. 243–5.

12 Vyvyan Adams (1900–1951) drowned on a Cornish holiday. As National Unionist MP for Leeds West 1931–45, he was active in the League of Nations Union, the Society for the Promotion of International Law and cognate bodies. In 1934 he urged on the Tory leader Leo Amery 'the great virtues of the Chinese and the mistake we should make if we offended them in order to placate Japan'. Amery commented in his diary (4 November 1934): 'Undoubtedly the Chinaman is for most of us a much more human creature than the Japanese. But I doubt whether politically anything can be done with him.'

13 The Independent Television Authority was created in 1954 by Act of Parliament to award and supervise the regional franchises for commercial television. Mary Adams had been appointed to its board earlier in 1965.

14 The Council for Industrial Design was formed by the Board of Trade in 1944. It opened showrooms in the Design Centre in Haymarket (1956–98), and guided consumer tastes towards products based on functional fitness and truth to materials. By 1965 its aesthetic was being challenged by Pop Art, psychedelia and romanticism. It was renamed the Design Council in 1972.

15 Basic English was devised in the 1920s by the Cambridge linguistic philosopher C. K. Ogden as an international auxiliary language which might promote world peace. Its emasculated vocabulary permitted only eighteen verbs. Subsequently the critic I. A. Richards tried to foist Basic English on Chinese students.

16 The bowl had been designed by David Douglas, 12th Marquess of Queensberry (b. 1929), Professor of Ceramics at the Royal College of Art 1959–83. It received the Duke of Edinburgh's award for elegance in 1964.

17 Latin: a judge of artistic taste.

am less sure. She also tends to drop names. But she is an invaluable lubricant of the party.

Then there is Ernie Roberts, assistant secretary-general of the AEU.[18] He is a clerical, not a manual type of trades unionist. His face is narrow, his lips dry and tight, and he speaks in a smooth, precise manner. He is friendly and has a subdued but discernible sense of humour, but he is close and austere. He is also rather puritanical: 'I don't smoke and I don't encourage others to do so'; 'I don't like tipping, nor do I encourage the habit'; etc. A kind of secularised non-conformist. Perhaps he is *communisant*. His friends in the academic world are Christopher and Bridget Hill[19] and Tommy Hodgkin.[20] He has travelled in Russia and all other communist countries in Europe, and takes communist trade unions seriously. Politically I suspect him to be pretty naïve, and his general interests seem to be narrowed into the compass of trades union organisation, to which he gradually reduces every subject of conversation.

Robert Bolt, the playwright, is the third, and I like him the best. He has a slight north-country accent, is, I believe, a Roman Catholic,[21] and qualifies for this company by being, or having been, an enthusiastic supporter of CND: indeed, he has gone to prison for the cause. His interests seem to me a good

---

18 See Appendix B, pp. 248–52.

19 Christopher Hill (1912–2003) was a historian of seventeenth-century English politics and religion. He joined the CPGB after visiting Russia, while a fellow of All Souls, in 1934; and remained a member until 1957. He was elected fellow and tutor in history at Balliol in 1938, worked as an officer in wartime military intelligence and in the Northern Department of the Foreign Office. Oxford sources of the Security Services suggested in 1954 that Hill was 'so publicly identified with his Communist role that he would find it very difficult to renounce the Party, especially as he is one of the few avowed Communist dons at Oxford, and much of his celebrity rests on his professional Communism' (NA KV 2/3943, serial 153a, 8 February 1954). He became Master-elect of Balliol in January 1965, and took office as Master on 29 September. His wife Bridget (1922–2002) joined the CPGB while a student at LSE. She was a fellow of St Hilda's College, Oxford 1961–68.

20 Thomas Hodgkin (1910–1982) was a grandson of A. L. Smith, Master of Balliol, and took a first in Greats there in 1932. He joined the CPGB in 1937 and resigned from open membership in 1949. Dick White described him as 'a man of extreme left-wing sympathies' (NA KV 2/3680, serial 7a, letter to V. Vivian, 20 May 1937). Elected as a fellow of Balliol and appointed as secretary of the Oxford Delegacy for Extra-Mural Studies, both in 1945, he resigned these positions in 1952 after disquiet about his influence in the college and university. An MI5 officer minuted: 'we consider him to be a communist and to have been guilty of using his position on various Appointment Boards to place communists in jobs where they would be able to spread propaganda for the cause' (NA KV 2/3681, minute 118, 22 May 1952).

21 Bolt was reared as a Methodist. Catholic sympathies were sometimes inferred from his portrayal of St Thomas More in his play *A Man for All Seasons*, but he had no Christian beliefs.

deal broader than those of the others, who both tend to reduce everything into their own little worlds, He is also gayer, more capable of enthusiasm. I have not yet penetrated his character, but I find myself most at ease in his company. How glad I am that he came! He came, as I did, at the last minute, replacing his fellow-supporter of CND, Vanessa Redgrave.[22]

And how do I qualify for this company? In fact I joined SACU by chance. Joseph Needham[23] invited me to join it, and I naturally do what he tells me to do. I venerate him; and I am interested in China, Chinese history, and the modern world. In joining, I felt that I was mainly giving my support: rather passive support too. I never supposed that the lot would fall on me. It has fallen because Maurica Bowra,[24] at the last minute, has run out, and someone – Needham probably – has proposed me as a substitute. So I have come. But I admit that I feel somewhat out of place in this company. They are all *croyants*.[25] Mary Adams believes in Women's Rights, Ernie Roberts in Trades Unions and perhaps something else, Robert Bolt in the RC Church. I alone, I feel, am the sceptic of the party. I am also the only member with any knowledge, however slight, of China, of Chinese history. This make me feel very exceptional, especially in the company of our Chinese guides, slaves to their own propaganda that Chinese history began in 1949.

---

22 The actress Vanessa Redgrave (b. 1937) was an activist in the Campaign for Nuclear Disarmament and in its militant offshoot, the Committee of 100. Instead of travelling to China she went to Rome in an effort to mend her marriage to the film director Tony Richardson. Dick White of SIS wrote to T-R (27 March 1968): 'Now we have our own Maoists, I should like your views as to who is the Chinese equivalent of Vanessa Redgrave.'

23 As an undergraduate reading Natural Sciences at Gonville & Caius College, Cambridge, Joseph Needham (1900–1995) lived in a frugal and earnest Catholic community in Cambridge Oratory. He later fell under the sway of Conrad Noel, whom he called 'Prophet of Christ's Kingdom on Earth' but better known as 'the Red Vicar of Thaxted'. He had an early interest in psychoanalysis ('At the B.A.'s table in Caius we talked exclusively of Oedipus complexes, anxiety neuroses, penis envy and Jungian archetypes'). Sir Vernon Kell made the first recorded MI5 enquiry about him to the Chief Constable of Cambridge in 1933.

24 Sir Maurice Bowra (1898–1971), Warden of Wadham College, Oxford 1938–70, withdrew from SACU's delegation because, as he explained in a letter to Evelyn Waugh, although he wished to see the Ming Tombs, he could not face doing so 'at the cost of first seeing infant schools, factories, crèches, girls doing bayonet drill and other neo-democratic activities'. He was consistently hostile to T-R: 'DON'T elect Roper', he urged at the time of the All Souls fellowship examinations when T-R was 22; and after T-R had engineered Harold Macmillan's election as chancellor of Oxford University, 'It is a pity that T-R should have so resounding a victory, as this is just what he likes most in the world, but with luck he will try something else soon, and fail' (Bowra to Isaiah Berlin, 20 October 1936 and 6 March 1960).

25 French: believers.

At 2.30 p.m. our guides collected us. They took us in two cars for a tour of the city. It was a frustrating tour. We drove, apparently aimlessly, along great suburban boulevards, and our guides pointed out, one after another, a series of identical, featureless, modern institutions, all built 'since Liberation'. 'How many inhabitants has Pekin?' we asked. 'Four million' we were told. But where were they? On either side we saw only fields of maize, or orchards, or vegetable gardens. 'Where', we asked, 'is the centre of the city?' But we never got a satisfactory answer. I suppose the real centres of population, being pre-Liberation, are not boast-worthy. 'What is that fine building?' we would ask, pointing to an exquisite tower with a shapely roof; but they did not know. Instead, they drew our attention to a featureless new block of flats. 'Workers' flats,' they told us. 'In your country there is no such thing. If flats are built there, they are only for Capitalists.' We began to expostulate, to qualify. It was in vain. 'It must be so,' we were told: 'it is a necessary consequence of the social system.'

Their ignorance, their complacency appalled us. Of Chinese history before 1949 they knew nothing, absolutely nothing. The most elementary questions found them quite without answer. To them 'imperial times' were all one: a kind of Dark Age before the Dawn of History in 1949. The only historic monument in which they had any interest was the monument to the Heroes of Liberation in the great square. It is a huge plinth containing a few gilded ideograms in the handwriting of chairman Mao;[26] and round its base are reliefs, in socialist realist style, representing scenes in the liberation of China, beginning with the Opium War. I'm afraid I was inattentive as every detail of these reliefs received its boring, propagandist commentary. I was far more interested in the skill of the kite-flyers who were flying kites of varying design – some made like birds, some like dragon-flies – far up in the sky over the square. But my inattention was noted and reproved. I am afraid that I got my first bad mark at that time.

Since then, I fear that I have earned another. Our guides and their interpreters came to dinner with us. At dinner the question of the Indo-Pakistani conflict over Kashmir arose.[27] How it arose was not clear to me; but once it had arisen, there was no escape. To Chi-Lou, casting the refuse of his food regularly on the floor beside him (his table manners are quite revolting), gave

---

26 Mao Tse-tung [Mao Zedong] (1893–1976), chairman of the Communist Party of China 1949–76.

27 Skirmishes on the disputed Kashmir frontier, which began in April 1965, had erupted into a full-scale war in August. Although the PRC supported Pakistan with armaments and diplomacy, Pakistan lost 3,800 men, 200 tanks and 20 aircraft before the United Nations cease-fire took effect on 23 September.

us 'the objective truth'. First came one sentence, then the translation. Then the sequence was repeated. Gradually it became clear that he was delivering a speech which might go on for a long time. It did. We were told that argument was impossible; that India, encouraged by American reactionaries, had attacked Pakistan in order to bolster up capitalism in India; that these 'objective facts' created a clean-cut situation and determined simple judgments. There was truth; there was error; there was right and there was wrong; and there could be no discussion. The face of To Chi-Lou, as he spoke, was a motionless mask; his voice a cold, metallic sequence of toneless, unintelligible sounds. We sat there, at the mercy of this remorseless bigoted hack. I ventured to ask him whether he had ever been to India or Pakistan. He brushed the irrelevancy aside. Robert Bolt ventured to suggest that truth was not so clear-cut. He was treated as a wayward child. I turned aside to my neighbour, Tsao-Kue-bing. All the time we had had no conversation, for he spoke no English. Suddenly he asked, in French, if I could speak French. With relief I answered yes, and from that moment I ignored the dreary bore opposite me and chattered away to my neighbour. I doubt whether this did either me or him much good, but at least it prevented a frontal battle. Seeing his audience disintegrate, To Chi-Lou said loftily that of course our Chinese hosts welcomed our criticism; but it was quite plain that this was a mere polite form, and we parted in teams of truce rather than peace: we resolved, it possible, to break away from this control by bigoted dunces, they clearly satisfied that we did not, either in ourselves or as representatives of our obscure society, merit any special consideration.

Robert Bolt told me of a remark by Bertrand Russell about India and China.[28] When you go to India, he said, you think that anything would be better than this, and that perhaps communism is the right solution for that dismal country. But there you go to China and, in the presence of that unbelievable self-righteousness, you begin to think that poverty, even Indian poverty, is preferable.

And yet I have omitted something, and that is something which struck me at once when I went into the airport at Pekin: the gaiety of the Chinese, a natural, spontaneous gaiety which no system can repress. In Russia no one seems to smile, but in China every face (except that of To Chi-Lou) seemed

---

28 Bertrand Russell (1872–1970), 3rd Earl Russell 1931, Fellow of Trinity College, Cambridge, Nobel laureate for literature 1950, had spent twelve months of 1921–22 as a lecturer at the National University of Peking.

to wear a smile.[29] The self-righteousness is no doubt, like so much else, a monopoly of the party.

Tuesday, 21 September

Having spent the two hours from 3.0 to 5.0 a.m. writing this diary, I could not sleep again (the beds in this hotel are rock-hard), so I came down early to breakfast and had been there for an hour when my colleagues joined me. The trades unionist is dissatisfied with our reception on ground of status: a subject on which he seems sensitive. Our reception, he considers, was second-class: when he went to Russia with a lot of MPs it had been first-class – they had gone first off the boat and been taken away in limousines. Here we were given no priority, only bouquets; the orangeade with straws which we were given in the airport was slightly *infra dig*; and the cars in which we were taken off could have been grander. Clearly he feels that the grandeur of the AEU has been slighted in his person.

We talked about last night's *contretemps* over Kashmir. How could that young man have had the self-assurance, I asked, to lecture us so dogmatically on subjects in which it was likely that we had access to better information than he, who merely repeated party propaganda? 'Oh, it is easy to do', replied Robert Bolt. 'When I was in the party, I was just the same'; and he described an event which, he said, made him sweat whenever he recalled it: how a friend, who had lived long in Russia, had lost his Russian girl friend to whom he was devoted, – she had disappeared without trace into a Russian concentration camp – and how Bolt, hearing the lamentations of his friend, had consoled him by assuring him, as a matter of objective truth known to himself (who had never been to Russia), that there were no Russian concentration-camps: they were all merely capitalist fictions. This was the first indication I had that Bolt had been a communist. He had been in the party, he explained, from 1942 to 1946.

The hotel is full of pamphlets, to be taken gratis by anyone who covets them. The theme of them all is constant: denunciation of Russia. Other themes – the creation of a new China, a new world, the war against imperialism, 'neo-colonialism' etc. – are incidental: the Russo-Chinese struggle is central. It

---

29 In 1954 Ayer was puzzled that the Chinese had a reputation for impassivity: 'they have, in the main, the gayest, most animated, most expressive features of any people I have ever seen, or ever expect to see'.

dominates all. I suppose the hotel guests are presumed to be delegates from communist countries who take the communist doctrine for granted and must be won from heresy within the movement rather than from infidelity without. There are also Albanian pamphlets, printed in Tirana, which seem, from the titles, to say the same thing.[30] But they have to be bought and I did not think them worth buying. This morning we went to the department store in Wang Fu-chin. It is far, far superior to Gum in Moscow,[31] in the variety of consumer good available; also, as far as one can compare, in prices.

I had telephoned the British Embassy early this morning and the acting *chargé d' affaires*, Michael Wilford,[32] had invited us all to lunch. We had a very pleasant lunch with the Wilfords and two experts on China, members of the Political Section, Alan Donald[33] and Timothy George.[34] They suggested concrete proposals for us to make in order to break away from the closed circle of ignorant party guides in which we are imprisoned. They invited us to a party tomorrow to meet Chinese students going to England and promised to introduce me, *sub rosa*,[35] to a heterodox historian, or at least to an historian who had studied in Paris and would, privately, talk to foreigners, Prof. Jang.[36]

In the evening we attended a 'banquet'. It was given for us in the Chuan Chu Te Restaurant. The presiding figure was Ting hsi-lin, the vice-president of

---

30 After Enver Hoxha allied Albania with the PRC in 1960, the Soviet Union imposed economic sanctions, withdrew its technicians, recalled eight submarines which it had given to Hoxha's regime, and broke diplomatic relations. Nikita Khrushchev made public jibes at the Chinese as 600 million Albanians.

31 GUM was the ugly state department store in Red Square opposite Lenin's tomb.

32 (Sir) Michael Wilford (1922–2006), born in New Zealand, brought up in Shanghai and Dublin, read mechanical sciences at Pembroke College, Cambridge, and joined Foreign Service in 1947. He was counsellor in Peking 1964–66, ambassador to Japan 1975–80. T-R's friend Sir Patrick Reilly wrote that Wilford had 'a firm and bustling competence which ... kept us all in order' (Bodleian Ms, Eng c 6921, f 24).

33 (Sir) Alan Donald (1931–2018), Third Secretary at Peking, 1955–57, First Secretary at Peking, 1964–66, Political Adviser to the Governor of Hong Kong, 1974–77, ambassador in Jakarta, 1984–88, ambassador in Peking, 1988–91.

34 Timothy George (b. 1937), Third Secretary at Peking 1963–6, Counsellor and Head of Chancery at Peking 1978–80, ambassador to Nepal, 1990–95. He belied Joan Robinson's claim in *Letters from a Visitor to China* that 'western diplomats live in the Legation Quarter chewing over their grievances and feeling superior about being white'.

35 Latin: literally, under the rose; figuratively, surreptitiously.

36 Not Jang but Chang Chih-lien, who taught world history at the University of Peking. In 1967 Red Guards denounced Chang as 'a stinking bourgeois professor' whose mind was polluted by 'reactionary ideas'.

the Cultural Association for Foreigners, a physicist who is also a playwright.[37] I sat next to him and found him an agreeable companion. There was also the secretary, Jen Ying Lun, whom we had met before at airport, and who appeared even more sinister on second meeting. There was a trade unionist,[38] no doubt to keep Roberts happy, and another playwright,[39] to keep Bolt happy, although Bolt's comment on him was that he would trust him not further than he could throw a double-decker bus. On my other side was the cultural *attaché* at the Chinese embassy in London, whom I found easy enough.[40] He is on two months' leave. After a lot of boring speeches, we dined on successive particles of Pekin duck. Then the disasters began. Mary Adams, who was sitting at my table (we were at two tables) on the other side of the Vice-President, spontaneously and gratuitously raised, once again, the question of Kashmir. Was there any news on that subject? she asked; and the Vice-President, having made some statement of alleged fact, asked her what her opinion was. At once she was off. The war, she declared, was absurd; India and Pakistan were brothers; we should all embrace in brotherly love ... then she turned to me, 'come on Hugh, support me!' It was the last thing that I was prepared to do. The woman is a ninny and it was absolutely clear that her remarks could only provoke dogmatic statements of the predictable party line; as indeed they did. So she waded deeper into the mire of her own making, gurgling, as she foundered

---

37 Ting hsi-lin [Ding Xilin] (1893–1974) studied physics and mathematics at Birmingham University in 1914–18. He wrote ten witty, frivolous plays between 1923 and 1940. In Mao's China he was professor of physics at Peking University and vice-chairman of the Chinese People's Association for Cultural Relations.

38 Doubtless Liu Ning-i (1906–1994), who is listed in Roberts's briefing notes. In 1950 he led a 'friendship delegation' to England which was described in *Tribune* as 'the worst mannered delegation ever to visit this country'. As chairman of the All China Federation of Trade Unions from 1958, Liu travelled exhaustively in Asia, Africa and Europe. Despite siding with the Red Guards in the Cultural Revolution, he was toppled by it.

39 This dramatist was probably Tsao Yü [Cao Yu; or Wan Jiabao] (1910–1996), director of the Popular Theatre Art League since 1949, who fell into disfavour during the Cultural Revolution but was rehabilitated after Mao's death. Another possibility is Lao She [Shu Qingchun] (1899–1966), who had been a lecturer at the School of Oriental Studies (later SOAS), 1924–29. Within months of the SACU visit, Lao was paraded through Peking streets by Red Guards, publicly beaten on the steps of the Temple of Confucius and drowned himself.

40 Either Chen Szu-chun or Cheng Yao-wen. Sir William Hayter, former ambassador in Moscow, had written in 1960 that Chinese diplomats were usually 'light-weight, empty, agreeable creatures. The characteristic of pre-Revolutionary Chinese diplomacy was great surface charm covering deep inner xenophobia. The superficial polish is now less; nothing else seems to have changed' (Sir William Hayter, *The Diplomacy of the Great Powers* (London: Hamish Hamilton, 1960), p. 65).

and sank under the pelting of their stony sentences, the fatuous moralities of a suburban drawing-room. I tried not to hear, but the only result was that I heard Roberts, at the next table, unctuously complimenting the Chinese on their liberal policy in Tibet.[41] At this point I realised that my English colleagues are as great an embarrassment as the Chinese bigots. Mary Adams is an opinionated mindless woman, useful enough when the need is for lubricating small-talk, but quite unaware of reality. Marxism, to her, is a closed book, and she is quite unfit to be our representative in this delicate position. Fortunately, her *bêtises* were finally ended by the necessity of presenting the glass-bowl, which she duly did in the speech of an MP's wife opening a bazaar. She dwelt unctuously in the fact that the bowl had been approved, by 'Prince Philip, Duke of Edinburgh, husband of our queen'. Then the bowl was unwrapped. As it emerged from its cocoon of paper, it seemed to me more boring than ever; but no doubt it will do for the taste of the Chinese People's Republic.[42]

When we got back, Bolt came to me, perspiring. The evening, he declared, had been absolute torture: a prolonged agony of laboured insincerity. His table had been worse than mine, for they had been more dependent on the interpreter, and they had had the bad interpreter. (One of our interpreters is very good, the other very bad). We sat down to relax over a drink. Then Roberts joined us. Bolt told him, pretty clearly, what he thought of his remarks about Tibet. That conversation drew itself out, and before long we were talking about East Germany. Roberts revealed himself as a supporter of the East German government and system. Bolt touched lightly on the Berlin Wall.[43] 'Whatever you may say', he remarked, 'you must admit that there is something wrong about the system which has to build a wall to prevent its beneficiaries from running away'. Then Roberts revealed himself in his true colours. First he minimised the wall: it was only a little wall in one city. Oh no, we pointed out, that little wall is merely the closing of a little gap in a long jealously guarded barbed-wire frontier right across Europe ... Then he tried to suggest that it was a double

---

41 The PRC's troops had occupied Tibet in 1949–50. The Dalai Lama fled when the PRC took full control of his country in 1959.

42 *SACU News* (December 1965) reported that Adams wanted to discuss the future of industrial design with the Chinese, 'but was unable to do so with anyone knowledgeable. She was also disappointed that the implications of the gift that was taken from SACU were not grasped.' The fact that Queensberry's bowl was a work of art 'specifically designed as capable of mass production ... did not seem to get across'.

43 The *Antifaschistischer Schutzwall* (anti-fascist bulwark or rampart) had been erected in 1961.

frontier, to prevent people moving to the East as well as from it. We soon disposed of that. Then he suggested that anyway there was no movement from the East at all: a few East Germans were temporarily seduced by the glittering lights of the West but they soon came back ... Then why build a wall to prevent them coming back? we asked. Then he sought escape into irrelevancy: 'I think it is best for the world that Germany be divided.' 'Perhaps', we persisted; 'but division does not entail a wall ...' So we pressed; so he wriggled; and the result was to reveal his true character. He is simply a narrow-minded, double-thinking fellow-traveller. As far as I can see, Anglo-Chinese understanding, to him, would mean unconditional surrender, lubricated by a few convenient dishonesties; to Mrs Adams it would mean a jolly chorus of meaningless trivialities about the rights of women, Basic English and simplified Chinese, forgetting (or rather, never realising) that China is a communist country.

Wednesday, 22 September

After the strain of last night I slept late and with difficulty got ready for our first appointment. We were picked up at 9.0 and taken to the Great Hall of the Peoples.[44] I protested. We would see the Great Hall of the Peoples often enough, I said, in the course of our stay (we had been assured of this at the Embassy); must we spend a morning in it? But it was no good: our orders were clear, and we had to obey. So we were taken to a vast building in familiar totalitarian megalithic style and made to savour, first, its pseudo-classical pillared front, then room after room – the Szechuan room, the Canton room, the Hunan room, with their coffered ceilings and red columns and wax flowers and expensive artefacts. Hunan being the native province of chairman Mao, our attention was particularly directed, in the Hunan Room, to an inscribed poem of the Master, in his own handwriting, only magnified a thousand-fold, on one wall, and to a huge painting on another, which represented a Hunan landscape containing his Birthplace and the Village School to which he went. And of course we had every detail of the Ten Thousand (or is it 20,000?) Seat Auditorium.[45] We were told exactly how many square or cubic feet every room occupied and how many ventilation-holes there were in the auditorium; but

44 This had been opened in 1959 at the west end of Tiananmen Square. Meetings of the National People's Congress and of the National Congress of the Chinese Communist Party were held there.

45 10,000.

when we asked the numerical strength of the National Assembly, our guide was suddenly ignorant and told us instead the weight of a marble monstrosity.

In the afternoon we visited the Imperial Palace and there, for the first time, I felt glad to be in Pekin. We went in by the Meridian Gate and were – at least Bolt and I were – bowled over by the impact: that huge, Cyclopean red bastion contrasting with the exquisite palace buildings above it; the succession of vast courtyards, the first of which is saved from bewildering uniformity by the artificial canal crossed by raised bridges; the harmony of the innumerable palace buildings; the majestic ceremonial rooms that form the dividing range between court and court. We spent two hours there, but they could only be exploratory. Once again, we had a hopelessly ignorant guide. She did not even get her dynasties right – the Shang, she insisted, were 1500 years ago, and she could not be persuaded to change the figure, on which all her chronology seemed to hinge.[46] This could have been very misleading as the labels are exclusively in Chinese. However she knew the correct claptrap, 'looted by imperialist aggression' etc. etc. We asked what training she had as a guide, and she explained with great complacency, as if it gave her added authority, that she was a high-school girl and had no training: she picked up her expertise by practice only. This explained a lot.

I have said that Bolt and I were bowled over, for Mrs Adams never shows any sign of aesthetic interest, in spite of the glass bowl and the Council for Industrial Design, and Trade Unionist Ernie Roberts spent the entire time giving, not receiving impressions. As we walked through those breathtaking courts he was continuously occupied in giving a lecture to our bigot guide To Chi-Lou, through the bad interpreter (whom Bolt has described as a presbyterian school teacher), on the subject of the British trade unions. This seems to be his only interest, and he emphasises it by distributing AEU badges to casually encountered Chinamen. The only remark which I heard him make about the palace was where we faced the most splendid building of all, the ceremonial throne room which forms the first cross-range. He said 'There is a garage just like that near my home at Beckenham. It's called the Chinese Garage'.[47] I could detect no trace of irony or humour in his voice as he made the remark. Then he returned to the subject of trade unions.

---

46 The Shang, or Yin dynasty, ruled the Yellow River valley during the second millennium BC.

47 The Chinese Garage was the local nickname of Langley Park Garage, which was actually designed in imitation of a Japanese pagoda. It dates from 1928.

Roberts fascinates me in a way. He is (or says that he is) one of the eleven children of a drunken miner. He is much the smartest of our party, wearing dapper suits and very carefully chosen and expensive-looking coloured shirts and ties. He is also much the most status-minded, and is always making comparisons between the treatment accorded to him in various communist countries (he seems to travel only in them). He clearly considers that he has a right to preferential treatment. The communist insistence on status is more intelligible to me after acquaintance with him: it is the generalisation, as a social pattern, of a human outlook individual in him.

At 5.30 Bolt and I went to a reception given by the acting *chargé d'affaires* for a number of Chinese students going to England. They go to an enterprising school at Ealing and then go on to universities in England. All but two are staying in London, but two are going to Birmingham, to study Greek (there is a sound Marxist professor of Greek at Birmingham, George Thomson).[48] I liked those students whom I met, and also the minister for higher education,[49] who was there too; and the action of the Chinese government in paying to send students to heretical England contrasts oddly with its bigotry in other matters. But Alan Donald assures me that the students are all hand-picked, hard and safe.

Then we were taken to an acrobatic performance by student acrobats in the theatre in Chung Shan Park (Sun Yat Sen Theatre, I think).[50] They were excellent, and the performance was a welcome relief from propaganda. Of course there was a little propaganda in it – a ridiculous fall-guy was presented as an American soldier, and there was some patriotic Mao-worship at the end. But the audience did not respond at all. They totally ignored the anti-American gesture, and when the Mao-worship began they sensibly deduced that the end of the performance was near and left to catch their buses. Propaganda, no doubt, is a compulsory game for intellectuals – and to be a Chinese intellectual

---

48 George Thomson (1903–1987) joined the CPGB and became Professor of Greek at Birmingham University in the same year, 1936. In *Aeschylus and Athens* (1941) he used Marxist ideas to interpret Greek drama. He was active alongside Joseph Needham and Joan Robinson in the China Policy Study Group, which published his pamphlet *Marxism in China Today* (1965) and his jargon-ridden book *From Marx to Mao Tse-tung: a study in revolutionary dialectics* (1971).

49 Probably He Wei (1910–1973), who had been appointed Minister of Education in 1964 and was disgraced during the Cultural Revolution, 1966. He had been Assistant Minister of Foreign Affairs, 1954–58, and ambassador in North Vietnam, 1958–62.

50 Ming emperors worshipped the gods of earth and harvest in the temples and at the altars of Chung-shan [Zhongshan] Park. It was renamed in 1928 to commemorate the revered nationalist Sun Yat-sen.

must be a terrible life–but others, it seems, contrive to ignore it and cultivate their gardens. Unfortunately, we are not allowed to meet the others.[51]

Bolt told me how Bertrand Russell nearly died in China.[52] He was in a coma. The doctor leant over him, listening, and said quietly, 'He's gone'. Where upon those inextinguishable eyes opened and that high voice was heard saying, 'I've never felt better in my life!'

Thursday, 23 September

Feeling exhausted by social strains, tourism and the heat, I contracted out of this morning's programme, which was a conducted tour of a primary school, and spent a leisurely and, I am sure, more rewarding time exploring on foot the back streets of Pekin, the places where the inhabitants (or at least a lot of them) live, and which our guides were so reluctant to show us. Almost immediately behind our hotel I found them, and soon I was lost in a fascinating labyrinth of enchanting hovels, all built in grey stone (it was one of the abuses of 'imperial times', our guide had told us, that the people had been obliged to build in grey; now, with the triumph of democracy, colours are free for all), all with heavy, ribbed grey roofs, some with majestic fronts and delightful details. There were imposing hollow facades, frontispieces of exquisitely carved stone, carved wood reliefs, armigerous gateways leading into alleys or courtyards, and stylised flora and fauna at every point: toad-like lions squatting on cottage doorsteps, proud, rampant lions on balustraded roofs, here a stone stork on a cottage chimney, there a caparisoned elephant in relief over a cottage door, festoons of fruit and flowers carved in relief over doors and windows. This labyrinth went on for ever and gradually merged into the bazaar area, from which I came out in front of the Chien Men, the great double Southern Gate of the old city.[53]

---

51 The theatres visited by the SACU tourists had 'proletarian audiences', Bolt told *SACU News* (November 1965). 'Young families with children, including babies at the breast. The children run about between the seats while the parents talk to one another. There is no politeness; they come to be entertained, and if they are not, they go on talking. The curtain goes up on a terrific babble, then the actors come on and have to get a hold of their audience. These ... audiences would give an English actor a nervous breakdown.'

52 Russell contracted double pneumonia, dysentery and kidney disease in 1921.

53 The two gatehouses inspected by T-R were reconstructions. The Boxer rebels had set fire to booths in the tunnel-like gateway between the gatehouses, where pedlars were selling such objectionably foreign goods as medicines, brass buckles, pipes, snuff and kerosene lamps. The flames engulfed neighbouring furriers, curio shops, jewellers and silk merchants.

There are two gates here, or rather gate houses, for each is a fortress in itself, mounted, like the Meridian gate of the palace, on a gigantic stone bastion with a tunnel-like gateway through it. Was this enormous bastion hollow or solid? We had asked this at the palace and had been told that it was solid; but it cannot be, I thought, and anyway that girl knew nothing. In the inner of the two gatehouses there are false doorways in the bastion at ground level, and a real door a little higher up, but still only half-way up the bastion. Through the cracks of this real door I could see the sky, which argued that the wall was at least largely hollow. But the outer gate-house has stone stairs up the bastion, and the iron gate closing the stairs was in one place ajar; so I slipped through and climbed up. I found myself on a level platform at the top of the bastion so in this case at least the bastion, whether hollow or solid, is enclosed all round and on top. A party of Chinese soldiers was sitting there. Their spokesman advanced, full of courtesy, very unlike an English soldier whose point of duty had been invaded. We had an entirely abortive but very genial conversation, from which I gathered that I was not allowed to inspect further and descended again. Then I returned through that fascinating labyrinth of old houses, discovering new details at every turn.

Yesterday, when we asked our guide what had been on the site now occupied by Tiananmen Square, the Great Hall of the people, etc. he had replied, with cold contempt 'old, broken-down houses'. I suppose they were like these houses, and I suppose these houses will go the same way soon.

When I had returned to the hotel, Robert Bolt came to see me. The visit to the primary school, he said, had been 'absolutely hilarious'. The school itself was technically excellent, the teachers charming and efficient, the children delightful, as all Chinese children are. The hilarity was caused by Mrs Adams. As has been quite clear to us from recent events, Mrs A. is as silly as she is complacent. She knows absolutely nothing about anything. She pontificates about art and is on the Council for Industrial Design, but is totally without taste. She is on the ITV authority but seems to know nothing about broadcasting. She talks knowingly about education – has just returned from Morocco, where she been 'examining the question of women's education' – but knows nothing about it either. She is really just a pushing, name-dropping busybody, and her *gaffes* become ever more outrageous. Yesterday, apparently, she gave our Chinese friends a brief talk on 'the Yellow Peril'.[54] Last night, when we

---

54 This phrase was popularized, if not coined, by William II of Germany. Originally applied to the Japanese, after their victory over China in the war of 1895, and increasingly current after the Boxer rebellion and the Russo-Japanese war of 1904–5, it expressed fears of Asian hordes overwhelming European Christendom. In the 1960s two other phrases expressed Western hostility to the PRC: 'Mao's flu' and 'Chinese heroin'.

learned that we were to be shown a film of the Indo-Pakistani war (or perhaps of the Indo-Chinese fighting in the Himalayas), she told us that it would be an occasion on which to raise again the discussion of the Kashmir problem. This after her follies at the banquet! She is incorrigible. And today, at the primary school, she was, Bolt tells me, at the top of her form.

The events began at the English lesson. The room was dominated by a portrait of chairman Mao, under which was written, in English, 'We love chairman Mao, chairman Mao loves us'. The children gracefully went through their drill for the benefits of the honoured guests. They sang a rhythmical chorus. The teacher beamed with gratification. Mrs Adams beamed too, like a memsahib graciously approving the obedient patter of the little natives (as Bolt says, she really has a 'colonial' mind). Then she asked what were the words of their song. The interpreter duly told her. The world visibly wobbled under her feet as she heard. Somehow it had never occurred to her that the little dears would be taught to sing anti-imperialist slogans. Then another class sang, in treble six-year-old voices, another welcoming ditty. 'And what are the words this time?' asked our now hesitant 'leader'. 'A Tibetan folk song', she was told, and signed with relief. But then she was told the words of it too:

> Bright shines the sun over Pekin
> For there resides chairman Mao
> Maker of the glorious people's revolution
> Destroyer of imperialist aggression …

Mary's face fell again. And it continued to fall as evidence followed evidence of indoctrination. At last, it seems, her ignorant complacency is beginning to tremble. But it has only strengthened her resolution to argue about Kashmir tonight. Surely, she thinks, the iron-clad, stone-faced, thrice-tested, justified saints of Marxism-Leninism will see reason where presented by a silly old memsahib from Surrey whose advanced ideas are sufficiently proved by her belief in the education of women and Basic English.[55]

'How on earth does such a woman get on to these committees?' I asked Bolt. 'She knows nothing about anything and is a prize ass. But I suppose she is useful as a lubricant.' 'Some of these lubricants are pretty gritty', he replied: 'the machine would run better without them.' However, I console myself that

---

55 Mary Adams had lived since the 1930s at Gloucester Gate on the perimeter of Regent's Park in London.

the party includes Bolt instead of Vanessa Redgrave. 'I don't know her,' I said to Bolt, 'but I suspect we would not have got on.' 'She would have driven you mad,' he replied: 'She is worse in her radicalism even than Ernie Roberts and sillier even than Mary Adams, and as tall as a giraffe.' Then I pleased myself by imagining the original party: Mrs Adams, Roberts, Vanessa Redgrave and Maurice Bowra. But I suppose Maurice would not have listened to anyone, just boomed away and got where he wanted.

In the afternoon we were taken to an arts-and-crafts factory. We had the usual lecture from the vice-director. ('vice', we decided, means 'party' – it was the 'vice-head master' who received my colleagues at the school, the 'vice-president' of the Cultural Association who entertained us, etc). Before Liberation, arts and crafts had been in the hands of capitalists who exploited the workers, damaging their health etc, etc. Now … etc. etc. They produced lacquer-ware, jewellery, irony-carving, jade-work, etc. etc. It was depressing to see the real skill and the patient training which went into the production of objects that were, on the whole, ghastly; but as Bolt remarked, all sensibility must have been extinguished by propagandist posters which faced the workers in every room. After the tour we had another lecture, on how the communist party under Chairman Mao had now created art in China after the long Dark Age of capitalism. 'Does the vice-director mean', we innocently asked, 'that art did not exist in China before Liberation?' I expected him to reply that it had flourished in imperial times but had degenerated in the last period of capitalism. But no: so feeble and conciliatory an answer was not to be expected from a vice-director. Art, he repeated, had not existed in China till 1949.

I dined with Bobbie and Natalie Bevan at the Szechuan Restaurant.[56] She had been at the Embassy party last night, and had reminded me that we had met with Randolph Churchill. They are on a party organised by two energetic and enormous ladies, Miss Molesworth and Miss Windsor.[57] They pay £750 apiece and have a month to, in and from China. They have not left Pekin except for excursions. Most of those who comprise the party are old ladies. The

56 Robert Bevan (1901–1974) joined a leading advertising agency, S. H. Benson, in 1923 after graduating from Christ Church, Oxford. He was chairman of Benson's, 1954–64, and a power in post-war English advertising. In 1952 he inherited his parents' art collection, which included works by Cézanne, Gaudier-Brzeska and Gauguin, and became a donor to the Ashmolean Museum. In 1946 he married the painter Natalie Sieveking (1909–2007), and lived from 1957 in a *menage à trois* with her and Randolph Churchill.

57 Beatrix Molesworth (1917–2014) was a partner with Miss Winsor in the International Services tour agency.

Bevans say that their lives have been saved by Jane Willoughby[58] and Caroline Jarvis,[59] who have come on the tour to get over various emotional or other crises. I spoke to Jane Willoughby this morning, having observed with interest that Ernie Roberts had been cultivating her for a good 15 minutes. I have since discovered (from Roberts) that she represented herself to be 'a welfare worker', and (from the Bevans) that he declared himself to be *persona gratissima* with the Chinese government, able to go (and to take her if she liked) anywhere in China. He poured scorn on the Embassy staff, as being confined to Pekin and environs, and represented himself as far more powerful and effective with the Chinese government. Thus each thought that the other was far grander (according to his or her ideas) than he (or she) was. I have not so far said anything to disturb this idyll, although the temptation may in the end prove too great. Our dinner was grand but not very good: however, by going out to dine I avoided the propaganda-film on the Indo-Chinese dispute in the Himalayas which was shown, specially for us, in the hotel. Our guides were somewhat piqued when I said that I must miss it: it had all been specially arranged, they said. But my answer is that I did not ask for it, and if they want to make special arrangements for us, they must first make sure that we are agreeable, and free.

Friday, 24 September

Bolt and I got up at 7.0 and went only by taxi with the Bevans, Jane Willoughby and Caroline Jarvis, to Tien Tan, The Temple of Heaven.[60] It is a wonderful series of buildings, as breathtaking as the palace itself. I could have spent the

---

58 Jane Heathcote-Drummond-Willoughby (b. 1934) succeeded her father, the last Earl of Ancaster, as 27th Baroness Willoughby de Eresby in 1983. The T-Rs occasionally stayed with her parents at Grimsthorpe Castle in Lincolnshire. She had been a Maid of Honour to the Queen at the coronation in 1953. Lucian Freud took her as the subject of his portrait 'Woman in a fur coat' (1967–68).

59 Caroline Jarvis (b. 1935) was a Lincolnshire neighbour of the Ancasters. Both her parents had worked in SIS during the war. After reading English at Newnham College, Cambridge, she worked at London Zoo, where she edited its zoological yearbook. In 1967 she married the tropical biologist Lord Medway, afterwards Earl of Cranbrook: they lived initially in the jungle of Malaya. She became a farmer, traveller to world zoos, and campaigner on issues of food quality and the survival of small shops.

60 The core of this complex was built in 1406–20. It was occupied, damaged and desecrated by Anglo-French troops (1860–61) and by the international forces that quelled the Boxer rebellion (1900–1). The grounds were opened to the public in 1918, and were described in 1932 by Ann Bridge as an 'untidy park, half wild spinney, half open space' (Ann Bridge, *Peking Picnic* (London: Chatto & Windus, 1932), p. 60).

whole morning there; and yet, if we were to comply with our official hosts and guides, we would never have seen it. As it was, we had to return after three-quarters of an hour for a quick breakfast in order to be on parade at 9.0. The parade, we understood, was for the Museum of Revolutionary History.[61]

We paraded one short: Mary Adams is indisposed, and has immobilised our good interpreter to supply her needs. Bolt thought that she was only suffering from a surfeit of umbrage at not being taken seriously enough. I fear she is anyway suffering from this. Bolt and I at least can endure the slights and inconveniences, the pretensions of ignorant guides and, for half the time, a useless interpreter. We can bear it because at least, though at this price, we have got to Pekin and can see the Palace, the temples, the country. But to Mary there is no reward, for she is interested in nothing: neither art nor culture nor people nor country. She only likes being busy and important, bossing some people, being courted by others, and seeming to be someone. And this, alas, has not happened.

By the time the rest of us had gathered for the parade, I had decided our policy. I told our guide firmly that we had not asked to see the Museum of Revolutionary History, and that, whereas we would be glad to see it, we must first see what we had asked to see, *viz*: the Museum of National History, which anyway was next to it and was a necessary introduction to it.[62] He replied that we could certainly move on to the Museum of National History if there was time after seeing the Museum of Revolutionary History. We pressed our point, he repeated his answer. Finally I told him curtly and firmly that there could be no question of seeing the Museum of Revolutionary History until we had seen the Museum of National History: we simply would not do it. Faced with this flat refusal, he collapsed, and we went to the Museum of National History.

It is an excellent museum: the only difficulty was that all the labels were in Chinese only, and we were hindered, not helped, by an idiot guide and a doltish interpreter (the presbyterian schoolmistress). The guide was a hopeless giggling peasant, who knew nothing at all. Whenever I asked for information from the interpreter, she consulted a curator and got lost in uncomprehending

---

61 The Museum of the Chinese Revolution [*Zhong guo ge ming bo wu guan*] had opened in 1961. Its propagandist displays began with the Opium War of 1840, and included the gallows where the Marxist pioneer Li Da Zhao was hanged in 1927, and the flag hoisted by Mao in Tiananmen Square on 1 October 1949.

62 The Museum of Chinese History [Zhong guo li shi bo wu guan] was divided into three didactic sections displaying primitive, slave and feudal societies. Replicas of objects held by other museums were mixed with genuine articles so as to clarify party doctrine.

conversation which she was incapable of rendering into English. At times I got very short with her, I'm afraid. 'I don't want an opinion', I would say, 'just translate the label'. But it soon became clear that she could not translate the labels for the simple reason that she could not read her own language. All she could do was to draw our attention to a succession of hideous modern statues which dominated the museum at recurrent points, and which all represented 'leaders of peasant revolts'. We soon learned to give them a wide berth. Finally, after two hours, we came to the preliminaries of the Opium War, and suddenly the curator, who by now was following us, and the interpreter came to life. The gramophone record was turned on. 'Imperialist aggression', 'capitalist exploitation', etc. – all the old phrases trotted out. But at least they could not trot far. The Museum came to an end at 1840 and at that date the Museum of Revolutionary History took over. But it was now after 12 o'clock. Our guide was bored stiff: he had followed us silently for over two hours, an inarticulate boor. Our interpreter had been reduced to order. We announced that it was now lunch-time. They did not demur; and we were saved.

In the afternoon (Ernie Roberts being involved with his Chinese trade unionists)[63] Robert Bolt and I were taken to a rural commune, Evergreen Commune, at the foot of the Western Hills. It is a market-gardening commune of 8100 households scattered in 112 villages. We visited the workshop, the communal school, the experimental farm, the orchards and vineyards, the pigs, the communal stores, and saw the irrigation system. All this impressed us greatly: it is far, far superior to the collective farm I saw near Moscow. But the most enjoyable encounter was with an old peasant who was the oracle on onions. All the young officials of the commune, party officials with white hands, deferred to him. He was the *paterfamilias* of the commune; and he had the venerable features and straggling beard and benign, intellectual look of Ho-Chih-Minh[64] and of those poets of the Han and other dynasties whose portraits we saw this morning in the Museum.[65]

---

63 In a letter to the *Morning Star* (19 July 1968), Roberts wrote that he met Kung Yung Ho, Liu Chin Mao, Wang Chia Ching and Chang Chaow, representatives of the All China Federation of Trade Unions: 'they showed a keen interest in the British Trade Union Movement, about which they were well informed'.

64 Ho Chi-minh (1890–1969) was prime minister (1945–55) and president (1945–69) of the Democratic Republic of Vietnam (North Vietnam).

65 The Han imperial dynasty reigned for 400 years from 202 BC to AD 221. It replaced the Qin dynasty, and was followed by the era of the six dynasties (AD 221–589).

In the evening we were taken to the circus in the Park of the Temple of Heaven.[66] There was a very enjoyable 'lion-dance', the lions being of the pantomime-horse variety. Otherwise it might have been a circus anywhere. I enjoyed the audience: I find Chinese crowds irresistible, so good-tempered and gay. There were some performing dogs who did a very engaging class-room turn. They are the only dogs I have see in Pekin. The girls (Jane Willoughby & Caroline Jarvis) told me that all dogs were destroyed and eaten in the famine of 1958; and that there is a commune which specialises in breeding dogs for human consumption.[67]

As we went round the Museum today, Ernie Roberts remarked (looking at a picture of an old emperor) that it looked as if mortar-boards had come from China. 'Perhaps', I said, 'and why not: examinations did.' 'Yes,' said the trade-union leader, 'and they knew the same tricks: how to make the examinations difficult in order to let the right people through.' The implication was clear: 'the right people' were the privileged, the sons of the establishment. But his real meaning was not quite clear to me, and I kept asking myself what he meant. I put it to Bolt. He thought that 'difficult' meant intellectually easy but socially esoteric. 'Perhaps this is what he did mean', I replied, 'but he *said* "difficult".' 'A Freudian slip' was Bolt's only solution of the enigma.

When we came back to our hotel after the circus, our guide To-Chi-lou ('Stoneface' as we have come to call him) asked us about certain projects. I insisted, as I have long done, that I wished to visit the *Academia Sinica* and I wished to see the head of the Historical Institute there, and (I now added) having been invited to China, I did not wish to go away without having done so. The usual excuses were made: there are so many foreign delegations, everyone is busy, etc. In the end Stoneface said, 'I will discuss it with Mrs Adams.' 'No', I said firmly; 'it has nothing to do with Mrs Adams: you must discuss it with me'. Mrs A's pretensions as 'leader of the delegation' have become insufferable. At London airport we were suddenly told that it might be convenient if we designated one of our number as our leader. To avoid embarrassment, I suggested

---

66 'The parks and gardens are full of what look like pieces of sculpture by Henry Moore, but are in fact stones which have acquired their odd shape naturally. They are much sought after, and have been brought to Peking from all over China. The Chinese have a great passion for what one might describe as natural deformities. A great many of the trees, for example, were groomed so as to look like the trees of their paintings. Even the goldfish, of which there are a great many on show in the public parks, are bred for strangeness' (A. J. Ayer, 'Impressions of Communist China', *The Listener*, 2 December 1954, p. 941).

67 The eating of dogs was supposed to improve men's vigour and to lengthen penises.

Mrs Adams, who is elderly and feminine and has some post on the committee of SACU (as on every other committee: the Consumers' Association, the Telephone Users' Association, the Patients' Association, etc.). Now the Chinese press refers to us as 'Mrs Adams' Committee' and we are announced as such whenever we go. Unfortunately, while she accepts the status willingly enough, Mrs Adams does not accept any obligations. She has acquired a bedroom for herself, but two bedrooms have been assigned to the three men. I, fortunately, am in one; but the other is shared by Bolt and Roberts. I regard this as intolerable and have been pressing for some time to get it rectified. The Chinese invited us; four people have always been expected; and they have no excuse for giving us only three bedrooms. I raised this matter again today, pointing out that the English tourists led by Miss Molesworth and Miss Windsor (who all have fine suites) are leaving today and that one room *must* be given to us. So far I have got nowhere. But Mrs A, comfortable in her private room, sees no need to lift a finger in such a matter.

Saturday, 25 September

This morning we went to the university of Pekin. We were met by a biologist who spoke good English and a professor of history whom I quickly discovered to be a worthless party hack.[68] Since his own student days he had spent twenty years in 'local government' and had only just come to the university to profess modern Chinese history 1919–1965. The biologist seemed to be a civilised scholar. We learned quite a lot about the university, which is 9,000 strong and specialises in producing teachers and research-workers in social sciences (including languages) and natural sciences. It is not to expand beyond 10,000, expansion in other subjects being met by the creation and growth of specialised institutes in Pekin. The university was founded on European models in 1898. We visited the laboratories, equipped with modern machinery from Leipzig, Japan and occasionally Shanghai; the historical department, which is strong in archaeology; the students' living quarters and the library. In the students' quarters Mrs Adams was on top of her form (she has recovered today, so we were duly introduced as 'the delegation under Mrs. Adams') and asked four Chinese girls what they thought of Queen Victoria. I heard a suppressed groan from Bolt and was able to intervene promptly and prevent the inevitable gramophone record about the Opium War, the cession of Hong Kong, and the

---

68 The biologist and party hack are both unidentifiable.

sacking of the Summer Palace (Mrs Adams, of course, has never heard of such things). In the Library the Librarian had set out an excellent exhibition of old books, including the printed catalogue of the Chinese books at Harvard and in the Library of Congress, which were designed as a text for the usual sermon on 'loot by U.S. imperialist aggressors.' 'Loot' of course is a tabloid word for any Chinese object which has been acquired, by whatever process, by foreigners and whose loss is subsequently regretted. I liked the librarian, who seemed a civilised man; and the little party twerp who dominated the history faculty had a charming and civilised young 'assistant' who showed us the archaeological work of the university. We also liked the biologist; but when we asked if he would care to come and dine with us one night, the invitation, as Bolt put it, went up like a lead balloon. We were told that it would be much better if we, as guests, were to dine with the biologist and others at the university. So the matter was dropped.

In the car going to the university, with Stone-face and the useless interpreter, I raised again the question of *Academia Sinica*. Stone-face asked what field of history interested me so that the right professor could be produced. I was determined not to leave the choice of my contacts to him or his superiors and said firmly that I wished to meet the President (*not* the vice-president) of the Historical Institute, and I would then discuss further contacts with him. From this position I refused to deviate. What will come of it is yet to see [*sic*]. On the way back I merely listened fascinated while Bolt, with infinite patience and persistence, tried to force a new party hack (a 'council member' of the Association) to face an interesting dilemma over the 'reformation' of the Pekin Opera.[69] It was like a sheepdog trying to force a sheep through an open gate. The sheep was very stupid – the blockish stupidity of all the officials who deal with us is infinitely depressing – but he was aware that he must avoid going through that gate at all costs. So the dialogue continued, made slower and more cumbrous by the useless 'presbyterian' interpreter, all the way to the hotel when the sheep escaped through the gate of the car instead.

---

69 Mao's wife Chiang Ch'ing [Jiang Qing] (1914–1991) had led an attack in 1963 on bourgeois ideology in Peking opera. In Joan Robinson's summary of 1969, 'The new opera are concerned with stories taken from the period of the long and multifarious struggles that led up to the Liberation, and contemporary themes such as the Korean War. Abandoning the subtlety and refinement of a palace art, they depict heroes and villains in strong, simple lines. They are extremely popular, and evidently have a powerful appeal to their audiences. The old opera was concerned with emperors, mandarins, court beauties and tales of magic. The common people in it were mainly treated as low-life comics. It glamorized feudalism, with its fascinating technique and gorgeous dress. The young generation had no sympathy for it' (*Cultural Revolution*, p. 49).

At lunch Mrs Adams was in fine self-important form, dropping important Christian names with liberal lips, and telling us that she had graciously endorsed some trivial requests we had made to our guides. Stone-face had reported them to her to make sure that the headmistress was not being bypassed by the schoolchildren. She reported this fact, and her condescension, with great smugness, and evidently now feels that we understand our proper place. I'm afraid she is the Lady Weir[70] of our party and we – that is, Bolt and I – lead her on in order that she may show her paces. Whenever she mentions 'Peter' or 'Julian' or 'Tony', we say 'Peter who?' etc; and as she adds the surname, Blackett[71] or Huxley[72] or Wedgwood Benn,[73] her crisp, toneless voice indicates condescension, if not contempt, for such social groundlings as ourselves.

After lunch, oh blessed news, we were free for the afternoon. So Bolt and I went back to the Palace and found the Ming paintings and the Sung and Ming pots (such as there are; for the best of them, I understand, were swept off to Formosa by Chiang Kai-shek).[74] For two hours we wandered through that

---

70 Weir is perhaps a misspelling of Wheare. Joan Randell (1915–2013) had married Sir Kenneth Wheare, Fellow of All Souls 1944–56 and Rector of Exeter College 1956–72. She was a versatile Oxford protester whose exploits included lying on the floor of the St Aldate's gas showroom, and standing outside the Clarendon Building reading aloud from Kenneth Clark's *Civilization* while undergraduates tried to occupy the building in a stunt about the university keeping personal files.

71 Patrick [not Peter] Blackett (1897–1974) was scientific adviser of the Ministry of Technology, which had been launched by the Labour government in 1964. At Cambridge, in 1925, J. Robert Oppenheimer had tried to poison him with an apple laced with toxic chemicals including cyanide. An experimental physicist, the creator of Operational Research during the Second World War, a specialist in cosmic rays, a pioneer of nuclear research, paleomagnetism and plate tectonics, Blackett received the Nobel prize for physics in 1948, was made a Companion of Honour in 1965, received the Order of Merit in 1967, a life peerage in 1969, and has a crater on the moon named after him. He defined a successful scientific laboratory as one in which ordinary people do first-class work.

72 Sir Julian Huxley (1887–1975), zoologist, evolutionary biologist, scientific popularizer and first director-general of UNESCO 1946–48, co-founder of the World Wildlife Fund 1961.

73 Anthony Wedgwood Benn (1925–2014), radical patriot and economic nationalist, first elected as a Labour MP in 1950, became the second Minister of Technology, working with Blackett, 1966–70.

74 'Generalissimo' Chiang Kai-shek (1887–1975) tried to rule China in 1928–49, and headed the government of KMT exiles in Taiwan, 1949–75. Lord Salter in 1947 called him 'a Chinese Cromwell' (*Personality in Politics* (London: Faber, 1947), p. 214). For Lord Vansittart, Chiang was 'first our enemy, then "not so bad", later "our heroic ally", finally a yellow dog in Formosa' (*The Mist Procession* (London: Hutchinson, 1958), p. 329).

labyrinth of courts, then we came back and, over tea, we discussed the impact of communism on China. The tension between China – historic China, Chinese society – and the communist party seems to me to be latent but constant. What surprises me most is the stupidity of all the party members we meet: the opaque, self-righteous solemnity, the parrot-like dogmatism, the absolute lack of understanding or self-criticism. Of course we are a second-class delegation. Perhaps if we were grander, we would have more intelligent guides: guides who would serve as conductors to, not insulators from the Chinese world. And yet Chinese society is a gay, sophisticated, self-critical society. Its poetry and art emphasise the insignificance of man in nature, the absurdity of his pretensions. How has this incredible reversal, this *Umwertung aller Werten*,[75] been imposed upon it? Or is it just a pendulum oscillation in the dialectic of Taoism[76] and Confucianism,[77] Ying and Yang?[78]

I asked Bolt about his own experience in the communist party. He explained how he had been drawn into it. He came from the borderline between the lower-middle class and the proletariat, of a non-conformist family, and both his class and his religion made him easy game. The communist agents at Manchester University preyed on his nonconformist conscience, his puritanism. At first the double-think shocked him; then he got used to it and almost adopted it; then he was shocked by it again and decided to reconsider his position. 'But it wasn't easy to slide out. Oh no: one felt a traitor, betraying a whole world, renouncing all friends and friendships. I had to take a long holiday in the Pyrenees before I could sort myself out and take the plunge.'

---

75 German: revaluation of all values (a phrase from Nietzsche).

76 Taoist philosophy saw humankind as an insignificant part of infinite and immortal nature. It upheld non-assertion, instinct, spontaneity, primitive bliss, privacy and disorganized multiplicity. It opposed purposive action, formality, hierarchies, war, taxation, punishment and conventional morality as unnatural restraints.

77 Confucius (551–479 BC) is the most revered person in Chinese history. His school of thought was proclaimed as the state cult in 136 BC. It taught the self-cultivation of humility, deference, docility, submission and subordination as the means to harmonious families, social decorum, political order and world peace. Confucianism remained China's dominant philosophical system for two thousand years.

78 Ying is a symbol of earth, femininity, darkness, passivity and receptivity. It exists in even numbers, valleys and streams, and is represented by the tiger, the colour orange and a broken line. Yang symbolises heaven, masculinity, light, action and penetration. It is present in odd numbers and mountains, and is represented by the dragon, the colour blue and an unbroken line.

In the evening he and I went to dine with Timothy George and his wife. A Frenchman, who had also been at Cambridge, Patrick Destiné (or Destenay?)[79] and his English wife[80] were also there. He is commercial attaché at the French Embassy. We released our feelings both about our Chinese guides and about our English colleagues. We soon discovered numerous things that Stoneface and co. have concealed from us: trivial things, but nevertheless concealed. I also had a long talk with Timothy about China. He is highly intelligent, knows Chinese, and is interested in China. He told me, *inter alia*, that the party has had great difficulty in recruiting intellectuals. The intellectuals acquiesce in the revolution because they recognise that a revolution was necessary and they also recognise that this revolution has produced important results. But they cannot bring themselves to support positively a movement so fundamentally alien to their ideas: they cannot identify themselves with it, and they do not join the party. This, if true, explains much. There are 17 million party members, and he insists that the intellectual membership is minimal. He also says that, during the 'hundred flowers' period, 1957–8, Pekin university in particular exposed itself as anti-communist and suffered accordingly in the 'rectification' of 1958. I remembered that at university we had been told that there were 'reforms' in 1958. But they did not mention this interesting background to the reforms.

Sunday, 26 September

A strong wind and some rain in the night left the air clearer than it has been since we came, with bright sun and a pleasant breeze. Our guides appeared at 8.0 and gave us some more plans. Tomorrow I am to go to the Institute of History. When others were asked if they were interested, Ernie Roberts said smugly, and seriously, 'I prefer making history to reading about it'. With what the Chinese call 'the broad masses of the people' on one's side, it seems,

---

79 Patrick Destenay (1938–1982) completed a two-year course in Chinese at St John's College, Cambridge shortly before France recognized the PRC in 1964. During the ensuing détente, he was appointed commercial attaché in Peking in March 1965, but was forced out by the Cultural Revolution. He headed the Chinese studies department at the University of Aix-en-Provence from 1972.

80 Anne Hawtrey (b. 1937) was daughter of the Clerk of Journals in the House of Commons. She married Destenay when he was at Cambridge in 1964. She prepared the English version of the compendious *Nagel's Encyclopaedia-Guide: China* (1968). This was the first guidebook to China published in forty years, and substantially the work of young Francophone sinologists who were enabled to visit the PRC during the Sino-French détente. Anne Destenay also translated the works of several French *sinologues* into English.

one is automatically a maker of history, especially if empowered as assistant general secretary of the AEU. Ernie also, it seems, has political ambitions: he told us that he had applied to be Labour candidate for Horsham at the last general election, but had been rejected by a committee of Labour members, dominated by George Brown,[81] on the grounds that he had appeared on platforms with Bertie Russell etc.[82] 'Of course I didn't want to get into Parliament', he explained – it would have been incompatible with his position of power in the Union, and anyway Horsham is unshakeably tory – 'but it would have given me a platform: they would have had to allow me, as a candidate, to express my views at party meeting on a national level.' The more I see of Ernie the more sinister this drab, power-loving mediocrity becomes, with his utter philistinism, his natty clothes, his smooth voice, his closed mind, his double-think. Bolt hates him; but he suffers more than I do, for he shares a room with him.

Today, being Sunday, we made an excursion into the country. We went to the Temples of the Sleeping Buddha (Wo Fo Ssû),[83] the Monastery of the Azure Clouds (Pi Yün Ssú),[84] and the Summer Palace.[85] Pi Yün Ssú interested me most. There are two splendid thug-statues – Hung and Ha they seem to be called – guarding the approaches; a gross, uncontemplative, corpulent Buddha which is nevertheless impressive; and some fine, clear-cut relief figures on the very top of the pagoda. But in general the Buddhist temples are full of debased superstition. Nearby there is a charming villa with an enclosed lake and a cloister round it. The Summer Palace I found disappointing: *bric-à-brac* of

81 George Brown (1914–1985), Labour MP 1945–70, Deputy Leader of the Labour Party 1960–70, First Secretary of State 1964–66, Foreign Secretary 1966–68. Patrick Reilly later wrote: 'By the time he became Foreign Secretary Brown was so soaked in alcohol that it took relatively few drinks to change him from a perfectly normal, likeable person to what I can only describe as a devil' (Bodleian Ms, Eng c 6925, ff 239, 252–3). Brown underwent a deathbed conversion to Catholicism.

82 In 1962 the Labour Party National Executive refused to endorse the parliamentary candidatures of Roberts at Horsham, and of Illtyd Harrington, later deputy leader of the Greater London Council, at Dover.

83 Wo fo si was one of the oldest monasteries in the Western Hills. It was renowned for a statue of a calmly sleeping Buddha, and for the rare trees planted in its courtyards.

84 Bi yun si was reached by climbing vast stony pavements towards the outer temple gate, which was guarded by huge figures of painted wood and plaster.

85 The imperial gardens and lakes of the Qing dynasty, which had been reconstructed by the Dowager Empress.

the Empress Dowager,[86] and no such impressive lay-out or exploitation of its marvellous position as could have been expected. But there are two delightful private theatres, where that wicked old woman watched no doubt unedifying performances without stirring from her room. The virtuous communist curator had little use for the Empress Dowager: 'She was a reactionary and spent her time flattering Western Powers in order to be allowed to oppress the people, as reactionaries always do', she said; and Stone-face moralised sententiously on the wickedness of imperial or aristocratic private as against democratic public theatres. Incidentally Bolt contrived, with great difficulty and after much persistence, to discover Stone-face's origins. They were rural, not urban. Millennia of peasant obstinacy lie behind his present privileged position in the party, to which he clings with trepidation; and Timothy George's statement is, to this extent, confirmed.

We suffer torture going round monuments with these abysmally ignorant guides. What would I not give for an educated *cicerone*! Fortunately Alan Donald has lent me Juliet Bredon's excellent book on Pekin.[87] Without it, I would be quite lost. Bolt and I also suffer torture from the incessant anilities of Mrs Adams and the pert, humourless jocosity of Ernie Roberts, who pleases himself vastly with his own philistinisms, like a professional funny man in a proletarian *char-à-banc*. These two between them are the ruin of any visit. Mrs Adams was so much worse today – positively feeble-minded – that we fear she may be in a state of physical and mental dissolution under the strain of age and travel: for certainly it has been a strain. An excellent lunch at the Summer Palace was spoiled by her, and we suffered from the after-effects too; for Bolt and I had conspired to escape and walk round the lake (about 4 miles) by ourselves. Timothy George had advised us to do this. When we announced our intention, there was a flutter of panic among our guides, but we were absolutely adamant: we refused to desist and we refused to be accompanied by them: nor, indeed, had they any desire to

86 Tz'u Hsi [Ci xi] (1835–1908), effective ruler of China from 1861, thought herself 'the cleverest woman who ever lived'. China was stricken by starvation, civil war and foreign invasion as a result of her misrule.

87 Juliet Bredon (1881–1937) was niece of Sir Robert Hart, Inspector General of Chinese Maritime Customs, whose biography she published in 1909. She married Charles Lauru, an official in the same customs service. In addition to *Peking: a historical and intimate description of its chief places of interest* (1922), she wrote a novel of peasant life, *Hundred Altars* (1924).

accompany us. Whatever Chairman Mao may have written about the necessity of physical culture for the regeneration of a people, has not penetrated to these weedy party hacks. But we could not refuse to be accompanied by Ernie, who also panicked at the thought of being left with Mrs Adams; and so, as we walked briskly round that enchanting lake, we did not enjoy the uninhibited conversation to which we had looked forward. However, we were compensated by one surprise. When we were on the far side of the lake, we suddenly saw a covered boat in the water beside us. We looked closer, and in it we saw Mrs Adams, reclining like Cleopatra in her barge. Beside her was the troupe of guides and interpreters, who had found this less energetic method of keeping us in view.

We got back to Pekin at about 5.0 p.m. in the evening. Bolt, Roberts and I (Mrs A being exhausted) were taken to the Pekin Opera. The old Pekin Opera has been 'reformed': i.e. the traditional operas, being regrettable relics of 'feudal' times, are being replaced by modern 'democratic' operas. With great difficulty we have discovered from our reluctant guides that *some* old operas, being 'good' – i.e., I presume safe – are not, or not yet abolished; and as the price of our consent to going to one 'democratic' opera we have been promised one traditional opera. Tonight was the 'democratic' opera – 'the Red Lantern', a tale of proletarian communist virtue in the struggle against Japanese aggression. The plot was simple, the characters the usual caricatures; but the action was excellent and the music effective. The orchestra sits behind a transparent screen on the stage, at the side (there used to be no screen but this, it was decided, diverted too much attention from the players): it consists of nine instruments, mainly strings, most of which are plucked: also a wood-instrument, a drum, a gong and cymbals. The star, the virtuous daughter of the railway-worker, was To Tiu Feng.[88] There was a splendid Japanese general, a type of voluptuous, cruel, effeminate, corrupt capitalist militarism, acted by O. I. Teng. The highly stylised form prevented the opera from the degeneration implicit in plot and characterisation: whenever that form was suspended, the degeneration was apparent, and there were *longueurs* of propaganda which would no doubt have been worse if one had understood the language. But the form – the music and the acting – saved the piece. How long it will save such pieces may be questioned. Bolt was not

---

88 The actors in this production have proven impossible to identify.

optimistic. 'Whenever stylisation and naturalism compete', he said, 'natural-ism always wins'.[89]

I forgot to mention that in the pagoda at Pi Yün Ssú there is a mausoleum, or rather cenotaph, of Sun Yat Sen,[90] who has now been given a place in the revolutionary Pantheon. One of the *Devotionalien*[91] there is rather bizarre: a steel and glass coffin sent as a present to him, when he had announced that he was dying, by the Central Committee of the Russian Communist Party. The coffin has a glass top, presumably so that the corpse could be exposed, like Lenin's, for veneration. It also has a steel lid to cover the glass when there is no need of such exposure. Unfortunately, by the time that this touching present had arrived, Sun Yat Sen was already dead and buried in Nanking. But his followers piously buried his hat and coat in the pagoda.[92]

Sun Yat Sen's son-in-law, Chiang Kai-shek,[93] seems never to be mentioned. There are posters claiming Formosa as part of China, and the Kuomintang is held up as a type of corrupt rule: but Chiang himself is unnamed. I understand that there is an open offer to him to return and become a privileged citizen

---

89 Bolt described a scene in *The Red Lantern* in *SACU News* (November 1965): 'The brave worker is being cross-examined by the cruel and inept Japanese commander, who stands behind the worker's chair attempting to corrupt him. He is alternately singing and chanting, moving in a very stylised way with his hands outstretched, his eyes staring, pacing and leaping about. Meanwhile the worker, the hero of the play, in order to demonstrate his bravery and indifference to all these blandishments, has been given an enormous briar pipe with a pouch of tobacco and matches. He is doing a lot of funny business with his pipe in a completely naturalistic way which, of course, absolutely destroys what the Japanese commander is doing.' This put the worker in command of the situation and made the Japanese commander look idiotic. It also made traditional Peking opera look foolish, 'because if you juxtapose on the stage highly naturalistic business with a highly formalised convention, there is no doubt, ever, which wins'.

90 The revolutionary nationalist leader Sun Yat-sen (1866–1925) led the KMT from 1912. After his death he became 'the patron saint' of Chinese nationalism, 'his writings became its Bible, and the ceremony of bowing to his portrait, which was made a feature of all public gathering wherever the Kuomintang held power, gave a flavour of religious devotion to party loyalty' (G. F. Hudson, *The Far East in World Politics* (Oxford, 1939), p. 218).

91 German: memorabilia (literally, devotional objects).

92 This story is garbled. Sun Yat-sen's embalmed corpse lay in the Diamond Throne Pagoda [Jin gang bao zuo ta] from his death in 1925 until its internment at Nanking in 1929. He was venerated with quasi-divine honours under the KMT and continued to be revered in the PRC as the founder of the Chinese republic.

93 Sun Yat-sen was not Chiang Kai-shek's father-in-law. The two men had married sisters: the daughters of Charles Jones Soong [Han Jiaozhun], a Methodist missionary and Bible-seller who joined the Shanghai anti-Manchu triad known as the Red Gang. They were the sisters of T. V. Soong [Soong Tse-ven or Soong Tzu-wen] (1894–1971), Kuomintang Minister of Finance (1928–34), Minister for Foreign Affairs (1942–45) and premier (1945–47).

of the People's China. Of course, any price would be worth paying for an abdication which would deprive the Americans of their legal rights to occupy Formosa.

Monday, 27 September

At last I was taken to the Institute of History. I was received by the Vice–Director, Hou Wai-Lu, a historian of modern China.[94] He had produced a parade, in the usual communist fashion. There were Ho Chang-Chun,[95] an expert on 'feudal society', i.e. 500 BC–1860 AD, but he specialised on Han and T'ang times; Chang Cheng-Lang,[96] an ancient historian; and Yao Chia-Chi, who works on the Yüan period.[97] The director of the institute is Kuo Mo-Jo,[98] who is also president of the Academy of Sciences (formerly Academia Sinica): he was not present. All the talking was done by Hou Wai-Lu, who soon revealed himself as a sound party man. He is (the good interpreter told me) 'a very well-known historian', and he alone, I soon discovered, had his works translated into European languages. He sat, voluble, beside me: the other three sat, mute, side by side, opposite him, like schoolboys facing the headmaster. I pressed them about foreign contacts, but it was obvious that they lived in a

---

94 Hou Wai-lu (1903–1987) had studied in France in the 1920s, translated *Das Kapital* into Chinese, and wrote a Marxist history of Chinese philosophy (1962), which subordinated the history of ideas to social awareness. In 1965 he was deputy director of Medieval History at the Institute of Historical Research.

95 Ho Ch'ang-Ch'ün published a study of the southern and northern armies of the early Han (1937). His later writings were overstrewn with quotations from Marx and Engels.

96 Chang Cheng-lang [Zhang Chenglang] studied Shang archaeology, bronze inscriptions and calligraphy, and interpreted ancient bandit heroes in Marxist terms.

97 Yao Chia-chi had been a historian of the Yüan period at Yenching University until it was shut by the PRC in 1952 and its campus seized for use by the new Peking University. As the 'Yenching Spirit' was wedded to humanism and liberal arts ideals, its faculty members were then subjected to 'thought reform' and mass criticism. After this ideological cure, Yao joined the Institute of History and Philology.

98 Kuo Mo-jo [Guo Moruo] (1892–1978) had trained in a Japanese medical school. He translated Spinoza, Goethe and Whitman, promoted vernacular writing, gained a reputation as a poet and joined the Communist Party in 1927. He held the presidency of the Chinese Academy of Sciences from its formation in 1949 until his death. During the Cultural Revolution, Kuo urged that all his previous works should be burnt and denounced former allies as counter-revolutionaries. Two of his sons supposedly killed themselves in 1967–68 while undergoing interrogation by Red Guards. By dint of sycophancy, Kuo was restored to political favour in 1969.

cloison ètanche.[99] I mentioned Étienne Balazs:[100] none of them had heard of
him, or of the *Annales*.[101] I asked after Wang Ling: they did not know where he
was, alive or dead.[102] It was quite clear that the machinery of foreign contact
was entirely in Party hands and there was nothing that scholars could do about
it, 'so long as foreign countries recognise two Chinas.' 'But my country', I said
smugly, 'has long recognised yours; why then is academic contact so difficult?'
'Diplomatic relations', I was told, 'are not yet normal.' 'But they can be used.'
'In 1959', came the reply, 'there was a sinological conference in Cambridge,
but our delegates only got their visas from the office of the British *chargé
d'affaires* two days before'. 'I only got my visa, from the office of the Chinese
chargé d'affaires,' I said, smugger than ever, 'on the very day of my departure.'
'That', said the vice-president, 'is different.' Then he returned to the question
of countries recognising 'two Chinas' and delivered himself of a long rigmarole
about the International Red Cross, which I did not understand–until next day,
when I read it all in the official Chinese news-broadcast to which, clearly, he
must have just listened. I felt sorry for those three sad scholars, if they were
scholars, who sat opposite me and only spoke if directly addressed, while their
vice–president who sat beside me, gave all the answers on their behalf. They
were obviously quite powerless. When I left, the Vice-President said, 'We have
heard of your work, Mr T.-R, and especially your work on *The Last Days of
Hitler*. Now you must record the last days of the new Hitler' (i.e. in the current
Chinese jargon, L. B. Johnson).[103] I did not condescend to notice this last

---

99 French: sealed compartment.

100 Étienne [Istvan] Balázs (1905–1963) was born in Hungary and wrote his doctoral thesis
at Berlin University on a subject beyond the bounds of traditional sinology: the economic history of the T'ang dynasty, 618–906. It drew on Marx and Weber, and was completed in 1933.
This pioneer work was original in its analysis and striking in its use of traditional sources for
new purposes. Nazi oppression drove Balácz from Berlin in 1935; he lived in Paris until 1939;
and went 'underground' during 1940–45 in a village in Tarn-et-Garonne, where he bred geese
and continued historical research despite great strain and fatigue. It was only in 1949 that he
achieved security by his installation in a chair for the economy and society of ancient China in
the newly formed sixth section of the École Pratique des Hautes Études (Sorbonne).

101 The journal *Annales d'histoire économique et sociale* was founded in 1929 by Marc Bloch
and Lucien Febvre. It rejected traditional lines of political and diplomatic history. Instead it
fostered interdisciplinary studies of climate, geography, demography and states of mind. T-R
admired the *Annales* school for its innovative thinking in the 1950s, but by the 1970s felt that
it had entered a phase of 'bureaucratic consolidation'.

102 Wang Ling (c. 1917–1994) trained as a chemist. Needham met him in China in 1943,
and employed him on the *Science and Civilisation in China* project, 1948–58. Wang Ling held
academic posts in Australia, 1958–83.

103 Lyndon Baines Johnson (1908–1973), 36th President of the United States, 1963–69.

remark. On the way out we passed through the library of the Institute. Among the foreign periodicals taken, I saw the *E. H. R.*[104] but not the *Annales* or *Past and Present*.[105] It looked as if they would take non-marxist staff provided it was safely dead, but history that had digested Marx or was merely *marxisant*, or 'revisionist', was excluded.

In the afternoon we were told that we were to visit a prison. I refused. 'Why this is prison nor am I out of it',[106] I said to myself, and Robert Bolt and I decided to see something of Pekin in freedom instead. So we took a taxi and visited the Yung Ho Kung, the Lama Temple,[107] by the north wall, originally the palace of Yung Cheng 'transformed for religious uses on his accession (1722) in accordance with the Chinese precedent that the birthplace of a sovereign shall never afterwards be used as a dwelling' (Bredon). The most impressive object in that series of courts and sanctuaries is a huge wooden Buddha, 75 feet high, rising through three storeys of the last shrine, all carved out of one gigantic cedar from Yunnan. It is hideous, like a swollen grotesque totem-pole huge as a mountain, κατά τ' ἔστυγον αὐτόν.[108] We then went to recover a sense of proportion in the Ta Ch'eng Miao or 'Temple of Confucius'; but it has been converted to some public use and was closed:[109] we were only able to visit the Kuo Tzŭ Chien, or Hall of the Classics,[110] next door. Then we walked in Bei Hai Park.[111] Our colleagues who had been to the prison afterwards reported that it was a very impressive modern 'reformed' prison.

---

104 The *English Historical Review* had been edited since 1965 by John Wallace-Hadrill (1916-1985), Fellow of Merton College, Oxford and historian of Merovingian France, whom T-R considered 'a niggler, a fuss-pot!' (Dacre 1/2/8, letter to R. W. Southern, November 1964).

105 *Past & Present: A Journal of Scientific History* had been launched in 1952 by members of the Communist Party Historians Group, but with support from non-Marxist social historians. 'We were analogous to the Annales' revolt,' recalled Eric Hobsbawm, 'and aware of the parallel'.

106 Spoken by Mephistopheles in Marlowe, *Doctor Faustus*, 1.36.

107 The Lama Temple (Yong he gong) was also known as the Palace of Eternal Peace, where the emperor rested while hunting.

108 Greek: 'and the sight of it filled me with horror'. Trevor-Roper adapted a passage from *Odyssey*: 10.113, κατὰ δ' ἔστυγον αὐτήν, 'the sight of her filled them with horror' (or disgust, loathing). The 'her' in the original quotation is Antiphates's oversized wife, who is described in the poem as being as big as a mountain peak.

109 It was occupied by a school of printing and therefore shut to visitors.

110 The former Imperial College (Guo zi jian), where the sons of high-ranking families were sent to study the Confucian classics, had been transformed into a municipal library.

111 The Northern Lake (Bei hai) on the western side of the imperial city was on the site of Kublai Khan's former palace. The lake had been re-dug in 1951, and a marble bridge built in 1956.

Alan Donald later told me that it was the standard prison which is shown to all visitors and no general deductions can be drawn from it. In the evening we were taken to a play. It was called (according to my French programme) 'Tam-Tam de Combat sur l'Equateur' and was about the struggle in the Congo, and the 'martyrdom' of Patrice Lumumba (Mme Lumumba, I hear, is in Pekin, no doubt to see it).[112] It was a grotesque piece of romantic proletarian propaganda and reminded me of that equally tedious ballet, 'Spartacus' by Khachaturian,[113] which Xandra[114] and I saw in Leningrad in 1957. American imperialists, brutal, degenerate and drunken, were opposed by Congolese nationalists, austere, virtuous and heroic.[115] When the news of Lumumba's murder was brought, the sky was darkened and the veil of the heavens was rent by topical lightning. This, observed Bolt, was carrying the cult of personality rather far but Ernie Roberts, whose narrow mind contains a glib half truth in reserve for every occasion, replied 'yes; just like the death of the last King' (George VI). The last scenes of the play were even more grotesque than the first, and the tedium generated by the propaganda was fortunately dissolved in pure hilarity. The

---

112 The Eisenhower administration in Washington and European governments had feared that Patrice Lumumba (1925–1961), the Congo's first elected head of state, would ally his nation with Soviet Russia and nationalize Belgian corporate interests. Harold Macmillan depicted him as 'a Communist stooge as well as a witch-doctor'. The covert operations, dirty tricks, bribery, sabotage and economic disruption of the CIA's Project WIZARD to destabilize and overthrow Lumumba were undertaken with SIS complicity. During the process of regime change he was tortured and killed in the secessionist state of Katanga. His dismembered body was dissolved in sulphuric acid by a Belgian police commissioner, who bragged on television that he kept two of Lumumba's teeth as mementoes. Lumumba's murder led to his canonization as the Pan-African martyr of anti-colonialism. In tribute to his memory Patrice Lumumba University was built in Moscow to educate young proletarians from Asia, Africa and South America. The earliest Lumumba graduates, drawn from 47 countries, received their degrees in 1965.

113 Aram Khachaturian (1903–1978) was an Armenian who served as secretary of the Union of Soviet Composers from 1957. He received the Lenin prize for composing the music of the ballet *Spartacus*, which tells the story of a slave uprising against Roman oppressors.

114 T-R had married Lady Alexandra ('Xandra') Howard-Johnston (1907–1997; *née* Haig) in 1954. 'Lady Alexandra is exactly like a mad English aristocratic lady in American fiction – absent-minded, distraught … and constantly puzzled and bewildered by everything that is going on' (Bodleian, Ms Berlin 246, Isaiah Berlin to Maurice Bowra, 2 April 1969).

115 *Tam-Tam de Combat sur l'Equateur* [*War Drums on the Equator*] dramatized the Congo crisis from the standpoint of a Leopoldville proletarian family. Some of the Chinese actors blacked their faces and wore tribal clothes. Others wore white face-paint and Western suits. The play began with grateful shouts of 'Freedom, Independence!' to celebrate the demise of Belgian colonialism. All too soon the Congolese people feel betrayed by the United Nations and accept the need for guerrilla resistance to European colonialism and American capitalism. The play closed with war-cries of 'Uhuru, Uhuru!'

play became a sort of high, moral fun-fare, with ridiculous stage-effects-jungle scenery, moving waterfalls, an aeroplane shut down by guerrilla rifle-fire, a terrified 'mercenary' descending by parachute, a perpetually moving waterfall in the background, and a scenic Armageddon with the voice of chairman Mao intoning eternal truths from Heaven: all the effects, said Bolt, of a Scunthorpe pantomime; but all taken with deadly seriousness by the communist Chinese, and hugely admired by Ernie, whose mind perfectly represents all the limitations of theirs (His chief complaint about *The Red Lantern* yesterday was that when tea poured out, real tea did not come out of the teapot).[116] On the way back to our hotel Bolt, with his infinite patience, questioned the good interpreter. (I regarded the whole thing as too pitiful, too grotesque for comment). Did she really, he asked, think that all Americans were like that, and that the U.N. was simply another name for the U.S.A.? She replied, quite seriously, yes, and supported her answer by remarks which showed that she – the most intelligent of the people who surround us – absolutely accepts, and believes that she believes, her own propaganda.

We have now had a full week in Pekin and I feel ready to generalise about our experiences. In many ways it is a disappointment. We were all led to believe that we would be received as an important delegation ('You will almost certainly meet Chou En-lai',[117] Bryan told me in London),[118] and we were explicitly told that, on arrival in Pekin, we would be independent of each other: we would each state our interests and we would each be taken where we wanted separately. None of this is true. It is quite clear that we are a second-class delegation – of what interest to the People's China is a committee in London? – and we are left to the mercies of block-headed ignorant guides who are no fit channels of communication. We are also forced to move as

---

116 Robert Bolt, in his *SACU News* interview (November 1965), accepted the play's analysis of the Congo crisis as part of the Cold War struggle for global dominance. Its message that nations seeking freedom from colonial oppression and capitalist exploitation must slay Soviet revisionism and US business imperialism was however put 'in extraordinarily crude terms. The US and the UN are absolutely indistinguishable, the UN is a sort of branch of the CIA, the Americans carry whips with which they incessantly beat the African, shoot them like dogs, and so forth. Yet, in some ways, as well as lending itself to propagandist plays, this convention takes the worst vice out of them; events on stage are presented in such black and white terms, so pickled and crystallised that they move you in the Brechtian sense as a satisfying pattern and shape which you can grasp.'

117 Chou En-lai [Zhou En-lai] (1898–1976), prime minister of PRC 1949–76, was 'le ‹contactman› du régime' (Bodard, *La Chine de la douceur*, p. 38).

118 Derek Bryan (1910–2003): see Introduction, p. 30.

a group, which is most exasperating, reducing our activities to their lowest common denominator. And this, thanks to Mary Adams and Ernie Roberts, is unnaturally low: indeed, they are about as sophisticated as Stone-face himself.

Mary Adams is unbelievably silly. Why, we ask ourselves, has she come to Pekin? Only, it seems in order that she may say that she has been there, and that the women of her numerous useless, busy committees, after hearing the steady trickle of translucent platitudes splashing among the suburban tea-cups, may say, 'how wonderful she is to have gone so far, and at her age!' Her conversation is of an incredible asininity. 'Do you know', she began slowly, *apropos* of nothing, to our Chinese guides the other day, 'what I mean by a Bikini?' Of course they did not, so she laboriously explained, thus merely convincing them that she was being gratuitously obscene. 'You will tell us, won't you', she said suddenly, while at luncheon in the Summer Palace, 'if anything serious happens in the world–if our Queen should be killed in a motor-accident?' But her *bêtises*[119] are innumerable. She has absolutely no function, no purpose here: she might just as well be in Surbiton. She has shown no interest in anything. What is shown to her, she immediately gets wrong. ('Is this the Forbidden City?', she asked, on being shown the Summer Palace four days after being taken through the Forbidden City). And yet, this wretched cretin is our 'leader'. That alone would make us a third-class delegation.

As for Ernie Roberts, he is really a sinister figure: a narrow, complacent, know-all who treads the funamulatory track towards the goal of power, invulnerable in the solid armour of hypocrisy, philistinism and double-think. He is convinced, absolutely convinced, of his own proletarian virtue, and smugly refers to his low income while enjoying a high standard of life, provided for him out of union funds. Has he not a snug bourgeois Victorian villa, standing in its own grounds, two cars (one – the union one – a Lancia),[120] natty suits (purchased at Simpson's),[121] expensive shirts (from Michael George),[122] a costly gold wrist-watch, fastidious tastes? When he was unable to eat much owing

---

119 French: idiocies.

120 The Lancia Flaminia sedan had been marketed in England since 1963 as a luxury car.

121 Alexander Simpson (1903–1937) developed the world's first self-supporting trousers, with an adjustable waistband which dispensed with the need for braces or belt. He used his profits to demolish the Geological Museum in Piccadilly, and to open on its site in 1936 an architecturally landmark shop selling expensive Daks brand clothes for men. These were more colourful and varied in fabric than other ready-to-wear lines.

122 The identification of Michael George has defeated even James Sherwood, the historian of London tailoring.

to diarrhoea the other day, he smugly explained to the Chinese that he had 'a worker's stomach' and could not eat like us capitalists;[123] and when Mary Adams, silly as ever, asked the Chinese whether they never said grace before meat, Ernie, smug as ever, said 'the British Workers' grace is 'For what we are about to receive *we* have worked bloody hard.' It is perfectly clear why *he* has come to China. It is the same reason for which he has travelled comfortably through every other communist country: so that he can have a growing stock of self-importance to propel him along his chosen road to power. In China itself he is not interested. *Caelum non animum* ...[124] The beauty, the strangeness, the excitement leave him cold. He asks no questions except about rates of pay. The remark about the Chinese garage at Beckenham, and the remark about making history not reading it, sum up his miserable philosophy: a philosophy of blinkered self-importance. What he is not shown he will not see and if, by chance, he is shown a monument, its only purpose to him is to be a background to himself: he gives his camera to a guide and then poses, with careful attention to dress and expression, firmly in front of it. He has often asked me to photograph him in such postures. Meanwhile, he distributes visiting cards and union badges to fix himself and his importance in the minds of those he meets. I often wonder when his supply of badges will give out. It seems inexhaustible.

Thank God for Bolt. I was cautious with him at first, having been told that he was a devout R.C. So he may be; but if so, he has been converted from Methodism to Popery, as he has been converted from communism to non-communism, without any of those repercussions which make so many converts more insolent than bawds. He joined S.A.C.U., as I did, through respect for Joseph Needham; and perhaps he owes his chance of coming here to his imprisonment as a member of C.N.D. He has a great respect for Bertie Russell, which endears him to me: so does his sophistication, his sense of humour, his understanding of politics, philosophy and literature, and his enthusiasm. In all these qualities our other two colleagues are totally defective. At first I *thought* I detected a latent sense of humour in Ernie Roberts, but experience has shown that I was wrong: that brief initial hint of humour must have been an accident.

---

123 In his memoirs of his childhood, Roberts recalled cabbage soup (the water left after the boiling of cabbage), bacon-bone soup and 'the luxury of "sop" – bread soaked in tea'.

124 Horace: *Caelum non animum mutant qui trans mare currunt* (They change their sky, not their soul, who rush across the sea).

By now Bolt has become my refuge, and I his. I shudder to think of my fate had Vanessa Redgrave not proved unable to come.

We need a refuge not only from our colleagues but from our guides and interpreters. Every one of them is ignorant and bigoted, and their chief function seems to be to keep us perpetually occupied in their company, without means of escape or leisure to devise it. First there is Stone-face, that lean blockish peasant, an empty-headed village know-all. He is constantly with us: the other guides vary, but not one of them can express anything except the crudest party handouts. Nor can any of them speak English. (I suspect them all to be quite illiterate). Consequently we need interpreters. The good interpreter is called Mrs Pai, alias Duck-bottom. (She began in skirts but has taken to trousers, which do not suit her shape but are no doubt necessary to show her revolutionary virtue). She speaks good English, but has the mind of a village postmistress and is a party bigot like the rest. The bad interpreter, the Presbyterian, has no redeeming virtues at all: she is ignorant, silly, smug and incompetent.

In this unpromising company any rational conversation is of course, impossible. One can only observe. What I observe is, above all, the tension – latent tension – between party and society. As a force of social regeneration one can only admire the Party. It has raised a ruined, atomised, contemned, country to a position of confidence and power from which the panicky Americans now cry that it seeks 'to dominate the world'. Its social achievement is extraordinary and I do not question that this achievement has won it the positive general support of all. On the other hand, the intellectual prison house which it has created is terrifying. None of the Chinese I have met can begin to think independently, nor do they even recognise that foreigners may see with eyes different from theirs. To them the whole world is jet black and pure white: those who see any trace of grey are the benighted, even if well-meaning, victims of a black social system. Argument, criticism, qualification are not wrong: theoretically they are right; but in practice they are absurd, a disease to which imperfect societies are entitled but which, in the self-righteous society of China, is a contradiction in terms. That there are other Chinese who think critically, I do not doubt; but we must not see them or know of their existences any more than they must know of ours. And lest we should know of their existence, all conversation, even with those whom we are allowed to meet, is strictly watched and carefully reduced to triviality. The character of our guides and interpreters by itself ensures such triviality anyway. So does the character of two of my colleagues. But even apart from that an atmosphere of terrorised conformity is created around them. Interpreters may not have direct conversation with us. If they do, they must explain it in Chinese to the guides as they go along. On one occasion, after the play on Sunday, Duck-bottom was alone with Bolt and me, and we brought her to express her views, which were of profound, not to say abject conformity. Even so, we sense that she is now uneasy with us. It is not that she uttered a single questionable thought. Clearly she cannot think at all. It was that she uttered.

How long, I ask, can this last, and whither will it lead? I read Chinese poetry, with its humour, its irony, its introspection, its sense of the ephemeral nature of humanity. I look at Chinese paintings, those pictures of giant Nature rising sublime and permanent above the little, transitory activities of men, even of emperors, who scurry to and fro on their little errands at the bottom of the canvas. Then I see the evidence – how can one avoid it? – of humourless self-righteousness and self-importance all around me, and I look at the modern pictures. In every shop, on every poster, they illustrate triumphant proletarian Chinese striding in procession up to the top of the canvas and waving their red flags on mountain peaks. It is the New Byronism, the Byronism of the masses, breaking through the weakened, formal crust of an Augustan, aristocratic civilisation. But how long can it last? Will not the pattern of centuries re-form itself, historical traditions reassert themselves, the old skin close again over this sudden eruption? Between Czarism and Bolsheviks there is the continuity of despotism. Between Frederick the Great and Hitler there is the continuity of militarism. But between imperial China and communist China I see no continuity, only a wide sudden breach, a total, emphatic reversal. When the revolutionary generation is over, and its achievement accepted, can its spirit survive?

But what of the meantime? What damage may this spirit do before it has expended itself, before that generation is out? Sometimes, when I see its manifestations, I think of nazism. The processions, the parades, the flags, the historical perversions, the leader-worship, the hymns of hate have as much of nazism as of communism in them. And yet I see, or think that I see, a difference. It is not merely the tension between people and party: the German people hung back from party extremism and yet, in the event, followed tamely into war. But the strident claims of nationalism, the clear demand for new frontiers, the open cult of violence, I re-assure myself, are not there. The Chinese Diaspora is not inflamed or mobilised; and although the permanent revolution is preached, I see as yet nothing that can be construed as a plan 'to dominate the world'.

There was a splendid piece of double-think from Ernie today. We were talking of the right to strike as an essential factor in peaceful change and Ernie had declared that the professional classes used it as readily as the workers. Robert Bolt had denied this, saying that school-teachers, for instance, had never struck, and governments exploited the knowledge that they never would.[125] The omniscient trade unionist, as always, had the reply. 'Certainly they have struck,' he said: 'they have withdrawn their labour by not entering into the profession, thereby causing a shortage of teachers.' So the natural law of the market, of laissez-faire, was quietly substituted for its opposite, the political right to organise against it. Then he beamed smugly at his own dialectical skill. 'You can see why he is so successful,' Bolt observed to me afterwards. 'You can see all those teak-headed trade-unionists listening to these ready sophistries and saying, They can't fault our Ernie ...'

Tuesday, 28 September

Bolt and I got up at 6.0 and took a taxi to the Tien Tan again.[126] It is really the most wonderful single thing in Pekin; and yet our guides have never even mentioned it. Had the Bevans not told me about it, we would have spent a fortnight in Pekin and never even seen it; and no doubt Mary and Ernie will do this, although it really doesn't matter whether they see it or not, they are so sunk in cretinous philistinism. We tried to see the Temples of Agriculture too,[127] but could not find it: its park seems to have become a housing estate and a stadium and nobody there even knew of it: so quick is human oblivion, aided by political purpose.

After breakfast Bolt was made by our guides to go to the Russian Embassy and get visas for our return. He must lose no time, they said, for the process is slow. This is sheer impertinence. Our passports were taken from us on arrival and we have never seen them since. The visas, if they are necessary, could have been requested a week ago. But instead we are kept in the dark, deprived of our passports, and then a week later, suddenly told to get moving because we have left it so late! When Bolt came back from the Russian Embassy even he

125 The National Union of Teachers called its first 'national stoppage' in the winter of 1969.

126 The Temple of Heaven.

127 The Temples of Agriculture (Xian nong tan) were built about 1530, and dedicated to the worship of the god of husbandry. After 1912, they were ruined by police and troops who were stationed in them. So little remained by 1949 that the PRC used the site to build a 30,000-seater stadium and a swimming-pool which could hold 4,000 swimmers.

was in a rage. He had spent an hour getting to the Embassy, partly because of a hopeless driver ('the original Pekin man'), partly because the whole of Pekin is in confusion today on account of the state visit of Prince Sihanouk, head of state of Cambodia: a decadent Parisian *littérateur* who walks the tight-rope between Saigon and Hanoi.[128] When he got there he found, what our guides had never told him, that photographs were needed. We had no idea where to get photographs, so we went out and tried to shop; but it was quite impossible, for the streets were either blocked by crowds of children ordered to turn out for a 'spontaneous' demonstration, or barred by police. Banners were everywhere, with most unproletarian slogans, such as 'Bienvenu S.A.R. Le Prince Sihanouk'; and in the end we returned to our hotel. There we found our guides, who instructed us to have lunch at once as we must leave at 1.30 for a great gymnastic show. Bolt and I said no: we had invited friend to lunch and they were not coming till 1.30. The sports began at 3.0 and we declared that we would find our own way there provided that they would give us our tickets. This led to the usual tussle, but we were adamant and won. They were very cross.

Our guests were the Timothy Georges and the Destinés [sic; Destenays]. We had a very enjoyable lunch together at the Jin Yang restaurant. Then we went to the Sports, arriving late enough to miss the speeches. They were not really sports, but 'calisthenics', a series of human *tableaux*. The entire vast stadium was full. Below us was the royal enclosure, containing the president, Liu Shao-chi;[129] the Prime Minister Chou En-lai; Prince Sihanouk, etc. Opposite was a huge section of the stadium in which everyone seemed to be identical. I reckoned that it contained 7,000 persons, all dressed in white. But as often as the human kaleidoscope in the arena changed from pattern into pattern, the bank of identical humanity opposite us also changed. By lifting in front of them (as I supposed) a series of pasteboards, the whole area was turned into one poster after another. There were slogans in bold red ideograms against a white background; there were coloured picture-posters of workers, peasants, intellectuals, of factories, cornfields and red flags; and of course, a gigantic

---

128 Norodom Sihanouk (1922–2012), the wayward King of Cambodia 1941–55 and 1993–2004, Head of State of Cambodia 1960–70, Head of Democratic Kampuchea 1975–76.

129 Liu Shao-chi [Liu Shaoqi] (1898–1969) was chairman of the PRC 1959–68. In 1965 he was Mao's designated successor, but within months he was denounced as China's Khrushchev and the top proponent of taking the capitalist road. He died in prison. Described by Humphrey Trevelyan as a 'sour-faced doctrinaire', prone to 'turgid and repetitive' doctrinal expositions.

portrait of chairman Mao, who alone was not personally present. (He is retired and, though only 71, – according to Tim George – 'a very old man'). After an hour and a half of this stuff, we become restive and decided to leave; and spotting a Swedish fellow-guest at the hotel moving down the stadium steps, we asked if he could give us a lift back. He could, via the Swedish Embassy; so we went with him, and Robert got his photographs on the way too. I always carry a stock, so I needed none.

The Swede is a writer called Zeitenholrn.[130] He has come here at the expense of a glossy Swedish woman's paper (he should meet Mary) called *Femina*. He will go on to Hong Kong and S.E. Asia, but has been excluded, he says, from Burma. 'It is a closed Buddhist state, and insists on absolute neutrality'. 'But you are a Swede', I replied; 'is anyone more absolutely neutral than he Swedes?' 'No', he replied, 'but here they class all Westerners as Americans'. He asked my name. When told, he confessed to having heard of it, 'Don't you write political *reportage?*' he asked. I didn't like the question but said, lukewarmly, yes. 'Perhaps,' I thought, 'he is remembering my exposure of Folke Bernadotte'.[131] But then he said, 'didn't you also write something on the last days of Hitler?' 'Yes', I admitted. 'Wasn't it a book arguing that Hitler was still alive?' he persevered. After which I allowed conversation to find other channels. His view of China seemed much like ours. 'There is an iron curtain within us all', he said – a curtain dividing admiration for one half of the achievement of the communist party from hatred for the other half.

In the evening we went again to the Pekin Opera. This time it was a classical piece, 'The Woman General of the Yang Family', a story of the Sung period. What a difference from the naturalistic propaganda of 'the Red Lantern'! It was a marvellous integration of music, dramatic action, ballet, acrobatics: absolutely stylised – but we had been told the plot and the conventions by Tim George – and brilliantly executed. The sets were beautiful. So were the costumes. It seemed incredible to us that the same directors could put on this miraculous performance and the dreary socialist realism of the 'the Red Lantern'. And yet, Tim George tells us, this 'classical' opera is being gradually pushed out and the few remaining pieces are only played, in effect, for two

---

130 Zeiternholrn, as also Zeitenhorn, Zeigenghorn and Zieternhorn, is unidentifiable from the catalogue of the National Library of Sweden.

131 Count Folke Bernadotte (1895–1948), United Nations mediator between the Arabs and Jews in Palestine, was murdered by Zionist terrorists. He was the subject of T-R's article, 'Kersten, Himmler and Count Bernadotte', *Atlantic Monthly*, vol. 191 (February 1953), pp. 43–5.

weeks in the year. Luckily we happen to be here during one of the weeks. On Saturday (2 Oct) they are playing 'the Monkey King', another classical piece. Robert Bolt and I have insisted on going. We get the usual answers: we shall try, we cannot tell, we shall tell you on the day …

As we left the stadium today, Robert Bolt said, 'doesn't it remind you of the late 1930s in Germany?' I demurred. In form, yes, I said; but the content seems to me less militant, less aggressive, less neurotic. Tonight Mary Adams, hearing this, said, 'but what of the slogans?' I confessed that, having no programme, I had not been able to read the slogans. She, who had had a programme, assured me that they were fire-eating anti-American war-cries. But I have not yet seen the evidence. (Later: having seen the slogans of National Day, I am satisfied that they are the same: mere tabloid formulae).

Wednesday, 29 September

Today we started at 9.0 a.m. for the Great Wall. As a guide (together with the inevitable Stone-face – or Cement-head as he is now more often known) we had a so-called 'dramatic critic' called Liu.[132] He came in the car with Robert and me, and I sat back and listened, fascinated, while Robert, with his infinite patience, questioned him on the Pekin Opera. His replies soon showed where he stood. 'Art', in his philosophy, was what pleased the People represented by the Party, which spoke through the Minister of Culture,[133] a hardened revolutionary fighter who was also Minister of Education and Propaganda. Robert, a skilful *retiarius*,[134] threw his silken net around the man, and drew it quietly tighter, and the man, an unskilful gladiator, hacked away with his blunt, short sword, never realising how completely he had been trapped.

The Great Wall was spectacular enough, as it rose and fell over the green and pink Loess mountains; but its effect was diminished by the crowds. Only one mile of it can be seen by foreigners; every foreigner in Pekin visits that mile; and at present, on the eve of 1 Oct, Pekin is full of foreigners, each of whom is beset by guides, interpreters, spies etc. Far more dramatic, to me,

---

132 Perhaps Liu Ye Yuan, author of a textbook with the English title *Drama Criticism and Appreciation*.

133 Lu Ting-i [Lu Dingyi] (1906–1996) was the Communist Party's head of propaganda 1944–52 and 1954–66. He had been appointed Minister of Culture in February 1965, but was disgraced in May 1966 and spent thirteen years in detention.

134 A type of Roman gladiator who disabled adversaries by capturing them in a net.

were the Ming Tombs,[135] which possess a whole romantic valley, or rather an open, almost circular area surrounded by jutting flanks of the Western Hills. The place is of wonderful beauty and serenity, and we had it, comparatively speaking, to ourselves. First we went down into the excavated tomb of the 13th Ming Emperor, Wan Li, who died in 1620.[136] It is the only tomb to be excavated and has yielded two museums full of treasure. The underground tomb-chambers are vast: never had I expected anything like this. Even the cold, half-congealed blood of Ernie seemed to warm *a little* on going through the museum – but rather, I think, at the value of the treasure (he is very money-conscious) than by any imaginative expansion. He began to think that perhaps there was something in antiquarianism after all.

When we emerged from those cold, dazing depths, Ernie & Mary demanded tea, while Bolt and I wanted to go on and see the tomb, or rather the monuments over the tomb, of Yung Lo, the Roi Soleil of the Ming Dynasty:[137] the emperor who built the palace of Pekin and the Tien Tan, and chose this majestic valley to be his family graveyard. Aided by the rabble of tittering guides, they had their way. I have by now adopted a policy, on such occasions, of sitting at the end of the table, to reduce the number of my neighbours. The small talk of Ernie, Mary, Cement-head, Duck-bottom, the Presbyterian etc. is more than I can bear, especially in such surroundings. But Robert, whose easy temper is now perceptibly giving way under the strain, suffered heavily. 'I have not come all the way to Pekin', he told me afterwards, 'in order to enjoy the conversational amenities of South Croydon'; and he added that Ernie's conversation was like 'a thin spray of bottled sauce spread over an otherwise delicious meal'.

In spite of this delay, we got to Yung Lo's tomb. Like everything of his, it has a magnificent simplicity and grandeur of design. The most striking building is the great shrine between the gateway to the graveyard and the tower before the tomb. It is the size of Westminster Hall – 225 ft by 90 feet as I paced it – and the green coffered roof is sustained by gigantic teak pillars,

---

135 The thirteen tombs of the last purely Chinese imperial dynasty, the Ming, which reigned 1368–1644. Bredon, whose guidebook was being used by T-R, described the Ming tombs as 'one of the largest and most gorgeous royal cemeteries ever laid out by the hand of man', and excelling the Egyptian pyramids.

136 Chu I-chun (1563–1620) ruled as Wan Li, 1572–1620.

137 Chu Ti (1360–1424), the third emperor of the Ming dynasty, who reigned as Yung Lo, 1402–24. Because of his atrocious cruelties and resultant unpopularity in Nanking, he shifted the capital to Peking.

made from whole tree-trunks fetched from Thailand and left unpainted. I felt overwhelmed by the beauty of it, and of its position in that enchanting valley, so open in itself, and yet enclosed by high but benign, misty hills. Yung Lo, to me, is now a real character, who touched nothing that he did not beautify and who saw the dramatic architectural possibilities of every spot which he chose to alter.

Tonight I dined with Alan Donald and his wife. They have a charming old Pekinese house in the centre of the city. He is a highly intelligent man. They had invited Professor Jang, of the University of Pekin, a westernized historian, educated in Paris, Marxist or marxisant, but sophisticated and not a Party member.[138] His wife was with him but left immediately after dinner for a family party. He pretends that his visits to the Donalds are clandestine and does not let them drop him at his door; but Alan told me to assume that anything I said might get into a report to the Party – in other words that his contact was permitted and its clandestinity a pose. We talked pretty freely and he was eager to question me on the Puritan Revolution which is a subject studied in Pekin. I found his views pretty close to vulgar Marxism, though sophisticated in presentation. I did not learn much from him: he was too eager to question me. But we had some historical discussion which served to show how much the Professors of the Institute had concealed. I also learned from the Donalds that no foreigner can go far outside Pekin (except by air to certain cities) without a permit, seldom granted to diplomats: a slavish imitation of the Russian system. Alan Donald offered to try to get Robert Bolt and me tickets for 'the Monkey King' on Saturday. I jumped at this: if he can do it, it will not only ensure places for us but put our guides in their place. They like to pretend that is it terribly difficult, to keep us on tenterhooks, and then, at the last minute, to produce the tickets with a parade of virtue.

Thursday, 30 September

I forgot to mention a typical conversation yesterday. We were returning from the Ming tombs to Pekin and somehow the evils of bureaucracy, of paper-work, were mentioned. I said genially to Liu, the alleged dramatic critic, that China had some responsibilities in the matter: it had invented both paper and bureaucracy. He took it very seriously and declared solemnly

---

138 Not Jang, but Chang Chih-lien.

that though there had been bureaucracy in imperial days, it had disappeared 'since Liberation'. Robert Bolt and I pressed him gently on this. Oh yes, he said, bureaucracy had now gone, or at least all its abuses had withered away because the citizen, if injured by an official, had instant redress. How? we asked, and we were told that he could always complain. But to whom? we asked, and we were told 'to the official himself'. Boggling a little at this we were assured that all officials, indeed all Marxists, believed in self-criticism and practised it daily; 'chairman Mao has said, "self-criticism and should be as regular as our daily work".' Thanks to this self-criticism, officials now could not go wrong. The patient Bolt then remarked that self-criticism, though we might wish to practise it, was in fact very difficult, at least if the criticism was real and profound, not trivial. He himself for instance found it very hard to accept fundamental criticism ... But Mr. Liu was not shaken. I whispered to Bolt the inevitable answer, 'that springs from the difference of social systems'; and barely had I whispered when Liu said aloud, like an echo, 'that springs from the difference of social system'. The idea of the self-righteous Chinese communists self-righteously claiming a monopoly of self-criticism amused me hugely.

This Liu is a perfect type of smug Chinese bigotry. Bolt asked him about the innovations in the drama. With heedless complacency, he walked into every trap. The new naturalistic drama, he said, was necessarily 'more profound' than stylised drama could be. We pressed him gently on this point. How did he measure profundity? Before long he was in hopeless knots, but quite unabashed. We left him explaining that even if characterisation was simple, language was more 'refined'; and he explained this refinement of language in great slabs of mindless tabloid jargon.

In general, we find that the Chinese are armour-plated, invulnerable behind a tough carapace of dogmas, platitudes and stock phrases, loosely strung together. From this armour every initial blow glances off, and they glory in their apparent invulnerability. Then, when one slips a blow in between the plates, one discovers that inwardly they are soft and flabby. Pierced, they collapse. The hard husk encloses a rotten kernel.

This morning we were taken to an 'art' shop in Pekin and shown the processes of reproduction of colour prints. Once again we were depressed by the waste of skill: the patient expertise which went into the making of hideous results. One remark by the director of the firm pleased me. He said, speaking of Old Masters, 'Since Liberation, reproductions are as good as originals'.

Free from 12.0 till 4.0 Robert Bolt and I decided to slip away and lunch by ourselves at the Jing Yang restaurant. We are both reduced to a neurotic state by the strain of China, our colleagues and our guides, from whom we simply cannot escape. It is maddening that Robert cannot speak any foreign language which would enable us to speak freely to each other in the presence of the interpreters. What wears me down most is the *trahison des clercs* of Ernie and Mary. They play the game of Cement-head, Duckbottom and the Presbyterian by laboriously interchanging fatuous small-talk with them. Thus a jolly time is had by all of them on the intellectual pond-bed and all efforts by us to establish the independence of the 'delegates' or to insist on a rational level of conversation are doomed from the start.

The great problem which faces us is, what shall we do on our return? It is clear that the only interest of the Chinese in SACU is as a communist 'front organisation'. It is equally clear that it can only be of real use to us of it is *not* such an organisation. If Robert and I make a fair report, we must force this issue. But the machine is controlled by Derek Bryan who is (I think) a fellow-traveller. If a showdown leaves the fellow-travellers (like Ernie) and the ninnies (like Mary) in command, as it well may, and if we then abandon the society, it will become what the Chinese want, but it will also become useless, for we shall expose it. On the other hand, to convert the society into something useful would mean one of us going on to the committee and taking a lot of trouble. Neither of us are eager to do this. The one thing that is clear to me is that the Chinese do not at present want 'understanding' on an independent basis. That smacks of 'revisionism', 'Titoism', 'Khrushchev's phoney communism', etc. etc.[139] But if we keep going, times may change; and the equivalent body for Anglo-Russian understanding does, I understand, do valuable work.[140] However, we will face this problem when we must: at present our chief problem is to keep sane.

---

139 Joan Robinson wrote: 'Khrushchev, who has to us certain sympathetic features, is the archetypal traitor to the Chinese, for he abandoned the international struggle against imperialism to butter up the Americans' (*Cultural Revolution*, p. 13).

140 T-R probably meant the Society for Cultural Relations between the Peoples of the British Commonwealth and the USSR, which had started in 1924 under the sponsorship of Julian Huxley, Maynard Keynes, Bertrand Russell, Virginia Woolf and others. This was distinct from the more political British-Soviet Friendship Society launched in 1927, which sought mass support from working-class communist sympathizers.

At 4 o'clock we were summoned to tea by the Chinese *chargé d'affaires* in London, Hsiung Hsiang-hui,[141] now on leave in China. I had met him at dinner with the Pakistani High Commissioner in London,[142] and had then learned that he was an old revolutionary fighter who had now received his reward. I decided that he was a hard party man who could be of little use to us. His tea-party was in the hotel. He giggled a lot, and it was not worth taking him seriously.

Then we were taken to a banquet in the Great Hall of the People, the preliminary feast of welcome to the visitors for tomorrow, National Day. It was a grim affair. I was furious from the start, for we were fetched at 5.40 and seated at table at 6.0 and then had to wait for an hour, the banquet being at 7.0. Also we were ordered about like schoolchildren by our guides. Moreover, even at this great banquet – there were 5,000 people dining – we could not escape our jailers: we were all together, plus two Danes and their jailers, at one table. I found myself imprisoned between Mary and the Presbyterian. I looked at Robert opposite: he was insulated between Cement-head and Duck-bottom. Good God, I exclaimed to myself, shall we never escape from these bores? But in that long hour's wait I did attempt some improvement. Seeing a Chinese guide, a peasant straight from the plough-tail, stuck speechless between Ernie and Mary, and the Dane stuck equally speechless between two monoglot Chinese, I suggested a switch. It would be a gesture of humanity, I said, and would enable two otherwise helpless prisoners to converse with their neighbours. Dead silence greeted my proposal. I knew that the wretched guides were simply afraid to lift a finger against any absurdity by the anonymous officials of the Party, so I maliciously persevered. They then said that it was impossible.

---

141 Hsiung Hsiang-hui [Xiong Xianghui] (1919–2005) was ADC to a Kuomintang general, 1940–43 but came under suspicion of communism. After studying political science at Western Reserve University, Cleveland, Ohio, 1947, his delicate facial beauty brought him work as a male model at a Manhattan arts-and-crafts centre, 1948–49. He entered the PRC's Foreign Ministry c. 1950, and was posted to London as *chargé d'affaires* (the senior Chinese envoy to Britain), 1962. He once told Humphrey Trevelyan that he had been a guerrilla fighter, and when a well-briefed Anthony Eden referred to him as such in Geneva, Chou En-lai roared with laughter. According to a report of 1966, 'he dresses in the best Savile Row style and is driven about in a Mercedes. He seldom leaves London, although he is known to have gone out of town to visit Sinophile Joseph Needham and Lord Montgomery.' Accused of revisionism and recalled to Peking, 1967; but rehabilitated by 1971 when he assisted Chou En-lai in negotiations with Richard Nixon and Henry Kissinger. As a reward, he was named as the PRC's first ambassador in Mexico, 1972.

142 Agha Hilaly (1911–2001) was posted to London as Pakistani High Commissioner in 1963.

'Some of us', I said smugly, 'believe that when a social arrangement is plainly irrational and does not work, it should be reformed.' Duck-bottom had to translate this; but the stone-faces remained stone. 'Very well', I said, 'then we must give up our plan of reform; but I yield with regret to the forces of blind reaction'. I'm afraid they didn't like this.

The dinner was a grim function. It began with a political speech by Chou En-lai and at the end there was an orgy of Mao-worship as Mao, looking old and infirm, mounted the platform before leaving. The 5000 guests chanted and clapped, 'Mao Tse-tung! Mao Tse-tung!' I looked at the Presbyterian. She was clapping her flabby hands above her head and her flabby face was dewy with hysterical emotion, like a German housemaid in ecstasy before the Führer. Duck-bottom said, more sedately, "There is an old Chinese song "A thousand eyes are fixed on Chairman Mao" ...'[143]

There is indeed. Bolt has acquired a book of such songs. It is called 'A Hundred Flowers Bloom: Amateur Song and Dance Festivals of China's National Minorities'. They bloom with remarkable uniformity. 'How I want to see Chairman Mao!' sing the Uighurs of Sinkiang. 'A silk scarf for Chairman Mao', sing the Usbeks. 'Chairman Mao is like the Sun', sing the Kelao.

As we left we ran into a Cambridge undergraduate, Graham Parry,[144] of Churchill College. His father is a travel agent and he had exploited this fact to travel through Egypt, India, China. He had followed the physical course of the

---

143 T-R kept an official press release describing how the speeches of Liu Shao-chi and Sihanouk 'were punctuated by stormy applause'. Liu declared at the banquet: 'on the international scene there are some people who neither dare to oppose U.S. imperialism themselves, nor allow others to do so. Among this sort are the modern revisionists. They are mortally afraid of U.S. imperialism. While professing support to the Vietnamese people, they are actually giving covert support to the peace talks scheme of the United States and trying to induce the Vietnamese people to capitulate. Being so obsequious to the U.S. imperialists, they yet have the cheek to style themselves anti-imperialists and want to squeeze their way into our Asian-African anti-imperialist ranks. The peoples of the world understand from their experience of defeating the German, Italian and Japanese fascists that such an appeasement policy, as adopted by the modern revisionists, far from checking U.S. imperialist aggression and defending world peace, will only inflate the aggressive arrogance of U.S. imperialism.'

144 [*sic*]. Graham Perry (b. 1945) was son not of a travel agent but of Jack Perry, whom T-R mentions elsewhere. This was the first of over a hundred visits that he made to the PRC. At Churchill he read history 1964–66, and economics, 1966–68. He was elected as secretary of the Cambridge branch of SACU in 1968, and decades later as vice-chair of SACU. After qualifying as a solicitor, in answer to an advertisement for 'an East End radical', he joined the firm of Clinton Davis, headed by the Labour politician Stanley Clinton Davis. He specialized in the arbitration of international commodity and sports disputes, and was visiting professor of dispute resolution at the University of International Business and Economics, Beijing, 2001.

revolution to Pekin. He seemed intelligent and I liked him, but he is returning home immediately after the celebrations tomorrow.

Bolt agrees that Duckbottom has had a fit of remorse for speaking to us openly, *in propria persona*,[145] the other night, though she strayed not a hair's health from bigoted conformity. Doubtless she has since washed herself with self-criticism.

Incidentally Alan Donald rang up this morning to say that he has got us tickets for 'the Money King' on Saturday. Our guides were visibly displeased by the news. Their standard technique is to refuse to promise anything and only to tell us what we are to do at the very last moment, thus preventing us from planning or from using our spare time. I simply decline to play this game and now that we have been to the Wall and the Ming Tombs, I don't care what plans of theirs I thwart; and I enjoy their mortification at seeing that if they won't fix what we want and tell us in advance, we can do it for ourselves.

Mary announced casually tonight that immediately after four weeks in China she is spending ten days in Prague, lecturing on Design to Czech Colleges of Advanced Technology, sent thither by the Council of Industrial Design. She also said that she had not in fact prepared any lectures (and of course will have no time to do so). I don't know what to marvel at most, her stamina and confidence or the idiocy of the Council in sending her. Bolt said that it was an illustration of 'Bolt's Law' which he discovered as a school teacher, *viz*: that confidence is in inverse proposition to knowledge. To this law, he added, there are *no* exceptions.

Friday, 1 October

Today is the great day, National Day, for which all Pekin has been preparing itself for the last week. The city is by now decorated and illuminated, the hotels crowded with delegations and visitors, and the crowding and the delegations have been the excuse made to us for every obstruction. We were paraded at 7.50 a.m. (as usual, insolently early) so that we could be in our standing places in the Tiananmen Square an hour and a half before the ceremony began at 10.0. The whole huge square was filled, like a gigantic flower-bed, with thousands of children holding sprays of artificial flowers, yellow, green and pink. Only the wide, straight east-west boulevard, the Champs Elysées of Pekin, was clear. We stood on the north side, looking south into the square, to the east of the

---

145 Latin: in her own person.

grandstand where stood Mao and company, and no doubt Prince Sihanouk, who is receiving the full treatment. In front of us huge posters carried the portraits of Marx and Engels, Lenin and Stalin, and, at the back of the square, Sun Yat-sen. Overhead, balloons like Chinese lanterns hung in the air with ideograms proclaiming 'Long Live Chairman Mao'. A poster of Mao himself hung immediately below him on the stand. The ceremony began with a political speech – the usual staff – by P'eng Chen, mayor of Pekin and a member of the Politburo.[146] Then came the procession. For two hours thousands upon thousands of Chinese filed past, filling the boulevard. At first all were waving above their heads wreaths or sprays of artificial flowers, so that the procession seemed a moving sea of changing colour. Among them moved great floats carrying symbols and images of China's resurgence, prosperity and new industries – and of course giant effigies of Chairman Mao, with two square slabs on each side of him which, it was explained to me, represented the four volumes of his theological works. Silken streamers and banners proclaimed long life to Chairman Mao and the usual slogans: hymns of praise to the communist party and its work, hymns of hate against U.S. imperialism and (Russian) revisionism. And, at intervals, clouds of balloons, with streamers and trailers, rose into the air and floated high up and away bearing the same messages. Altogether it was a delightful procession. There was no militarism about it, and hardly any military. The soldiers who lined the streets were unarmed. Even the slogans of hate seemed purely conventional. It was callisthenic, not aggressive. Flowers and balloons dominated it, and all the new technological virtuosity of China seemed to express itself, as under the Sung or the Ming, in brilliant pageantry, fantasy and *feux de joie*.

When we got back to our hotel we found that, once again, we were not to be free. Those insufferable bores, our guides, and one of their block-headed superiors, were to be with us at lunch. As we sat there, drenched with childish propaganda, slowly and imperfectly interpreted, I thought of Hotspur's outburst about Owen Glendower:

> I had rather live
> With cheese and garlic in a windmill, far,
> Than feed on cates and have him talk to me
> In any summer-house in Christendom.[147]

---

146 Peng Zhen (1902–1997) was deposed from both posts in 1966.
147 Shakespeare, *Henry IV Part 1*, 3.1.156–9.

In the end I could stand it no longer, and since Mary would do nothing (by her sycophancy she positively encourages them to persecute us), I left the table at 2.15, and went to bed for the afternoon. I afterwards discovered that I had left at an apt moment. I was so blind with fury that I had not noticed the significance of it. Ernie Roberts had proposed a toast of world peace. I was annoyed because his proposal, quite unintentionally, by its suddenness, wrecked my manoeuvre to break up the table which was on the point of success. But apparently the chief party functionary had slipped in a rider 'after the defeat of colonialism'. Even Ernie was furious at this injection of politics into an unpolitical toast, and all my colleagues were delighted by my gesture of leaving, although in fact I deserved no credit for it.

In the evening we went back to the Tiananmen Square for the fire work display. The fireworks were sent up to a great height by mortars, but when they exploded they were, I thought, tamer and less various than our own. Mary, as 'leader' of 'Mrs Adams' delegation', was invited to the Grandstand and came back purring, having shaken hands with Chou En-lai.[148] In the hotel we discussed the policy we should adopt on our return. Mary regards me as Public Enemy no. 1, who has no right even to be a member of SACU, since I don't (she says) believe in Anglo-Chinese understanding. I believe in it on a far solider, more rational basis than she who is a mere toady of any govt. which will invite her. Her refrain is, 'We are guests'. I reply 'yes; but that does not entitle our hosts to beat us about the head during the meal.' She also accused me of causing a day to be wasted on the Wall and Ming Tombs, which might (I suppose) more profitably have been spent exchanging small-talk with a vice-director of Old Folks Homes. 'Scholarship,' she added sententiously, as one who has a profounder understanding of the world, 'is not enough'. 'There are more things in Heaven and Earth, Horatio ...'[149]

At lunch today Duck-bottom admitted that she had marched in procession on National Day. But she said that she preferred standing in the Square, holding a spray, as a schoolgirl, 'because then I could look at Chairman Mao all the time'. Duck-bottom is also, I fear, very cross at our finding our

---

148 For Chou En-lai, wrote Simon Leys, 'no interlocutors ever appeared too small, too dim or too irrelevant not to warrant a special effort on his part to charm them'. This experience was shared by 'thousands of enraptured visitors – primary school teachers from Zanzibar, trade unionists from Tasmania, Progressive Women from Lapland'.

149 Shakespeare, *Hamlet*, 1.5.184–5.

own way to the Opera tomorrow. She has now produced a vast number of tickets, which – since the misunderstanding is clearly deliberate – we shall ignore.

At lunch today I questioned Tsao Kue-bing, the second guide, who sat next to me. We can communicate in two languages, French & Italian, but he has nothing to say in either. He is simply another party blockhead. But I discovered one thing: he too is of peasant origin; so T. George's theory is once again supported.

Saturday, 2 October

A morning of mind-bending boredom. We were told to parade at 9.30 to be presented to 'the Heads of State'. Civility required conformity, and we conformed. We were taken to the Great Hall of the People and were placed at a table in a large room. 55 other delegations sat at 55 other tables. We were expected to drink wine and eat food. With us, inevitably, were our gaolers, Cement-head, Duckbottom, the Presbyterian, and the party hack who had presided at lunch yesterday and whom we now know as Smooth-face. We sat for nearly two hours, bored stiff while canned music filled the air and Mary nattered to the Presbyterian. Then we were photographed shaking hands with a vice-premier, the minister of culture and the president of the host Association, subjected to a speech in five consecutive languages, and at last dismissed. Even the fellow travelling Ernie (Bolt and I have noticed) is beginning to find all things Chinese a little less rosy than he did; and this morning marked a further stage in his conversion.

Tomorrow we are to go to Loyang, and then to Sian, before Bolt and I leave on 9 Oct. Our hearts rise at the thought of leaving Pekin, but sink again when we recollect that we shall still be beset by this dreary troupe of bores to whom, we now learn, Smooth face will be added. All of them are illiterate boneheads; none of them have been to either place. They can give no local help even if they should want to, which of course they will not; and now – a new horror – they will presumably have all meals with us too. Thus what is an occasional torture in the capital will be permanent torture in the provinces; and there will be no Embassy as an escape.

The afternoon was spent by Bolt and me in various forms of frustration. Going to the Russian Embassy to collect our visas and finding it shut, so that we had to pursue the consul to his home. Going to the Museum of Chinese Art only to find that it was a Chinese Tretiakov: socialist-realist post-liberation advertisements.[150] But we saw Matteo Ricci's astronomical instruments (if they are his) still poised on the city wall.[151]

In the evening Robert and I went to the Pekin Opera with Alan Donald who had also invited a charming Chinese couple, the Tsaos.[152] Mr Tsao teaches Alan & other diplomats Chinese. We dined very well in a restaurant in the NE corner of the old city, the opera being nearby. It was not in fact 'the Monkey King' in its entirety, but four scenes from four operas: one which has been translated by Pearl Buck as (I think) 'the Paradise of All Good Men';[153] one on the Righteous Judge, called (I think) 'An Event in Mulberry Town';[154] the other two were 'The White Serpent',[155] and 'the Monkey King'.[156] The last pleased me most but Tsao, who can appreciate every detail, prefers 'The White Serpent'. He was a splendid interpreter: I see how easily, with increasing knowledge of the symbolism, which is as sophisticated as Mandarin language, one could become a devotee of this stylised Opera.

---

150 Construction of the National Art Museum of China had been completed in 1963.

151 Matteo Ricci (1552–1610), Jesuit missionary in China from 1583, translated Euclid's books into Chinese, wrote religious and scientific treatises, advanced cartography, mapped the heavens, and built astrolabes, quadrants, celestial spheres and sundials.

152 This is perhaps a misspelling: the Institute of Foreign Affairs interpreter, who attended the former French prime minister Edgar Faure on his visit to China in 1958, was named Tsia.

153 Pearl S. Buck (1892–1973), Nobel laureate for literature of 1938, translated the Chinese classic *Shui Hu Chuan* as *All Men are Brothers* (1933). Its heroes are men who have been driven from organized society by their brave defiance of corrupt magistrates and officials. Their virtues are similar to those of Robin Hood's band of robbers, wrote Alan Clutton-Brock: 'They are easily pleased and easily offended, but show great kindness to the poor and loyalty to their comrades. Their affection for each other appears to be supported by a distaste for the company of women' (*Times Literary Supplement*, 28 December 1933).

154 Bao Zheng (999–1062) was a judge of celebrated incorruptibility and detective skills. After his death, he became the subject of numerous tales and plays.

155 The Legend of the White Snake is one of the great folk-tales of China. A boy who has been sold pills of immortality vomits them into a lake, where they are eaten by a white serpent, which is thus imbued with five hundred years of magical powers. After the white snake saves the life of a green snake, they assume female human form. A tortoise who is jealous of the white snake's magical strength becomes a Buddhist monk, and begins a campaign of vindictive persecution. After many ordeals, the white snake defeats the terrapin-monk, who takes refuge in the stomach of a crab.

156 The Monkey King, or Sun Wukong, is a legendary Chinese figure possessing formidable magical powers.

In the interval we met the Indian *chargé d' affaires*, Mehta,[157] who speaks the most perfect Eton-and-Oxford (I think he was at Cambridge) English, without any Indian intonation. He is about to go back to India. We spoke of Chinese self-righteousness. He said that it gets worse and worse: the manner in which the ultimatums to India over Sikkim were presented was that of an over-lord to a vassal. The Chinese now state that they will only attend conferences provided that acceptance of their whole policy, set out in detail, is guaranteed in advance. Mehta is evidently a great fan of mine, which is always flattering. He told Alan how delighted he was to meet me. On leaving I asked him to give my love to K. P. S. Menon Jun, my pupil.[158] He said, 'we are all your pupils'. Naturally I liked him.

After the performance we went to the Donalds' house and talked. We discovered that guests invited to official functions are required to be in position at different times according to their status: the least important to be there first. This explains the early hour at which we were summoned to the banquet on Thursday and the parade on Friday. Alan also told us that dramatists (& presumably other writers) are ordered by party officials to incorporate explicit topical political statements in their plays at particular points of the text. He gave us full details of this process of 'responsible' writing, from a dramatic writer whom he knows and whom he has invited us to meet if we are back in time on Friday. We also discussed the future of SACU. He asked why we joined. I said, for three reasons: (1) because I admire Needham, who invited me; (2) because I have genuine interest in China; (3) because I think there is a danger of people in England treating China as a remote, hostile abstraction, whereas it is 650 million people, with a great history, in the middle of a great social experiment: in fact, I fear a kind of McCarthyism. Robert said his reasons were precisely the same. We agreed that, though the Chinese clearly envisage SACU as only useful if it is a 'front-organisation', we ought to try to

---

157 Jagat Singh Mehta (1922–2014) had been educated at Leighton Park School, Reading and St John's College, Cambridge. Appointed as India's *chargé d'affaires ad interim*, i.e. head of mission, in 1964 (diplomatic relations had been reduced after the India-Chinese war of 1962), he imbued solidarity into a legation that was beset by Chinese animosity. Foreign Secretary of India 1976–79 until he fell from Indira Gandhi's favour.

158 Kumar Padmanabha Sivasankara Menon senior (1898–1982) took a first-class degree in history at Christ Church, Oxford. He was India's first Foreign Secretary after independence, 1948–52, ambassador in Moscow 1952–61, and then in Peking. His son K. P. S. Menon junior (1921–2016) was Indian ambassador in Tokyo during the early 1980s, and in Peking during the mid-1980s. He served as Foreign Secretary of India, under Rajiv Gandhi, 1987–89.

keep it going, as a holding operation against better times. Afterwards, Robert told me that our task would be difficult because Mary will certainly try to damage us (and especially me) in SACU on her return – not because she is a fellow-traveller. but because she is a mindless, self-important silly who is furious with us for having clear ideas when she (she thinks) is getting on so well and creating Anglo-Chinese understanding by nattering trivialities to Cement-head and Goose-bottom. However, we shall be back three weeks before her and should be able to stop that.

Sunday, 3 October

I have got a bad throat and all the symptoms of trouble from sitting in the cool courtyard of the Donalds' house after the hot theatre last night, I fear. However, I must hope to control it, though today's circumstances were not propitious. We got up at 6.0 and caught the 7.30 train to Loyang. Happily, our forebodings about the train were not justified. We – the four of us – had a carriage to ourselves, & the *troupe* (Goose-bottom, Cement-head, smooth-face and the Presbyterian) were in another. The train was clean and the first-class carriages comfortable – very Russian, with curtains and antimacassars. The second-class carriages were very different, & crowded like cattle-trucks, which forced Ernie into some repulsive double-think. We travelled all day over a vast brown plain, with the Western Hills on the right. It seemed almost empty: but here and there we saw ploughs drawn by men or animals, seldom by tractors. The agricultural revolution looks less impressive here than just outside Pekin. Just after dark we crossed the Yellow River by the huge new railway-bridge. As we crossed it, Mrs Adams told our Chinese guides that in England all we know about the Yellow River was that, in flood-time, it carried thousands of corpses to the sea.[159] She was surprised that they did not like this – just as she was surprised, yesterday, when they did not appreciate her remark that we called human monsters 'mongol children' ('I explained to them that is was only a *name*, because they were deformed ...'). Soon after 10.0 p.m. we arrived in Loyang and were taken to the hotel, where I took two dispirins and went straight to bed. The anilities of Mary and the sanctimonious double-think of

159 The Yellow River, or Huang, is the second longest river in Asia, after the Yangtze, and the sixth longest on the planet. Raymond Dawson wrote in 1967 that 'mass national awareness' in England of China was limited to a few geographical features: 'the Yangtze and its league-place among the world's largest rivers; the Yellow River changing its course, overflowing its banks, and drowning myriads of peasants'.

Ernie have become so intolerable that Robert and I spent a good deal of time sitting in the dining-car to avoid their company. At lunch Mary described her visit to the Chinese Medical Association in Pekin.[160] I allowed my attention to lapse, but it was suddenly aroused, as I was pursuing a particularly slippery sea-slug round the bowl with my chopsticks, by a statement that 'they find stainless steel contraceptives the most effective'. I asked Robert afterwards if this was really what she had said. He replied that is was: she had interrogated the Chinese minutely on this delicate subject. As Robert said, her purposeless interest in other people's business is positively impudent. He also told me that Ernie had stated that he had no particular interest in England: 'I am a citizen of the world'.[161] The thought of that prim, purblind, parochial creature claiming cosmopolitanism was too much for me, and from now on I shall think of him as 'the Citizen of the World'. But in fact, I suppose, there is a sense in which he can claim the title. He is a universal type: the type of smug, narrow-minded go-getter whose meritocracy is communism. That is why I dislike both meritocracy and communism. Give me a ruling class which at least, knowing that there is no damned merit about it and having tasted a liberal education, claims no personal tribute and can sustain some standards of taste.

Incidentally Mary, who equally, and with equal justice, would claim to be a citizen of the world told me the other day that Felix Topolski[162] had wanted very much to come to China, 'but I was firm and blocked him'. I asked why. She said, 'because I didn't think his art *avant-garde* enough'. I did not reply, what I felt *viz*: first, that such a consideration was irrelevant; secondly, that *avant-garde* art is anyway not acceptable in communist countries; thirdly, that even if it were, she is no judge of art (or anything else). She said today that what surprised her most in China was the elegance of the clothes. There is no

---

160 Mary Adams met the obstretician and gynaecologist Lin Chiao-chih [Lin Qiaozhi; Kati Lin] (1901–1983), who had trained in London, Manchester, Vienna and Chicago, and delivered over 50,000 babies.

161 Roberts was active in the Movement for Colonial Freedom. 'My interest in international affairs is all-embracing,' he wrote at the end of his life. 'Many trade union officers wear blinkers when it comes to their brothers and sisters overseas; I have always been an internationalist in the best sense of the word – fighting for the establishment of socialism throughout the world, not only within the confines of my own country' (Ernie Roberts, *Strike Back* (Orpington: Ernie Roberts, 1994), p. 179).

162 Feliks Topolski (1907–1989) worked as an official war artist during the 1940s, and was an inquisitive world traveller. His commission by the Duke of Edinburgh to paint murals of Queen Elizabeth's coronation will not have recommended him to Adams.

elegance at all. Any Japanese can be recognised here at once precisely because the Japanese are elegant and the Chinese are not.

About an hour after leaving Pekin, the *troupe* came into our compartment with grave faces and said that there was news item which they thought we should know. There had been a coup in Indonesia. A group of 'reactionary officers', 'in league with the C.I.A.', had planned a *coup*, but this had been frustrated by a junior officer, one of Soekarno's guards, called Un Dun (or some such name).[163] The reactionaries had failed and Un Dun was at the moment master of the situation. Soekarno himself was in protective custody.[164] Nothing more was known. We asked when and how this was known and were told that the Association had known yesterday but the public had not yet been told. We deduced more from this reluctance to tell the public than from the facts stated, and we speculated why they had decided, or been told, to tell us. Ernie did some rapid double-think in order to conclude that England was no more honest.

The hotel at Loyang (the Loyang Hotel) is frowsty. We have sitting-rooms but no baths, only showers and lavatories which smell of drains. It is bran-new but seems already in decay. Service is poor, the furniture heavy and characterless. Nothing seems Chinese. If anything, it is like a Russian provincial hotel – that hotel in Vladimir.[165]

---

163 Lt. Col. Untung bin Syamsuri (1925–1967), battalion commander of the Presidential Guard, led the rebels who in the small hours of Friday 1 October 1965 blockaded the presidential palace, seized control of Jakarta's telephone exchange and wireless station, shot dead three Indonesian generals in their homes, and took three other generals to an air force base where they were shot or stabbed to death. Untung was described by Sir Andrew Gilchrist, Britain's ambassador, as 'a brave but not very intelligent soldier who did well in the West Irian campaign, simple and austere in his personal life, a man genuinely sickened by corruption in high places'. The *communiqué* which Untung issued after the *coup*, with its 'hysterical condemnation … of "generals and officers who lust for power, ignore the wretched fate of their men, live in luxury at the latter's expense, and humiliate women", had the mark of a man who was swayed more by grievances and personal jealousies than by anything else' (NA FO 371/180320, despatch 13, Djakarta, 8 October 1965, Sir Andrew Gilchrist) Untung denied that he was a member of the Indonesian Communist Party [Partai Komunis Indonesia, or PKI], which was then the largest in the world outside countries under communist rule. He lost military control of Jakarta within a day.

164 Soekarno is T-R's spelling of Sukarno, the political name of Kusno Sosrodihardjo (1901–1970), first president of Indonesia 1945–67. His leftward-leaning, nationalist economic policies were antipathetic to foreign investment: Harold Wilson accordingly told the US president Lyndon Johnson that he was 'crooked and irrational'. The CIA and SIS were active in deception, bribery and disruption targeting both Sukarno and the PKI.

165 In 1957 T-R had stayed in Vladimir in Intourist's newest hotel, which was already decaying and infested with bedbugs.

Monday, 4 October

But indeed, all Loyang is characterless. I begin to see what Michael Meyer[166] meant when he said that all Chinese towns outside Pekin are like Bolton. Loyang was the capital of nine dynasties, from the Chou to the T'ang.[167] But that old city has been swallowed up in a giant new industrial town: its population has grown from 50,000 to 600,000 'since Liberation'.[168] It makes tractors and bull-dozers,[169] and the local propagandists – i.e. the local branch of our host Association – are very proud of it. The members of that branch came to call on us this morning. Their leader was a jolly, friendly trade-unionist, a refreshing change from Smooth-face & Cement-head; and they outlined their plans for us for our two-day stay.

This morning we went to the caves at Lungmen. These are 'Buddhist caves' – some 2000 in all, we are told – all in the limestone cliffs on either side of the river Loho, cut out and filled with statues and carvings by the Sui, Northern Wei and T'ang emperors. Some of the statues are very impressive and the caves-walls are covered with reliefs and inscriptions. But our pleasure and interest in seeing them was *almost* marred by the female curator who led us round and whose commentary, as Bolt put it, was like a constant waterfall of stale garbage falling on our heads. All the old stuff was poured out. The caves were hewn out by 'the power of the ruling class', but the works of art were made 'by the wisdom of the labouring people'. The whole achievement was 'the super-structure of the feudal system'. Buddhism was 'the opium with which the ruling class doped the people'. Finally, every missing head (as well as some carved reliefs which undoubtedly were sold to America) was 'looted by US imperialists' or 'destroyed by reactionary Kuomintang warlords'. At one point I ventured to ask why such people should want to knock off heads from

---

166 Michael Meyer (1921–2000) co-edited *Eight Oxford Poets* (1941) while reading English at Christ Church, Oxford. He lectured in English at Uppsala University 1947–50, translated the plays of Ibsen and Strindberg, and wrote their biographies. In 1957, at the instigation of Graham Greene, he made a long Asian tour. Before visiting the PRC, he was asked by SIS to note the types of aircraft that he saw on airfields.

167 The Chou [Zhou] dynasty ruled 1046–256 BC, succeeding the Shang dynasty (1600–1046 BC). After the era of the six dynasties ruling rival states (AD 221–589), the Sung emperors ruled a unified China 589–618. The Sung were followed by the T'ang dynasty, which ruled AD 618–906.

168 Anne Destenay's edition of *Nagel's Encyclopaedia-Guide* gives Loyang's population as 100,000 in 1953 and 400,000 in 1963.

169 The tractor plant had been built in 1955–59 with Soviet aid. Its seventeen workshops were in 1965 producing caterpillar tractors of the 'East is Red' brand.

states, and was promptly told, 'to demonstrate their reactionary nature just before their fall'.[170]

However, in the afternoon, we were refreshed. We were taken to the Kwang-ling museum, which is a new museum for objects excavated at Loyang installed in the temple of Kwang Yü (a fine Ming temple built by Wan-Li in honour of Kwang-Yü, a national hero of C4 A.D.).[171] Here we were shown round by a young curator, a graduate of the department of archaeology of Pekin University, who was not only intelligent, scholarly and attractive but also avoided all propaganda. Only once did he pay tribute, or rather lip-service, to the compulsory orthodoxy. Referring to the loss of certain objects, he said that they 'had been looted by U.S. imperialist, etc.' The hurried, perfunctory way in which he threw out those no doubt obligatory words, and the casual, contemptuous addition of the 'etc.,' warmed our hearts towards him.

Then we went to the White Horse Temple (Bai-mal-sa, or something like that).[172] This is a fine Buddhist temple, of Ming style, but Han foundation, with a pagoda rebuilt (we were told) in Sung times. I found the temple most attractive. It stands in its own grounds, which the monks cultivate (for it is an 'active' monastery, with 15 monks at present) and so is surrounded by orchards and vegetable-gardens, all well-kept, and formal cypress hedges, beautifully trimmed. The gentle, pastoral atmosphere surrounding those stately but simple buildings – for in spite of their carved gables and painted coffers there is an essential simplicity in them, different from the urban, metropolitan splendours of the temples of Pekin – charmed me; and had I been alone, I could have stayed there happily all day. But alas, I was not alone. There was Mary, there was Ernie, there was the troupe. They all behaved like a vulgar charabanc-party. Ernie once again became the funny man. He had himself photographed sitting in the lotus-flower, and kneeling in mock-devotion before the Buddha. Mary made asinine low-brow comments followed by her short, mechanical

---

170 *Nagel's Encyclopaedia-Guide* recorded that 1,352 caves had contained 97,306 statues, 3,608 inscriptions, 750 niches, and 39 carved pagodas. 'All this was sacked by 19th and 20th-century antiquarians. The heads of nine-tenths of the statues have been damaged or removed; marks left by saws are clearly visible. The Chinese lay particular stress on an adoration scene, which was in the Ping yang cave and is now in the United States.'

171 During the levelling and terracing required for Luoyang's new industrial districts, ceramics, painted pottery, kilns, tomb figurines, bronzes, mirrors and weapons were discovered. These were housed in a former temple dedicated to Guan Yu, a third-century general who was made a god of war.

172 Monks of the Dhyana school still lived in Bai ma si.

bray of a laugh. And every asininity was duly translated by Goose-bottom or the Presbyterian for the benefit of Smoothface and Cement-head, so that everyone, including the poor 75-year-old monk who led us round, could share the joke. Robert and I were so embarrassed that we detached ourselves, as far as we could, from the Party; but alas, it could not be far enough: our guides saw to that.

In the evening we were to go to the local opera; but after discovering that it was a modern opera about the love of a communist girl for her commune, I contracted out. It had been wet all day, and my health is low, and had got lower with rain and mortification; and so I thought myself better in bed. After the experience in the monastery, Robert told me that he had had enough of China and only looked forward to being in England. I now feel the same.

At lunch today we were talking of Chinese indifference to England in general and us in particular.[173] Mary said, 'they don't even ask us about the subjects in which we are specialists.' I was wondering what subject she was going to claim as her own speciality, when she went on: 'They never asked me about the kind of contraceptives used in England.'

Two new tabloid phrases for the traveller in the People's China: (1) 'a superstitious object' = anything connected with a church or temple or religion; (2) 'a cultural relic' = anything worth saving from Antiquity – i.e. from before 1949.

Tuesday, 5 October

I had a bad night and stayed in bed all morning which the others went to the tractor factory. I got up for lunch, but retired to bed again afterwards, while they went to a bull-dozer factory. I was tempted to accompany them, but the risks are too great, especially as we have to spend tonight in the train (This is very tiresome: we had hoped to travel from Loyang to Sian by day, to see the country; but now we shall miss the country and have the discomfort of a night on the train). When they returned, they reported that they had also been shown two Han tombs as an extra. I brought my diary up to date and read Hume's *Essays*.[174] I had supper in my rooms while the others were entertained

---

173 'In the entire visit no one asked me a question about England,' Bolt told *SACU News* (November 1965). 'Their interest in the rest of the world is slight.'

174 The Enlightenment philosopher and historian David Hume (1711–1776) was among T-R's best-loved authors.

by the local Association in the dining room. Then we caught the train for Sian.[175] I was feeling very low, but I am like a wounded straggler in an army retreating through hostile country: I must stay with the army or I am lost. I had a dreadful night in the train, made worse by Robert's pipe: he is a continual pipe-smoker and, like so many smokers, is quite unaware of the feelings of non-smokers (all the rest of us are non-smokers). However, I got through it and by the time we reached Sian, at 7.0 a.m., felt slightly better.

Wednesday, 6 October

At Sian we were met by the usual deputation from the local Association. The weather was dull, cold and wet. We were taken to our hotel, 'The People's Building', a vast concrete structure, newly built but already, as usual, showing signs of its hasty construction: ill-fitting windows, warped doors, amateur repairs. We each have a perfectly good suite, but the beds, as always, are hard and the water-supply is uncertain. At first glance, Sian, like Loyang, might be Bolton; but from the fifth floor of the hotel (where we are) temple-roofs can be seen among the offices and factories. Sian is the capital of Shensi province and has (we are told) 1,600,000 inhabitants. It was the capital of China under the Western Chou, Western Han, Sui and T'ang dynasties.

As we were finishing breakfast, an English girl of about 23 came up to us. She is the wife of an Englishman who teaches English in a school here, having learned Chinese at the School of Oriental and African Studies in London.[176] She comes from Bristol and is sensible, intelligent and civilised. (Alan Donald told me that some of the English schoolteachers here are the best ambassadors we could have; but some, he added, were a dreadful liability). Her husband is on a two-year contract, and she does a little teaching too. She said that he was promised opportunities of study as well as teaching, but these have not materialised. She also said that there is positive resistance to any attempt to teach anything about England. The Chinese only want the English language and it must be entirely divorced from English ideas, English history, English life. The language is useful not as a means of penetrating English culture, but

---

175 Sian (Xi'an) had been China's capital for 970 years. Under the PRC's first Five Year Plan, the city underwent swift industrialization, its population rising from 490,000 in 1949 to 1,600,000 in 1965. Cotton textiles, electric instruments, nitrate fertilizers and plastics were its main products.

176 The experiences of English-language teachers in the PRC can be gleaned from Ronald Price, *Education in Communist China* (London: Routledge, 1970).

simply as a means of communicating Chinese propaganda to Africans and Indians. She also said that she had never discovered an educated Chinaman in our sense of the word. The 'intellectuals' do not think or even want to know how to think. They merely repeat a jargon which they do not understand. This has been our experience too. It may, of course, only mean that we move on the same low level. She said that she was maddened by the nonsense that Chinese children were told about England: 'I never realised how English I was and felt, till I came out here.' At these words a look of smug contempt settled on the face of the Citizen of the World, who, however, said nothing.

After breakfast we were taken to the Bell Tower,[177] a Ming building very similar to the gate-houses of Pekin: i.e. it was a two-storeyed building placed on a huge and apparently solid bastion with a tunnelled carriageway through it. We had the usual lecture from a doltish female curator. The building was effected by 'the power of the ruling class'; its beauty was due to 'the wisdom of the labouring people'; it had been damaged by 'Kuomintang reactionaries', etc. etc. The furniture in the two storeys was heavy, debased Ching: 'Trust-House Ching',[178] I said to myself; but at that moment Mary spotted it 'what beautiful, *beautiful* furniture!' she exclaimed, and she flitted about exclaiming, with great assurance, 'this is the first *good* furniture we have seen in China'. I fear that we may now have a rash of later Ching furniture from the Council of Industrial Design.

Indeed Mary was in first-class form today: so much so that, when we came to the Tayen or Wild Goose pagoda,[179] Robert and I (though I was feeling very feeble) climbed 250 steps up to the summit to be out of reach of her asinities and the acute embarrassment they cause us. The pagoda is a most beautiful building, built in C.7. by or for the monk Hiuan-tsang. He had travelled in India and had returned with Buddhist sutras, which were translated and kept there. It stands in temple grounds, cultivated and restful, with little temple buildings, and from the top there is a splendid view over the whole city, with its old gates in the four quarters. This visit filled the rest of the morning and we returned to the hotel for lunch.

---

177 The Bell Tower (Zhong lou) had been restored by the PRC.

178 The Trust House chain owned medium-sized provincial hotels with traditional furniture and plumbing. These exemplified Sigmund Freud's diagnosis: 'the English, having created the concept of comfort, then refused to have anything more to do with it'.

179 In 652 the pilgrim Hiuan-tsang [Xuan Zang] had a pagoda built in order to house the precious Buddhists texts which he had brought from India. After much rebuilding the Big Goose Pagoda (Da Yan Ta) was seven storeys high.

In the afternoon we went to the Museum, which is an extension of the old temple of Confucius.[180] It is a wonderful museum. Even the tabloid idiocies of the curator, made drearier and more protracted by the slow, fumbling efforts of the Presbyterian translator, could not diminish its impact. There were the usual Shang bronzes, Han and T'ang earthenware, Sung and Ming Pottery; but what made it so striking was two departments: the house of stone statues and 'the Forest of Stone Tablets'. The former was a collection of stone sculptures, mainly Han and T'ang, of extraordinary power and vitality: horses, lions, bulls (a charming bullock-calf in repose), and a gigantic, sullen old rhinoceros, with lowered head, little forward eyes, and heavy stone pleats in his neck. There were six splendid T'ang horses, carved in relief: a series, some standing, some at the gallop, with stirrups dangling; and a relief of an ostrich with neck curled back. The strength, grace and tension of these great stone figures kept me there long and drew me back afterwards. I was enchanted by them. The rhinoceros, incidentally, might have been by Epstein: Epstein at his best.[181]

The Forest of Stone Tablets is an amazing collection of texts beautifully carved on flat, tombstone-like slabs of black stone. It might be black granite or black marble: they called it 'blue-stone'. They are – we were told – perfect texts of the classics, mainly Confucius, thus carved to provide a *textus receptus*[182] for students. There are 224 tablets and a total of 650,000 ideograms inscribed on them. They were moved here, to the temple of Confucius, in 1090, and other stone tablets, containing commentaries and filling *lacunae*, have been added to them. Among these others is the famous Nestorian inscription of the 7th century discovered by the Jesuit in 16 [*sic*],[183] and long regarded as a Jesuit imposture. I was very excited to find this, and since the curator knew nothing about it, gave a little lecture on the project, not omitting the names of Voltaire and Gibbon. How I would like to return, alone and unguided, to this museum! But alas, everything has its price, and the price of this visit was the cold. Although I wore my thickest clothes I shivered with the cold which

---

180 The Historical Museum housed in the former Temple of Confucius (Kong miao) had been enriched by many objects found in recent excavations.

181 The stone carving by Sir Jacob Epstein (1880–1959) was rooted in primitive sculpture, unlike his modelled bronzes which were in the baroque tradition.

182 Latin: received text.

183 Álvaro de Semedo (1585/6–1658), a Portuguese Jesuit, was (c. 1625) the first European to see the Nestorian Stele. This was a limestone monument erected in 781 and inscribed in both Chinese and Syriac with text recording the existence since c. 635 of Christian communities in a few northern Chinese towns. It had been buried in 845 and was unearthed by Chinese workmen c. 1623–4.

was constantly exhaled by those cold stone statues and cold stone tablets, and felt my state sinking all the time. Then, when all was over, Mary would not go. It was not that she was interested: she hardly looked at the museum: she was exchanging small-talk – very small-talk – with the oafish Presbyterian. As for the works of art, she expressed herself summarily (as always) on them. 'In point of fact', she said to me, 'apart from your Nestorian tablet, there's nothing here that we couldn't see better in England!' My heart shrank as she uttered these words. 'What came she forth for to see?' I asked myself.[184] But of course it was a purely rhetorical question. She came to increase her self-importance and to tell the Chinese about industrial design, consumers' associations, women's rights, Basic English and contraception. No doubt she will have an opportunity of extending herself on these topics tonight, when she has insisted on meeting some university students. The rest of us have refused to join her in this, knowing perfectly well that such a meeting is useless for practical purposes.

Poor Mary! Her deceptions are constant. At the museum, since she found the statues, tablets, etc. all so boring, she bought a rubbing of an engraved stone representing the monk Hiuan-tsang; for he at least had got into her head at the pagoda this morning, and will no doubt come out of her mouth back in Kensington. Afterwards she was mortified to discover – simply because she had declined to listen at the time – that this engraving, alone of everything in the museum, was modern, having been executed in 1933. By the time we were all at dinner in the hotel, she was thoroughly grumpy. Of all places in China, Loyang and Sian seemed to her the least worthy of being visited. But of course, she hastily added, it was the British Embassy that had recommended them. That explained all.

For Mary hates embassies. This had come out in Peking, when I had observed that it was decent of Michael Wilford to ask us all four to lunch the very first day. 'Not at all', she had retorted; 'it's his business.' I denied this, and she then let fly at embassies in general as being quite useless institutions: a consulate was all that was necessary: the rest could be covered by journalists. What did those young men do except enjoy themselves and entertain the sort of visitors whose company they enjoyed, like Hugh Trevor-Roper? She had made this last remark in so waspish a way that I had deduced her general motive. I fear that, normally, she is not much noticed, on her travels, by British embassies and the fact that she had been invited to the embassy in Peking under my aegis was an added mortification.

---

184 See Luke 7.24.

At dinner Ernie reported that he had picked up some news from Indonesia. Ever since Sunday we have regularly asked our guides whether they have heard any more from Indonesia, and always they say no. But Ernie had caught 'the Voice of America',[185] and, though it was jammed, had heard it say that Soekarno was back in power and that student-demonstrations in Jakarta had demanded the banning of the communist party for having murdered five generals. Now a pattern begins to emerge. I deduce that Un Dun – though our guides never whispered so much – was acting for the communist party of Indonesia, and that this *coup* was an attempted communist take-over.[186] I also deduce that, to justify the *coup*, he had claimed that there was a 'reactionary' plot in league with the CIA, and that, in his moment of power, he had quietly disposed of those adversaries whom he had conveniently accused. If this is so then the motives of our guides, in telling as what they told us on Sunday, become clear. At that time they believed that the take-over had succeeded, and although the Chinese govt. was not spreading the news till they could be sure of success, their superiors had instructed them to prepare us for the best, and perhaps observe our reactions. Happily we gave no hint of any reaction. I feel very inclined to ask them tomorrow if they have still no news from Jakarta, and then, when they deny any, innocently to give them ours.[187]

After dinner I went straight to bed. Robert and Ernie were taken to the local opera (modern). Mary had contracted out, to interview her students. I don't suppose she will get anything from them, but I shudder to think what they will deduce about us about 'Mrs Adams' Delegation'.

185 The US government had financed its external broadcasting operation, the Voice of America, since 1942.

186 Sir Andrew Gilchrist, ambassador in Jakarta, reported in a despatch of 19 October 1965: 'Agents of a political party as monolithic and disciplined as the PKI do not do this sort of thing unless they have a firm directive from the top. It seems best to discount any theory which establishes the PKI as having plotted a major uprising or bid for power on the 1st of October, with Untung and his men in the position of their shock troops. The unreadiness of the PKI and the general incompetence of the proceedings … are far from characteristic of a communist plot' (NA FO 371/180320, DH 1015/215).

187 British 'political warfare' experts spread propaganda against both the PKI and Sukarno after Untung's uprising. This aided the forces of General Muhammad Suharto (1921–2008), whose men massacred some half million suspected communists in Sumatra, Bali and Java over the course of a few months. Officials in London ignored these killings, and took satisfaction in the success of their covert operations in achieving the collapse of Sukarno's government. Suharto replaced Sukarno as president, and established his New Order regime. During thirty years of autocracy, he embezzled up to 15 billion US dollars.

Thursday, 7 October

I slept for twelve hours and feel a bit better, but still have a bad throat and cough, so I decided – now that we have seen the pagoda and the Museum – to detach myself firmly from excursions to schools and cotton factories. I think – or at least Robert tells me – that I did well. Apparently the rest of the party had an excruciating propaganda talk from the director of the cotton factory, and Mary excelled herself in self-importance on the subject of design, but unfortunately revealed that she did not realise that there was a difference between printed and woven design. This may limit the usefulness of her lectures to the Czech colleges of technology. But Robert says that he was impressed by the real democracy – or at least equality – within the factory. This corresponds with what I have observed elsewhere and it seems to distinguish China from Russia. Timothy George told me that Mao has successfully insisted, against the army leaders, that there be no permanent officers' ranks in the army;[188] and differentiation of classes (by wages etc.) is one of the crimes most constantly imputed to Russia in the propaganda literature. I also asked Robert about the operas which I had missed, both here and at Loyang. He said that they had been tediously moral – i.e. political – well produced and pleasantly informal – i.e. the audience were gay and noisy. But naturalism and stylisation cannot long co-exist. All I got from Mary on the subject of her meeting with the students – of whom there were eight – was that they had all chosen to learn English in order 'to help to build a new China', and that when she asked whether they wanted to know anything about England, they all replied, 'No'.

After lunch I again contracted out of all activity, leaving the others to go to visit a naturally warm bathing pool. When they came back it transpired that they had been obliged to bathe in it, no doubt in fulfilment of the instructions of chairman Mao, of whom we had seen a fine full-scale socialist-realist painting in the Museum of Chinese Art in Pekin, robed in something between a bath-robe and the gown of a Confucian sage, exhorting some handsome and athletic young socialists, of either sex, to take the plunge. It also transpired that Mary had been back on her pet subject, cross-examining everyone on contraception.

---

188 'In the vein of Long-March nostalgia, the government in 1964 abolished all insignia of rank, which, however, is a mixed blessing to a private, for it makes officers and noncoms feel they have to work doubly hard at acting and shouting like officers' (Koningsberger, *Love and Hate in China*, p. 101).

Our plans were to fly back to Pekin tomorrow.[189] This would have allowed me to go early to bed and escape grim functions tonight: a 'banquet' in the hotel given by the Vice-president of the local association. But when we discovered that there is no certainty that any Chinese plane will fly (like the Russians, they are far more limited by the weather than we are), and that if the plane does not fly, we shall miss our plane home, we decided to go on the night train, which leaves Sian at 10.20 tonight and takes 24 hours. This was a nuisance, but a necessity: and it was a double nuisance because it meant that I had to sit up and could not avoid the dinner. However, the good Goosebottom insisted on fetching a doctor, who gave me some magical pills, and I prepared to face the dinner.

It was dreadful. The Vice-President (a sly, shrivelled party hack) began with a long, provocative speech. He described Sian in the usual cant terms: formerly 'a consumer city of landlords, capitalists and bureaucrats', now an industrial city of workers etc. etc. He attacked 'U.S. imperialist aggression', announced that China must reply 'tit for tat' (this has become a continuous cant phrase since Chou-En-Lai used it in his speech on 1 Oct), and finally attacked Britain for supporting U.S. aggression 100%. Bolt made a good and careful reply. I was feeling too low to speak much, and I suffered a good deal from sitting next to Cement-head and having to dodge his discarded chicken-bones, but I remarked that 100% was not true and referred to our diplomatic recognition of China. The Vice-President then stated that Britain was 'double-faced': we recognised China and yet did not give the 100% support to Chinese policy which he seemed to think that such recognition implied. Ernie made smug little remarks to advertise his own proletarian virtue. Mary nattered. Bolt gently told him that since they asked for criticism, we found it difficult to accept the self-righteous attitude of the Chinese. The Vice-President said that the Chinese believed in criticism and self-criticism and compromise; but they would never compromise on essentials, for right was right and wrong wrong, and they were right, 100%, and we 100% wrong. We were glad to escape to the night-train.

Friday, 8 October

All night and all day in the train. Robert & I had to share a carriage with Smoothface (who snored) and the Presbyterian; but on the whole we have done

---

189 T-R had stipulated when he accepted SACU's invitation to visit the PRC that he must return to England by 9 October, when the academic term began in Oxford. Bolt had also pre-arranged his return by that date.

better than Mary and Ernie who not only have each other but also the granitic peasant Cement-head and the virtuous puritan Goose-bottom. They are going on today to Shanghai and to enjoy each other's company for another week. I'm afraid we often solaced ourselves by thinking of their flight. Smoothface is basically idle and the Presbyt. totally incompetent, so they can agree on a certain amount of relaxation, but Cement-head and Goose-bottom will keep each other constantly up to the mark, and Mary & Ernie really hate each other. Though they sit on the same intellectual pond-bed, once either of them starts to move they conflict. Ernie has hitherto been kept in some control by Robert and me, but now he will break out in all his odious dishonesty. (Incidentally he is also breaking out into ever new sartorial elegance: recently he has been wearing a natty hacking-suit, with long jacket and slanting pockets, such as is worn by pseudo-hunting men in road houses). Mary though outwardly syco-phantic to the Chinese is really furious at their refusal to treat her as important and makes occasional waspish outbursts. Now that her status had sunk further – for 'Mrs Adams' delegation' now consists only of Ernie – she will be more furious still. 'They will probably come to blows', Robert said smugly. Robert and I, who have rediscovered the old pleasure of truancy from our guides, have now recovered the equally old pleasure of breaking up for the holidays, and I'm afraid that the pleasure is heightened by malicious thoughts about those still at school. Poor things, we say, as we imagine the incidents of next week, do they really deserve it? But then we reflect that they are less sensitive than we are, and need no pity.

We passed through the same country as before, but having more daylight saw more of it, especially between Loyang and the Yellow river: brown earth, small fields – whether communal or private – and many cave-villages. At Pekin we were met by the usual delegation, together with Berger,[190] an English busi-nessman whom we had met in London. He is a fellow-traveller if not worse and, coming to our hotel and keeping us up late, this to persuade us that our experiences were a-typical. We did not believe him.[191] There is also another

---

190 Roland ('Ro') Berger (1904–1991): see pp. 26–7.

191 'When I arrived I heard at second-hand of T-R's objectionable behaviour but also of some ham-handling on the part of the Association,' Berger wrote from Peking in a letter of 11 October to Jack Perry (Bryan papers). 'The Association people ... seemed quite satisfied with the reactions of the four members and with the programme they had arranged for them. But I could tell that ... the itinerary had followed a stereotyped formula. T.R. and Bolt returned from Loyang and Sian late on Saturday and left early on Sunday morning. I met them at the station and went back to the Hotel with them for a chat. Despite reports of T-R's boorishness and bad manners, I found him quite friendly and affable.'

English businessman who imposes himself on us. He is called Silver;[192] & is, no doubt like Berger, Jewish and fellow-travelling.[193] But Silver is large, loud and thrusting, an intolerable man: I prefer Berger.

Incidentally, on the train today I asked Smooth-face innocently whether there had been any news of Indonesia since his communication of 8 Oct. 'None at all', he replied.

Saturday, 9 October

We got up at 5.0 and were taken to the airport by Smooth-face, Presbyterian, and the parrot-like Secretary, and full complement of others. Even at breakfast at the airport, even at 6.30 a.m., we were not spared: the Secretary was dinning party cant into our ears. In the car on the way to the airport the Presbyterian handed us our tickets, but a quick glance from Smooth-face checked her and she at once took them back. Only at the last minute were they given to us and only then did we know our flight numbers. We are to fly to Moscow, via Irkutsk & Omsk, and then catch a BEA flight, at 6.15 p.m. Moscow time direct to London. All the frustrations of three weeks evaporate as we think of discarding these wretched Chinese gaolers and sleeping tonight at home.

We flew back over those grim, horrible mountains. The Great Wall looks even more impressive from the air than from the ground: one sees it creeping along those knife-edges of rock. In the early morning sunlight, which sharpened the shadows, that criss-cross of razor-edges cut into the very mind and imagination. I found the mountains south of the Gobi desert hateful. Then I settled down and waited to see the northern edge of the desert, the gentler hills which announce the return of the north Eurasian plain (they were sprinkled with snow now), and the friendly waters of Lake Baikal. When we reached Lake Baikal, I prepared for a brief wait at Irkutsk.

Alas, Irkutsk is a place of ill-omen for us. Suddenly, it was announced that we could not land at Irkutsk, owing to 'the weather', and that we were being taken to another airport, to wait there till the weather had improved at Irkutsk. We were told to draw our curtains, not to look out of the window, nor to leave our seats. Through a crack in my curtains I saw that we were landing at a military airport, bristling with planes: then the stewardess came round carefully

---

192 Adolphe ('Adolf') Silver (1913–1978) had been a Labour member of Hampstead borough council in the 1940s. He was leader of the Waste Trade Federation.

193 An intelligence report on Berger, compiled in the Warsaw embassy, noted: 'he is of Jewish descent but does not admit it' (NA KV 2/4236, serial 196a, 24 November 1948).

closing all such cracks. I asked her innocently the name of the airport. It was a 'disused airport', she said. We sat there imprisoned, immobile and darkened, for two hours while the roar of fighter-planes taking off commented on the 'disuse' of the port. Then we flew to Irkutsk for customs etc., and lunch. We left at 2.0, seriously worried whether we would get to Moscow in time for our connexion to London. But the stewardess reassured us: all going well, she said, we would still get to Moscow in seven hours, which would mean at 4.0 p.m. (Moscow time).

She was right. We flew swiftly over Siberia – much of it a waste mass perforated with lakes, like the North American Shield, stopped in Omsk (a grim city in the infinite plain, surrounded by huge fields dotted with clumps of yellowing birches: it made me think of Saskatoon), and landed in Moscow, in heavy rain, at 4.0 pm. Immediately, we sought out the BEA counter.[194] I wanted to telephone or telegraph Xandra to meet us at London airport. But the BEA desk was closed, and soon we learned the reason. There was no BEA flight, nor any flight to London, we were told, till Tuesday. There were no flights anywhere from Moscow tonight and none tomorrow either. Those worthless Chinese had simply deceived us. They had booked us on Tuesday's flight and by holding back all information, and only giving us our tickets at the last minute, had prevented us from finding out. As our only instructions to them had been that we *must* be back on the 9th (whenever we left China) we found this unforgivable. But we had to admit that, by now, it was also farcical.

What on earth could we do, kicking our heels in Moscow for at least two valuable days, with no Russian, no Russian money, no preparations? We were taken to a transit hotel in Leningradskii Prospekt. I telephoned the Embassy. Humphrey Trevelyan[195] had left but I was advised to speak to his secretary, Andrew Wood,[196] who, I was assured, was on duty. I duly spoke to him. I was sorry, I said, to trouble him but I understood that he was on duty till 8.0 p.m. 'I am the Ambassador's secretary', he replied, very frigidly, as if ambassador's

194 British European Airways was a Crown corporation (i.e. state-owned) founded in 1946. By the early 1960s it was the world's largest passenger airline outside the United States. It was merged in 1974 with the British Overseas Airways Corporation to form British Airways.

195 Sir Humphrey Trevelyan (1905–1985), Lord Trevelyan 1965, *chargé d'affaires* Peking 1953–55, ambassador to Egypt 1955–56, to Iraq 1958–61, and to USSR 1962–65; High Commissioner in Aden, 1965. His recipe for a fulfilling posting was: 'Not too civilized, too much work, hard climate, a spice of danger.'

196 (Sir) Andrew Wood (b. 1940), was first posted to Moscow in 1964. He returned as Head of Chancery in the embassy, 1979, and served as ambassador to Russia and Moldova, 1995–2000.

secretaries were too grand to be on duty. I told him our position mentioning that we had not even got visas for as long as two days. He told me that we had better apply to Intourist: it was they who would have to extend the visa and I might as well apply direct. He was so uncivil, so cold, so utterly unforthcoming, that I decided to trouble him no more and acquiesced. But then a new problem arose. We had no roubles. It was after 5.0 on Saturday. The Bank at the airport had been closed. The Transit hotel refused to change our money. We could not even take a taxi to find if anyone else would. We could not buy a drink to calm our tempers. I could not send a wire to Xandra to explain our delay. So there was nothing for it but to telephone Mr Wood again. He was an official; we were British subjects; our predicament was his business, however grand he thought himself to be. 'Don't apologise for troubling him this time,' Robert said; but I forgot myself, and did. It did not make any difference. Without waiting to hear me, Mr Wood told me to wait while he spoke to someone else. I overheard him laboriously explaining about the visa. Ultimately I called him back. 'You have not waited to hear what I wished to say', I said, this time rather coldly, for I had had enough of this young man with his jack-in-office manner; and I added that we had no Russian money and could not get our money changed. 'I believe you will be in the Embassy till 8.0', I said. He replied, 'I suppose I could stay in till then'. 'I will not keep you longer than it takes to find a taxi', I said. 'I propose to come straight to the Embassy in a taxi. I shall ask you to pay for the taxi. I shall also ask you to let us have a few roubles.' Once again he did not let me finish. 'We are not empowered to advance money', he said, with the frigidity of a high official brushing off an importunate mendicant, 'except in certain circumstances …' This time it was I who cut him short. I put down the receiver and we resolved to ask no help from the Embassy but to stay, if necessary, immobile for 48 hours in the ghastly transit hotel. But we went downstairs and ordered a bottle of Russian champagne; to be paid for, somehow, tomorrow. Then, at about 8.30, we began to go to bed.

Soon afterwards there was a knock on the door and a young man came in. He introduced himself as Rodric Braithwaite,[197] from the Embassy. We did not ask what force had propelled him hither, nor did we so much as mention

197 (Sir) Rodric Braithwaite (b. 1932) served in Moscow 1963–66, and was a visiting fellow of All Souls 1972–73. He was the first British ambassador to Russia (as distinct from the Soviet Union) since the Bolshevik revolution seventy years earlier. In 1992–93 he chaired the Joint Intelligence Committee.

Wood. He at once paid for our champagne and lent us some roubles. He assured us that there were means of leaving Moscow tomorrow. He telephoned from our room and established that there was a KLM flight to Amsterdam at 8.10 a.m.[198] Nobody could be found at the KLM office, but he promised to go on trying. Meanwhile he advised us to go to bed, prepared to rise at 5.45 if he could get us on the plane. He would do everything necessary, and would ring back if he had been successful. So he left us and we went to bed. At 11.30 I found myself shaken violently out of a deep, deep sleep by Robert. The excellent young man was there too. He had come in person to say that he had got us on to the plane. He gave us exact instructions. He gave exact instructions in Russian to the hotel. He ordered a taxi. He gave us his telephone-number and insisted that, in any difficulty, we telephone him: he would drive us personally to the airport at 6.15 a.m. if necessary ... Profuse in our thanks for this uncovenanted help, this sudden warmth after the winter frost of Andrew Wood, we bade him goodnight and went to sleep again, serene in the knowledge that tomorrow, even if we do not get to London, we shall at least be in the 'decadent', civilised West, in Amsterdam.

Sunday, 10 October

Our internal clocks disordered by so much flying, we were both up at 4.0, filling in our diaries. At 6.15 the taxi came. At the airport the Dutch girl who acted for KLM seemed an angel of light. For the first time for three weeks we found ourselves dealing with a foreign official whose instinct was evidently to help, not to obstruct, who did not have to be approached sideways, or upside down, whose immediate reaction was of rational co-operation, not suspicion of our motives and oblique calculation of distant consequences. Once on a Dutch plane, our spirits rose. Even at Warsaw, where we landed, we felt almost free. In Amsterdam, which we reached at mid-day, we felt intoxicated by the sensation of liberty. I telephoned Xandra. We ordered and drank a bottle of Krug. At 1.40 we were on the plane to London. By 3.15 Robert, Xandra and I were in the Ariel Hotel[199] drinking tea, and Robert and I were competitively

---

198 KLM [Koninklijke Luchtvaart Maatschappij; literally, Royal Aviation Company] made its first scheduled flights to London in 1920.

199 The Ariel was England's first dedicated airport hotel. It was built by the caterers J. Lyons to profit by the opening of Heathrow airport's Oceanic Terminal handling long-haul international passengers.

insisting that nothing, nothing, nothing would ever lead us back to China, or indeed to any communist country, except a personal invitation at the highest level: a level which would eliminate all possible contact with people like Mary Adams, Ernie Roberts, Cement-head, Smooth-face, Goose-bottom, Presbyterian, and all those vice-directors, vice-presidents, vice-chairmen, vice-headmasters, etc. etc. But I must let my emotions settle before making a report to SACU or writing, as I will, an article of the *Sunday Times*.

PART TWO

LONDON AND OXFORD, 1965

Wednesday, 15 December

When I arrived back from China I thought, at first, that I had done with it: with it and with SACU. The emotional strain, the frustration, of my visit to that land of bigots and parrots was a guarantee against my return to it, and what, I asked myself, was the purpose of SACU? To us – or rather, to me – it seemed clear enough, when in China, that to the Chinese at least SACU has no purpose except in so far as it might be converted into a communist front organisation, and that the most we could do, if we had the time and the energy to do it, was to prevent this from happening and to keep the society in being until such time as the Chinese themselves, having outlived their Stalinist period, were willing to accept it on other terms. But would the Chinese even consider co-operating with it in the meantime? Would they not rather, in that case, seeing that it was not totally theirs, drop all interest in it and, by ignoring it, cause it to die? This indeed did seem the most probable development; and that being so, I expected gradually to drop out of a dying organisation.

However, I said to myself, I shall not drop out without testifying to the truth. The *Sunday Times* had telephoned to me on 18th Sept and had caught me on the airport at Copenhagen. They had asked me to write for them on my return. At that time I had given no promises. I was to be the guest of the Chinese government. Perhaps their hospitality would inhibit me from writing freely. However, after a week or so in China, I revised my view. The Chinese government, I decided, was not treating me as a guest. It is true, it was paying my expenses. But I was giving up three weeks of my time. I was submitting to all the discomforts of distant travel. I was doing this not because the Chinese government was paying the cost of my dislocation but because it had offered to show me whatever

I wanted to see in China. This it had not done. It had merely imprisoned me in a group of low-grade morons, prevented me from meeting intelligent persons, and subjected me to continuous small-talk worthy of a charladies' tea-party. For this I felt no sense of obligation. So I changed my mind, dropped my reservations, and decided to write an account of China for the *Sunday Times*.

After my return I wrote it with great care. I sought to express the full horror of Chinese propaganda and Chinese conformism. But at the same time I sought to show that once one had got past that barrage of propaganda, once one had seen through the language of conformism, there was a positive achievement which, at least, had to be respected. And I added that, in my opinion, China was opportunist but not, or at least not yet, aggressive. The American fears of a Chinese conquest of the world seemed to me, at present, absurd.

Having written this article and sent it to Frank Giles,[1] I went up to London to report to 24 Warren Street.[2] But before going there, I called on Richard Thistlethwaite.[3] He gave me some interesting details about SACU. Then Dick White came to lunch at the Savile.[4] We had a merry old talk, and after lunch he offered to take me to my meeting. But I thought that to arrive at the HQ of a communist front-organisation in the limousine of the Chief of the Secret Service might be indulging my sense of irony too far; so I declined, and took a taxi instead. At 2.30 I reported, and gave my account to Joan Robinson[5] and Derek Bryan. It was a brief factual account; and at the end of it I confirmed that

---

1 Frank Giles (b. 1919), Foreign Editor of the *Sunday Times* 1961–77 and Editor 1981–83.

2 The address of SACU's London office.

3 Richard Thistlethwaite (1917–1985) was educated at Bootham, the Quaker boarding-school in York, before matriculation in 1935 at the Queen's College, Oxford, where he was Lady Elizabeth Hastings Scholar and obtained a first in PPE in 1938. He was awarded a Laming Travelling Fellow at Queen's in 1938. He served as a District Security Officer in Palestine during the 1940s; then as the Security Service's first liaison officer in Washington DC; was apparently posted to Singapore, 1955–59; then headed its Anti-Communist section in London or was head of operations in London. Elected to the Athenaeum in 1964, many of his letters were written on club notepaper, and T-R sent his replies to Thistlethwaite there. After retiring from MI5, Thistlethwaite was assistant registrar of the General Medical Council, 1971–72.

4 Sir Dick White (1906–1993), Director General of the Security Service (MI5), 1953–56 and of the Secret Intelligence Service (MI6), 1956–68.

5 Joan Robinson (1903–1983) studied economics at Girton College, Cambridge, where she came under the Marxist influence of Maurice Dobb. Lecturer in the economics faculty at Cambridge, 1937; elected a fellow of Newnham College, 1962; professor and fellow of Girton College, 1965; the first woman to become an honorary fellow of King's College, 1979. The Nobel economics laureates Amartya Sen and Joseph Stiglitz both encountered her in Cambridge in the mid-1960s: Sen found her 'brilliant, but vigorously intolerant'; Stiglitz, who was her pupil for one 'tumultuous' term in 1965, found that she did not brook contradiction.

I would speak, together with Mary Adams, Robert Bolt and Ernie Roberts, at the public meeting in Church House, Westminster, on 16 Nov. Joan Robinson suggested that I should emphasise the 'positive' rather than the 'negative' side of the visit: in other words, that I should flatter the Chinese.

That was 28th Oct. Three days later the *Sunday Times* published my article. It dominated the 'Week-End Review'; but when I saw it, my heart sank. A huge headline had been imposed on it, 'The Sick Mind of China'. Of course, I said to myself, they will be furious – and rightly. Such a title bore no relation to the content of my article. It was unjust and offensive. I wrote at once to Frank Giles to protest. But of course it could do no good. It was too late. There was nothing for it but to await the reactions, knowing that those reactions would be more violent than they need be thanks to a headline which I could not defend and against which my protest would be in vain.

My forebodings were correct. The reaction was violent. However, I resolved to stand firm. My resolution was fortified by discoveries which I kept making about SACU and its real character, and the real character of its guiding spirit, Derek Bryan.

The first thing that I discovered concerned the circumstances in which SACU was founded. It seems that originally there had been a China Friendship Society which was run, more or less openly, by the communist party. But when the Russians and the Chinese parted company, the pro-Russian faction packed the general meeting and voted the pro-Chinese faction out. The pro-Chinese faction there upon abandoned an anyway discredited body and set up a new cover-organisation, SACU. They also run another society, the China Policy Group, which publishes a pamphlet, *The China Broadsheet*. This pamphlet is manufactured by Bryan, in his house in Holden Road, Finchley; but since SACU was founded, the theoretical (though not the real) address of the office has been changed, lest the office of SACU be blown by its apparent identity.

For Bryan, it now appears – and on him I now have an excellent source in Valerie Pearl,[6] who herself lives in Holden Road and knows him well, having her-self (unless I am gravely mistaken) a Marxist if not a communist past – whatever he may appear to be in metropolitan London, in Finchley is a hard communist,

---

6 Valerie Pearl (1926–2016) was daughter of a Labour MP, and a doctoral student of Christopher Hill's. T-R helped her to recast her dissertation into her first book, *London and the Outbreak of the Puritan Revolution: city government and national politics, 1625–43* (1961). In the mid-1960s she was a lecturer at Somerville, but was not appointed to a fellowship because of her insistence on living, for family reasons, in Barnet rather than Oxford. She was a frequent correspondent of T-R's, co-editor of the *festschrift* presented to him in 1981, and ended her career as principal of a Cambridge college.

or at least a crypto-communist. I once said to Peter Swann,[7] of the Ashmolean, who like me is a member of the council of management of SACU, that Bryan had the shifty look of a crypto; but he thought he was only permanently worried by having to run so chaotic an organisation as SACU. Now, however, I feel certain. SACU is indeed run by him – by him and Joan Robinson is my guess – but it is not quite so chaotic as it seems: it is dedicated, not indeed to communism but to Chinese communism. For Bryan, like Needham, as it seems to me, has reached his political views through his sinophil views: both are communists, or *communisants*, because they are sinophils, not sinophils because they are communist. Ernie Roberts, of course, is the other way round.

Nor is this all. In the days after my visit to London, I studied carefully the structure of the society and I noticed certain interesting little facts. The Council of Management, on which I sit, consists largely of harmless public figures. There are three MPs, Dame Joan Vickers,[8] Jeremy Thorpe[9] and Philip Noel-Baker.[10] There are grave academic figures: Sir Gordon Sutherland, Master of Emmanuel College, who is Hon Treasurer;[11] Pulleyblank, the Professor of

---

7 Peter Swann (1921–1997) established the Department of Eastern Art within the Ashmolean Museum in 1963, and was responsible for buying major works of Chinese art before the Cultural Revolution.

8 Joan Vickers (1907–1994) was elder daughter of Winston Churchill's stockbroker. She trained as a Norland nanny, rode well to hounds, and when she wanted to go into politics sought Churchill's advice. He advised her to wear a pretty hat and to join the London County Council. She did both. After defeating Michael Foot at Plymouth, Devonport in 1955 by 100 votes, she held that marginal constituency until, after boundary changes, David Owen ousted her in 1974. She sat in the House of Lords 1975–90. A formidable figure, the only woman of her generation to speak in Commons debates on the armed forces, she owed her successes to determination rather than charm. She sported a severe blue rinse, and enjoyed being nicknamed 'La Truite au Bleu' at the Council of Europe. When she espoused the cause of prostitutes, Lord Hailsham dubbed her 'the non-batting captain'. She was one of the first women parliamentarians to visit the PRC, and chaired the non-Marxist European-China Association.

9 Jeremy Thorpe (1929–2014), President of the Oxford Union 1950, MP for North Devon 1959–79, Leader of the Liberal party 1967–76.

10 Philip Noel-Baker (1889–1982), Lord Noel-Baker 1977, was a Labour MP who held senior ministerial posts in 1945–51. Stuart Hampshire was briefly his civil service assistant after the war. Awarded the Nobel prize for peace in 1959.

11 Sir Gordon Sutherland (1907–1980) was wartime secretary of the Unexploded Bombs committee, Director of the National Physics Laboratory, 1956–64, an expert on infrared spectroscopy and Master of Emmanuel College, Cambridge, 1964–77. He had a fine collection of Chinese porcelain. His visit to the PRC in 1962, as a member of a Royal Society delegation, strengthened his admiration for the Chinese people and their culture. He discouraged Derek Bryan from approaching Charlie Chaplin and Spike Milligan to be sponsors of SACU lest it bring ridicule on the society.

Chinese at Cambridge;[12] Nicholas Kurti, reader in physics at Oxford;[13] Peter Swann, and myself; and there are others. But the Council of Management meets only once a quarter. More regular meetings are held by the General Purposes Committees, sitting under the sinister chairmanship of our old double-thinking friend Ernie Roberts. Some of the members of this committee are harmless members of the Council of Management – as, for instance, our old feather-headed friend Mary Adams. But there are some members of the G.P. committee who nestle only in that protective shade. They are Roland Berger, who visited our bedrooms on our last night in China and who, next day, I have now discovered, sent a telegram to SACU advising that the public meeting fixed for 16 Nov be cancelled, lest our accounts should do more harm than good, and three other dim creatures, Perry,[14] Ash[15] and Timberlake.[16] All these, I now find, are 'hard' communists; and Berger is the director, and

12 Edwin Pulleyblank (1922–2013) was a Canadian who spent three wartime years at Bletchley Park, where he learnt Japanese. He was appointed lecturer in classical Chinese at SOAS, 1948, and professor of Chinese Studies at Cambridge, 1953–66. He visited the PRC in 1954 as adviser to a Labour Party delegation. 'Pulleyblank is an excellent man but inarticulate, as he admits; and of course all professional sinologists are paralysed by fear of being excluded from China if they express themselves too rashly' (T-R to Kurti, 8 April 1966, Kurti papers H937).

13 Nicholas Kurti (*né* Miklós Kürti, formerly Karfunkel) (1908–1998): see Introduction, pp. 39–40.

14 Jack Perry (*né* Isidor Perisky) (1915–1996): see pp. 23–5. He was, like Deng Xiao Ping, an ardent bridge player: in the 1990s he sponsored the Lords and Commons annual bridge match, and chaired the Chinese Bridge Federation.

15 William ('Bill') Ash (1917–2014) had been educated at Highland Park High School, Dallas. In 1934, as an intern journalist, he saw the bullet-ridden corpses of Bonnie Parker and Clyde Barrow. After graduating from the University of Texas (Austin) in 1938, he became a railroad hobo, enlisted in the Royal Canadian Force in 1939, piloted RAF Spitfires in 1941–42, was shot down over France in 1942, and spent three years trying to escape German captivity. Steve McQueen's character Virgil Hilts, 'the Cooler King', in the 1963 film *The Great Escape* is reputedly based on Ash. After the war Ash studied Marxism with the Birmingham professor George Thomson, before going to Balliol in 1946 to read PPE. He worked for the BBC external services in India for four years during the 1950s, but was eased out under political suspicions. He then became a novelist and radio dramatist (remarkably he adapted *The Golden Bowl* for radio). In 1968, after the CPGB rejected his application for membership, he and Reg Birch co-founded the Communist Party of Britain (Marxist-Leninist) (CPGBML). 'Thought to be a hard-core crypto-communist operator, but I don't know enough to say whether this is true or not,' Trevor-Roper noted in 1966. Dacre 13/3, List B [May 1966].

16 Percy Timberlake (1916–2004) read PPE at Hertford College, Oxford. In wartime he was a Ministry of Information official and RAF education officer; but was perhaps debarred from postwar employment as a civil servant by his political affiliations. He joined BCPIT as Berger's assistant in 1953. In 1954 he organized the 48 Group of businesses willing to flout the trade embargo on mainland China. Seven years later the Security Service rated him 'a secret member of the Party'.

Perry and Timberlake are members, of BCPIT – the British Committee for the Promotion of International Trade: an organisation set up under communist inspiration for trade with communist countries.[17] Joan Robinson, I understand, is closely connected with it. It has been proscribed by the Labour Party and denounced in Parliament as a communist body.[18] There are some reasons to suspect that it may be the real paymaster of SACU.

After making these discoveries, I started looking more critically than before at the various papers I had received as a member of the Council of Management. I found that, in June, a 'budget' had been presented. It was an extraordinary document. For the twelve months ending in April 1966 the estimated budget was some £9000. Of this no less than £4250 was expected to come in from a 'general appeal' *urbi et orbi*,[19] which however had never been launched, and another £1500 was to come from 'advertisements'. I looked through SACU News, which incidentally is edited by Mrs Berger,[20] and found no sign of any advertisements. So £5750 out of £9000 – nearly 2/3 of the whole budget – was ascribed to fictitious sources. I looked further; and then I found an interesting remark. Mrs Robinson, introducing the Budget, was recorded in the Minutes as saying that if the result of the Appeal should fall short of the expected amount, 'certain business firms and individuals' (unnamed) had volunteered to stump up. I felt that I could name the firms (or rather the firm) and the individuals. It seemed likely that SACU was secretly financed by BCPIT.

---

17 T-R mistook the name of the British Council for the Promotion of International Trade. It was an offshoot of the communist World Peace Council, and solely interested in developing business relations with communist countries, with the exception of Yugoslavia.

18 A Labour MP, Harold Davies, who was well-travelled in south-east Asia, had asked the Foreign Secretary in 1953 whether BCPIT 'was a Communist front organization'. Anthony Eden's parliamentary reply stated: 'It is public knowledge that a number of the members of the council are (or were until recently) either members of the Communist Party or closely associated with bodies which are generally recognized to be Communist "front organizations" and are proscribed by the Labour Party. The fact that some highly respectable persons are concerned with it is a measure of its success as a "front" organization. These members in fact provide the "front"' ('Trade Organization a Communist Front', *The Times*, 19 November 1953, p. 12).

19 Latin: to the city and the world.

20 Nancy ('Nan') Whittaker (1914–1998), who was Berger's second wife, was summarily dismissed – as politically suspect – from her first job, in the Bank of England, in 1940. After working in the Ministry of Information during the war, she transferred to the peacetime Ministry of Fuel and Power. On the basis of telephone checks on her, John Cuckney reported: 'Nancy BERGER is very likely responsible for collecting the Party registration forms from civil servants' (NA KV 2/4237, serial 259z, 6 April 1951). In the 1960s, as London representative of the New China Press Agency, she attended daily Foreign Office briefings. She wrote books on nutrition, women's status and children's rights.

Soon after coming to these conclusions, I had a letter from Robert Bolt. He had seen Bryan and he now wrote to warn me of the impending party line. 'I *think*', he wrote, 'that his argument is going to be that our closely restricted tour was the consequence of your "hostility" which the Chinese somehow "sensed" – which is ridiculous, since you weren't hostile till made so by their treatment of us, and indeed aren't simply hostile now ...' I soon discovered that his forecast was quite correct. Joan Robinson, in a letter to the *Sunday Times*, made precisely this point ('it was wonderfully funny', Valerie Pearl wrote to me, 'to see the stage army moving into action in the *Sunday Times*'), and afterwards Needham made it in correspondence with me. But I am moving too fast. I must pause on the great day, 16 Nov, the day on which we were all (since Berger's telegram had failed to stop it) to make our report to the faithful in Church House, Westminster.

By that day, my view of SACU was pretty clear. I saw it as a communist 'front organisation' managed, in effect, by a triumvirate of Berger, Joan Robinson and Bryan, using the Council of Management as a façade and actually operating through the General Purposes Committee, where the infamous Ernie Roberts could be trusted, as chairman, to follow the lead of Berger, Perry, Ash, Timberlake. I suspected that the finances of the society were guaranteed by BCPIT – whether from the profits of trade or from a concealed Chinese subsidy was not yet clear. And I had heard from Nicholas Kurti that Sir Gordon Sutherland, who is a friend of his, was furious because the 'budget' had been drawn up and accepted without reference to him, the Hon. Treasurer. I therefore decided, before the public meeting, to check a few facts, and for this purpose I called, in the morning, at 24 Warren Street and put some questions to Bryan.

First, I asked about the General Appeal. This, replied Bryan, had not yet been launched. When would it be launched? I asked. He told me that a meeting was to be held with 'the Hon. Treasurer, Sir Gordon Sutherland'; but the meeting had not yet been held and clearly no appeal could be launched this year. The prospect that such an appeal would raise £4250 by April 1966 seemed to me remote. Then I asked him how it was that a telegram of congratulation had been sent to the Chinese People's Association for Foreign Cultural Contacts on National Day, 1 Oct, in the name of the Council of Management – for this had been reported in Mrs Berger's *SACU News*. He looked furtive and said that the Council of Management had voted it. I drew his attention to the Minutes which made no reference to any such proposal. (In fact it was a proposal by the General Purposes Cttee, against which Kurti had protested in writing). Then I asked to see the Constitution, of which he produced the draft (we are to vote on it at the next Council meeting). I noticed that it contained no reference to the General Purposes Cttee. So I asked whether I was right to assume that the GP Cttee was a sub-committee of the Council of Management. He agreed. Then ought not the Council, I asked, to receive minutes of his [*sic*] meetings? He agreed that it ought. Finally, I asked to see the Library. He was a little put out of this and apologised for its vestigial character. It was in fact a room stacked with Chinese government propaganda – those same anti-Russian pamphlets which I had seen in every Chinese hotel – and nothing else. After this I left to give a somewhat uninhibited talk on China at Chatham House.[21] Then I went to the Garrick Club[22] and wrote to Sir Gordon Sutherland to draw his attention to certain financial facts and speculations. At 4.0 p.m. Robert Bolt came there to tea and we planned the next move.

Bryan had asked us to meet in Church House an hour before starting-time. I had been prepared to come half an hour early and could not adjust my programme at the last minute; for I had promised to call on Princess Coocoola of Sikkim at 6.0.[23] So I had asked Bryan what was the preliminary business. 'To fix the order of speakers', he had replied. 'Oh, in that case it is easy', I had said: 'my vote is for alphabetical order – always the best and least invidious.' I had deduced that he had not liked this (it would in fact give the last word to me), but I had been firm. Now I told Bolt that I was convinced that the Administration would want Ernie Roberts to speak last. He agreed that we should insist on the alphabet, and promised to hold out until I arrived.

In due course I arrived. 'Coocoola had given me champagne and I was feeling in confident mood; but I was determined to be prudent and moderate. I found Bryan and Mrs Robinson in the committee room, together with the

---

21 T-R's talk (entitled 'China Today') was given to a general meeting at Chatham House (the Royal Institute of International Affairs). No transcript was made.

22 T-R had been elected to the Garrick in 1965, but resigned his membership after joining the Beefsteak in 1966.

23 Princess Pema Tsedeun Yapshi Pheunkhang Lacham Kusho (known as Coocoola) (1924–2008) was the daughter of the eleventh Chogyal of Sikkim. In 1941, at Lhasa, she married the governor of the Tibetan city of Gyantse. With her low, clear, musical voice and delight in good talk about the arts and politics, she was the equivalent in Lhasa to Lady Colefax in London. When travelling the bandit-ridden trade route between Tibet and Gangtok, with her small children crammed in windowed boxes on mules, she rode with a rifle across her shoulder and a revolver in her pocket.

three speakers to whom I came as a fourth, and K. W. Wedderburn,[24] who was to be our chairman. Also there was Berger, who of course had no *locus standi*; but as in Pekin, he was *auch dabei*.[25] The argument about order of speaking was still going on. Bolt was being firm for the alphabet; Mary Adams preferred the alphabet; I added my voice to theirs; and Wedderburn, as chairman, voted with the majority. But Ernie Roberts, in his soapy voice, declared that he had good (but apparently unavowable) reasons to speak last, and Joan Robinson, stating that 'the alphabet is a very artificial thing', supported him, and Berger supported her. We would not yield. Thereupon Joan Robinson tried a fast one. 'Well', she said confidently, 'it seems clear that the general view is that Mr. Roberts should speak last'. However, she did not get away with it. We declined to agree. In despair, Berger intervened *en maître*.[26] He snapped that Roberts *must* speak last. Still we, being the majority, and the parties concerned, would not yield. Meanwhile it was 7.30 and the faithful were waiting in the hall. We could not disagree for ever. Finally, the deadlock had to be resolved by casting of lots. When we went in, the order of speaking was, Mrs Adams, myself, Roberts, Bolt. This proved a very good order. I had anyway resolved to be brief and unprovocative. Ernie Roberts was corrupt and his speech was mere feeble propaganda. Bolt, in the closing speech, was excellent and said all that I would have said as well as exposing Ernie's tricks. But the real events of the evening were not the set speeches: they were the noises from the floor.

From the beginning the audience had shown its mood. Every time that my name was mentioned – and it was mentioned pretty often – there were boos and hisses, and the boos seemed to get louder, and the hisses shriller as the evening wore on. Xandra, who had rashly come to the meeting, found herself sitting in the middle of the anti-Trevor-Roper claque and almost had to join in the boos and hisses in order not to be lynched by her neighbours as a black-leg. Even the moderation of my own speech did me no good: I noticed that Joan Robinson, who sat next to me, did not even simulate a perfunctory clap when I sat down. In question-time the anti-Trevor-Roper parts became even more vocal, especially since Bolt defended me against gross misrepresentation. Finally, a crisis was precipitated by my most outspoken enemy, Joan Robinson.

---

24 Kenneth William ('Bill') Wedderburn (1927–2012), Lord Wedderburn of Charlton 1977, sat on the Council of SACU. He had been Fellow of Clare College, Cambridge 1952–64, and was Professor of Commercial Law at LSE, 1964–92. He advised the Labour Party on employment law and industrial relations. He joined T-R as a FBA, 1981.

25 German: also there.

26 French: as master.

It began at 9.55 – the chairman having stated that the meeting must be over by 10.0. Joan Robinson, having chosen her moment well, rose to her feet and read a letter from Needham the gist of which was to deplore my article and indeed me. I did not mind this. I felt that I had expressed my views in the *Sunday Times*, publicly, and he had every right to reply publicly. His language was civil. But when Joan Robinson had finished reading, a man rose in the hall and demanded to know how I contrived to remain a member of SACU after writing such an article. It seemed to me that if anyone was to answer such a question, it was I; but before I could answer, Joan Robinson was on her feet. On behalf of all those present, and all members of the society, and 650 million Chinese, she publicly apologised for 'Professor Trevor-Roper's bad manners': bad manners, I understood her to mean, in criticising the Chinese.

I was furious. I at once said to Wedderburn, aloud, that it looked as if the meeting was to end on an offensive personal note, and I requested him to suspend the closure. He at once agreed. Meanwhile pandemonium broke out in the hall. Hitherto there had been an anti-T-R group but no pro-T-R group. Now the pro-T-R group suddenly revealed itself, clamouring to be heard. I waited for the chairman to allow someone to speak but he firmly forbade all speech from the floor. I had not intended to speak – I was still clinging to the vestiges of my carefully maintained moderation. But now there seemed to be no alternative. I had demanded an extension. The extension had been granted. The chairman forbade anyone else to speak. So what could I do but fill the gap? As I rose to my feet, I savoured the delicious irony of it. Mrs Robinson had fought tooth-and-nail to prevent me from having the last word. Now, by her own action, she had forced me to have the last word. Obviously, I said to myself, I must seize the opportunity turns suddenly thrust upon me ...

At that moment I felt the fatal symptom. First the veins opened like sluices. Then a sudden refreshing flush of blood coursed through them. I felt the ebullition of Coocoola's champagne. Then came that brisk snap near the aorta; and after that I knew nothing, or perhaps I merely cared for nothing. All I could afterwards remember was the sensation of words rolling out of my month, loud, unambiguous and infuriating. What they were, I do not know. When I sat down, the whole place was in uproar. Several people came up and congratulated me. Among them were Stephen King-Hall[27] and Isaac

27 Stephen King-Hall (1893–1966), Lord King-Hall 1966, compiled the first Admiralty manual on cruiser tactics. After serving as a torpedo lieutenant on Royal Navy ships of the China squadron, 1921–23, he wrote *Western Civilisation and the Far East* (1924) and *The China of*

Deutscher[28] – an enjoyable pair. A reporter from the *Manchester Guardian* asked me if I would now resign from the society.[29] I replied: 'never resign; always wait till you're kicked out'. Meanwhile the table covered with Chinese propagandist literature was deserted. The begging-bowl received no alms. No one joined the society. And Xandra and I escaped by taxi to the Savoy Grill for a late dinner. Robert Bolt came separately to join us: we had agreed that we should not go away together, lest any suspect collusion.

For the next fortnight the repercussions rolled in. Mrs Berger denounced me in *SACU News*. In the General Purposes Committee, Ash demanded my expulsion. From the faithful in their local cells the same demand poured in. But I knew I was safe. Bryan admitted to Valerie Pearl that, for all my crimes, I would do more good than harm inside the Society – which seemed perhaps a sinister observation; and Mrs Robinson wrote me a postcard which did not indeed offer a word of apology for her onslaught, but firmly commanded me to stay. I replied with an indecent sea-side postcard, telling her that I had received so many fan-letters that I was thinking not only of staying but also of running against Ernie Roberts for the chairmanship of the General Purposes Cttee. And I wrote a longer and graver missive to Needham explaining my position and standing firmly in it.

The truth is, I can't help liking Joan Robinson. She is, or seems to me to be, a kind of romantic anarchist, a rebel against authority, perhaps against her parents' world (she is the daughter of General Sir Frederick Maurice:[30]

Today (1927). King-Hall resigned as a naval officer to become a researcher at the Royal Institute of International Affairs (1929–35). He tried to educate public opinion as a BBC broadcaster and by starting the *King-Hall* Newsletter in 1936. He was an MP, 1939–45. He predicted in 1961 that before 2000, 'the Chinese People's Republic will be the most powerful nation (militarily and industrially) in the world'. Soviet Russia, the United States, and perhaps Japan and India would ally against 'the common menace of a China whose ambitions may include control over large areas of Central Asia, South-East Asia and the Indian sub-continent' (Sir Stephen King-Hall, *Our Times 1900–1960* (London: Faber & Faber, 1961), pp. 332, 334).

28 Isaac Deutscher (1907–1967) joined the outlawed Polish communist party in 1927, but was expelled in 1932. He fled Warsaw for London in 1939. Ten years later he published a biography of Stalin, whom he praised for equipping Russia with atomic piles instead of wooden ploughs. Three acclaimed volumes on Trotsky followed (1954–63). After the Sino-Soviet split, his writings supported Moscow against Peking.

29 The *Manchester Guardian* had been renamed as the *Guardian* in 1959. Its editorial offices had moved to London in 1964.

30 Major General Sir Frederick Maurice (1871–1951) was Director of Military Operations at the War Office, 1915–18, co-founder of British Legion 1921, and Principal of the Working Men's College in London, 1922–33.

compare Michael McCreery).[31] I infinitely prefer her to Bryan: Bryan who, within a fortnight, was telling Valerie Pearl that, though an enemy of the People, as a matter of fact I was quite right, and who was denouncing, as the real enemy, his old ally Ernie Roberts not for *being* but for so obviously *seeming* to be a twister! Bryan, Valerie says, is 'a very able politician.'

In the month which followed the famous meeting, information, or indications, continued to come in to improve my knowledge, or idea, of SACU. I was involved in correspondence with Needham, with Sutherland, with Kurti. Needham took up the argument long ago adumbrated by Bryan and destroyed in advance by Bolt, *viz*: that I had been 'hostile' to the Chinese from the start. He announced that he would read my letter and his answer to the Council of Management on 13th December. I replied that my letter was personal to him and was not to be divulged. Sutherland told me that he had resigned long ago as Treasurer – in writing to Bryan on 28 June. (And yet on 16 Nov. Bryan was still pretending to me that Sutherland was Treasurer, and nothing had been said at the meeting of the Council of Management on 18 Sept!). Kurti gave me further evidence of Bryan's duplicity. Thereupon I wrote to Bryan and gave notice that, at the meeting of the Council of Management on 13 Dec., I wished to raise three subjects: our visit to China, finance and the constitution. I was determined either to expose, or to bring to order, the finances and the General Purposes Committee. In order to do this, I wrote also to Jeremy Thorpe, and when he proved an ally, I authorised him to show my letters to Dame Joan Vickers.

While thus preparing for battle, I suddenly learned that a branch of SACU was being founded in Oxford. A meeting had been held in Norham Gardens, to which I had not been invited. The next step was a lecture with slides, by a

---

31 Michael McCreery (1929–1965) was a renegade Etonian whom T-R had liked as a Christ Church undergraduate in the early 1950s. They remained in remote but friendly contact until 1962–63. McCreery, whose father was a general, worked for the CPGB from 1956. Two years later he began teaching at London's North-Western Polytechnic, where the Principal failed to get him dismissed on political grounds. In 1963 he founded the Committee to Defeat Revisionism for Communist Unity, which strove for the dictatorship of the proletariat, mass revolutionary mobilization and liberation struggles on Albanian and Maoist models. The CPGB suspected that his magazine, *Vanguard*, was funded by Berger (NA KV 2/4251, serial 797a, Lascar Top Secret, 21 May 1964). He was killed by cancer, April 1965. His brother Charles was a friend of T-R's stepson James Howard-Johnston in the 1960s.

Dutch medical couple called de Haas,[32] on Friday 3 Dec. in Nuffield College. I decided to go, in order to see what was afoot. The organisation was in the hands of Raymond Dawson,[33] university reader in Chinese, and it seemed that Bryan, by-passing the three Oxford members of the Council of Management (Kurti, Swann and myself), had got in touch with him direct. He afterwards told Valerie Pearl that Dawson was an excellent man, an ally against Trevor-Roper in Oxford.

The lecture by the *Ehepaar*[34] de Haas was pathetic. They had spent three weeks in China visiting hospitals. They were entirely uncritical and simply repeated the well-worn propaganda themes.[35] I don't think they made any converts. The audience consisted mainly of middle-aged Oxford citizens. As the lecture had been on the last Friday of term, there were practically no undergraduates, and I don't think that the silver-collection yielded much. Next day I got a letter from Dawson. He apologised for the standard of the lecture and asked if I would give the opening lecture to the Oxford branch of SACU next term, on 11 Feb. Hearing that he was seeing Bryan in London tomorrow, I hastily wrote back accepting before Bryan could warn him off. Afterwards I spoke to Dawson on the telephone. He said that Bryan was demanding 75% of all local takings for HQ in return, presumably, for HQ's services in providing lecturers like the de Haas. I urged him to yield to nothing since the Council of Management is meeting next week. He had not realised –i.e. had not been told – that Kurti, Swann and I are on the Council of Management. He told me that he had grave reservations about Bryan and was doubtful about

---

32 Jacob Hendrik ('Joep') de Haas, Professor of World Health at Leyden University, and his physician wife Hermana de Haas-Posthuma visited China in 1964, 1967 and 1971. They published their findings in 'Sociomedical Achievements in the People's Republic of China', *International Journal of Health Services*, vol. 3 (February 1973), pp. 275–94. Their other publications were on infant mortality and paediatrics.

33 Raymond ('Ray') Dawson (1923–2002) was elected an exhibitioner at Wadham College, Oxford in 1941. Invalided from wartime service as a RAF navigator, he took a Japanese language course at the School of Oriental and African Studies in 1945 before returning to Oxford in 1948 for the Honours School of Classical Chinese. He was appointed Spalding lecturer in Chinese at the University of Oxford in 1957, spent six unfulfilling months in China in 1958, and was Fellow of Wadham, 1963–90 (thereafter emeritus). Under the name of 'Setsquare' he composed crossword puzzles for the *New Statesman*.

34 German: married couple.

35 An ex-CPGB member of the Oxford branch reported: 'People like the good, dear de Haas's are no good here. The poppycock talked by people like that sounds ridiculous to the people listening, who are students of the subject' (SOAS, Peggy Garland to Derek Bryan, 26 April 1966).

SACU from the moment when he heard that Bryan – whom he had known as an undergraduate at Cambridge – was its secretary.[36] He had not liked the propagandist tone of SACU's official documents. We agreed to keep in touch.

About the same time – Sunday 5 Dec – Kurti, Swann and I met by arrangement in the Ashmolean. Kurti was outraged by the puerility of the de Haas lecture. Swann reported that he had been to a SACU week-end party to lecture on Chinese art. He had come back in the train with two girls, one French, one English, both *devôtes* of the Party, or at least the movement. But that had not stopped them from admitting to him that it was a relief, with his lecture, to get away from politics. So it seems that SACU Chinese cultural meetings are heavily political. This is confirmed by the minutes of the last meeting of the General Purposes Committee which now, for the first time, as a result of my pressure, are being circulated to the members of the Council of Management. There I read not only that Mr. Ash had moved my expulsion from the Society (a proposal which it is not within the powers of the GP Cttee even to discuss) but also that someone – Ernie Roberts presumably – urged the addition of five more Trades Union sponsors, of whom one is a known communist (Lawrence Kirwan)[37] and two others are fellow-travellers. This was agreed by the Cttee, which had been attended by the whole gaggle of fellow-travellers *plus* the ridiculous Mary Adams.[38]

But it is not only the minutes of the GP Cttee which are now being circulated. On Saturday 11th Dec I received a letter from Pulleyblank, the Professor of Chinese at Cambridge, whom I don't know at all but who is also a member of the Council of Management. He sent me, for information, a copy of a long letter which he had addressed to Bryan, being his comments

---

36 Bryan had matriculated in 1932 at Sidney Sussex College, Cambridge, where he read modern languages.

37 Lawrence Kirwan (1910–2000) joined the Labour Party in 1931 as a communist infiltrator. He was leader of a communist cell within Reuter's news agency in London at the time of the outbreak of the Korean War. After being dislodged from Reuter's, he ran the Hungarian News and Information Service in London: 'Of all the English language publications of the so-called "people's democracies" issued in London, *New Hungary*, edited by Lawrence Kirwan, is perhaps the best-produced technically and the most servile politically' (*The Newsletter*, 2 August 1958, p. 197). President of the National Union of Journalists, 1966.

38 On 7 December Maurice Bowra wrote to Isaiah Berlin: 'I have had a slightly ghoulish dinner with the Trevor-Ropers, in Oriel. I could not make out whether the main dish was goose or mutton. Poor Xandra was in a tizzy the whole time and more than usually inconsequent, while Hugh boasted of his rudeness to the Chinese while he was their guest in Peking. They would soon see through him' (Bodleian, Ms Berlin 246).

1. Hugh Trevor-Roper at the time of his election as Regius Professor of Modern History at Oxford, 1957.

2. Mary Adams at BBC television centre at Alexandra Palace, 1949.

3. Robert Bolt at the time of his sell-out play, *A Man For All Seasons*, 1960.

4. Ernie Roberts at the wheel of his car.

5. Lady Alexandra Haig (afterwards Trevor-Roper), 1939.

6. Joseph Needham, chairman of the British-China Friendship Association, which was proscribed by the Labour Party, and then of the Society for Anglo-Chinese Understanding, 1949.

7. Joan Robinson, a delegate at the Moscow Trade Conference, and a zealous supporter of Maoist economic planning and social engineering, 1959.

8. Lord Boyd-Orr, President of the communist front organization called the British Council for the Promotion of International Trade, 1942.

9. The Oxford physicist Nicholas Kurti, Trevor-Roper's ally and confidante in SACU intrigues, 1989.

10. Imperial Palace, Peking.

11. Chinese garage, Beckenham, which Ernie Roberts likened to
the Imperial Palace.

on my correspondence with Needham of which copies had evidently been 'circulated' by Bryan. Circulated to whom? I naturally asked myself – for this was the correspondence of which I had explicitly and in writing forbidden Needham to circulate my part. I had not even been informed that it was now being 'circulated'. I asked Kurti if it had been circulated to him. It had not. But afterwards Mary Adams admitted that it had been 'circulated' to her. I can only conclude that Bryan had it circulated to those members of the Council of Management who, he thought, would be brought over to his side by such documents – and would not tell me. If so, he has miscalculated. Mary Adams still natters her outdated platitudes from Bryan's pocket, but Pulleyblank has come out firmly on my side. He also asked Bryan to place his views before the Council of Management – to all of whom, no doubt, he supposed that the correspondence had been 'circulated'. This, needless to say, has not been done.

So we come to Monday 13 Dec, the day of the Council meeting. I had luncheon with Roderick MacFarquhar,[39] the editor of the *China Quarterly*, and Ivan Morris,[40] *chez* Solange in Wardour Street (it is part of a plot to bring Ivan Morris to Oxford). They told me that Raymond Dawson is very sound and confirmed my view of Bryan. I asked MacFarquhar if he would come and speak to the Oxford SACU. He said No: the Chinese govt refused him a visa to visit China, so he would not go out of his way to oblige their British agency. He spoke highly of Pulleyblank, and of his courage in coming out on my side, since he too was dependent on Chinese goodwill for a visa. I told them the true history of SACU, which diverted them. I said that, having agreed to be a sponsor, and having thereby appeared publicly as a supporter of the society and perhaps led others into it, I could not quietly slide out of it: my divorce, if it were to come, must be as public as my marriage. But before contemplating divorce, I must make a serious effort to make the marriage work; so I was fighting to keep the society to its avowed purpose. 'Do you think you will succeed?' they asked, incredulously. I had to admit that I did not: how could a miscellany of distant amateurs, busy in their own field, meeting only once a

39 Roderick MacFarquhar (1930–2019) read PPE at Oxford, edited *The China Quarterly* 1959–68, was non-resident Fellow of St Antony's College, Oxford 1965–68, Labour MP 1974–79, Director of the Fairbank Center for Chinese Studies at Harvard University 1986–92. His many works include *The Hundred Flowers Campaign and the Chinese Intellectuals* (1960) and *China under Mao: politics takes command* (1963).

40 Ivan Morris (1925–1976) gained his BA at Harvard, and his doctorate from SOAS. He was an interpreter sent to Hiroshima after the nuclear bombing, and held faculty posts at Columbia University 1960–73. T-R's plot was apparently successful, for Morris was elected as a fellow of St Antony's College 1966.

quarter, hope to control an organised, devout party? However, I said, I would try; and then, if I failed, I would go out carrying with me as many of the non-communist sponsors as I could. Like Samson, I would bring the pillars of the temple down with me.

The meeting of the Council of Management was at 5.30, in the House of Commons. Sutherland was not there, but Pulleyblank unexpectedly was. Once again, I was determined to be moderate. I wrote out the words 'Moderation! Moderation! Prudence! Prudence!' on a piece of paper and kept in front of me as a standing guide to speech. I began, when the minutes had been read, by questioning the reference to Sutherland which implied that he was Hon Treasurer. Bryan wriggled hard, but I obliged him to admit enough facts to damage him in the eyes of all. Then we settled down to the draft constitution and Kurti pointed out that there was no reference to the General Purposes Committee. We wrote it into the constitution as a sub-committee of the Council with additional members, to be nominated by the council. The administration wanted them to the co-opted, but we scotched that. We also fixed their tenure at one year (subject to reappointment). This was a good beginning. Then we turned to finance. We appointed Horsley,[41] a Hull business-man, and Kurti as joint treasurers. We blocked the issue of the appeal on the grounds that we had not been admitted as a charity and that it was imprudent to launch an appeal to the public when our own finances were so questionable that our Hon. Treasurer had resigned. We then went into the actual finances – very different from the 'budget' of June. The balance sheet showed from £2800 I think (I am writing all this from memory) from 'donations'. It was explained to us that some donations from business firms were necessarily anonymous owing to the danger of black-listing. We said that anonymity might be admissible in public but that every member of the Council of Management must be in a position to know the source of any donation above £20. Thereupon Ernie Roberts lifted his plaintive, sanctimonious, hypocritical voice. 'I'm a democrat', he whined, 'I don't like privilege. If 19 members of the Council of Management are to have a right to know, I want every member of the society to have the same

---

41 Alec Horsley (1902–1993) got a third-class degree in PPE at Worcester College, Oxford (1924), of which he became an honorary fellow in 1981. After a spell with the Colonial Service in Nigeria, he joined (in 1932) his father's Hull-based company, which imported Dutch condensed milk for wholesale. He expanded this into a conglomerate known successively as Northern Dairy and as Northern Foods. As a Quaker, he joined CND and the Committee of 100 on their formation; supported prison reform; and was a benefactor of the Department of Peace Studies at Bradford University. Thistlethwaite thought him 'politically naïve'.

right: anything else is privilege, undemocratic, undemocratic …' Of course the crook really meant that he wanted equality of ignorance, not equality of knowledge: the 19 members of the Council were to be kept as ignorant as the society; only the administration was to know the true source of our funds. But we swatted him down, as we also swatted down the proposal that the limit for secret donations be raised to £100.

Altogether it was a good day's work. Provided we can work it, we now have a constitution which does not allow the obvious tricks. But I hardly hope that 'we' can work it: I fear it will be worked by 'them': the constant, central devotees of the 'movement'. The meeting lasted 2½ hours. At 8 o'clock Pulleyblank had to rush to Liverpool Street for a train. I was sorry: I would like to have talked to him. Instead I went and dined at the Beefsteak, returned late to Oxford, and next day set off to Chiefswood where I am writing this account.

Incidentally, about three weeks ago, I received a letter from a Mrs Collier in Edinburgh (her husband is a well-known fellow-traveller) asking me to be a sponsor of the China-Scotland society which aims, it seems, to tell the Chinese about Scotland.[42] I enjoyed the thought of anyone trying to interest those smug, self-contained oriental bigots in Lallans poetry, bogus tartans and the battle of Bannockburn. I also enjoyed the evidence of Scottish backwardness. Just at the time when the *devôts* of SACU were clamouring for my expulsion, here and their Scottish equivalents asking for my patronage. I replied prudently saying that I would be glad to sponsor their society if possible, but that as they would not expect me to sponsor it without first knowing what I was sponsoring, I would like to know about (a) its constitution, (b) its finances. Since then I have had no further communication from Mrs Collier.

I forgot to mention that, during the Council meeting, Mary Adams, Ernie Roberts and I had to make short statements about the visit to China. My statement that our movements were closely controlled brought Ernie to his feet. 'Not at all, not at all!' he cried in his toadying, querulous voice. We were perfectly free. Why, 'we were allowed to go to lunch with the British *chargé d'affaires* …' I told him, rather sharply I fear, that I did not need such 'allowance'. I fear that Bryan did not enjoy this exchange. His view is that Ernie lets the side down by too openly betraying his fellow-travellers.

---

42 Elsie Collier was the first secretary of the Scotland–China Association, which was founded in 1966. She resigned when a few years later she and her husband Johnny (d. 1998) went as teachers to Guangzhou. They were co-authors of *China's Socialist Revolution* (1974). Like SACU, SCA members opposed the CPGB's support of Moscow against Peking after the Sino-Russian fissure.

PART THREE

HISTORY OF A
FRONT-ORGANISATION, 1966
The Suppressed *Encounter* Article

No doubt I should never have joined SACU. Even in the egg the chick should have been obvious. In retrospect, the whole history is something of a farce. It is a tale, as Oliver Cromwell once observed, when he too had been deceived by virtuous professions and unctuous Welsh saints, 'of my own simplicity and folly'.[1] But perhaps it is also a moral, a cautionary tale. So why should I not tell it? It is also, I suspect, a classic tale: a standard history of a Front-Organisation.

Of course I always knew that there was a risk. Any society which aims at 'Anglo-Chinese understanding' is bound, in the nature of things, to contain many members whose loyalty is to a political system rather than to 'under-standing'. And of course I knew that Dr Needham, the Chairman and Founder of the Society, who first solicited my support, is himself ... well, I said to myself, politically somewhat naïve. I was prepared, at that time, to be charitable: to suppose that it was mere *naïveté* that had caused him to expose himself so incautiously during the Korean War. But in spite of this, the risk, it seemed, was worth taking. Dr Needham is a great scholar: I venerate his work. The Fellows of a Cambridge College have since elected him as their head. My own relations with him had previously been good. Indeed, I had been fortunate enough, a few years ago, to be of some service to him. So, on

---

1 Cromwell described as 'a story of my own weakness and folly' the summoning in 1653 of the assembly of eager Puritans derisively known as Barebones' Parliament, in which Welsh zealots were conspicuous.

the whole, I decided to take the risk. Not only had Dr Needham, in his letter of invitation, promised that SACU was a 'new' society, dedicated solely to the supply of 'accurate information' about China, undistorted by the 'misconceptions' and 'misrepresentations' of politics. Human vanity, complacency over his previous indebtedness to me, confidence that we belonged to the same academic fraternity combined to sway me. 'This time', I said to myself, 'as Neville Chamberlain said of Munich, 'he has promised to *me*'.[2]

So I accepted Dr Needham's invitation and agreed to be a 'sponsor' of his society. In sponsoring it, my own mind at least was clear. I was sponsoring what Dr Needham had so exactly defined to me: a new society devoted to objective understanding of modern China. And by 'understanding' I meant, of course, understanding with the mind, the sympathetic but independent critical mind. Surely, I said to myself, this is a worthy purpose: to cross the frontiers of ideology, to accept the difference of social systems, to recognise that each system, theirs and ours, is legitimate within its own context, to admit objective (even objectionable) facts on both sides, but to resist those who, on account of those facts, misled by detachable circumstances or ideological prejudice, would repudiate understanding altogether, sacrificing it either to bigoted opposition or slavish adulation. This was my interpretation of 'understanding', and I think it is that of many honest persons who have agreed to sponsor or join the Society.

To Dr Needham, however, as I afterwards learned, the word 'understanding' evidently has a somewhat different meaning: a meaning which, unfortunately, he has never made quite so clear. There were other things also which he did not make clear when inviting my support. With a stringent economy of language, he omitted to mention that the Society was 'new' only in a somewhat refined sense of the word: that it was in fact the continuation, under another name, of the old British-China Friendship Society of which he had also been Chairman. As long as the Communist Party of Great Britain was united, this old society had been happily united under his control: but when rifts had opened between China and Russia, that society had been riven too and Dr Needham and his party had found themselves outvoted by the 'Russian revisionists'. That, I afterwards discovered, was the real origin of Dr Needham's 'new' society. No

---

2 'Of course, I knew from the start that I must walk warily. I knew my Needham. But I am afraid I did think, vainly, like Chamberlain at Munich, that "this time he has promised to *me*." For not only had I good personal relations with Needham, but I had, a few years ago, raised no less than a thousand pounds for him in order to sustain *Science and Civilisation in China*. So I thought he would hardly try openly to cheat me, and that I could rely on his assurances' (T-R to Geoffrey Hudson, 31 May 1966).

doubt Dr Needham thought that a new name and a new official address made it new, and that this old history was irrelevant. All the same, I wish that I had been allowed to decide its relevance or irrelevance for myself.

Thus I found myself a sponsor of the Society. So far, I was no more than a sponsor. But can one stop at being a sponsor? Sponsorship is a public act, and although many of my fellow-sponsors seem to take a different view, I interpret it as entailing continuous responsibility. I cannot understand the happy-go-lucky attitude of those public men who give away their names effortlessly, permanently and unconditionally. I am not, by nature, what the Americans call 'a joiner'. I am reluctant to sign corporate letters. I like to define my own views and take personal responsibility for them. Consequently, having given my name, I was determined to watch the Society, and I was glad when Dr Needham gave me an opportunity of doing so at close quarters by inviting me to serve on its Council of Management, or governing body. I accepted this further connexion with the Society in the summer of 1965. Soon I discovered that I was to stop not even there. I was to go further.

For in September 1965, when I had just returned to my home in Scotland from a congress of historians in Vienna, the telephone rang and the Secretary of SACU, Mr Derek Bryan, asked me whether I would go, in four days' time, to China. The invitation was rather sudden, – it was due to a sudden cancellation. The time was not very convenient for me. Still, it was an opportunity. What were the conditions? I asked. There were none, he assured me, none at all. I would go as a sponsor, with three other sponsors; but in Peking we would all be separated and taken separately to pursue our separate interests. We would be shown whatever and whoever we wished to see.[3] The time would certainly not be wasted. The visa? That would present no difficulty. It would be arranged within twenty-four hours. Such speed seemed to me remarkable and required similar speed from me. I took twenty-four hours too, secured confirmation of the various promises, and then decided to go.

---

3 Bryan told T-R that he would meet two veteran Marxist historians, Hou Wai-lu and Chien Po-tsan [Jian Bozan] (1898–1968). Chien had studied at the University of California in the 1920s. He was chairman of the department of history at Peking University from 1954, and the university's deputy president from 1962. While accepting that historians must interpret their material according to Marxist-Leninist methodology, he criticized the dogmatic categorizations of Marxist historiography. He might have interested T-R, even if their exchanges were sanitized by official translators; but they were kept from meeting, despite Bryan's promise. During the Great Proletarian Cultural Revolution, Chien was so venomously persecuted that he and his wife killed themselves.

Two days later, I was in London and the Secretary took me to call on the Chinese *chargé d'affaires* in London, for tea and a little propaganda before starting on the long journey. On the way back, I asked the Secretary who was the British *chargé d'affaires* in Peking. He replied that he did not know, which struck me as odd, and then changed the subject. 'You will be received on a very high level', he assured me. 'You will probably meet Chou En-lai'. I got the impression that the British Legation in Peking was not popular in SACU.[4]

At London Airport the four 'delegates' assembled. First of all, there was the Vice-Chairman of the Society, an elderly but vigorous lady who, it soon transpired, knew everybody in public life by their Christian names: as well she might, for it seemed that she was not only Vice-Chairman of SACU but Chairman or Vice-Chairman of fifty-seven other committees, councils, authorities: the Independent Television Authority, the Council of Industrial Design, the Consumer's Association, the Patients' Association, the Telephone-users' Association, the Lavatory-users' Association, the Joiners' Association[5] ... Her views were advanced (or had been in 1920) and her energy commanded respect: she had just been to Morocco to advise the Queen of Morocco on female education[6] and was fitting in her visit to China between lecturing in London on contraception and in Prague (extempore) on industrial design. Naturally, with all these interests, she occasionally became confused and some-times seemed to mistake her audience. Her eloquent little discourse on the 'Yellow Peril' and her informal chat on Mongol babies, for instance, had no doubt gone down very well with the Kensington Telephone-users. They would be less well received when she gave them (extempore) to the Chinese People's Association for Cultural Relations.

----

4 Members of the British legation, like the rest of the diplomatic corps in Peking, were for-bidden to venture more than 30 kilometres beyond the city without a special permit. Reciprocal restrictions were imposed on the Chinese Minister and his staff in London. This was a less onerous confinement, as Chinese diplomatists seemed 'indifferent to the British scene outside the Legation in Portland Place, apart from regular Sunday visits to Margate to sit on the sands in summer' (Gelder, *Memories for a Chinese Grand-daughter*, p. 210).

5 Adams was chairman of the Telephone Users Association, deputy chairman of the Consumers' Association, and an activist in the National Council for the Unmarried Mother and her Child, the Women's Group on Public Welfare and (as the author of a book on heredity) the Galton Foundation.

6 Adams had probably met Princess Lalla Aicha (1931–2011), president of the Union Nationale des Femmes Marocaines, sister of the ruling King Hassan II of Morocco, and her brother's ambassador in London, 1965–69.

Then there was the Trades Unionist, a man of remarkable dialectical ingenuity (provided he was assured of the last word). He represented the A.E.U., but I think it was some time since he had touched an engine. Although conscious of his fellowship with the oppressed workers of the world, and always ready to emphasise the modesty of his cash income and the narrow capacity of his 'worker's stomach', I am glad to say that his material hardships now seemed over: he would tell us, with natural pride, of his expensive cameras, his Lancia car (bought from a declining peer), and other benefits conferred by a grateful Union. He was also by far the best-dressed of our party. I particularly admired his costly suits and tasteful ties, his natty suitings (especially his elegant hacking-suit with vent and sloping pockets). He too was a great traveller, at least in Eastern Europe, on fraternal visits. Thanks to these visits, he had risen above vulgar prejudice: he was, he once told us, 'a citizen of the world', and like the Apostle he had an enviable gift of being all things to all men, congratulating the Chinese on their liberalism in Tibet and explaining that the Berlin Wall had been built to prevent the otherwise uncontrollable influx of hungry west-Berliners into the *Schlaraffenland*[7] of the East Zone.

Finally, there was the dramatist. He was also, like me, a substitute. Suffice it here to say that in those three ghastly weeks in China his company saved my sanity. But for it, I often reflect, I would doubtless have ended in a Peking lunatic asylum, being exhibited to the Vice-Chairman and the Trades Unionist to show the excellence of the People's lunatic asylums; and they would have believed it.

These formed the rest of the party of Sponsors. But others had kindly accompanied us to the airport, to see us off. There was the Secretary, Mr Bryan, a former diplomatist whose skill in the diplomatic art of polite evasion I was afterwards to have many opportunities of admiring. No man more skilful at skating round a difficult point, sliding over a difference, disappearing in clouds of courteous ambiguity and leaving his hearer momentarily satisfied, ultimately none the wiser. With him was another character whose position was not explained to me. He was not a Sponsor, or a member of the Council, or an official. He was evidently a businessman, who knew China well. He was officious, helpful, suave. His name was Roland Berger.

'I think', said the Secretary, as we waited for our plane, 'that you would find it useful to elect a "leader" of the delegation. Of course it is a pure formality ...' Obediently we elected the Vice-Chairman. 'And I think', he added, as a

---

7 German: the land of Cockaigne.

photographer appeared, 'that you had better not exhibit the title of that newspaper'. Obediently, the Trades Unionist hid his copy of *The Daily Worker*.[8] Then the formalities were over, and we were off, via Copenhagen and Moscow, to Peking.

In Copenhagen, as we waited, I was suddenly called to the telephone. It was the editor of an English Sunday newspaper, who had heard that I was going to China. Would I write something on my return? he asked. I was cautious. I was a guest, I explained: perhaps civility would inhibit me from public expression. Perhaps I would have nothing to say. So I would promise nothing, at least as yet. Ten days later, after due deliberation, I would change my mind.

I am writing about SACU, not about China, and therefore I shall not dwell upon our experiences in China. Indeed, even if it were relevant, there is no room here: my China diary – necessarily reserved for posthumous publication – fills 150 quarto pages. But some things I must say, for it was in China that my eyes were opened – not about China itself, although I contrived (I think) to see a good deal even through those prison-bars, and to hear something even through the twittered banalities of remorselessly circumscribed conversation, but about SACU.

How shall I ever forget the horror of those three weeks? From the moment of our arrival, when we were greeted with a set propaganda speech by a delegation from the People's Association for Foreign Cultural Contacts, to the moment when, with a great sigh of relief, the dramatist and I waved goodbye to the same delegation from the window of the airliner that was to take us to Moscow, the four of us were prisoners. Prisoners of each other – for all the promises made in England were quickly forgotten; prisoners of our 'guides' and their interpreters, whose conversation never rose above the iterated conformity of an infant Sunday school.

It was a prison-routine too: we were never told in advance what was to happen to us. Only at night, when we were released in our hotel, were we told when to parade next morning. Only at that parade were we told how we were to spend our day. And how we spent it! Passed off from parrot-cage to parrot-cage, hearing the same endless tabloid monologue; cut off, as it seemed, for ever from the world of dialogue and sense; kept waiting whole mornings, or whole evenings, in slow filling rooms, to hear the same gramophone-record played by a larger or louder human gramophone, or to be photographed in the presence of a slab-faced Vice-chairman … *Horresco referens*.[9] However, there

---

8 The *Daily Worker* was founded by the CPGB in 1930, and renamed *Morning Star* in 1966.
9 Latin: I shudder to relate.

were occasional escapes. I must admit that, once I had learned the system, I contrived to play truant a good deal. To that truancy I owe whatever of pleasure and information I gained during three weeks in China.

The very first night, during dinner, we had a warning dose. The war between India and Pakistan was in progress. 'On this subject', said our gaoler-guide, after a long preliminary expectoration, 'I wish to say a few words'; and he said them, slowly and at great length: for he had an impediment in his speech. They were deferentially and literally translated. There were two moral concepts in the world, said our gaoler as he tossed the half-chewed *detritus* of his dinner on the floor around him: Right and Wrong. Pakistan was right, India was wrong. China always supported what was right. *Ergo* ... At that time we had not yet realised our position and some of us even ventured to comment. We soon learned that commentary was not expected. It was impertinent. It was also useless. We never repeated our error.

For the next three weeks that phrase, 'On this subject I wish to say a few words', would strike a chill to our hearts. Together with the expectoration, it was the invariable sign that we must be silent and listen to a monologue from our gaoler. And what a gaoler! 'Cement-Head' we familiarly called him: it had taken 4000 years of docility in the paddy-fields to produce that abject, earth-bound, inarticulate obstinacy. But there was no escape from it, no alternative contact, no possibility of emancipation.

For of course we had not been fetched to China to 'understand'. Our Chinese hosts – it was clear – did not for a minute suppose that we might have any independence of mind. We had been fetched, not to examine or discuss, but to offer fraternal greetings on a political anniversary. On 1st October the new Son of Heaven, 'Chairman Mao', was to receive the acclamation of the whole Celestial Kingdom and the tribute of those Outer Barbarians who submitted to his rule. To swell the tribute and show the extent of the rule, we too had been fetched, and while paying our respects might enjoy, at a proper level, the imperial hospitality. We were like a party of devout Irish peasants for whom the local nuncio had very decently arranged a jaunt to Rome on the occasion of some Feast of the Church. On arrival, a very low-grade capuchin had been deputed to show us a few churches, relics, processions and to exaggerate, for our benefit, a few puerile miracles. We might even, from a great distance, see the Holy Father receiving the homage of the Faithful. But of course we were not to argue, or expect to meet anyone above the rank of a sub-prior, or run loose in the Holy City. We must remember our place. Viewed from Peking, England is remote and small; the communist party of England is insignificant even there; its pro-Chinese fraction is a minority even of it; and we, its delegates, must not give ourselves airs.

I must admit that some of my colleagues were more tolerant of our fate than I was. The Vice-President seemed not to mind in what direction she was being carried, provided she was in the swim, or at least afloat; and she was happily endowed with a flow of light conversation which, being equally useful as a background *continuo* on any of her 57 committees, did not need adjustment even for China. The Trades Unionist basked in his sense of cosmopolitan identity with the Toiling Masses, and from the sloping pockets of his hacking-jacket extracted A.E.U. badges for all comers.[10] But the Dramatist and I found the pressure, in the end, quite intolerable, and after three weeks we left our colleagues in Sian and took the train to Peking to return to England.

Arriving back in Peking, close on midnight, we were met by the usual group of officials. But with them, this time, was a familiar face from England. It was the assiduous Mr Roland Berger, who had so kindly seen us off from London and was now, with equal kindness, eager to set us off from Peking. He escorted us back to our hotel, insisted on accompanying us to our bedrooms, questioned us about our experiences. Since we were due to rise at 5.0 a.m.to catch our plane, we would have preferred to sleep, but we answered his questions. We admitted that, in some ways, our experiences had been deceptive. He seemed most concerned. This was not at all typical, he assured us; and he was profuse in bewildered sympathy. I afterwards learned that, next day, he had sent a telegram to Headquarters advising that the public meeting at which we were to describe these experiences, and which had been arranged by the Council of SACU, should be cancelled. It surprised me, at first, that a mere private member of SACU should think that the Secretary, on his advice, should overrule a decision of the Governing Body of the Society. But I soon got used to such surprises.

By the time when I left China my mind was made up on two matters. First, I had decided to write, and to write freely, on my experiences. No feelings as a guest now inhibited me. Hosts, I said to myself, have duties as well as guests. If a host organisation, prompted by considerations of its own interests, invites busy people to give up a month of their time and to travel thousands of miles,

---

10 'I know old double-think Ernie well, having had three weeks of him in China,' T-R wrote to Kurti, 25 December 1965. 'I regard him as a sinister, crooked, narrow-minded, sanctimonious, hypocritical petty politician. He has no interest in China at all: only in harnessing all communist and fellow-travelling votes in the AEU & in the Trade Unions to his own little bandwagon' (Kurti papers H936).

that organisation incurs obligations which are not met by merely paying the expenses of such dislocation. Therefore I would write about China, objectively I hoped, but without artificial restraint. Secondly, I had decided to look more closely into the organisation that sent me to China.

For after all, if the Chinese has treated us as an uncritical delegation of half-baked tributaries, that was not to be charged to them. They are a highly intelligent people and other visitors have had other experiences. I am not disposed to judge China by my personal contact with Cement-Head but by my wider reading, and by the intelligent conversation which I discovered, and discover, outside the mental prison-house of the People's Association and SACU. Our treatment clearly resulted from the account of us, and of our organisation, that the Chinese received from the central office of SACU: for it was that central office which had made all the arrangements. Clearly, if the Chinese had misunderstood our position and purpose, SACU could be accused of misleading them. Or perhaps it was not the Chinese whom SACU had misled. Perhaps it was we. In any case it seemed that SACU spoke with two voices. While one voice was assuring us that it was a 'new' society seeking 'accurate information' on China, another voice was assuring the Chinese government that it was a docile instrument of official Chinese propaganda.

I duly wrote my article, which appeared in the *Sunday Times* of 31 October 1965. Unfortunately an improper and indeed offensive headline was put upon it.[11] This was a great shock to me and I protested at once, in writing. I also informed SACU of my protests. Apart from that, I believe that the article was fair. A fellow member of the Council of SACU, and a distinguished orientalist, described it in writing as 'an important contribution to the cause of Anglo-Chinese understanding'. However, I soon realised that, whatever its title, the masters of SACU would anyway have been enraged by it. It is enough to glance

---

11 Roberts tried to make quick amends for the *Sunday Times* article 'The Sick Mind of China'. On 8 November he wrote to the General Secretary of the Chinese People's Association for Cultural Relations with Foreign Countries: 'The opportunity to see for myself the very great problems that you inherited from past destruction by imperial powers, by the centuries of neglect from your own feudal lords and capitalists and other reactionary elements in your country prior to 1949 was greatly appreciated. There is ample evidence of the better, more secure and happier life of the people of China. They are now both well-fed and well-clothed. The problem of education, housing, health and cultural development is being tackled by your Government in a most energetic and successful way.' Countering T-R's complaints, he declared: 'every opportunity was given to me to visit any place that I was interested in. Information I asked for was made readily available by the guides and interpreters that you so kindly arranged for me to have' (Roberts papers; cf. Roberts, *Strike Back*, p. 180).

at the monthly periodical which they began to issue at this time. This periodical is called *SACU News*; it is characterised by abject mindless conformity, and is edited by Mrs. Roland Berger. Several correspondents, having read my article, warned me of my impending fate. 'You have understood China only too well', one of them wrote: 'they will SACU'.

The first sign of such reaction occurred at the public meeting which Mr Berger had not succeeded in cancelling. This took place at Church House, Westminster, on 16 November 1965. When I arrived, fortified for the ordeal with half-a-bottle of champagne, I found my three fellow-travellers in a committee-room together with Professor Joan Robinson, the Deputy Chairman of the Society, Professor Wedderburn as chairman of the meeting, and the Secretary. Also, in an indefinable capacity, there was the ubiquitous Mr Roland Berger. The subject under discussion was the order of speaking. Most of those concerned were in favour of alphabetical order (which incidentally would have put me last), but the Trades Unionist declared that he had something to say which, by its very nature, must come last. However, as he could not explain this necessity, he made no converts. Only Mrs Robinson supported him: 'the alphabet', she declared magisterially, 'is a very artificial thing', thus implying that God or Nature had obviously intended the Trades Unionist to have the last word. My arrival gave one more vote to the majority, which was overwhelming. Seeing her cause sinking, Mrs Robinson tried the effect of surprise attack: her father had not been Director of Military Operations in World War I for nothing. 'Well, we can't go on arguing', she said (for already the hall had filled up and the audience was waiting) 'I see that the general sense of the meeting is that our Trades Union member should speak last'. I could not but admire the boldness of her attempt; but she did not quite get away with it. The voice of dissent rose again. Then, suddenly, the hitherto silent Mr Berger spoke up. But it was not now the suave Mr Berger of London Airport and Peking railway station. The old insinuating voice had changed. The persuasive, emollient oil had dried up. The mask of affability had fallen. His eyes flashed and he spoke *en maître*. 'Mr Roberts must speak last!' he rapped. At that moment I began to realise where real power in the Society lay.

The Trades Unionist did not speak last. In the end, the deadlock had to be solved by the casting of lots. The lot fell on the Dramatist. Then we filed, somewhat exhausted by this preliminary debate, into the hall.

It was a strenuous meeting. Every time my name was mentioned – and it seemed to mentioned deliberately for this purpose – boos and hisses rose from the Hall. My wife, by an unfortunate chance, had placed herself in the middle of the Opposition and found herself painfully exposed. Safe on the daïs, I was determined to be very uncontroversial. I placed before myself a warning card inscribed 'Prudence! Prudence! Moderation! Moderation!' I spoke briefly and, I believe, very moderately. During question-time the fatal name of Trevor-Roper continued to recur. So did the unflattering accompaniment. Finally, two minutes before closing-time, a crisis was precipitated. Someone delivered a challenge to me from the floor. I was meditating whether to accept it when the Directrix of Operations rose purposively to her feet and in the name of the whole society apologised to all China for 'Mr Trevor-Roper's bad manners'.[12]

At that moment hubbub broke loose in the hall. For the first time in the evening, I found that I had supporters. At the same time I felt the fatal symptom. The strain of moderation had been too great. There was a sudden, curious snap in the aorta, an outward rush of blood, a failing of the sight, a delicious flushing sensation of champagne circulating in the veins. I found myself on my feet. I felt the taste of words rolling out of my mouth. What words they were I do not know, but I doubt if they erred on the side of moderation. I think I told them the terms on which I would continue to sponsor the Society. Then I escaped from the noise and tumult. Only fragmentary memories survive in my mind. Two people came up to support me. They were Lord King-Hall and Mr Isaac Deutscher. I took this as a good omen, a sign of my own objectivity.[13] A newspaper correspondent asked if I would resign. 'Never resign: always wait till you're kicked out!' I replied summarily, quoting someone, I forget who – Disraeli perhaps, or Salisbury. Then I left.

In the Savoy Grill, dining late that night with the Dramatist, we considered the future. He decided to have nothing further to do with the Society. Its character was clear, only too clear, and he was bored with it, bored stiff. After the horrors of that Chinese visit, surely one had drunk the cup of Tedium to its dregs: why should one go on? Perhaps he was right. But my fundamental puritanism rebelled against this easy escape. Had we not accepted a public position as sponsors? Perhaps members had been drawn to the Society by our

---

12 One of the questioners who spoke against 'The Sick Mind of China' was Jack Perry's son Graham. T-R's myopia probably prevented him from recognizing the Cambridge undergraduate whom he had recently met and liked in Peking. Graham Perry no longer remembers the substance of his remarks: conceivably he delivered the challenge that brought Joan Robinson into action.

13 'I was pleased at the end when two men came up and congratulated me. One was the rogue Communist Isaac Deutscher, the other the rogue Conservative Commander Stephen King-Hall. Swamped by the orthodox, I like to be in the company of rogues' (T-R, 'Myth of Chinese Utopia', *Independent*, 3 June 1989).

patronage of it. Could we now, having been to China as its representatives, slide quietly out? For him it was easy, and fair: he was not on the Council: there was nothing he could do. But I was on the Council. I decided that as long as I held a position of responsibility I would work to keep the Society to its proper course. Only if I should be plainly defeated would I throw in my hand and then, as I legally must, disown the Society as publicly as I had owned it.

Two days later I wrote a grave letter to Dr Needham. I explained my position. I explained the terms on which I had agreed to sponsor, and would still sponsor, his society. But I also told him my reservation, and I suggested – perhaps too charitably – that I had some fears that 'both your and my good faith may have been abused'. Dr Needham's reply was somewhat testy. 'I am glad', he wrote, 'that you intend to remain a member of SACU; I only hope that this will not lead other people to leave it ... I am satisfied that the original purpose of the movement has been well served. Nobody's good faith has been abused in any way'.

So what next? I asked myself; and I decided that my first duty was to examine closely the body of which I was a member, a governor, and a patron. How was it financed? Where was the centre of power, of decision, of policy? While looking into these matters, I would be constant in my duties and seek to forward the original aims of the Society.

First, I looked at the finances. Five months ago, a 'budget' had been issued. I had not, at that time, scrutinised it. Now I did. I found it a very strange document. In the first year, I noted, a very large income was expected from sources which, as far as I could see, could not conceivably yield a penny within that period. How could a 'Special Appeal' yield £4250 by 30 April 1966 when even now, in November 1965, no proposal for such an appeal had yet come before the Council? How could 'advertising in journal' yield £1500 when there were no advertisements whatever in the journal and no proposals to include them? And what was the meaning of £400 'anticipated profit on October 3rd [*sic*; October 1st] China National Day Celebration' when in fact October 3rd [*sic*] had now passed and there had been no such celebration in England? Perplexed by these entries, I wrote for enlightenment to the Hon. Treasurer elected by the Council, Sir Gordon Sutherland. Sir Gordon replied that he was no longer Treasurer. Immediately after seeing 'that ridiculous budget', which had been drawn up without reference to him, he had sent in his resignation. That had been on 29th June, five months ago ...

I looked at the Council papers. The Council had met since 29th June – in September. But the resignation of the Treasurer had not been reported. The

Council was to meet again soon, on 13th December; but the agenda, when it appeared, contained no reference to the vacancy of the Treasurership. In documents and in conversation the Secretary allowed us all to assume that Sir Gordon was still Treasurer. Meanwhile, who was in fact handling the finances: the mythical Appeal, the mythical advertisements, the mythical profits from National Day? It all seemed very odd, and I decided, at the next Council meeting, to raise the matter.

Meanwhile, what of the real centre of power? More and more, as I looked into the matter, I found that the Council of Management was used, if at all, as a mere rubber-stamp for decisions taken elsewhere and carried out by committees which seemed to have formed themselves in the dark and whose membership and proceedings were not communicated to the Council. The most important of these committees was the General Purposes Committee. One day I tackled the Secretary on the subject. Was not the General Purposes Committee subject to the Council? He agreed that it was. Then should not the minutes of its meetings be sent to the Council? He agreed that, constitution-ally, they should. The minutes were then produced and one of the first thing I noticed was that the Committee had discussed a proposal for my expulsion from the Society. Constitutionally, the committee had no right even to dis-cuss such a matter and it should, of course, have been ruled out of order by the chairman. The Chairman was my old travelling-companion, the Trades Unionist. The proposal was made by Mr Ash, the American author of *Marxism and Moral Concepts*.[14]

This experience caused me to look a little closer into the structure of the Society. First, of course, there was the Council. Its members were largely public figures. The Council, naturally, overlapped with the General Purposes Committee; but I noticed that it was mainly the leftward end of the Council which extended into the Committee. Mrs Robinson was there; so was the Trades Unionist; and so, incidentally, was the Vice-President; but then she could never be kept off any committee. But the most interesting members of the General Purposes Committee, I soon found, were those who sat in its shadows, outside the sunlit Council. It was in this darkened penumbra that the ubiquitous Mr Berger had his seat. Beside him there were Mrs Berger, Mr Ash (who had proposed my expulsion), Mr Perry, and the Society's accountant

---

14 Ash wrote that he learnt the theoretical application of Marxism to morality from George Thomson, and the practical application of Marxist morality to working-class conditions from Reg Birch.

Mr Tallon, who incidentally was married to Mr Perry's daughter.[15] Mrs Tallon herself also worked in SACU Headquarters.

The more I examined the working of SACU, the clearer it became to me that the centre of power lay not in the Council but in the General Purposes Committee, and that the real managers of SACU – those who secretly organised the finances and maintained the link with the Chinese government – were in the 'inner ring' of the General Purposes Committee: Mr Berger and his friends. Between the well-advertised public figures who sat on the Council but not on the Committee, and the well-concealed operators who sat on the Committee but not on the Council, there was little, if any, contact. The right hand did not know what the left hand was doing.

I decided that it was my business, as a governor, to know what I was governing, and as a sponsor to know what I was sponsoring. I therefore made discreet enquiries; and what I learned soon convinced me that the structural faults of SACU did not arise merely from the natural difficulties of an amateur organisation in its first year. I also observed that my enquiries did not seem welcome to the occupants of 24 Warren Street. The Secretary, indeed, was always courteous and diplomatic – although somehow, at the end of our conversations, I found that we had hovered around or away from the point on which I had meant to alight. But the Directrix of Operations – a lady whom, in spite of everything, I can still respect: for her opposition, if blunt and graceless, was at least open – made no concessions to the enemy, and Mr Berger, who was often to be found at a well-covered desk in G.H.Q., would give me, on these occasions, a baleful Levantine glare. However, I was not deterred. SACU, after all, was not a secret society: in seeking to understand its workings, and to keep it to its original purpose, I was only performing my duty. So, when the Council next met, on 13th December 1965, I was prepared to open up two questions: first the question of the various committees which seemed to have escaped from control, and especially the General Purposes Committee; and secondly, the finances.

We had a well-attended meeting on 13th December – the fullest Council meeting that I ever attended. I contrived to raise the question of the

---

15 David Tallon (b. 1940), then an accountant at Deloitte's, had married Jack Perry's daughter Jillian in 1964. He was far from Maoist sympathies, and as respectable as his father Claude Tallon, who served on the Corporation of London's Court of Common Council, and as chairman of the Gresham Club in Abchurch Lane. David Tallon was senior editor of *Inland Revenue Practices and Concessions* (1984), and became senior partner of an accountancy firm specializing in private client tax planning.

Treasurership, and after some evasion, it had to be admitted that for the last six months there had been no Treasurer. This was a surprise to most of those present. There were also some surprises about the finances. The provisions of the old budget, it was now admitted, were unreal. But as the expenses remained real, the question had to be faced, where was the missing £6000 coming from? With all other sources abandoned, there only remained 'donations'. The question was, whence were these donations to come?

We agreed to touch the Sponsors. But would the sponsors fill so large a deficit? It seemed unlikely. Those who are most prompt to give their names to a cause often regard their names as gift enough. However, said the Directrix of Operations, there was another possible source. Certain friendly businessmen might well contribute – provided they were protected by anonymity: otherwise they might be blacklisted. Some of us did not like the anonymity and were not convinced by the argument. Businessmen who trade to China are well-known (I have never had any difficulty in identifying them), and mere anonymity of private donations will not conceal them. We insisted that from the Council there must be no secrecy: the governors of the Society at least must be able to know the sources of its finance.

The issue was strongly contested. Above the general murmur a high, querulous lilt could be heard: 'I'm a democrat! I don't like privilege!' it was saying, and I recognised at once the unctuous tones of my old friend the Trades Unionist. 'If 19 members of the Council are to know, I say that every member of the Society must know. Either everyone or no-one'. Of course he meant 'no-one', he meant only those anonymous persons who already handled the finances. Such was the meaning, to him, of 'democracy', freedom from 'privilege'.

We prevailed. The details of all donations, we insisted, must be available to all members of the Council. It was objected that some donors had already received guarantees of anonymity. Such guarantees were of course invalid, since the Council had never authorised them. We insisted that the Secretary write to such donors and ask for a release.[16] Then we insisted that the constitution of the Society provide for the proper definition of its committees, limitation of their powers, subordination to the Council.

It seemed a victory; but the last victory in always with those who execute, not those who decide. Between that Council Meeting and the next (which was thinly attended, for it occurred during the General Election campaign)

---

16 'The insistence that a record of donations should be maintained seems to have restricted SACU's fund-raising activities' (Thistlethwaite to T-R, 25 March 1966).

the Secretary had contrived to re-write the constitution, omitting some of our provisions, and the new text – 21 printed foolscap pages – first appeared on the table of the meeting itself, so that no one had time to read it. When I afterwards sent for the financial books, I was shown an exercise-book into which an unknown hand had transcribed a few names and sums. Nothing before December 1965 was recorded; nothing that was recorded was authenticated. All that could be deduced, by comparing all available documents, was that in December a spring had been touched and within two months £3000 had flowed in, of which two-thirds came in the names of 21 persons.

Meanwhile SACU was founding its local branches. Energetic persons were active in Hampstead, Barnet and elsewhere;[17] groups were formed, lectures and films shown, week-end courses organised. At every turn, the list of 'sponsors' was shown, and before so impressive a list, local authorities surrendered, facilities were granted. But who were the organisers, who supplied the basic membership? Who chose the films and the lectures? It was fairly clear that, in general, and naturally, the local activists would be the survivors of the old China Friendship Society, the already mobilised pro-Chinese fraction of the local communist party or those persons who, through support of China, had drifted into that position. Friends in the various branches kept me informed of events and I was amused to see the same pattern constantly repeating itself. As for the lectures, films and week-ends, they were pure political propaganda: Chinese films on Tibet, or on the great callisthenic display 'in Praise of the Revolution'.[18] I had actually witnessed this last display in Peking: it was there that my neighbour, the Dramatist, had turned to me and said, 'Doesn't it remind you of Germany in the 1930s?' All these lectures, films and week-ends were organised, centrally, by the ubiquitous Mr Berger.

However, there was one local branch which differed from the others; and as it was by the events in this eccentric branch that my own history was determined, I shall turn, with some relief, from the conformists to the nonconformist. The

---

17 Valerie Pearl, who reported on the Barnet branch to T-R, thought that Berger and Ash were even 'bigger crooks' than Bryan. 'The more I see of our local branch the more I feel it resembles the American Communist party, in consisting of no-one but agents and counter-agents!' she wrote on 18 May 1966. 'As for the rest of SACU, I have never met an organisation with so many committees and so little democracy. The rank and file is *never* consulted at any level' (Dacre 13/3).

18 At the second National Games held at Peking in September 1965, the mass callisthenics was called 'A Song in Praise of the Revolution', and included such songs as 'Tightly grip the gun in your hand'.

non-conformist branch was that which was founded at Oxford; and it was non-conformist, basically, for one reason. Whereas other branches, inevitably, were based on the relics of a local political organisation, the Oxford branch was based on the resident Orientalists of the university.[19]

At first, it seems, attempts had been made to begin on a different basis. At least, my old fellow-traveller, the Trades Unionist, had paid an unpublicised visit to the university and spoken to students there. But this had led to nothing. When the branch had been founded, the Central Office had tried again, and had sent down a well-chosen pair of lecturers, with slides, to give us a start. But this also had been a failure. The lecturers were a Dutch medical couple who had spent three weeks in China and had swallowed everything. While his wife operated the projector, Dr de Haas regurgitated what he had swallowed. I could recognise the very sentences of the People's Association as they came up, crude, undigested gobbets from his too receptive stomach. His message was, in his own words, that 'China is Heaven, the rest of Asia is Hell'. After that we decided that we could do better ourselves, whereupon the Secretary at Headquarters decided that we were unsound and must be watched. I noticed him watching in person one evening, sitting secretly at the back of the hall in which I was speaking.

But the event which precipitated the crisis was the proposed Oxford week-end school. Our Oxford chairman had taken great trouble to organise this school, and to procure well-qualified speakers for it; but when the details were reported to headquarters so that they might be announced in *SACU News*, the reaction was imperious. The arrangements, we were told, were not satisfactory. Our subjects were unsuitable, our speakers too highly educated, and we would do better to accept speakers and subjects from headquarters. Why had two Fellows of St. Antony's College been invited to speak?[20] Why were

19 Its members included the quantum chemist Charles Coulson, Fellow of Wadham, then Rouse Ball Professor of Applied Mathematics at Oxford and Chairman of Oxfam; Sir Noel Hall, previously Director of the Administrative Staff College at Henley, the earliest business school in England, and currently Principal of Brasenose; the Nobel laureate Dorothy Hodgkin; Sir Harold Thompson, Fellow of St John's, Professor of Chemistry and later Chairman of the Football Association.

20 These were Geoffrey Hudson (1903–1974) and Evan Luard (1926–1991). Hudson won the Davis exhibition in Chinese in 1923 while an undergraduate working towards a first in Greats. He was a fellow of All Souls, 1926–54, and thereafter of St Antony's, where he directed the Far East Centre. His first book was *Europe and China: a survey of their relations in history before 1800* (1931). Hudson was wartime head of the Far Eastern section of the Foreign Office's research department. After the war he was a luminary of the *China Quarterly*, and contributed articles on Sino-Soviet relations to *Foreign Affairs* (1957–60). Luard was a former diplomat in Peking, author of *Britain and China* (1962) and Labour MP for Oxford 1966–70 and 1974–79.

Russo-Chinese relations to be discussed? Why had we not chosen speakers who had been to China? (In fact, eight out of the nine had been to China) ... The writer of this authoritative letter was Mr Roland Berger.

Naturally when Mr Berger's letter was read in the Oxford Committee, on 25 April, there was an outcry. Who was Mr Berger? Was he a member of the Council? He was not. Then what was his position? And what was the authority of the Council? As a member of the Council it was clearly my duty to reply; and so, as question followed question, I gave the answers. Some members found them dismaying. What, they asked, was one to do? 'That depends,' I answered, 'on your position in the Society. I have a particular position. I am a Sponsor. My sponsorship has been public. If the Society betrays its promises, I cannot slip out privately. I must disown it as publicly as I owned it. But that would be an extreme act. Before contemplating such an act, one must make an effort to correct the Society, to bring it back to its original avowed purpose. For that reason I shall stand for re-election to the Council at the Annual General Meeting next month, on 21st May'.

Of course, knowing my SACU, I took it for granted that there would be *a spy* in our midst, so I was not surprised to learn, soon afterwards, that on the very next day one Mr Nicholas Bateson[21] had given a full and highly coloured oral report to his Masters.[22] I felt sure also that, even without such a report, those Masters would already have settled to get rid of me, if they could, when the elections took place: for naturally I had expressed my views to them too. And I did not doubt that, from their central position, they could achieve this result: 21 May, the date of the Annual General Meeting, was a Saturday, and whereas the Faithful of Hampstead and Barnet might be persuaded to spend a summer Saturday afternoon in London, more rural members, I thought, would not. However, no battle is lost until it has been fought, and in spite of these discouragements I decided to fight. So did my friends, whose genially

---

21 Nicholas Bateson (b. 1935) was son of F. W. Bateson, Fellow of Corpus Christi College, Oxford, former agricultural correspondent of the *New Statesman*, and author of the Fabian Society study *Towards a Socialist Agriculture*. He was an undergraduate at St Catherine's College, Oxford until 1958, and then a graduate student at the University of North Carolina until his support of Castro in Cuba led to the cancelling of his stipend. See Introduction, pp. 44–6, for his revolutionary activism at LSE. Later he became a civil servant.

22 Correspondingly, on 27 April, the Security Service received 'a fascinating report' of the meeting from a source who had attended (Dacre papers 13/3, Thistlethwaite to T-R, 28 April 1966). Bateson telephoned Needham in Cambridge on 26 April, and at Needham's suggestion sent a written report to Bryan: SOAS, Bryan papers 99/1/5/4, Bateson to Bryan, 28 April 1966.

and freely given support greatly encouraged me. Then, on 15 May, only six days before the election, Fate intervened. A well-informed article about the Society appeared in the *Sunday Times*.[23]

I confess that, when I saw the article, I had misgivings. It would, I thought, alarm the *Bonzen*[24] and cause them to call up their reserves: and their reserves were more accessible, and perhaps more disciplined, than mine. Nor did the article take me completely by surprise: the author had telephoned me (among others) before and had told me some of the facts which he had discovered. Whatever my reservations, it was no part of my business either to persuade or dissuade an enterprising journalist who had made interesting discoveries, and I had contented myself with referring him to the Secretary. What the Secretary had told him, I do not know. What I do know – for all has since been leaked or dragged into light – is the reaction of the *Bonzen*. Without seeking for evidence or confirmation, either of Mr Bateson's letter or of their own fancies, or stopping for self-criticism as prescribed by Chairman Mao, they decided that I had written the article – or at least they decided to fix it on me and thereby force me off the Council.

Their first plan was evidently to denounce me at the Annual General Meeting. For this purpose they asked Mr Bateson to send in a written account of my Oxford statements, reiterating his previous oral report, suggesting that I had written the article in the *Sunday Times*, and giving them explicit authority to use his letter in public. Mr Bateson complied with zeal.[25] Indeed he excelled himself; for when the letter was afterwards revealed (much against his will),[26] every other member of the Oxford Committee independently declared it a gross falsification or distortion of the facts. The letter ended by stating that there was no point in 'appeasing Mr Trevor-Roper': the only safety lay in his expulsion. At the same time the Secretary approached an old friend

---

23 The article entitled 'Battle to Control China Society' was by John Barry, who had read PPE at the Queen's College, Oxford. He stated that 'a powerful group in SACU is trying to run it wholly as a pro-Communist organisation', and that their machinations were based on 'standard Communist-style committeeship'. Barry was a persistent and ingenious ferreter of secrets. As a pillar of the *Sunday Times* 'Insight' Team, he was threatened with prosecution by Lord Chief Justice Widgery if the findings of journalistic research into Parachute Regiment misconduct at the time of the Londonderry shootings were published in 1972. He went to Washington DC as National Security of *Newsweek* in 1985.

24 German: bigwigs.

25 SOAS, Bryan papers 99/1/5/4, Bateson to Needham, 18 May 1966.

26 Bateson was forced to read aloud his letter at an Oxford branch meeting at the insistence of Kurt Mendelssohn (1906–1980), Reader in Physics at Oxford from 1955.

of his on the Oxford committee[27] and asked her for a similar letter 'to be read at the Annual General Meeting'. She however refused. As she afterwards explained, she did not think 'for a moment' that the statements which she was asked to make were true. The *Bonzen* were thus left with Mr Bateson's letter, which, in the end, they decided not to use. Perhaps it was too extreme. Perhaps they thought that I might attend the meeting (as I did) and might refute the document (as I certainly would have done). So foolish a letter might prove a boomerang, and rather than risk disaster, the *Bonzen* decided to adopt a subtler and more devious method of assassination.

The article in the *Sunday Times* had suggested that the Council, as the result of the elections, would now move to the Left. The *Bonzen* decided to prevent any public appearance of such a move. For this purpose, certain steps had to be taken. The faithful must be urged to vote for two Opposition MPs (Dame Joan Vickers and Jeremy Thorpe) whose names inspired confidence but who, inevitably, had been unable to give attention to the Council's business. At the same time the well-known communist Mr Reg Birch,[28] for whom the entire Barnet branch had been urged to vote (I possess the leaflet) was prevailed upon to stand down. This would give the necessary 'moderate' look to the elections. That done, Trevor-Roper could be isolated and detached, and who would notice the real, positive result of the election: the quiet election to the Council of such relatively unknown figures as Mr William Ash and Mr Roland Berger.

But how was Trevor-Roper to be isolated? The chosen method was simple; it was to be by secret denunciation. On 19 May the Chairman (Dr Needham), the

---

27 Margaret ('Peggy') Garland (1903–1998). She and her physician husband were 'pros-elytising Reds' until they left the CPGB in 1947. Thereafter, so her cousin Patrick White, the Nobel prize-winning Australian novelist, recalled, 'Peggy switched from this to that: from Marx to Mao, to the I Ching, even British Liberalism.' Her interest in Anglo-Chinese understanding ensued from her visit to the PRC for a peace conference in 1952. 'The conference itself was very well-arranged and ran on the principle that only unanimous agreement was good enough,' Garland recorded. 'If a delegate disagreed with a proposal or even one word of a resolution, the Conference was held up until either the delegate or the entire Conference changed its mind.' She did not mind this coercion. 'There was absolutely nothing that any human being with the slightest feelings of goodwill towards his fellow man would not have agreed with.'

28 Reg Birch (1914–1994) was associated with Ernie Roberts as a divisional organizer of the AEU. He had been elected to the CPGB national executive in 1956, but was expelled some ten years later as punishment for his preference for Albania and China over the Soviet Union. After meeting Bill Ash at the Chinese Legation, they founded the Communist Party of Great Britain (Marxist-Leninist) in 1968. Birch was the only Maoist ever to serve on the general council of the Trades Union Congress, 1975–79. He was a wily fomenter of strikes which he intended as sabotage of capitalism. He disliked democracy, saying that the use of ballot-boxes made workers lazy. In order to avoid being understood by his enemies, he was deliberately incomprehensible and incoherent.

Deputy Chairman (the Directrix), and the Vice-Chairman (who could not be left off even this little committee) signed and sent out a hastily stencilled letter in all directions but one.[29] It informed the recipients that the article in the *Sunday Times* could be presumed to be by me, deplored 'this introduction of McCarthyism into the Society's affairs', and urged the recipients not to extend their just detestation of me to the useful Opposition MPs who were also candidates for re-election to the Council. How many copies of this letter were sent out, I do not know. All that I know is that it was sent out in haste, in order to influence the election: as the Directrix afterwards wrote, it was essential to get it out 'before Saturday'. But at the same time it was apparently necessary that I should not know about it until after Saturday, and my own copy was therefore skilfully held up, so that I only received it on my return to Oxford from the annual general meeting. Thus although I spent the whole of that day, Saturday 21 May, in the company of the three signatories – in the morning at a Council meeting, in the afternoon at the Annual General Meeting – not one of these three colleagues even hinted that they had issued a defamatory document behind my back.

Such was the plan of the *Bonzen* of SACU. It succeeded – at least in the short run. At the Annual General Meeting the myth of a 'broad base' (or at least a broad face) was carefully preserved. In speeches from the Throne, the Deputy-Chairman carefully emphasised the importance of re-electing the Opposition members of parliament, and the Trades Unionist no less carefully deplored the views of 'Professor So-an-So'. I think they must have been surprised when I was found to have secured 63 votes – only three too few for re-election. But I know pretty well whence all those votes came. They were not the votes of the Faithful but of the independent spirits who had joined the Society for the election only, or had travelled from Oxford or elsewhere on a summer Saturday afternoon in the vain hope of bringing SACU back to its avowed purpose.[30] I must also admit that the margin was, in strict honesty, by one vote too favourable to me. This does not in the least reduce my sense

---

29 CC, Dacre 13/3, Joseph Needham, Joan Robinson and Mary Adams to Sponsors of SACU, 19 May 1966.

30 In gratitude for a hilarious 26-page letter from T-R describing the SACU meeting of 16 November, Sheridan Hamilton-Temple-Blackwood, 5th Marquess of Dufferin and Ava (1938–1988), art dealer and gallery trustee, brought fifteen friends whom he had induced to join SACU in support of T-R. These included the *Evening Standard* journalist Maureen Cleave (b. 1941), whom John Lennon had recently told in an interview that the Beatles were more popular than Jesus. In addition, Valerie Pearl assembled a voting party of ten. The Oxford contingent included Conrad Asquith (b. 1945), then a Christ Church undergraduate, subsequently a television and film actor.

of gratitude to the enterprising lady who, being well trained in the politics of Northern Ireland, and finding a spare voting-paper on the floor, showed her zeal in the cause by voting for me twice.[31]

I must admit that I enjoyed the Annual General Meeting. I enjoyed it as part of the *comédie humaine*. I enjoyed the unpredictable episodes – the Trotskyite leaflets which were thrust into my hands denouncing impartially the unholy trinity of Needham, Bryan and Trevor-Roper. I also enjoyed the predictable episodes: the impotence of the Chair in that tumultuary gathering; the high canting voice of the Trades Unionist, dripping with double-think; the dry, military bark of the Directrix. 'And who is that?' asked a young friend from Scotland who had turned up to vote,[32] looking towards the back of the hall where a confident, vigilant figure stood, erect against the wall, and through the disorderly files darted his experienced eye. It was of course Major-General Roland Berger.

When I got back to Oxford that night, I found a copy of the circular letter in which Dr Needham and his two lady friends had denounced me as a McCarthyite.[33] At first I was amazed by such an action. I wrote at once to all three, pointing out that their facts were untrue and their statements defamatory; and I asked to whom the circular had been sent. After six days, having received no explanation, apology or information from any of them, I decided that from now on all relations and obligations between me and the three signatories were broken. They had sinned against the most elementary rules of human behaviour. They could expect no mercy, and I, for my part, could no longer be a member of a society of which they were the principal officers. I therefore used my right of reply and sent to the Sponsors of SACU a documented statement of my reasons for dissatisfaction with the Society. At the same time I sent a formal letter of resignation to Dr Needham. Like so many other letters on serious matters, it has remained, to this day, unacknowledged.

My resignation from SACU did not pass without some repercussions. The *Bonzen* found themselves, for a time, on the defensive. In order to justify

---

31 Serena ('Lindy') Guinness, Marchioness of Dufferin and Ava (b. 1941), artist and *chatelaine* of Clandeboye.

32 John Baillie-Hamilton, Lord Binning, afterwards 13th Earl of Haddington (1941–2016), Patron of the Centre for Crop Circle Studies, student of the paranormal and editor-publisher of a periodical, *Bird Table*, dedicated to preserving small songbirds from cats.

33 'I suspect that Robinson's was the master hand: the rough, rude, graceless manner is hers; but Needham is the chairman and has signed' (T-R to Kurti, 26 May 1966).

themselves, they were reduced to reading out, to the new Council, the denunciatory letter sent by Mr Bateson. But this did them no good, for the two Oxford representatives,[34] who alone knew the facts, were able to state that Mr Bateson's letter was a gross travesty, and the three signatories were ordered by the Council to send a letter of apology to me. This they have never done, and the Secretary, by judicious misrecording the order in the minutes, has sought to save them from that embarrassment. In an attempt to shore up the blasted credit of Mr Bateson, the Secretary also tried to persuade his old friend on the Oxford committee to write, or to say that she had written, an 'independent' letter confirming his allegation. But once again, as she writes, 'I naturally refused'. This refusal did not stop the Secretary from writing an official document stating that she had sent precisely such a letter.

So much for the history of my relations with SACU. From now on, I have no interest in it. I regard it with contempt: a squalid, dishonest society which thrives by public fraud and private denunciation. But the larger question remains. How far can such organisations do good or harm? What function do they perform, good or bad, in the cause in which I, for one, still believe: Anglo-Chinese understanding? In order to consider this question, it is necessary to look at SACU as an organisation: to see the structure, the function, the real purpose of the society which so many people have innocently, and from the best motives, joined, supported and served.

The basic fact about SACU is that, like all front-organisations, it has a double structure. There is a public front – the list of Sponsors, the Council – and a private core: Mr Berger, Mr Bryan, and their friends. It is a private core which alone knows the facts, alone controls the machine. This is apparent to any mere councillor who attempts to penetrate the *arcana imperii*.[35] A straight question is put: at once the secret alarm-bells ring, the defensive smoke-clouds are discharged. It is just like China itself. In China, whenever we asked an innocent question, we could sense the immediate reaction. 'What is he after?' they seemed to be saying: 'how can we evade the question? What is the minimum we can say without committing ourselves to anything?' When the Dramatist and I arrived in Amsterdam on our way home, and received, from an airport official, a straight answer to a straight question about flight-schedules, we felt that we were in another world. For the last month we had known nothing like

---

34 Dawson and Kurti.

35 Latin: state secrets, literally secrets of the empire.

this: we had almost forgotten that straight answers existed. Since then, I have often felt the same emotion on emerging from 24 Warren Street.

And what are the *arcana imperii* of SACU? Basically they are two: finance and contact with the Chinese government. It is perfectly clear that contact between SACU and the Chinese government is close: SACU can obtain a visa by return of post. But no ordinary member of the Council knows how this contact is maintained. No documents are ever shown, no facts ever stated, no questions fairly answered. Equally, no ordinary member of the Council – not even the Treasurer – knows how the £6000 worth of donations is raised, what letters are written, in what terms, to whom; who responds, and why. The Council may demand information, but none is given. Elaborate delaying actions are fought; half-revealed truths are quickly covered up; time, oblivion, bureaucratic muddle are called in to help. In the end, the questioner wearies or allows himself to be fobbed off with general assurances, and the particular details remain a close secret in unidentified hands.

Whose hands? For myself, I have no doubt. SACU is controlled – inevitably – by whoever raises the £6000 *p.a.* which saves it from bankruptcy. Theoretically this £6000 comes in by voluntary donations; but even voluntary donations do not flow in spontaneously. They have to be solicited, and not everyone can solicit them. In this case it requires no great acumen to discover the immediate source: Dr Needham himself, under pressure, has revealed it. The Society, he has said, is supported by 'donations from business firms who are eager to make a thank-offering for trade with China'. This answer naturally provokes another question: why should such a thank-offering take the form of donations to SACU? Once again, the answer suggests itself. The thank-offering is not made to SACU or to the Council of SACU – that mere list of names from *Who's Who*: it is made to a far more important figure: Mr Roland Berger.

The secret of Mr Berger's power is that he is the executive director of a private organisation: the British Council for the Promotion of International Trade. Through this organisation, small British exporting firms find their way to the rich Chinese market, and they find it the more readily because Mr Berger, though (alas) unpopular with successive British governments, holds views which endear him to the Chinese government. Naturally his business friends are grateful for his help and will show their gratitude in concrete form. In making 'donations' to SACU they are not necessarily supporting the declared aims of the Council of Management: they are gratifying Mr Berger. Inevitably this gives Mr Berger great authority in the Society. Whatever the

Sponsors, the Council, the Annual General Meeting may think or decide, it is he who, secretly, pays the piper and therefore he who, secretly, calls the tune.

What tune does he call? For answer, we only have to look at the instructions which he sends out, the Chinese films which he shows, the lecturers whom he chooses, the week-ends which he organises. One only has to look at Mrs Berger's poor broadsheet, *SACU News*: that distant echo of the rasping mendacities of *Peking Daily News*[36] and the Hsinhua News Agency,[37] softened and trivialised for English ears. In Mr Berger's hands, SACU is an organ of Chinese propaganda in England. No wonder the Chinese government is delighted with it and opens its carefully controlled market to his friends.

What good does this do to Anglo-Chinese understanding? In my opinion it does none: it only does harm. And since I believe Anglo-Chinese cultural relations should and could be improved, on a basis of mutual respect, I end by explaining why I believe that the destruction of SACU, as at present organised, is a necessary stage in such improvement.

When two societies are as different as our own and Chinese, 'understanding' can be based either on independence or on servility; but when one of these societies is apprehensive and aggressive, it will always prefer to deal with a servile fifth-column rather than with an independent body. The Russians, whose revolution has been matured by time and events, how recognise that good relations, in cultural matters, are better achieved by independence and mutual respect. But the Chinese have not yet reached that stage of development. Their society is Stalinist at home, Leninist abroad. Real achievements are masked not only by foreign misrepresentation, but also by a gross cult of personality in China and by shrill, blundering, self-defeating intervention in the rest of the world. In these circumstances, so long as there is an uncritical organisation, like SACU, the Chinese government will prefer to invest in it. And the more they invest in it, the more it will acquire a monopoly of interpretation, and the more difficult it will be to place Anglo-Chinese understanding on a proper basis.

A good instance of this process is the matter of visas. Every serious student of China naturally wishes to visit the country. But visas are not granted easily. Indeed, the more serious the student, the more likely the refusal. SACU, on

---

36 This had been founded in 1909 as an English-language newspaper under American inspiration. T-R may have meant the *People's Daily*, the official mouthpiece of the Communist Party, published in Peking since 1949, and with numerous foreign language editions.

37 The Red China News Agency had been founded by the communists in 1931, but in 1937 changed its name to the Hsinhua [Xinhua] News Agency, or New China News Agency.

the other hand, seems to have no difficulty of this kind. Therefore it is natural for orientalists to join SACU, not in order to learn about China but in order to get there. Unfortunately, once in SACU, such members will soon discover the price they must pay. Any independence of mind will put them, and may well put their visa, at the mercy of that private denunciation which seems an essential part of communist social life. Thus the result of their action will have been merely to build up an organisation which makes access to China dependent upon political subservience and thereby to reduce the chance of any rival organisation which may aim at understanding on the basis of mutual respect.

For this reason – because I believe in real understanding of and with China – I now believe that it is essential for such an alternative body to be set up, and for those persons who, like myself, trusting the promises of Dr Needham, originally gave their support to SACU, to withdraw that support and give it to some other body: a body which does not rely upon secret funds, dishonest methods and private denunciation.

PART FOUR

TAIWAN AND CAMBODIA, 1967

Saturday, 25 November

I have decided to revisit China. That is, after the horrors of communist China, I have decided to visit what remains of non-communist China, or at least Taiwan. I was first invited there long ago – in 1955 I think. At that time I refused, partly through other preoccupations, partly through fear of air-travel: a fear so strong that, in general, I would forgo travel rather than accept it as a gift on those terms. (Afterwards I was rather ashamed, when I heard that Lady Violet Bonham Carter[1] had replaced me: she thought nothing of air-travel, and indeed, returned by continuing her air-journey round the world). Some years later, I was invited again, but again refused: by then I was thinking about [going to] communist China and I realized that to have been to Taiwan might prevent me from visiting Peking. But now I have been to Peking and my desire to revisit it is very weak; nor would I on any account be readmitted there now. So when a third invitation came, I accepted, especially since the invitation was expanded to include Xandra. In order not to lose part of the vacation, or to waste leave of absence in a term, we settled for the end of November, immediately after six weeks of full term;[2] and we arranged to fly direct, by the new Trans-Asian express – the SAS DC 8 jet which flies from Copenhagen to Bangkok, stopping only at Tashkent – on Saturday 25 Nov 1967. Two days before (23 Nov), I went to London and took the opportunity of lunching with

---

1 Lady Violet Bonham Carter (1887–1969), Baroness Asquith of Yarnbury 1964, Liberal party orator and activist, sought T-R's help in 1962-63 after accepting a 'terrifying invitation' to be the first woman to give the Romanes lectures at Oxford.

2 The residence requirement of the Regius Chair was a minimum of six months of full term.

Dick White at the Fontainebleau Restaurant in Northumberland Avenue. He had written to ask for a meeting – obviously in connexion with the Philby affair and its recent publicity.[3]

Originally he had suggested eating at the Garrick. Then, at the last minute, he had changed the place. As he explained, if he and I were seen together in the Garrick, speculation would at once be generated. I told him that I had often wondered with what eyes he was now scrutinised by the witnesses in the Garrick, since his identity had been exposed in the Press. He said, 'I have never dared set foot in the place since then'. We had a long conversation on the subject, and I told him that I might well write something on the subject, although I had withdrawn my preface from the 'Insight' book on hearing that the publishers (André Deutsch)[4] were going to include something by le Carré, i.e. David Cornwell.[5] Dick condemned Cornwell to me. He had been for a time in the Old Firm. When he wrote the book, Dick asked him what he would do with the profits. He said that he proposed to found a Pestalozzi school;[6] of which, since then, Dick added drily, nothing has been heard. He also told me that the *Sunday Times* had tried to bribe, with a large sum of

---

3 On 1 October 1967 the *Sunday Times* published an article revealing that 'the Third Man', Philby, had been SIS's 'chief anti-Soviet spy' (1 October 1967). On the same Sunday, Patrick Seale's front-page article in the *Observer* described Philby's career as 'an unmatched success story in espionage'. Seale's article was largely accurate in its facts, but misled by Philby's insidious Marxist class analysis. It claimed that his impact was 'a judgement on the complacent values of a ruling élite, bound together by a friendly old-boy network ... his friends were always ready to believe him. They meant well: they were made fools of.' White wrote to J. C. Masterman on 5 October: 'The Philby stuff in the Sunday papers has been very tiresome. The general position taken, I think, by both the *Observer* and the *Sunday Times*, is that the brilliant work of the war was sacrificed and nullified in the years immediately after peace by the traitors in our entrails.'

4 André Deutsch (1917–2000), who was born and educated in Budapest, came to London after the Anschluss and was likened to a mitteleuropa leprechaun. He became the best-known London publisher at Frankfurt's book fair.

5 David Cornwell (b. 1931) read modern languages at Lincoln College, Oxford 1952–56, during which time he became a Security Service infiltrator of such groups as the Oxford University Communist Club and the Anglo-Soviet Friendship Society. His obvious inquisitiveness made him suspect as an informer. After further cultivation by Thistlethwaite, he joined MI5 full-time in 1958, transferred to SIS in 1960 and resigned after publication of *The Spy Who Came in from the Cold* in 1963. T-R wrote to his agent A. D. Peters (7 January 1968): 'I have already seen, in proof, Cornwell's preface to the Deutsch book, and I think that it is awful: mere nihilistic froth. It is well-written, but the content seems to me deplorable, and factually wrong.'

6 Johann Pestalozzi (1746–1827) founded an international boarding school at Yverdon in 1805. The first principle of his curriculum was that clear thought was instilled by accurate observation of actual objects. The Pestalozzi method emphasized drawing, writing, singing, physical exercise, field trips, cartography, model-making and collecting.

money, one of his young men to exchange jobs. He blamed much of the history on the bad relations between Press and govt., which have been exasperated by the inept handling of the D-Notice affair by Wilson.[7]

I told him that I was fascinated by the Philby affair, partly because of my own involvement, partly by the mere psychological problem: how can any man, being an intelligent man, devote his whole life to so negative a satisfaction as the secret destruction not merely of the impersonal system around him, but of all the personal relations – relations of friendship, dependence, trust – which have been built up, in good faith, around him? This, to me, is the central problem. But there are other problems too. Is Philby really intelligent after all? Sharp, shrewd, superficially sophisticated – yes; but is (or was) he in any sense intellectual? By contrast with the other members of the Firm he did of course seem to be an intellectual; but did he in fact read, could he in fact think? Looking back, I have to admit that I have no evidence. Except for one reference to Marx, he never mentioned a book in my presence, nor could I ever get him to talk on serious topics: he would always keep conversation on a superficial plane, in ironic, Aesopian language, as if he knew of the differences which would divide us should we break the surface on which, till then, we could happily and elegantly skate. (Christopher Hill, I find, is just the same, although, with him, I know the depths: with Kim, I now feel, they did not exist). And what harm did he really do us? Of course there was the Volkov affair which, as Dick told me, viewed in retrospect in 1951, personally convinced him of the truth.[8] But what else?

---

7 Under a longstanding arrangement with the Newspaper Proprietors' Association, a D-Notice was a formal letter circulated confidentially to newspaper editors, the BBC and television companies by a committee composed of government officials and media representatives. These letters requested that certain topics or stories, usually involving national security, would not be published. An article by an untrustworthy snout, Chapman Pincher, in the *Daily Express* (21 February 1967) reported that copies of all telegrams going to or coming from foreign destinations were undergoing scrutiny in the Ministry of Defence. Pincher denied that his cable-vetting story was covered by any D-Notice, or that he had been officially told that it was. After an official inquiry, the Wilson government on 19 May issued a White Paper on the subject. The law lord and security expert Lord Radcliffe discredited the White Paper in a House of Lords debate on 6 July.

8 Konstantin Volkov (d. 1945) was a NKVD agent working under consular cover in Istanbul. His offer to tell SIS all that he knew of NKGB headquarters and overseas networks, and to name Soviet agents, in return for political asylum and £27,500, was reported to Philby in SIS. He delayed acting on Volkov's offer, betrayed him to Moscow, and was thus responsible for his kidnapping and liquidation.

Dick told me that when he took over MI6 he was dismayed to find Kim still on the strength, but had sent him to the Middle East to be out of the way. Harold Macmillan[9] agreed that he could do less harm there. The *Observer* were told that he was (nominally) working for SIS: David Astor's denials were untrue – D. A. simply would not face the facts on that issue.[10] It was true that the *Observer* was not told of the suspicions against Kim – suspicions which, in Dick's own mind (as he told me in 1952) were certainties. In 1963 Dick sent Nicholas Elliott[11] out to confront Kim with the evidence. The purpose was simple. In Beirut, outside British jurisdiction, Kim might have admitted the facts, especially to Elliott who had previously been his strongest defender in the office but who was now himself converted. Elliott was to offer him an amnesty in exchange for a complete revelation of what he had done. But Kim would not play. Later, when he had arrived in Moscow, he sent a message to Dick saying, 'You have won this round, but I assure you that I will win the last'.

Dick told me that Kim was receiving a great deal of money. (I had asked him how one of his sons was able – as announced in the newspapers – to live in Leicestershire, hunting and steeple-chasing). An Anglo-American film company had offered him any sum he liked to name, to be paid to his nominees, for his consent to a film about his life, of which he was to be the hero and the censor. His son John, who visited him in Moscow, was paid £40 a week by the *Sunday Times*.[12] Dick said that this was the first money he had ever earned.

---

9 Harold Macmillan (1894–1986), Earl of Stockton 1984, was Foreign Secretary April–December 1955 and prime minister, 1957–63. By the time that Philby reached Beirut as the *Observer*'s stringer in August 1956, Selwyn Lloyd had succeeded him as Foreign Secretary. White had been transferred from being Director General of the Security Service to be chief of SIS in June 1956.

10 David Astor (1912–2001), editor of the *Observer* 1948–75, was naïve about counter-intelligence matters, and (perhaps as the result of medication for depressive anxiety) forgetful. Probably he was told that Philby was working for SIS, and that Philby's job as Middle East stringer for the *Observer* was cover; but Astor may not have understood what was being said or have blanked its meaning.

11 Nicholas Elliott (1916–1994) was the long-serving SIS officer who was supposed to have told Astor about Philby's continuing work for the service. T-R thought him 'an agreeable poop' (letter to Ted Harrison, 18 September 1995, Dacre 10/43).

12 John Philby (1943–2009) was then a freelance newspaper photographer. He later had a one-man joinery workshop near King's Cross.

He had been in prison for confidence tricks.[13] Dick is obviously angry about Kim's surfacing in Moscow, fearing that it may – indeed must – be part of a Russian game to destroy confidence in ourselves. This is consonant with recent decisions of the Politburo. The process would be helped by the present nihilistic attitude of the Press and other 'media', and could be continued by the similar surfacing of Blake. I felt that he was indignant, partly, because he was inhibited from revealing our own successes. Penkovsky, for instance, supplied us with 10,000 documents ...[14]

I told Dick that nothing would make me defend the wartime SIS. I told him the story of Philby's obstruction of our political discoveries in 1943–4, which now assumed a new colour.[15] I said that I personally was convinced that he was being groomed to be C. My reasons were, first, that he held, one after the other, all the most appropriate jobs, and secondly, that there was no one else who could conceivably have been chosen. Dick said that he was convinced too. (It was after this that he told me of Kim's message from Moscow: perhaps he meant that 'the first round' was the rivalry for the post). I said that, soon after the war, I had come to the conclusion that the prime function of important communist agents in the West was, in general, not to supply information, which might blow them, but to ensure their own survival and promotion, so that they might be in key positions at any time when action was needed. He agreed, and drew from his pocket a piece of very interesting evidence which supported my view.

---

13 In 1964 John Philby was fined £15 and placed on probation for two years for stealing, with two friends, a radio, alcohol, cigarettes and cash with a total value of £75 from a sports pavilion at Greenwich.

14 Oleg Penkovsky (1919–1963), a Soviet military intelligence officer codenamed HERO and IRONBARK, was recruited by SIS in 1961. He supplied almost 5,500 exposures on a Minox camera providing up-to-date material on Soviet intercontinental ballistic missiles and chemical warfare programmes which resulted in major revisions of NATO strategy. In 1962 he was arrested during the Cuban missile crisis after an indiscreet visit to the hotel bedroom of the SIS courier Greville Wynne. He was tortured during a long interrogation, and killed with horrifying sadism.

15 In 1942 Stuart Hampshire, one of T-R's staff in the Radio Analysis Bureau (RAB), produced a report 'Canaris and Himmler' arguing, on the basis of decoded messages, that there was an intensifying power struggle between the Nazi party and German general staff. Philby in SIS vetoed its circulation. Two years later Philby suppressed another report from RAB about opposition to Hitler within the German military.

He told me that this policy was being pursued very successfully at present in France.

I left him at 3.0. His last words were, 'It is a pleasure to discuss these problems on a sophisticated level after discussing them, at an abysmally low level, with the Prime Minister[16] and Colonel Wigg!'[17]

On Saturday morning (25 Nov) Xandra and I were taken to London airport and flew to Copenhagen: then we boarded the crowded Trans-Asiatic jet. As always, I was terrified; and as on my journey to Peking, I took with me some allegedly sedative pills to calm the nerves. But as on that previous occasion, my irreducible puritanism intervened and I declined to take them, and gradually, with time, I found myself more at ease. We flew past Riga and Moscow and landed, in the small hours, at Tashkent. There we waited for an hour or so, in a typical Russian airport, bran new, unfinished, but already in decay; then we flew, still in the dark, over the Western Himalayas, past Lahore and Delhi, and when dawn broke I looked down on the infinite brown plain of India and the brown course of the Ganges. We passed near Calcutta, over the deltas of the Ganges and the Brahmaputra, and then the sharp, ribbed, forested hills of Burma, to the mouths of the Irrawaddy. Then suddenly the land was flat, green and fertile and we were gliding in towards Bangkok, where we left our plane. It was to fly on to Singapore: we were to change to a Thai International plane and fly, via Hong Kong, to Taiwan.

At Bangkok we were met by a Mr. Lim and given the full, or relatively full, treatment. Xandra was fascinated by the elegance and charm of the Thai women, and when we boarded the Thai plane, and she was given a mauve orchid and a mauve fan, and found that even the lavatory was tastefully decorated in mauve, she was more delighted still. We flew over Cambodia to Vietnam, crossing the coast at Hué, on the war-front, and then direct to Hong Kong: hundreds of white skyscrapers growing, like crowded toadstools, out of the island-rocks. Then an hour's flight took us across the sea and up the coast of Formosa, whose central mountains rose on our right. We landed at Taipei

---

16 Harold Wilson (1916–1995), Lord Wilson of Rievaulx 1983, Labour Prime Minister 1964–70 and 1974–76, knew little of intelligence matters before taking office, but soon yielded to the temptation to be a do-it-yourself intelligence analyst.

17 George Wigg (1900–1983), Labour MP 1945–67, Paymaster General 1964–67, purveyed parliamentary gossip, reported Cabinet plots, boasted of fixing journalists and confided dirty secrets to Wilson in letters headed 'Absolutely Personal' or 'Top Secret'. He thereby convinced Wilson that he was expert in espionage and counter-espionage. One of his anxieties was the security risks posed by foreign *au pair* girls. Wilson retired Wigg from government office on 12 November 1967, and consoled him with a life peerage.

at 5 o'clock, in a lurid sunset, and were met by Mr. Eddy Ti-Chiang Hsia of the Govt. Information Office,[18] who is our guide. He took us to our hotel, the Ambassadors, where (neither of us having slept a wink on the plane) we went straight to bed at 7.30 p.m.

Monday, 27 November

We woke at 6.0 and had breakfast in our room. At 8.50 Mr. Hsia collected us and we were taken to call, first on Mr. James Wei,[19] Director of the Government Information Office, who is our host, – a very gay, likeable character, with an excellent sense of humour; then on to Prof. C. T. Wu,[20] the director of the Institute of International Relations.[21] This is a kind of Chatham House; but soon, as I questioned Prof. Wu, I decided that there were differences between the two institutions. Prof. Wu's office is divided into three sections: international affairs in general (which seems the smallest of the three), Russian and Eastern European affairs, and mainland China. It has relations with West Germany (the Free University of Berlin[22] and the Forschungsinstitut at Munich),[23] the Hoover Institution at Stanford,[24] and organizations in Seoul and Tokyo. It is

---

18 This may be the Eddy Hsia interviewed in Bridget Kendall, *The Cold War: a new oral history of life between east and west* (2017). 'The Communists just wanted to kill as many people as possible, for whatever reason they could find,' Hsia recalled of the rural districts south of Shanghai where he lived before taking refuge in Taiwan in 1949. 'My mother was killed by Communists … She was an innocent woman … I cannot understand, I cannot forgive, I cannot forget.'

19 Wei Ching Meng, known as James ('Jimmie') Wei (1907–1982) left Shanghai for Taiwan in 1949. There he acted as Reuter's correspondent, and founded the ROC's first English-language newspaper, *China News*, in 1949. He was managing director of the Broadcasting Corporation of China 1954–66, head of the Government Information Office 1966–72 and director of the Central News Agency 1972–78.

20 Unidentified.

21 The Institute of International Relations had been founded in 1953 as a government 'think-tank', and by 1967 was linked to the National Chengchi University (the National University of Governance). The latter was the Taipei successor to the KMT's Central School of Party Affairs at Nanking.

22 The *Freie Universität Berlin* was founded in West Berlin in 1948, with US financial aid, as a Cold War substitute for Frederick William University, which lay in the Soviet sector. The latter's students were liable to detention, abduction, forced labour or liquidation.

23 An agglomeration of research institutes in the humanities, industrial research and development, and social sciences had been created in Munich, by different initiatives and endowments, during the twentieth century.

24 The Hoover War Library, collecting books and documents on the recent European war, was opened on the Stanford campus in 1922 at the instigation of the 31st US president Herbert Hoover. It was renamed the Hoover Institution in 1959.

a private foundation and its funds are private. These facts alone convinced me that it is financed by the CIA, and I tactfully forbore to press the subject further.

Of course I don't mind this in the least. I cannot become indignant over the CIA. The furore over *Encounter* and the CIA seemed to me farcical.[25] I had always – ever since the Berlin Congress for Cultural Freedom in 1950 – taken it for granted that *Encounter* had funds from the CIA, but since it never refused to publish anything of mine, and I did not write in the CIA interest, why should I object? The function of writers is to write, not to quibble at the source their publisher's income. I cannot understand why Isaiah Berlin[26] and Stuart Hampshire[27] make such a fuss about the ideological and financial virginity of *Encounter*. Dick White, who shares my view, was equally puzzled when we were discussing the matter on Thursday. I said that I thought it was simply the difference between Christ Church and New College.[28] Nevertheless, I did not want to get involved with Prof. Wu in such matters, so I raised no further questions with him, but inspected his institution and dutifully admired his card-index, his library and his publications. Then I was introduced to Mr. Li,[29] of the section dealing with mainland China, and we found ourselves closeted with him: Xandra, myself, Mr. Hsia, two other members of the Institute, an oldish man in a pale grey suit, who was never introduced but who sat in the distance, his eyes perpetually twitching, occasionally taking notes, and a jolly

25 The monthly London magazine *Encounter* was covertly funded by the CIA from its launch in 1953 until 1964. Thereafter its expenses were met by the *Daily Mirror* tycoon Cecil King. In March 1967 two American journals published articles confirming the rumours of covert CIA funding. (Sir) Frank Kermode (1919–2010), who had been ignorant of the arrangement, resigned as co-editor in May.

26 Sir Isaiah Berlin (1909–1997), Fellow of All Souls 1932–38, 1950–66 and from 1975, Fellow of New College 1938–50, President of Wolfson College 1966–75, opposed both Marxist determinism and the Soviet Union. He objected to the clandestine funding of a periodical which had, he felt, vaunted its independence: he would not have been troubled by an open subvention.

27 (Sir) Stuart Hampshire (1914–2004) had joined the staff of T-R's Radio Analysis Bureau (afterwards Radio Intelligence Service) in 1942. He was a fellow of All Souls 1936–40 and 1955–60, and of New College, 1950–55. In 1967, by when he held a chair in philosophy at Princeton, he tried to raise money to launch a new magazine which Kermode nicknamed *Counter Encounter*. He was warden of Wadham College, Oxford, 1970–84.

28 Christ Church (the college of White and T-R) had a reputation for hardy worldliness. New College, where Hampshire was a fellow, was reckoned more finical.

29 Li Tien-min [Li Tianmin] (1909–1993) was a Chinese Nationalist legislator until he fled to Taiwan in 1949. There he became a professor at National Chengchi University. He wrote a series of biographies of PRC leaders, including Chou En-lai, Mao Tse-tung and Deng Xiaoping.

English naval officer who appeared from nowhere and spoke Chinese.[30] It was clearly expected that I should question Mr. Li.

I asked him particularly about the launching of the Cultural Revolution in 'mainland China'. People speak of it as being mounted by Mao. But how was it mounted? It was an attack, explicitly or in effect, on the Head of State, the Politburo, the Party. No party Congress would have supported it – at least, none was summoned to depose Liu Chao-Shi because, we are assured, none would have done so. The effective Party government in the great majority of provinces resisted it, with success. Mao himself, by all the evidence, was out of touch. He had withdrawn, according to the official statements at the time, to be the philosopher of the revolution. According to his own later version, he had been forced out. The Red Guard in the schools cannot have been organized by the Party. They cannot have been organized by, or through, the teachers, who are their victims. By what mechanics, then, were the *Thoughts of Mao* generalised, the Red Guards organised, the attack launched? But on this crucial matter I could get no light from Mr. Li. He was very long-winded. He spoke of the People's Liberation Army;[31] but that, I observed (and he did not deny) was only called in long after the attack had been launched, and it was called in reluctantly as being itself divided. He spoke of the 'cult of personality', the desire of the young to avoid being taught. Finally, he fell back on the Secret Police. I did not find his explanation convincing.

The naval officer gradually revealed himself. He was from the British consulate and is regarded by the Chinese as unofficial naval attaché. His name, I think, is Nicholls. He had expressed an interest in the Institute, and Mr. Hsia (who, I see from his card, is a commander in the Chinese navy) had invited him to join us. He took us afterwards to the consulate, but the consul (Bray)

---

30 Robert ('Bob') Nicholls (1928–2011) served on Royal Navy vessels intercepting illicit transports to Palestine until 1948. He was then transferred to naval intelligence and the interrogation of individuals detained off the coast of Korea. During the Malayan emergency he commanded a sea defence motor-launch for two years. He took a Chinese language course at SOAS, 1958, followed by a further course at Hong Kong University. Appointed in 1964 as naval intelligence officer on the Commander-in-Chief's staff in Singapore, Nicholls provided Indonesia-related intelligence product gained from interrogations, sources and signals intelligence. In 1966–68 Nicholls was naval liaison officer in the British consulate in Taipei gathering economic, political and military intelligence. In 1968 he moved to Canberra, where he joined Australia's Naval Intelligence Directorate.

31 The People's Liberation Army of the PRC.

was out.[32] Then he invited us, together with the Hsias, to dinner tomorrow. We would have preferred to be invited alone, for greater freedom of conversation.

We had lunch in our hotel and then, at 3.0, we went to see the Confucian temple, built 'about 60 years ago' – in the last days, then, of official confucianism, in standard style with suitably late Ch'ing frills. I gather that there has been some revival of Confucianism since 1949 – understandably as the KMT gropes for an ideology against communism. Close by was a Taoist temple which was full of animation. Some new part of it had just been completed and groups of women were singing, in two separate parties, at two different altars. One party was dressed in pale blue, one in black, and they were accompanied by gongs and other musical noises. Mr. Hsia seemed to us somewhat contemptuous of Tao-ism as a vulgar degradation of its own original form, now admittedly more widespread than Confucianism, but largely among country bumpkins: these women, he said, were housewives from the country, volunteers representing their localities in celebrating the new shrine. He himself, as an official, was no doubt a secular confucian conformist.

As we came out of the Taoist temple we heard, among the discordant polyphony, yet another noise, and looking across the courtyard we saw a covered wooden stage and on it some splendidly dressed figures. It was an opera: a visiting company was performing in the open air, having been hired by a group of public benefactors to entertain the public, who were standing in the courtyard among the vendors of fruit and vegetables: a sort of Chinese Covent Garden, combining both an opera-house and a vegetable-market. The opera was about three kings of the Warring States time, and was in the Amoy dialect: an Amoy version, presumably, of a standard classical opera. The King of Wu had a magnificent red beard and red roses in his crown. His mother sat gravely in the centre of the stage, and animated arias were interchanged between her and the three kings, while the whole side of the stage was crowded with musicians and a few others who were perhaps privileged spectators, perhaps the donors of this public treat: a kind of orchestra and royal box combined. I was fascinated and could have spent the rest of the afternoon there; but I fear that our guide is not a lover of Chinese opera, or very knowledgeable about it: he is a correct, tidy-minded, rather humourless official; and anyway, we had

---

32 Raymond Bray (1922–1988) began his official career in 1939 as an Inland Revenue tax officer. After military service, during which he learnt Japanese, he was transferred to Customs and Excise and then to the consular service in 1948. He held posts in Yokohama, Kobe and Tokyo before his transfer to Taiwan in 1964.

another appointment at 4.30: we were due at the Agricultural Exhibition Hall of the National University. There we saw an excellently arranged exhibition to illustrate agriculture and land-reform; but I still regretted the opera.

Mr. Hsia told us that he was from Shanghai: he could not understand the Amoy dialect and himself spoke Mandarin with strong Shanghai accent (This arose out of a complete failure of comprehension between him and an old man who only spoke Amoy). His father, he said, had been killed by the communists in 1950 and he had come, via Hong Kong, to Taiwan to join the KMT forces. Xandra, with her knowledge of naval officers,[33] doubts whether he will be a conduit leading us to the arts.

Tuesday, 28 November

In the morning we went to the National Museum. It is a fine building, in classical Chinese style, set in a magnificent position in the hills outside Taipei. It was completed two years ago, to house the imperial treasures brought from Peking.[34] We were received by the deputy director Chuang Shuang-yen[35] (the director is away, in Greece).[36] He was a charming old man who had lived for years with the collection, following it from place to place, as he explained to us over the tea: first in Peking, then in Chungking, then back in Peking, then in Nanking, finally in Taipei. Most of this time, it seemed, the collection had been in boxes: only two years ago had it been finally unboxed and exposed, by rotation, in this splendid new museum. We spent the whole morning there, and could have spent much longer, among the Shang and Chou bronzes, the Sung and Ming porcelain, jade and paintings, the Ch'ing enamel. The Han and T'ang periods were hardly represented: it was not their turn, we were told, for exhibition. I hope we may return before we leave: perhaps we may escape from a factory to this more congenial place.

---

33 Her first husband had been a naval officer: Rear Admiral Clarence ('Johnny') Howard-Johnston (1903–1996), sometime director of the anti-submarine division of the Admiralty.

34 Chiang Kai-shek diverted hard-pressed resources during the crisis of 1948–49 to evacuating the collections to Taiwan. By doing so, he defended his claim to be still the legitimate ruler of all China, and scored a propaganda blow against the communists.

35 Chuang Shuang-yen was vice-director of the National Palace Museum for several decades.

36 Chiang Fu-ts'ung [Jiang Fucong] (1898–1990), a historian of the Song dynasty, studied philosophy at Peking University and librarianship in Germany. Under the KMT he was director of the Central Library, 1940–65, and director of the National Palace Museum, 1965–83.

After lunch we had a somewhat heavy course of lectures. First, we were taken to the Council for International Economic Co-operation and Development, where Mr. Charles Z. Yeo[37] took us, once again, through the history of land-reform and described, with fluent eloquence and tumbling statistics, the economic miracle of Taiwan, adding that all this was directed by faith that 'mainland China' would ultimately be recovered: without that faith, he seemed to imply, all this effort would be in vain. He seemed really to believe that 'mainland China' was heading for collapse and would surrender at discretion to the gnomes of the Taipei. Then we were carried to the Sino-American Joint Commission on Rural Reconstruction and had a heavier lecture from Mr. Moses Hu.[38] It was very boring. He spoke very deliberately. 'Would you please sit on the other side of the table', he began, 'so that you can see the blackboard'; and having asked permission to remove his coat, he armed himself with a chalk and wrote every date, and much else, on the board for our benefit. It was all very tedious and I'm afraid that at one moment he caught Xandra yawning. At the end of his lecture he revealed that he was a Presbyterian – doubtless his parents or grandparents had been converted by the famous Canadian mission-ary Mackay who was a great figure in these parts.[39] I thought I detected a trace of the Scotch pulpit in his discourse.

Flattened by these experiences we returned to our hotel; but not for long. An hour later we had to be ready to go out to dinner with Commander Nicholls, who lives at Tamsui, forty minutes away by car. Our guide Eddy Hsia came to collect us with his wife, who is charming and elegant. She is Chinese, born in Japan, where her father was in business, and works in the Japanese embassy in Taipei. We drove out of Taipei along the Tamsui river – a splendid wide river, as it seemed in the dark – through the town of Tamsui (where another open-stage opera was in progress) and finally mounted a steep bank, past the old Dutch fortress in which the British consul holds sway, but which we could

37 Charles Z. Yeo was senior specialist at the Council for International Economic Co-operation and Development, which had been formed in 1963 as successor to the Council for United States Aid in Taiwan. It co-ordinated economic policy in ROC, promoted industri-alization and developed the infrastructure.

38 The Sino-American Joint Commission on Rural Reconstruction was funded by the US government, 1949–79. It oversaw reform of land holdings and farming methods, agricultural education, irrigation, flood control, fisheries, forestry, improvements of crop and animal stock, rural credit and contraception. Moses Hu was an expert in rural development.

39 The Presbyterian evangelist George Mackay (1844–1901) settled at Tamsui, north Formosa in 1872. He published a religious memoir-cum-guidebook, *From Far Formosa*, in 1896.

not see, and arrived at the commander's elegant colonial house – formerly the house of Mackay himself, who clearly looked after himself in patrician style. When we entered it, we found a somewhat colonial society too: three self-assured memsahibs, in shapeless, characterless clothes, were raising their voices in confident banality and two large Anglo-Saxon dogs squatted in central positions and indecent postures in the room. My heart sank as I entered, κατὰ δ' ἔστυγον αὐτάς.[40]

The party consisted of the jolly commander and his wife, who was American, and two American couples, the Partridges and the Deans.[41] Partridge was at the American Embassy, a career Foreign Service man who had been in Hong Kong and elsewhere in the Far East for some years.[42] He was likeable and intelligent. Dean was a lawyer in some American organisation, and although I hardly had any conversation with him, he seemed sensible too.[43] The commander also is intelligent behind his jollity. But the three American ladies were unbearable. They completely overpowered Xandra, totally ignored the charming Mrs. Hsia, and interchanged loud local reminiscences among themselves, using the reluctant Xandra as a captive audience. Even at dinner Mrs. Partridge[44] would not allow her to converse with her masculine neighbours but belaboured her across the table with egotistical information. I suffered similarly from Mrs.

---

40 Greek: 'and the sight of them filled me with disgust'. Simon Malloch notes that 'them' must refer to the dogs, which were presumably bitches – αὐτάς is a feminine form. For the second time in these journals Trevor-Roper adapted *Odyssey* 10.113, κατὰ δ' ἔστυγον αὐτήν, 'the sight of her filled them with horror' (or 'disgust').

41 In the passage that follows T-R confuses the Partridges and the Deans.

42 This describes David Dean (1925–2013). Dean was a US naval aviator 1943–48 before studying English history and literature at Harvard. He joined the US Foreign Service, was posted to Kuala Lumpur 1951, and mastered spoken Mandarin and Cantonese while attending the US Foreign Service Language School in Taichung, 1957–59. He served in Hong Kong 1959–62, and was deputy director of the East Asian & Pacific Bureau Office of Asian Communist Affairs in Washington, 1962–66; political counsellor, and sometimes acting *chargé d'affaires*, at the US Embassy in Taipei, 1966–69; deputy chief of mission in Peking, 1976–78; and director of the American Institute in Taipei, 1987–89.

43 This describes Benjamin Waring Partridge II (1915–2005). Partridge received a doctorate of jurisprudence from the University of Miami in 1948. He commanded a US naval vessel in the Pacific during the Korean War. Afterwards he served as a naval lawyer in the Philippines, Iceland, Rhode Island and finally Taiwan (1954–68). During the 1970s he was chairman of the Vermont State Environmental Board and director of state planning. He co-authored five books with his wife, including *China Sea Round-up* (1960) and *Rendezvous in Singapore* (1961).

44 By 'Mrs Partridge' T-R means Mary Alice Dean, director of the Young Women's Christian Association in Taipei during the 1980s.

Dean,[45] who was an author too, having written fifteen children's books: she now had an irresistible spiritual urge, she said, to be a historian and do serious *re*search and write serious history, of which not enough, apparently, was being written; did I not agree that the art of the children's fiction writer would reanimate my flagging subject? I'm afraid I did not greatly encourage her.

I escaped from the ladies for some time both before and after dinner (the dinner was in the American style, with a very long wait before it) and had some interesting conversation with Partridge.[46] He told me that the economic reforms in general, and the land-reform in particular, were of genuine Chinese origin, not imposed by the Americans, but of course they could not have been realised on the mainland ('if only we could have begun ten years earlier', Mr. Yeo had said this afternoon, 'there would have been no communism in mainland China') where the KMT depended too much on the landlords: any serious attempt to impose it these might have led back to war-lordism. Formosa was *tabula rasa*: the local landlords were unrepresented in the central KMT government which arrived in their midst and which consisted of sophisticated metropolitan intellectuals. Even so, it had taken the shock of the Korean war to put the American effort behind them. Ironically, the main beneficiaries had been the local landlords. The immigrant officials had benefited merely by their official pay-rise; the local landlords had invested their compensation in the new industry and become the new Taiwan entrepreneurs. I said that it was like the Scotch Highland chiefs after 1745.

What will happen when Chiang Kai-shek dies? At present his mystique is a powerful force – and he is prudently investing in it, becoming a sage who looks forward to a distant rather than an immediate future. But on his death tensions, at present muted, between local and central interests may be felt. Chiang's successor as elected President of China, which is at present his undisputed position, will be elected by the rump of the old KTM Central Congress. When the govt. moved to Taiwan it brought with it a quorum of that Congress; but of course the rump shrinks annually and at the time of Chiang's death (through the legal quorum may be reduced) it can hardly claim to be representative. No doubt it will elect the present Vice-President C. K. Yen;[47] but the international status of 'the Republic of China' can hardly be the same.

---

45 By 'Mrs Dean' T-R means Cora Cheney (1917–1999), who had married 'Ben' Partridge in 1939. She wrote novels for children, compiled folklore collections, including *Tales from a Taiwan Kitchen* (1976), and became history columnist for the *Brattleboro Reformer*. After ordination as an Episcopalian priest at the age of 65, she used a portable altar adapted from her ironing-board when visiting parishioners. She led a pro-abortion campaigning group of elderly women who always paraded in their Sunday finery carrying parasols.

46 T-R doubtless means Dean, not Partridge.

47 Yen Chia-kan (1905–1993) succeeded as President of Taiwan, 1975–78.

We got home just after midnight. I was ashamed at the way in which those three American women treated the charming Hsias, whom they simply ignored for most of the time, booming their parochial vulgarities across them. It was like a scene from *A Passage to India*.[48] And their clothes ... the contrast with the elegant Mrs. Hsia was emphasized visually as well as vocally and mentally.

Cmdr Nicholls told me – I didn't know whether to believe him or not – that the land-reform project was lifted from a Japanese scheme of 1939. He admitted that he had not seen the scheme, and said that he wanted to find it. I suspect him to represent SIS in these parts: he seemed always so vague about his functions. At one point I said something implying as much, and he ignored the remark, which could be seen as confirmation.

Wednesday, 29 November

We began with the handicrafts shop: a necessary visit. It was not much better than its equivalent in Peking, but Xandra bought a Ming doll and a kite (in Red China they would not have had the kite, kite-flying being a reprehensibly individualist pastime). Then we went to the Academia Sinica,[49] which is some way out of Taipei, in pleasant rural surroundings. We were received by the president, Dr. Wang Shih-chieh,[50] an old man (he had taken a graduate degree in economics in London during the first world war). He reminded us of Wallace Notestein.[51] But he was not much help to me. He insisted on reminiscing about his trivial experiences on a visit to England in 1943, when he had stayed at Claridge's, and although I continually tried to recall him to the Academy, he would not answer the call. Even when I was quite explicit

48 E. M. Forster's novel (first published in 1924) about the incomprehension and injustice meted out to a Moslem doctor in India by colonial officials and middle-class women.

49 Academia Sinica was founded in 1928, and relocated to Taiwan in 1949. Its campus had been at Jiouhjunang since 1954.

50 Wang Shih-chieh [Wang Shije] (1891–1981) graduated in economics and politics at London University in 1917. The University of Paris awarded him a doctorate in 1920. He became professor of comparative law at Peking University in 1921, and KMT minister of education 1933–36. Described as 'mellow, sedate' when he succeeded the Chinese premier T. V. Soong as Minister for Foreign Affairs in 1945, he and Soong were reckoned 'the two principal members of the Chinese ministry' (*Manchester Guardian*, 19 August and 16 September 1945). He retired as MFA in 1948, was appointed minister without portfolio in Taiwan 1958, and president of Academia Sinica 1962.

51 Wallace Notestein (1878–1969), Sterling Professor of English History at Yale 1928–47, was venerable, studious and poised in appearance.

and said that I wished to visit the Institute of History, I got no response: he just maundered on about biographical trivialities. Finally he suggested that we might like to see the archaeological museum of the Academy. I was reluctant, thinking that anything of value would have gone to the National Museum and only unimportant stuff would remain in this out-of-the-way place. However, I was wrong. It contained a large number of the oracle-bones excavated by the Academy at An-yang in the 1920s, and two wall-painting from Turfan, as well as Shang and Chou bronzes and some very early black pottery – pre-Shang I think. These restored my waning good-humour: but for them I would have regarded the visit as a complete waste of time.

After lunch we were to visit the Taoyuang farm area, about an hour's journey to the south of Taipei, to see the Farmers' Association and peasant families. But when we arrived at the town of Taoyuang, we found the whole place in ferment. It was the day of a great local festival, for the temple had been restored, and the entire population was pouring into the town for this celebration, which was to culminate in a great virtual slaughter of hogs and unconstrained eating and drinking. Of course there was no life at all at the Farmers' Association, whose offices were closed. However, in spite of our protests, the General Manager was found, and having taking time to put on his tie, presented himself before us. He had held his post for thirty years, was gross and heavy, with a great roll of too, too solid flesh protruding over the back of his collar, and his answer were in the form of brief, porcine grunts. We did not learn much from him. Then we were taken – still protesting somewhat, for we felt that we were spoiling their holiday – to see some 'typical' peasant families.

The first family consisted of thirteen persons, three generations. All seemed delighted to see us and we were introduced ceremoniously to the three generations (including one infant on its sister's back) – but not to two kinsmen who sat apart and were somehow regarded as outsiders. We fully expected to be presented no less ceremoniously to the water-buffalo who, as Eddie Hsia said, is always regarded as one of the family; but the water-buffalo had been sold a few days ago and replaced by a tractor.[52] As we went into the house, we were faced by the altar for the cult of the ancestors, with a great glazed inscription, like a poster, behind it, and bric-à-brac of all sorts on it. Beside it was the living area, and opposite that a recess containing the farm implements, the bicycles and the new tractor. We were made very welcome and given special rice-cakes,

---

52 A year later T-R wrote of 'that most enchanting of creatures, the Asiatic water-buffalo' (*One Hundred Letters*, p. 159).

made to celebrate the successful garnering of the rice harvest. Then we passed on to another family.

This second family was smaller. Only one man worked the ground. He was an only son, aged 25. His old mother kept house and his young wife was in the kitchen preparing what seemed a lavish meal. There were five children, all small. Outside the house everything was neat and well cultivated. The rice was piled on the drying ground and had been covered with straw for the night. There were vegetables and flowers. The house too was spacious and prosperous. As we went in, the altar faced us. Beside it was a large print of Confucius with extracts from the Analects. Then room led into room, all clean and tidy, with sewing machine and electric cooker, until the house merged imperceptibly into the farm and after the kitchen we found ourselves suddenly in the pigsties. When we went to take our leave, the old lady pressed us to stay to dinner. But we made our excuses and set off towards Taipei. As we returned through Taoyuang, past another open-stage opera, the town was in chaos: vehicles were pouring into it from all sides and the police were distracted. All the way back to Taipei we drove against a continuous crocodile of cars, hondas,[53] pedicabs, all flowing remorselessly into Taoyuang for the feasting. It was a weary journey; but we got back at last, and since we were both exhausted and have instructions to be ready to leave tomorrow at 7.0 a.m., we dined early and went straight to bed.

All through the day, if ever my mind was vacant, there flew into it, like a great dirty bluebottle-fly, the disagreeable thought of those three hard, empty, charmless, inelegant American women; but now, when that thought first approaches, I open the other side of the mind and in rushes the more pleasing thought of those charming hospitable Confucian peasants, followed by an imaginary water-buffalo, to drive it out.

Thursday, 30 November

We had breakfast at 6.0 and were ready at 7.0, to set out on an expedition to the Taroko Gorge on the eastern side of the island. Unfortunately this morning was cold and wet (hitherto it has been warm and dry) and the expedition looked like being a fiasco. I had thought that we were going by car and so was somewhat dismayed when I found that we were to fly. But there was no argument with fate, and we duly climbed into a crowded old DC 4 of China Airlines and

---

53 i.e. motor-cycles.

bumped through thick rainclouds to Hua-Lien halfway down the east coast.[54] There the weather was better and we set off in a hired car towards the gorge.

We had not gone for when the incidents began. A few days ago, a terrible typhoon hit the Hua-Lien area. Everywhere there was evidence of it: landslides, trees and buildings thrown down. Only a few miles out of Hua-Lien we found that the bridge which carries the main road over a great wide river had been swept away and we had to make a detour and ford two separate arms of the river. We got through ourselves, but a smaller car behind us stuck in the water, and as it belonged to the same company as ours, and the cars of that company had been ordered to go in convoy, we had to wait half-an-hour or so until a tractor with ropes had hauled the car out to safety. Then we continued our journey up the gorge where a new highway, which took five years to build, has at last been completed, cut through the marble rocks in order to provide a road link between the east and west coasts of Taiwan.

It was a dramatic drive, through great galleries cut in the mountain. Cascades of water fell to right and left of us and the detritus of landslides periodically blocked our way. The wall of the rock was covered with ferns; here and there were inscriptions or temples commemorating those who had been killed making the highway, and gardens with camellias and poinsettias in flower, but also heaving damaged by the typhoon. At the head of the gorge a new Buddhist temple was being built and there was a restaurant where we had lunch. Then we came back the same way.

I did not have much confidence in our driver. He drove faster than was necessary (for we were in no hurry) or seemed to me safe, skidding round corners of that curved, precipitous mountain road. But any time that we had needlessly gained we soon lost again. When we reached the river, the level had risen, and in the middle of the second watercourse we stuck fast. Water poured into the car and into the engine. A group of men who were waiting for such profitable emergencies ultimately pushed us through for NT $ 20 (20 New Taiwan dollars), but the driver struggled in vain to make the engine re-start, and ultimately a Chinaman in a taxi gave us a lift to the airport. We arrived at 2.0 and the plane did not leave till 3.0; so when our own driver ultimately reappeared with his restored car, we filled in time by visiting a local marble-factory. Then we boarded the plane and bumped our way, again through thick rainclouds, back to Taipei.

---

54 A Douglas DC 4 propeller-driven passenger aircraft in the fleet of Taiwan's China Airlines, established 1959.

We arrived tired and cold, for the temperature had dropped sharply during the day; but fortunately we had time to rest and recover before dinner, for we were dining out with Mr. James Wei. We dined at the Green Leaves Restaurant. Unfortunately there was no private room, Mr. Wei explained to us on arrival, but he had chosen it for the food, which was the best in Taipei. This seemed rational. We had a very gay dinner party. The other guests, apart from us and Eddie Hsia, were 'ambassador Cheng',[55] Lin Yu-tang,[56] George Yeh,[57] a Mr. Chiang,[58] two professors both called Li or Lee, but spelt differently in Chinese, (Li-Shi[59] and Li Tung-feng[60]) and a young painter called Hu Chi-Ching.[61]

55 Chen Ching-men (b. 1894), generally known as C. M. Chen or Keng Tan Tiang, was educated at Raffles Institution, Singapore 1902–10, Dulwich College 1910–11, and St Catherine's College, Cambridge 1913–14. He was secretary of the hydrographic department of the KMT naval ministry before transferring to the Ministry of Communications, c. 1926. He worked as traffic manager of major Chinese railways, had charge of KMT transportation in Singapore and Manila at the time of Pearl Harbor, and went into hiding from the Japanese for three years. As director of communications in Taiwan (1945–50) he had charge of railways, highways, harbours, shipping and airfields. He acquired the ambassadorial prefix by his role in the KMT mission to Japan, 1950–52. When T-R met him he had been chairman of the state-owned China Merchants Steam Navigation Company for nine years.

56 Lin Yutang (1895–1976), who attended the universities of Shanghai, Harvard and Leipzig, had taught English literature at Peking University 1923–26. Harold Acton found Lin 'a staid, stilted little man' who 'specialized in a Rotarian brand of facetiousness'. Lin deprecated national assertiveness: 'the prospect of 400,000,000 million meek Chinese people learning to be "cocky" and "stand on their rights" rather confuses and frightens me' (*My Country and My People* (1939), p. 397).

57 George Kung-chao Yeh [Ye Gongchao] (1904–1981) was educated in Illinois, Maine, Massachusetts and at the University of Cambridge. He was a jovial, voluble head of the English department at Peking University 1935–41; London representative of the KMT's Ministry of Information, 1942–45; director of the European department of the KMT's Ministry of Foreign Affairs 1946–49; first Minister for Foreign Affairs of the ROC, 1949–58; ambassador in Washington, 1958–61; minister without portfolio, 1962–78.

58 Probably Chang Kia-ngau [Zhang Jia-ao] (1889–1979), who was KMT Minister of Railways 1935–37 and of Communications 1937–43. He had been educated at universities in New York and Japan. During 1947–48 he held the presidency of the Central Bank of China.

59 Li Ji (1896–1979), or Li Chi, was awarded a PhD in anthropology at Harvard in 1923. In 1928 he was appointed head of the newly established department of archaeology in Academia Sinica, and led the excavations of Yinxu. In 1949 he moved to Taipei, where he ran the departments of archaeology and anthropology at National Taiwan University.

60 Li Dong-fang (Orient Lee) (1907–1998) was awarded a doctorate in history by the University of Paris in 1931. He taught history and philosophy at the universities of Peking, Tsinghua, Fudan and finally Chinese Culture.

61 Hu Chi Chung (1927–2012) was a cartographer in the Chinese National Marine Corps who settled in Taiwan in 1950. He joined the Fifth Moon Group of contemporary Taiwanese artists in 1961. Its members blended the bold brush-strokes of traditional Chinese calligraphy with the shapes and colours used by European and American contemporary artists.

George Yeh I already knew: he is a member of the Savile Club, and he was introduced to me there long ago, as he told Xandra, by H. G. Wells.[62] He is now minister without portfolio in the Cabinet. 'Ambassador Cheng' was ambassador in Cyprus. He had been educated at Dulwich College and St. Catherine's, Cambridge, and looked and spoke like an English colonel, but overdid the colloquialisms: 'd'you mind if I peel off my coat?', 'Here's how!', 'I'm afraid I must scram now', etc. One of the professors Li (Li Tung-feng), who has anglicized his name as Orient Lee, presented me with various works in Chinese, but I had no direct conversion with him. The other (Li Shi) was the head of the Institute of History and Philology at the Academia Sinica and had been in charge of the excavations at An-yang: I enjoyed his conversation which was scholarly, well-informed and sophisticated. The painter was an abstract painter-rather in the style of David Cortez de Medalla's Filipino cousin:[63] he brought reproductions of his paintings with him and Xandra wants to organize an exhibition for him in London or Edinburgh.[64] Mr. Chiang had been a minister, then President of the Bank of China, and now presided over a glass-factory. He had lost his voice, so I can say no more about him. George Yeh had been invited to dine with the Vice-President C. K. Yen,[65] but came to us instead for dinner and went on to him afterwards; so he left fairly early.

We had a delicious dinner and animated conversation on all topics. Afterwards I had a political discussion with Mr. Wei. We spoke about broadcasts to mainland China, which he directs. He told me that they receive regular responses. At first, listeners on the mainland communicated through addresses in other countries, but now they write direct to Taiwan and the Post Office officials in red China simply turn a blind eye and send the letters to Hong Kong, whence they are forwarded. He seemed quite certain that the letters are genuine and are not controlled or tampered with. The Taiwan government

---

62 Herbert George Wells (1866–1946), novelist, scientific popularizer and political gadfly. At a dinner given by Chinese students in London to celebrate the fourteenth anniversary of the republic of China, Wells expressed his 'shock' at the nationalist movement in China. 'China is a civilisation, not a nation. We must prepare for a great cosmopolitanism, or else for a triumph of the rat and ant in humanity.' He predicted that by 2025 'a United States of Europe, a great America and a great China [would stand] as the three pillars of the world' (*The Straits Times*, 16 November 1925).

63 David Medalla (b. 1938) was a kinetic and participatory artist. In 1967 he launched Exploding Galaxy, a group of painters, musicians, performance poets and dancers attuned to hippy counter-culture.

64 No exhibition was organized.

65 Yen Chia-kan (1905–1993), vice-president of ROC 1966–75 and president 1975–78.

now has a well-developed network of agents in mainland China. At first they were organized from Taiwan, but now the headquarters are on the mainland. He was quite confident that the apparent support for the communist government is unreal: the Chinese have always masked their private dissent by a show of public conformity; and he gave historical illustrations from the end of the Sung and the end of the Ming dynasties. He offered to show me the contemporary evidence at his office, and I hope that, in our crowded programme, I shall have this opportunity.

We broke up at 9.15 after an entertainment lasting 2¼ hours and containing, in that time, a hundred times the pleasure and instruction provided in the four-hour session among those American memsahibs.

Friday, 1 December

We went first to the Fu Shin Chinese Opera School where children from the lowest age were learning to perform.[66] The school was cramped and primitive and musicians and singers were practising in competition with each other in bare rooms surrounded by elementary wash-basins. The singers sang with their backs to the music, as on the stage: the instruments are the Ku-Chin or Chinese violin, the guitar and the flute. We have asked to be taken to the opera, and we now hope that we shall go tomorrow: Mr. Hsia is clearly unmusical and unknowledgeable on these subjects, but I think that our insistence has prevailed. Afterwards we went to a nearby pottery factory, and then back to our hotel, as I must prepare a lecture for this afternoon.

This little chore came as a surprise. I found it stated as a fact in our itinerary that I would lecture to the history students of the University of Taiwan this afternoon,[67] and again tomorrow to the history students of the College of Chinese Culture.[68] Which of course I am willing to do; but I wish I had been given notice: since we were here, we have not had a moment's leisure in which I could prepare a lecture. And anyway, what was I to lecture on? I asked Eddie Hsia, and he thought it should be on History. But what history do they know? Can I refer to Machiavelli and Hobbes, Queen Elizabeth and

---

66 Pupils at the Fu Sheng (Fu Xing Ju Xiao) opera school in Taipei sang in Hokkien dialect rather than in Mandarin.

67 The Taihoku Imperial University had been founded by the Japanese in 1928. After Chinese sovereignty was regained in 1945, it was renamed the National Taiwan University.

68 The Chinese Culture University had been founded in 1962 as a private university on a suburban campus near the Yang Ming national park.

Oliver Cromwell, Descartes and Galileo, when speaking to Chinese students in Formosa? I thought not. Even if I talked in general terms, how could I be sure of being intelligible to them? I suspected that their intellectual level would be low, and their English bad: that it would be like talking to American sophomores, but in a language that they did not understand. However, I applied myself to my task. I prepared a lecture which I entitled 'Some Reflexions on the Study of History', and which seemed to me ideal for my purposes. It was clear and concrete, and yet it made no arcane allusions, quoted no esoteric European names; it took its illustrations from modern times; and there were a few happy references to China and Chinese history. Altogether, I said to myself, as I folded up my notes and went down to lunch, I could not have done better.

In fact, it soon became clear, I could hardly have done worse. We arrived at the university at 2.30: an American style campus fringed by ugly buildings in European late colonial style, the ugliest of which had been built by the Japanese. In the Arts building, the ugliest of all, we were met by an elderly professor, and went through the usual tea-drinking ceremony in strained silence. Then I was taken to a dreary lecture-hall, which was crowded with impassive oriental students. The professor made a speech in Chinese. Then I mounted the rostrum, tried to persuade myself that an enjoyable marriage of minds was about to take place, and began.

Every word fell absolutely flat. I tried to animate my discourse by evocative gestures. The faces remained utterly stable. I brought forward my happy quotation from Voltaire about the Chinaman in Holland and Bossuet's *Universal History*.[69] Not a laugh, not a smile, not even a light in a single eye. In despair I cut out a choice passage which I thought would be too difficult for them. I abbreviated the lecture. I lowered the level. I improvised new simplicities and spelt my words slowly, reducing the felicitatious polysyllables to blunt short words. But it was no good. When I ended – a fine clear peroration – there was absolute silence, except for the continuing noise of lessons being learned by rote and repeated in chorus as in a primary school, next door. Then I folded up my notes emphatically, stuffed them in my pocket, and fixed a deliberate

---

69 Voltaire describes a Chinese visitor to Holland in 1723, 'who was both a learned man and a merchant, two things that ought by no means to be incompatible; but which, thanks to the profound respect that is shown to money, and the little regard that the human species pay to merit, have become so among us'. The Chinese finds a copy of Bossuet's *Universal History* for sale in a shop, and is dismayed by its scant reference to the splendours of China's dynasties, arts and literature.

eye on the Chairman. That at least established my point, and they applauded. The chairman then made a speech in English thanking me for my lecture on European history since the 16th century and then perplexing me still more by recapitulating some of the things that I actually did say. Then we broke up, and Xandra and I went first to Hu Chi-Ching's exhibition; then to a tailor who is to make me a tropical suit for our visit to Angkor; after which we returned to our hotel.

I felt in a state of depression and collapse. No doubt yesterday was anyway too much for us. It seems inconceivable that we are not both ill after that long, cold, wearisome expedition which certainly was not worth the exertion it entailed. As it is, I have a cough and am anyway feeling in pretty precarious health. The weather is cold again today; and this fiasco, and the thought that I must repeat it tomorrow, lower my morale still further. What went wrong? I ask myself. Vanity forbids me to suppose that there was anything wrong with the lecture; so I conclude that they could not follow it: they simply do not understand my English. Then how can tomorrow's lecture be anything but a fiasco too: a fiasco for which we must get up early and perhaps tip the wavering balance between health and illness? For we were both ill before leaving England – I had a week in bed, – and we both arrived taking a course of antibiotics to keep us from relapse. On arrival at our hotel, we went to bed till dinner. Then Xandra went out shopping with the Hsias – the elegant Mrs. Hsia had been mobilised to show her the way round the *couturiers* of Taipei – and I received a visit from the younger brother of my Taiwanese Oxford protégé, Chen.[70] He came bearing gifts from his parents and stayed for a short time. Then I retired to read and write: to read Douglas Hurd's *The Arrow War* and to write this diary.[71]

---

70 T-R's visitor Yuan Chin-shen wrote (8 August 1969): 'I greatly enjoyed talking with you and have a vivid recollection of your friendliness and scholarly manners' (Dacre 1/2/13). His elder brother was a junior member of Hertford College, Oxford.

71 *The Arrow War: an Anglo-Chinese confusion, 1858–1860* had recently been published. Douglas Hurd (b. 1930) served under Humphrey Trevelyan and Con O'Neill when they were *chargés d'affaires* in Peking during the 1950s. In 1967 he was starting a political career which culminated with his period as Foreign Secretary in 1989–95. Hurd quoted Lord Elgin's parting salvo to the English business colony in Shanghai: 'Uninvited, and by methods not always of the gentlest, we have broken down the barriers behind which these ancient nations sought to conceal … the rags and rottenness of their waning civilisation. Neither our own consciences nor the judgment of mankind will acquit us if when we are asked to say to what use we have turned our opportunities, we can only say that we have filled our pockets from the ruins we have found or made.'

When Xandra came back, she said that I was not to be too downcast about the lecture. According to Eddie Hsia, no Chinese audience 'responds' to a lecture: they sit and politely listen. All the same, there was a dead-pan quality about that audience at the university, and no polite assurance can overcome that discouragement.

Saturday, 2 December

Xandra woke up with violent sinus-headaches, so we decided that she should stay in bed and avoid the ordeal of my lecture at the College of Chinese Culture. I got up and breakfasted alone downstairs, with the raucous voices of three American women preaching their strident inanities to the entire restaurant from the next table. As I winced, I caught a sympathetic glance from the polite Chinese waitress. Then, at 8.30, Eddie Hsia appeared, and we motored, through mist and heavy rain, out of the city and up into the mountains, past the villas of millionaires (and of Lin Yu-tang), till we came to the College, poised obviously in a splendid position but now wrapped in mist. It is a private college, with 8000 students, both undergraduate and graduate, founded five years ago by a Dr. Chang Chi-yun, formerly Minister of Education.[72] Connected with it is an Institute of Advanced Studies. Ever before I entered the lecture room I was struck by the difference between this college and the university which I visited yesterday. The architecture was modern, sometimes classico-modern, the halls clean, the general atmosphere was of efficiency. I had a large audience, and I watched it carefully: it never responded, but it was closely attentive; the attention encouraged me, and I gave them the full treatment, neither abbreviating nor lowering the level. At the end I felt that the lecture, this time, was not only better in itself then yesterday but also a success.

Then I was taken by car further into the hills and found myself in the War Academy, among buildings of even greater elegance and opulence commanding a whole valley to themselves. I was received by Dr. Chang Chi-yun himself, who, having founded the College and the Institute, with funds largely from the Chinese Cultural Foundation, is now director of this War Academy, or Imperial Staff College. He was a charming, courteous, cultivated man, and

---

72 Chang Chi-yun [Zhang Qiyun] (1901–1985) was a historian and geographer who had been a research fellow at Harvard in 1943–45. He served as Taiwan's Minister of Education in 1954–58 and as Minister of Atomic Energy, 1955–58. After his political retirement, he devoted himself to compiling his monumental *Five Thousand Years of Chinese History* and to the foundation of the Chinese Culture University.

he showed me over the college and the library, presented me with some of his works on Chinese history, and then took me to a magnificent neo-classical palace, the Sun Yat-Sen Memorial Hall. Everything here was on the most lavish scale and most elegantly decorated: splendid reception rooms, a large and a small auditorium, a dining room to hold 1800 banqueters, a suite of rooms reserved for visiting heads of state. The whole building, Dr. Chang said, had been built in eight months, on 24-hour shifts. Inevitably I was reminded of the Great Hall of the People in Peking, with its vast auditorium and banqueting hall, also built in record time; but what a difference between the gross solidity, the heavy proletarian bombast of that hideous metropolitan megalith and this graceful palace in the hills! I was enchanted by it, and flattered too when Dr. Chang pressed me to come and dine there and speak to 'a group of ministers'. I wriggled hard – for when can I find the time? – but he pressed harder, and in the end I surrendered, perhaps rather to the flattery than to the force, and it has been fixed for Thursday, after our return from Kinmen (Quemoy).

I am somewhat perplexed both by the War Academy and by Dr. Chang. The War Academy is clearly something more than a mere war academy: it seems to be the cultural as well as the defensive centre of the government. It is obviously a holy of holies. Eddie Hsia told me that he had only once been there before. I was told by Dr. Chang that the Council of Defence meets there, under the Presidency of Chiang Kai-shek, and that three cabinet ministers (none of them service ministers) are graduates of it. Its library is far more than a military or war library. And Dr. Chang seems, at times, out of place there – or would be if it were only a war academy: for he seems to be the representative, above all, of Chinese culture. He is also the President of the newly founded China Academy, which seems far more dynamic then the Academia Sinica, and Chairman of the Editorial Board of its quarterly review, *Chinese Culture*.[73] In fact, he seems to be the driving force in the movement to unite the revival and defence of KMT China with the revival and defence of traditional Chinese culture in a new age. I found him a fascinating personality, and this whole problem, and my desire to see deeper into it, encouraged me to accept his invitation for next Thursday.

When I got back to the Hotel, Xandra was still unwell and merely had soup and toast for lunch, in bed. So, being alone, I went to the Szechuan restaurant, for which I have always hankered but from which her frail stomach has hitherto debarred me. Resisting the lure of 'bull's-penis soup', I settled for some highly

73 *Chinese Culture* had been published since 1957.

spiced shrimps and meat, with pepper and garlic, and then set out alone for a second visit to the National Museum. I spent two hours there, concentrating exclusively on the paintings, of which the Sung and Yüan paintings delighted me most – and especially, I think, the Yüan. I liked to think that at the time when the early Italian and Burgundian painters were producing crowded religious scenes, or hunts or battles, these scholar-painters of Mongol China were indifferent alike to divinity and to humanity, at least in their public forms, and painted Nature, uncontaminated by either. There were some charming earlier paintings – especially two anonymous works of the Five Dynasty period,[74] 'deer in an autumn grove' and 'deer among red maples' – but of all those exposed for views the four Yüan masters pleased me best. The later Ming and early Ch'ing paintings seemed to me suburban by comparison. I could not resist buying a copy of a delicious Sung picture (the original was not exhibited) of 'Herdsmen fleeing from a storm', for the sake of the water-buffaloes and the straw-clad herdsmen perched on their backs. There was also exhibited a Ch'ing picture of a herdsman on a water-buffalo, by Yang Chin, 1644–1728, which showed no change in the herdsman's straw skirt in 800 years.

Xandra got up in the evening and we went, with Eddie and the elegant Mrs. Hsia, to the opera: by continuous gentle pressure we have achieved this success. The performance was given by the Armed Forces Opera Troupe, for the benefit of some visiting and newly decorated S. Vietnamese generals. The entire audience, except for ourselves, was military, and at the end of the performance we were presented to the general, general Wang (Xandra as *La fille du maréchal*).[75] Three pieces were played: first 'Reunion in an Old City', a story of the Three Kingdoms period, whose hero, the King of Wu, I recognized as the same rose-crowned red-faced prince whom we had seen in the open-stage opera in the Taoist temple courtyard. Then came a mere dance, followed by 'the White Serpent', which I had seen in Peking. The first seemed a little wooden to me, but I fear that I am setting too high a standard in comparing it with 'The Female General' which I saw in Peking. The last was marvellously done, as a brilliant acrobatic performance. I love the Chinese opera: its majestic gait, its ceremonialism, its symbolism, its combination on artificial gravity

---

74 The period between the fall of the Tang dynasty in 907 and the founding of the Song dynasty in 960.

75 Xandra was introduced as the daughter of Field Marshal Haig to Wang Sheng (1915–2006), then deputy director of the General Political Warfare Department, the intelligence and covert military branch, and head of the department from 1975. His enemies accomplished his exile as ambassador to Paraguay in 1983.

with acrobatic virtuosity. But the Hsias, I'm afraid, do not share this taste. Charming and elegant though they are, they are fundamentally suburban in their tastes: they prefer (as they admitted) 'Western movies'.

Sunday, 3 December

Xandra, who had revived last night, and enjoyed the opera, was in a poor state again this morning, and stayed in bed. We are due to leave for Kaohsiung at 12.15, so our plans remained in some suspense till her state should be clear. I got up and packed in anticipation; then, at 10 o'clock, I received a visitor. He was called Nguyen [blank space], and his surname is evidently pronounced Ruã.[76] He is a friend of Chen, who had written to him, asking him to call on me.

I found him enchanting. He is a graduate student at Taiwan university, study-ing ancient Chinese thought (Chou to Chin dynasties).[77] He came from the mainland in 1948, at the age of six. His father was a merchant. His mother died when he was two, his father soon after the migration. He had a sister 20 years older than himself, and two brothers, also much older than himself, one an officer, the other a teacher; of whom however he sees little. He lives entirely alone: that is, he lives in a dormitory of the university and studies, and wishes to go on studying, supported by scholarships eked out by occasional small contributions from his brothers, or one of them. I felt sorry for him in his solitude, but he was not sorry for himself: he felt free, he said. He had attended my lecture at the university and encouraged me by his praise of it, and he asked me a series of very intelligent questions. I was sorry when he left, sorry that I should probably not see him again. I found him infinitely attractive, a pure spirit, like some young Taoist disciple seeking wisdom in solitude. In discussion about the lessons of history I told him that there were no short cuts, and he seemed positively pleased at the thought of a long and difficult way.

Xandra decided to get up and risk the expedition to Kaohsiung. We set out with some trepidation, for it was clearly the expedition to Taroko on that cold day, and the waiting in the draughty aerodrome at Hua-lien, that brought her down and me half-down; and today too is cold and wet and the journey is by air. However, we faced it. We flew by FAT (Far Eastern Air Transport),[78] in a

---

76 Impossible to identify.

77 The Chou dynasty dates from circa 1122 BC: the Ch'in dynasty ruled 221–107 BC.

78 Far Eastern Air Transport had operated regional aerial services from Taipei and Kaohsiung airports since 1957.

two-engine plane, and soon we passed out of the rainclouds into clear sky and saw sharp, serrated, thickly forested hills to the east as we flew southward over the coastal plain of Taiwan. When we emerged from the plane at Kaohsiung airport, the air was hot, very hot, and we motored through sugar-cane plantations and banana groves to the city, which is the second largest city in Taiwan (700,000: Taipei being 1,200,000). After settling into the Grand Hotel – a luxurious modern hotel on the edge of the broad river Aihoa – we were taken on an expedition to Tainan, the ancient capital of Formosa, Koxinga's capital.[79]

It was a disastrous expedition. The taxi was small and uncomfortable. Eddie sat in front with the driver, Xandra and I behind. For all our adjurations, the driver repeatedly lowered his window and Xandra wilted in the draught. In order to show us some 'reconstructed landholdings', the driver took us off the main road on to a bye-road, and then told Eddie that it was quicker to stay on the bye-road which would also bring us to Tainan. It was not. We bumped and jolted in that cramped, unsprung car, through groves of bananas and sugar-cane, soya bean and papaya. The dust poured in through the ever re-opened window. We stuck behind a constant succession of deliberate water-buffaloes, slowly pulling gigantic loads of sugar-cane. The sun declined and it became cold. Xandra's face became more pinched, her expression more hopeless, as she involved her nose in a thin gauze scarf and sighed that, deluded by the heat, she had left her coat behind. When we reached Tainan, it was already darkling. We went into Koxinga's temple, but its quality had disappeared with the light. When we re-emerged, feeling thoroughly cross (for the long return-journey was still to come), the taxi had disappeared altogether. Ultimately we were told that, while stationary, it had been hit by a moving car and that the driver had gone in search of a garage or the police, or his assailant. Not one knew when he would reappear. We shoved Xandra into a shop to keep her out of the draught and the shopkeeper gave her a chair. After about ten minutes Eddie, seeing her distress, went in search of the taxi. Where he had disappeared from sight the taxi appeared from the other direction. By the time we had re-assembled all our force, it was dark. We looked reluctantly at Koxinga's castle but absolutely refused to do more, telling Eddie that we would prefer to come again tomorrow, omitting a factory, and see Taiwan by daylight. To this, happily, he agreed.

---

79 Tainan was founded by the Dutch East India Company as a strategic outpost and trading station called Fort Zeelandia. The pirate Koxinga [Zheng Chenggong] (1624–1663) expelled the Dutch colonists in 1661–2, and established the kingdom of Tungning in south-west Formosa. Tainan subsequently became the capital of the Taiwan prefecture until 1887, when Taipei replaced it as the provincial capital.

So we put Xandra in the front of the taxi and drove straight home. The journey took an hour (it had taken two hours to come), and both the hour and the two hours, and the visit between them, were a waste of time: we would have done far better to rest in the hotel, where I could have been writing my diary and Xandra could have recovered from the air-journey and been better tomorrow. As it is, she may well be worse.

We dined in the hotel – a dull American dinner – and after it we did what we should have done before it. I wrote these words and Xandra went to bed.

Monday, 4 December

My first appointment today was to visit the Kaohsiung Export Processing Zone at 9.0 a.m.[80] We decided that Xandra should miss this and have breakfast late and in bed. I appeared for breakfast at about 8.0 and found Eddie sitting at a table with a pleasant-faced young Chinese who, it transpired, had been with him in the Navy. He was a local boy and now kept a store in his village near Kaohsiung. They were both eating a gigantic American breakfast of two fried eggs, bacon and four great batter puddings which they covered with butter and syrup. Eddie is really very Americanised: he has none of the native Chinese tastes, and always goes for the most revolting of American dishes. After breakfast we went to the KEPZ as planned.

It is a peninsula, on reclaimed land in the harbour, and consists of a duty-free factory area, surrounded by a protective perimeter. Some of the factories are built by the state and leased to manufacturers; some are built by the manufacturers to their own taste, on land for which they pay a ground-rent only. But all manufacture [is] for export only and thus [*sic*] find it convenient to use this duty-free enclave. I was taken through two factories by a Mr. Thomas T. C. Kuan,[81] who had Toynbeean ideas about history[82] and submitted them very respectfully to my criticism as we drove from factory to factory. The first factory was run by General Micro-Electronics, a subsidiary of Philco-Ford.[83] 450 girls,

---

80 The export zone had been opened in 1966.

81 Unidentified.

82 Arnold Toynbee (1889–1975), sometime professor of international history at the LSE and director of studies at the Royal Institute of International Affairs, had arrayed his philosophy of cyclical history in his twelve-volume *Study of History* (1934–61).

83 Philco, a leading US manufacturer of record-players, air conditioners, refrigerators and space electronics, had slid into financial trouble when it tried to diversify into computers. It was bought by the Ford Motor Company in 1961, and reconstituted as Philco-Ford in 1966.

working in day and night shifts, with their eyes glued to microscopes, carried the manufacture of transistors through the 18 stages of their construction. I walked along the benches and at each stage the personnel supervisor, Mr. Yih-Shou Lee,[84] made me look through the microscope and see the minute organism gaining an infinitesimal cell here, correcting its internal structure there, until, at the end, a three-pronged object not much bigger than a pin emerged to be a single component in a computer. I naturally thought of Adam Smith's chapter on the manufacture of pins by subdivision of labour, but my heart sank as I thought of those human lives engaged in a kind of micro-monotony, those eyes ruined, those minds contracted to a pinpoint through a microscope. How great, I asked Mr. Lee, was the turnover, secretly hoping that he would say that none of the girls lasted for more than a year, so that I could then imagine them spending the rest of their youth in more agreeable, or diversified, or natural, or varied pursuits; but he replied proudly that it was only 0.1% (or some such figure). The girls, he said, seemed to like the work: the factory was air-conditioned, they had tea-breaks of ten minutes every two hours … so I saw them, in my mind, being gradually conditioned to enjoy their termite-life, like battery hens who find nothing really so or cozy or unexacting as their battery. Then I was taken to another factory, where two floors were filled by young men making children's clothes. There was a flannelly fug throughout both floors. I contrived not to scrutinize the detail, but returned with Eddie to the hotel, picked up Xandra, and we all went to an orchid-nursery in the suburbs of Kaohsiung.

Eddie was out of his element in anything so close to nature as a plant-nursery, and unfortunately the owner of the orchidotrophy[85] was out: there were only garden-serfs who seemed to be so specialised in their labour that none knew anything beyond his little province of weeding or watering; so, apart from admiring varieties which were unlabelled and unidentifiable, we gained little from our visit. Then we returned to our hotel and, after, lunch set out, once again, for Tainan.

This time we went straight, and arrived there at about 3.0. First we visited a Roman Catholic Church built like a Chinese temple: a very bizarre mixture which should, I suppose, have dated from the 17th century, from the times of the great controversy about Chinese ceremonies, but which in fact was very modern. Then we revisited the temple of Koxinga in better light and at greater leisure – a typical temple standing in a great courtyard and with a gatehouses and surrounding

---

84 Unidentified.

85 T-R's coinage for a place where orchids are nourished.

walls all painted red, and with Koxinga's effigy, like a Buddha, domination the central temple – and 'Koxinga's castle', in similar style, but rebuilt with a good deal of Ch'ing detail, including a series of stone turtles sustaining inscribed slabs, some of them inscribed also in Manchu, set up by K'ang Hsi. But the building that pleased us most was the temple of Confucius, which had no Ch'ing frills, no Buddhising vulgarities of personality-cult but a delightful, impersonal, quiet atmosphere, enhanced by the great, shady banyan trees growing in front of it, under which old men were sitting, while students sat under the outer walls of the temple, painting, and children a little further away, were noisily playing, in contrast with the quiet inside the walls. We dawdled there, enjoying the place; but were then urged on the Eddie, for surely we must visit Fort Zeelandia, the Dutch fort which Koxinga had conquered, and which was some way out of the town.

We agreed, and found ourselves being driven down a road which ran between two arms of water. On our left was what seemed a canal, filled with fishing-boats: a delightful sight; on our right, wet paddy-fields. Ultimately we came to the castle: a thoroughly disappointing mixture of uninteresting ruin and banal reconstruction. The Japanese had rebuilt the brick terrace; a hideous square tower of modern concrete had replaced, and presumed to represent, Fort Zeelandia. We declined to waste time there. But the journey was not wasted, for our way back was even more delightful than our way down. We passed through the town, or village, of An-ping, to which the tower belongs. The town lay on our left, and already the fish-market (which seems equivalent to the town) was in full activity; while on our right was now the canal, or waterway, down which another fleet of fishing-boats was moving, in ceremonial procession, with red and green lights, towards the sea. So we returned to Taiwan and (after looking at another unrewarding Buddhist temple) went to the railway station to catch the train to our next staging post, Taichung.

It was a very comfortable journey: a very clean train, with attendants constantly supplying face-towels, tea, etc. The journey lasted three hours, during which I began *Middlemarch*: a novel which, I'm afraid, I haven't read but which James has first recommended, then lent to me.[86] I took it to Rumania in March

---

86 James Howard-Johnston (b. 1942) was T-R's stepson. In 1972 he became Fellow by Special Election of Corpus Christi College, Oxford and was elected in the same year as Labour councillor for the South Ward of Oxford borough council. He represented that ward on the new county council, 1973–77, and East Ward in 1981–87. He served as deputy leader of the Labour group, 1981–85. He was university lecturer in Byzantine studies at Oxford, 1971–2009. His research as a historian of Byzantium AD 500–1100, especially interested in historiography and relations with Armenia and Bulgaria, drew him deep into Islamic history.

of this year, but it returned unread. However, this time I have determined to read it. His loan of *Wuthering Heights* alleviated the horror of life in 'mainland China'; why should not *Middlemarch* enhance the pleasure of Taiwan?

We reached Taichung at 8.00 p.m. and went to the Railway Hotel – a second-class international hotel. The Grand Hotel at Kaohsiung was first-class international: there we had a spacious room with a sitting room opening out from it, and although the windows would open, the air-conditioning worked. Here we had all the disadvantages, none of the advantages, of 'international' status: the room was cramped, the windows were sealed; the air-conditioning machine, when we at last got it to work, discharged such a fearful draught, and did it with such hideous groans, that we soon turned it off again, preferring to be stifled. In addition, the food was revolting. Altogether we had a disagreeable dinner and an uncomfortable night, after a long and tiring day, we began to think, looking at our programme for tomorrow, that we would have done better, as well as gained a day, if we had cut out this visit to Taichung.

Tuesday, 5 December

When we woke this morning, my first thought was that Xandra should forgo the morning's visits – to Tunghai University, to the Provincial Assembly and the Provincial Government. She was tired with travel, had set out with sinusitis, and now complained of a skin rash, perhaps caused by eating fish, perhaps by Dr Mullins's precautionary antibiotic pills.[87] But how could anyone spend a restful morning in that disgusting hotel? It seemed inconceivable; and she herself could not conceive it. So we decided to undertake together the full programme, came down to breakfast at 7:30 and at 8.0 was ready to set out to Tunghai University, prepared for a dull morning of official interviews followed by a disgusting lunch at our hotel. Then we were to go on, by train, to Taipei.

Our fears were happily confounded. Tunghai University was delightful.[88] It is some way out of Taichung, in a most beautiful position, and it is quite different from any other college or university which we have visited. It is a private university, a protestant missionary foundation, the residuary legatee, in a sense, of the 19 protestant missionary colleges of the mainland which have now been dissolved and destroyed by the communist revolution. We were

---

87 David Mullins (1923–2011), who had read medicine at Trinity College, Oxford, 1942–48, was in general practice in Woodstock Road.

88 Tunghai University was a private institution founded by Methodist missionaries in 1955.

received by the President, Dr. Wei,[89] a genial, jovial man who wore a light khaki suit, the uniform of the college. He wore it, he explained, to encourage the students to wear it too, and not to compete in sartorial expense. The students, we observed, did not much follow his example. But what delighted us most was the design of the place: both the lay-out which was rural, and the architecture, which was a wonderfully successful blend of modern and classical, western and Chinese: elegant, spacious, functional buildings which yet, with their identical Chinese tiled roofs, their trellis and lattice-work, and other details, had a traditional character. The central feature of the place was 'the Mall', a paved causeway rising by gradual steps up sloping ground. On either side of it were 'colleges', i.e. faculty buildings, but not lining it or crowded upon each other: they stood back and each seemed isolated among its trees. Behind them rose the pointed spire of the new chapel given by the late Henry Luce, in memory of his father, who had been a Presbyterian missionary in China and who died in 1940.[90] This was a very modern design: externally simply [*sic*] to curved planes, as of intersecting circles, narrowing towards a point at their intersection, which point was the spire; but internally the whole surface of the walls was patterned with lozenges, which diminished as they rose higher, thus breaking up the surface and lightening the impression. Beyond the chapel the hills of central Taiwan rose above the trees. As we saw them, they were emerging from the morning mist: delicate outlines in the soft Chinese light, as in a Chinese painting. The whole lay-out, both in general and in detail, is the work of a Chinese architect in America called Pei.[91] He has been commissioned, Mr. Wei told us, to design the Kennedy Memorial Library at Harvard. After we had been taken round the college, we had tea with Mr. & Mrs. Wei in their house which, like everything else – the staff houses, the retirement cottages for the staff, etc. – was charming. Then we left, in a good mood, to visit the Provincial Assembly and Government.

---

89 Wu The Yao (1915–1994), who had been awarded a Harvard doctorate in political science in 1946, was President of Tunghai University, 1957–71.

90 Henry Winters Luce (1868–1941) was a Presbyterian missionary in China, 1897–1928. His son Henry Robinson Luce (1898–1967) founded *Time* magazine in 1923, *Fortune* in 1930 and *House and Home* in 1952.

91 The Luce Memorial Chapel is a tent-like cone, which was built in 1962–63 at a cost of 125,000 dollars. I. M. [Ieoh Ming] Pei (1917–2019), one of the finest twentieth-century architects, designed it.

These were also both in normal surroundings. The province of Taiwan, in Japanese times, had been governed from Taipei; but with the arrival there of the national government, the administrative congestion had become too great and the provincial capital had been moved to Taichung. The Assembly was in session when we arrived, but the Speaker gave over his place to his deputy and came to entertain and inform us. Then we went on to another village where the provincial government has its offices. We were placed in chairs and given a recorded briefing, by an American voice issuing from a machine, while a young man with a wand stood before a service of panels, pointing in turn to tables, diagrams, statistics. We felt that we could have dispensed with this process, especially since the full text of the 'briefing' was already in our hands. However, we were grateful to our host, Mr. Chou Tien-kou,[92] the Director of the Office of Information there, for he afterwards invited us to lunch in Taichung and thus saved us from the horrors of our hotel.

I must admit that, during the 'briefing', my disengaged mind had been dwelling chiefly on these horrors; for I could not think what I could possibly eat off that menu, and yet to fast would have offended Eddie. Last night, though hungry, I contented myself with soup and an omelette – the only thing that looked (on the menu) eatable: it was totally uneatable in fact. To escape from this disgusting diet to the delights of Chinese food was therefore a pleasant surprise, and in fact we had a very enjoyable luncheon-party which crowned and terminated an unexpectedly pleasant morning in Taichung.

At 3.0 p.m. we took the train to Taipei, arriving there at 6.0. We dined in our hotel, and then the Hsias appeared and took us to our respective tailors to collect my linen suit for Angkor, Xandra's Chinese evening dress for Scotland.

Wednesday, 6 December

We had breakfast at 6.0 a.m. and were taken at 7.20 to the military airport to be flown to Kinmen (Quemoy) where we are to stay the night.[93] At the airport, a Captain Lee took charge of us.[94] He is a captain in the Army. His English was not good. After some conversation, he told us that he spoke French too, and thereafter we conversed mainly in French; but it was doubtful whether his

---

92 Chou Tien-kou published a study of Taiwan's industrialization strategy in 1985.

93 The Kinmen archipelago was the ROC territory closest to the mainland, and had been the object of hostile PRC action, especially in 1958.

94 Lee is untraceable.

French was any better. However, between English and French we understood each other well enough. We had rather more conversation with him then we had expected, for the plane, which was due to leave at 7.40, did not leave till nearly 10.0; which drew many laments from Xandra, thus unnecessarily made to rise several hours before her preferred hour.

We flew in a lumbering freight plane, crowded with Chinese soldiers returning to duty in Kinmen. We sat along the sides, wearing Mae West life-jackets, as in war-time.[95] We flew south as far as Taichung, then to Penghu (the Pescadores),[96] where we dropped very low over the islands – flat islands of red earth, closely cultivated. From then on we flew very low, under the enemy's radar-screen, and protected by fighter-cover, until we landed in Kinmen, after a flight of an hour and forty minutes.

At Kinmen we were taken to a little reception room at the airport and presented to the commanding general who was awaiting us.[97] He seemed somewhat anxious and was continually called to the telephone. Xandra said, 'I think something has happened'. Being trained in security, I forbore to show any curiosity, but she did not hesitate, and elicited a reply. 'The military situation has suddenly become very tense', we were told. It seemed that reconnaissance had shown a great build-up on the communist side. In fact, Kinmen had called Taipei to stop our plane from coming, but too late. However, since we were there, we were to receive the full treatment, and we all – the General, the captain, Xandra and I – got into jeeps and were driven to the little town of Kinmen where there is a HQ with a hostel for visitors. We were shown to our room, sat down to tea, and then had an excellent Chinese lunch with the General. But all the time the General was being called to the telephone. Finally we were told part of the problem. Nothing, it was thought, would happen today; but it was questionable whether any plane would fly to Taipei tomorrow. If we cared to stay for a few days, we would be welcome, but if we wished to be back in Taipei by tomorrow night, it would be best to leave this afternoon: a plane could go at about 4.0 …

We agreed that it was best to leave this afternoon and the General gave orders accordingly. When it was confirmed that a plane could take us, the afternoon was devoted to seeing Kinmen. Eddie had told us that we would

---

95 The swelling curves of life-jackets issued during the Second World War led to the preservers being nicknamed after the curvaceous Hollywood film star Mae West (1893–1980).

96 The archipalego in the Taiwan strait.

97 Unidentified.

be surprised by what we would see: the vast underground fortifications, the military preparedness; and I was ready to admire a Vaubanesque system of defence.[98] But we saw none of this; and since clearly it had been intended that we should see it –it was implied not only by Eddie's remarks but also by the document we had had to sign at Taipei, in which, among other things, we had declared that we visited Kinmen by our own will and absolved the Republic of any responsibility for our death or injury there – we could only conclude that the sudden frontier tension made a visit to that (western) side of the island inadvisable. Instead the General took us to see an old folk's home, a school, a distillery, the local museum, and a summer-house on a lake built, on the order of the president, for this entertainment of the troops and inhabitants. The old folk's home was enchanting. It was built in the rough form of a large, indented quadrangle. At the centre of one side was the formal gateway: opposite it were the public rooms. The rest of the quadrangles consisted of almshouses, each for two persons, married couples or two single persons. In the centre was the temple. The buildings were all painted pale blue, the window frames brown and yellow: only the great gateway and the pillars of the temple were red. The inhabitants were all dressed in dark blue. They gathered to give us a great welcome and we visited some of them, including an old lady of 102, in their almshouses.

At 4.0 we arrived at the airport and sat in conversation in the reception room. The General was charming throughout, took infinite trouble, and though continually called to the telephone and clearly concerned by the military developments, seemed entirely at ease as a host. He presented Xandra with two jars of Kinmen porcelain and me with a bottle of Kinmen wine. We never discovered his name: I did not dare ask because one of the things which, in my signed declaration, I had promised not to do was to photograph 'the name of the general'. At about 4.30 we were told that the plane was ready to take off and we went aboard.

It was not the plane that had brought us. That had already returned. The general had ordered a special plane for us alone: Xandra, myself and Captain Lee, who returned later with dozens of bottles from the distillery. It was a somewhat similar freight-plane, and we flew very low, with fighter-cover, as before. The plane was darkened, and we sat in silence, on opposite sides, in our

---

98 Sébastien Le Prestre de Vauban, later Marquis de Vauban and Maréchal de France (1633–1707), military engineer responsible for building or strengthening the fortifications of some 300 French cities after 1667.

Mae Wests. I felt back in 1943. As we left, a Chinese colonel had explained about the fighter-cover: it was very easy, he said encouragingly, to get shot down so near to the mainland. We flew back more directly, cutting out the Pescadores, and kept low almost till we reached the coast of Taiwan. Where we landed at Taipei, and the door of the plane was opened, the ground staff gave a great cheer. We did not know how to interpret this.

By 7.0 we were back in our hotel, and glad to be back. Clearly, if we had stayed the night in Kinmen, we would, in the circumstances, have been both embarrassing and embarrassed. As it was, we had seen the place – although not the fortifications – and we had gained a night. At Kinmen, we would probably have had to rise early and then, as today, wait long. As it is, we can enjoy a long night and tomorrow is an unexpectedly free day in which I shall have leisure to prepare my speech to the War Academy.

Thursday, 7 December

Today we relaxed: woke late, and lingered long, Xandra in bed, I writing up this diary. Then we went to the consulate, called on the jolly Commander Nicholls and the visa-office, and there discovered that our ambassador in Bangkok is Tony Rumbold.[99] How silly of us not to have found this out before! We returned to our hotel and sent him a wire in the hope of seeing him over the week-end; for our plan is to fly to Hong Kong on Saturday, spend the inside of the day there, and then fly on that night to Bangkok, where we shall stay till Monday. On Monday we go on to Angkor.

In the afternoon I went to the Historical Museum. It was a disappointment. It was not, properly speaking, a historical museum at all: it was simply a local museum. Its nucleus was the provincial museum of Honan, many of whose contents had been brought here (consequently some good Han and T'ang objects from Loyang). On this nucleus other treasures had accumulated, and until the imperial treasures were exhibited in the National Museum it had served as a very adequate museum; but now it is totally eclipsed. However, I did learn something, for one set of rooms was decorated as a replica of the

---

99 Sir Anthony Rumbold (1911–1983) was elected as a fellow of the Queen's College, Oxford in 1933 before entering the Foreign Office in 1935. He was minister at the Paris embassy in 1960–63, ambassador at Bangkok 1965–67, and at Vienna 1967–70. T-R's friend Sir Patrick Reilly wrote of him: 'Rumbold, with great ability and generations of diplomacy behind him, should have gone quickly to the top of the Service ... He seemed content to be Ambassador in Bangkok and Vienna: but neither post was worthy of him' (Bodleian, Ms Eng c 6921, ff 22–23).

Tun-hwan caves in Sinkiang of which I had not known. They were apparently discovered by accident by a Taoist hermit in 1900 and are cavern-temples, Buddhist in inspiration, of the T'ang-Sung period. They contained, apart from the wall-paintings, 1700 early printed books. Tun-hwan added to Turfan make Singkiang, historically, even more interesting.

In the evening we went out to Yang Ming Shan for my speech to the War Academy. Chang Chi-yun was our host at dinner. The other guests included Li Tung-feng (Orient Lee), W.G. Goddard and Mrs Goddard,[100] ambassador Wu Nan-ru,[101] Dr Sung (Dean of Research at the Institute of History in the College of Chinese Culture),[102] and Mr Chai (Chang chi-yun's secretary). Goddard is an Australian by birth, formerly professor in China, now – aged about 80 – director of the Institute of Pacific Relations in the China Academy.[103] He is the author of an excellent book on Formosa which the Rosenthals[104] gave us before leaving Oxford and which we have both read.[105] He spends half the year here, half in England.

After dinner we went into a large hall where the audience was awaiting us. It was a military audience, colonels and upwards. Chiang chi-yun introduced me and then, to my surprise, presented me with a scroll and declared that I had been elected an Academician of the China Academy. Though greatly flattered, I could not help feeling that there was a comic element in this, for the document referred to my important contributions to Chinese studies. However it is a

---

100 William George Goddard (1887–1986) was a Methodist preacher in New South Wales and Queensland 1908–14, lived in Japan during the 1920s, broadcast weekly commentaries on Asian and world politics for a Brisbane radio station in 1930s, and from 1954 was a lobbyist for Taiwan in London, acting through the Office of Free China Information in New Cavendish Street. He married his second wife Jessie MacLennan (a New Zealand radio commentator) in 1953.

101 Wu Nanru (1898–1975) had been *chargé d'affaires* of the Chinese Embassy in Moscow during the 1930s, and ambassador to Switzerland in the 1940s.

102 The Far East Research Institute had been founded in 1962, and was renamed the College of Chinese Culture by Chiang Kai-shek's decision in 1963. It was re-designated the Chinese Culture University in 1980. 'Dr Sung' is possibly Jao Tsung-i (1917–2018), an expert in oracular bone inscriptions, bone divination, epigraphy, bamboo and silk texts, and calligraphy.

103 This institute had been founded with a fanfare in 1966, but did little or no work.

104 Albrecht ('Albi') Rosenthal (1914–2004), Oxford bookseller specializing in Spanish and Portuguese literature, Judaica and the history of art, bought the renowned music firm of Otto Haus in 1955. He was president of the Oxford University Orchestra, and a member of the council of the Bodleian, to which he gave his collection of Mozart manuscripts.

105 Goddard's *Formosa: a study in Chinese history* (1966) contains shameless flattery of Chiang Kai-shek, and presents Taiwan as a Chinese settler society similar to the early British settlers in Australia, and thus providing a model for future Chinese civilization.

move in the game of one-upmanship. I can play it against Charles Boxer who, with for greater justice, finds himself a Fellow of the Academia Sinica;[106] and may it not serve also to enrage the SACU gang? After responding, I hope, in suitable terms, I delivered my lecture, which was translated, with great fluency, by ambassador Wu. I called it 'historical reflexions on the Cold War' and the burden of it was that the cold war would be won not by sacrificing permanent traditions to temporary ideological postures but by political and military containment, patience, and preservation of traditional culture: for in a generation the situation will be changed beyond recognition even if the present political divisions (Germany, Korea, Vietnam, China) are permanent. I don't know how well my meaning got through the translation or went down with the audience. Afterwards there were a few questions; then we left. As we left, Goddard came up to me and congratulated me. He was very glad, he said, that I had spoken as I did: 'they are generally fed with ideas of reconquering the mainland'; and he agreed entirely with me. Chiang Chi-yun said to me, 'as a historian, I agree with you'; but what reservations were implicit in this statement I could not tell.

Orient Lee came back with us in the car. He was excellent company; learned, gay, sophisticated. He told us that he was to dine with Arnold Toynbee when the Sage passes through Taipei on his way from an apotheosis in Japan to an apotheosis, I suppose, in Manila. He is stopping for one night only, and staying with Lin Yu-tang. I'm afraid I was rather irreverent about the Sage. Lee asked me to give one concrete instance of his method. I referred him to the Toynbeean tables of cycles of war and peace. 'Oh yes', said Lee, 'I was very impressed by those tables'. I drew out some of the details. Lee is a learned man and saw the consequences at once. 'I'm afraid I was impressed at the time', he said; 'now I am ashamed'. We told him not to mention my name at Lin Yu-tang's dinner-party; it might sprinkle a thin powder of ill-flavour over the birds-nests and the sea-slugs.[107]

---

106 Charles Boxer (1904–2000) served in the Lincolnshire regiment, 1923–47. He was seconded in an officer exchange to the Japanese army, 1930–33; joined the military intelligence department of the War Office, 1935; became an officer in Far East Combined Bureau, running British military intelligence from Shanghai to Singapore until 1941, when he was captured in the fall of Hong Kong; Japanese prisoner-of-war, 1941–45; Professor of the History of the Far East, SOAS, 1951–53.

107 T-R had criticized Toynbeean postulates of cyclical history in 'Arnold Toynbee's Millennium', *Encounter*, volume 8 (June 1957), pp. 14–28. Philip Toynbee called this, in a letter of 8 July 1957 to Donald Maclean, 'a savage and mad attack on my father' (NA KV 2/4157, serial 1013a). Maclean replied from Moscow: 'I'm all for bashing your father's theory of history but I, like you, was staggered by the accusations against Toynbee-Messiah ... I don't know about Trevor-Roper except that he is a frenetic anti-catholic which I welcome' (NA KV 2/4158, serial 1028a, undated, intercepted 21 August 1957).

Friday, 8 December

At 9.0 a.m. the Vice-Consul telephoned: he was very sorry, but he had mis-informed us. The ambassador in Bangkok is not Tony Rumbold but Sir Neil Pritchard:[108] the consular handbook was out of date. But Sir N.P. had wired to invite us to dine on Sunday and offered to help with hotel accommodation. We were dismayed, for we had sent a genial, brief, almost imperative telegram, addressed only to 'the British ambassador', on the assumption, never made clear in the text, that he was Tony. What must he have thought on receiv-ing it? I told the Vice-Consul (who admitted liability for the error) that he must explain the facts and sweeten our names before we arrive. Meanwhile we accepted the dinner, to which we feel ourselves self-invited strangers.

At 9.30 a young man from the *Taiwan Daily News* (Edward Hsu, I think)[109] came to interview us, and stayed about two hours. Like all Chinese here, he was desperately curious about mainland China, and once he knew that I had been there, he questioned me more about it than about our visit to Taiwan. Then we had lunch and afterwards paid another visit to the National Museum, looking once again at the paintings and at the porcelain. We returned to our hotel at 3.30 and spent the rest of the afternoon packing and preparing for tomorrow journey.

We dined with the Hsias at the Shansi Restaurant – a most enjoyable res-taurant, full of Chinese conviviality and Shansi food – and afterwards said goodbye to Mrs Hsias whom we like enormously. Indeed we have been very lucky in our guide: both the Hsias are friendly and civilised. Eddie's conven-tionalism and penchant for American way of life are redeemed by his urbanity and friendliness and his wife is not only elegant but also charming: she and Xandra get on really well together.

Saturday, 9 December

Eddie took us to the airport, where we said goodbye to him and took the Thai plane to Hong Kong. There we had eight hours to spend, and we followed the practical advice of Mrs. Nicholls, the American wife of the jolly naval com-mander, and took a taxi straight to the Peninsula Hotel, which engaged a driver

---

108 Sir Neil Pritchard (1911–2010), a graduate of Worcester College, Oxford, was high commissioner in Tanganyika 1961–63 and ambassador to Thailand 1967–70.

109 Edward Hsu wrote a weekly column, 'Taiwan as seen by Foreigners', for *Taiwan Ribao* (the *Taiwan Daily News*).

to show us the colony. He was a maddening driver, of the vulgar democratic Americanised kind. 'Call me George', he instructed us, but we had no occasion, or indeed opportunity, to do so, for he never ceased to pour unintelligible syllables into our ears as he drove us, first to the ferry from Kowloon to the island of Hong Kong, then round the island, through the city and to Repulse Bay and Aberdeen. I'm afraid we really hated Hong Kong. First there was the hideous vulgarity of the place, the philistinism of the architecture, the suburban way of life. Then there was the dreadful contrast of wealth and poverty: the ghastly vulgar palaces of Chinese manufacturing millionaires, tasteless, repellent, beyond belief, and the miserable wooden shanties in which refugees from the mainland have been living for ten years beside them, without, apparently, a twinge of social conscience. When I looked at that contrast, I felt a hatred of the British Empire – of the Scots and Mancunians and dissenting manufacturers and utilitarian radicals who made it – and the contrast between Hong Kong and Taiwan made me ashamed. Taiwan is a society, Hong Kong an interest. I also felt increasing contempt for the jolly Cmdr. Nicholls. I was surprised, at dinner with him, when he suggested that the present reforms in Taiwan might have been devised in fact by the Japanese in 1939. I know no grounds on which to credit the Japanese with such projects and he himself did not claim to have seen any evidence. He repeated this suggestion more emphatically and precisely when we saw him on Thursday: the present development of Taiwan, he said summarily, was simply the continuation of the Japanese plans. Then he said casually that at least, in going to Hong Kong after Taiwan, we were doing things in the right order. What did he mean? we asked. He explained that Taiwan was so seedy and Hong Kong so lively and prosperous, that Taiwan would have been a dreadful come-down after Hong Kong. I was astonished at such a statement at the time, having seen Taiwan; I am more astonished still, now that I have seen Hong Kong.

However, at Aberdeen we had an excellent sea-food lunch at the Sea Palace. We then returned to Kowloon, but had not time or daylight in which to visit the New Territories. Xandra was also determined to shop, and for two hours of frustration I followed her back across the ferry to Hong Kong and through its streets in search of a store which had advertised Italian silk parasols with scarves to match in the Taiwan paper. Ultimately we found the store, and the parasol, but my temper was almost lost in the process, as we stumbled from one blank Chinese face to another (for the advertisement had given no address) and then went to the wrong ferry. I was afraid that we would miss the plane to Bangkok for the sake of the wretched parasol.

In fact we caught it. It was the TWA plane. We flew the same way which we had come, across the war-frontier of Vietnam – searchlights shining and artillery firing beneath us – and landed in Bangkok at about 9.30. We stayed in the Oriental Hotel.

Sunday, 10 December

We woke up in Bangkok and found that our room looked out over the river. It was an attractive room, and the view cheered us. We were also cheered by a very civil letter from Sir Neil Pritchard which welcomed us and showed that all had been explained, and a note from Robert Swann,[110] who had called in person last night, hoping to take us out for dinner. He telephoned again this morning, as we were having breakfast in our room, and we agreed to go sightseeing with him this afternoon. However, one piece of news which he gave us was disconcerting. He told us that tomorrow is a holiday, and unless we already have Cambodian visas, we can hardly get them before Tuesday. As we are booked on a plane tomorrow morning, this may be serious.

There has been a muddle about our visas. In London, where every authority wanted our passport at once, we were told by the travel agency that it would be best to get the Cambodian visas in Taiwan, where we had plenty of time. In fact this was wrong advice. Cambodia has no diplomatic relations with Taiwan. So the British vice-consul in Taipei sent a cable on our behalf to the consul in Bangkok, giving all the necessary details, and asking him to take the necessary steps against our arrival. When we called at the consulate at Taipei on Thursday, we asked if there had been any reply. The vice-consul admitted that there had not, 'but my cable', he added – without much conviction, I thought – 'did not really call for a reply'. Thus, after Robert's news, it was clear

---

110 Robert Swann (1929–2001) was an old Etonian convert to Catholicism. As a scholar of Christ Church, Oxford he preferred race-meetings and the bridge table to books. In 1953–55 he was third secretary at the British Embassy in Bangkok, where he was described as doing 'para-diplomatic work'. He left government service to teach English at Bangkok University, but returned to England after contracting polio. In August 1965 he was appointed secretary-general of Amnesty International, which was soon embroiled in rows after publishing accurate but hotly contested reports of the torture, under interrogation, by British forces of Arab detainees in Aden (1966). His position was further shaken by revelations that Amnesty had accepted cash from a shadowy source called 'Harry' (probably Her Majesty's Government) for the relief of the families of political prisoners in Rhodesia. He left Amnesty in July 1967, and taught English in Bangkok and Rabat until his appointment as secretary general of the Parliamentary Association for European-Arab Cooperation, 1974–88.

that everything depended on the consul, and what he had done on receiving the cable from Taipei. At least he had had plenty of time to act, for our cable had been sent nearly a fortnight ago. The consul's name is Mr. Boyes.[111]

Having failed to find his secretary, or the duty officer, I rang the consul's home. His American wife answered for him. He was out, she said. But if he had been asked to act, we could be sure that he had acted. Anyway, he would ring us after lunch. With that, for the time being, we had to be content; and we took a taxi to the centre of the city and walked through the Sunday Sanam Luang market, where Xandra was happy for two hours goggling at silk and printed cotton designs, etc. Then we wandered round a temple – the temple of the reclining Buddha – and came back to our hotel for lunch.

After lunch the consul rang. He was very calm and self-assured. He had done nothing, he said smoothly, for there was nothing that he could do: applications for visas had to be made in person. Now that we were here, we could apply, but not before Tuesday, and hardly in time for Tuesday's plane to Cambodia – if indeed there was such a plane on Tuesday. It would be best to assume that Wednesday was the earliest day on which we could leave Bangkok. I felt furious, because of course he could have done something. He could at least have alerted the Indonesian [*sic*] consul. And even if nothing could have been arranged, he should have replied to Taipei explaining the position – saying that we must apply in person and that Monday was a holiday. We could then easily have come a day early and settled everything before this long week-end. However, the wretch had simply done nothing and said nothing, and we are now in a fix. I tried at least to cancel our flight tomorrow, but even this was impossible: no answer could be obtained from Burma Air Lines, even at the airport. We were fixed in our fix.

At 4 o'clock Robert Swann arrived. He had with him a young cousin, Peter Wellby, just down from Ch Ch: doing V.S.O. in Malaysia.[112] He took us in his

---

111 William Boyes (1910–1985) had postings from 1944 in Baghdad, Managua, Damascus and Kuwait before serving as Consul in Chicago, 1960–64, and in Bangkok from August 1964.

112 Voluntary Service Overseas began in 1958 when sixteen young volunteers went, at the Bishop of Portsmouth's request, to teach English in Borneo. This was the start of a social movement which led to some 21,000 young people volunteering for overseas service in the next thirty years. Peter Wellby (b. 1946), who read English at Christ Church, 1964–67, was not bashful: in convincing disguise, he had been one of the first six women to dine as guests in Hall at Christ Church; he toured France and Italy in the cast of an Oxford University Dramatic Society production of *King Lear*; and played the Wind in Picasso's play of the same name. Afterwards head of English and housemaster at Sherborne School 1971–2000, Principal of the Anglican International School in Jerusalem 2000–2003, and Director of the Copenhagen International School 2003–2010.

car to the centre of the city and we visited a couple of monasteries. One was 'the Marble Temple' built by King Chulalongkorn.[113] One part of it, called the Song Panuat building, has engaging frescoes, *circa* 1900, illustrating the life of Chulalongkorn as monk and king. Then we returned to our hotel. Robert was in excellent form and we had a great deal of gay conversation. (His cousin hardly spoke). He made it clear that Boyes was not much of a friend and advised us, in our predicament, to do what we could with the ambassador tonight.

At 7.45 the ambassador sent his car for us. It was a small but most enjoyable party. The other guests were Ronald Scrivener,[114] first secretary I think, and his wife (formally married to Christopher Hohler and the mother of Frederick Hohler),[115] and the new British Council man, David Cardiff.[116] Robert had spoken highly of Cardiff, but we found him rather flat. We greatly liked both the Pritchards and the Scriveners. The Pritchards have arrived very recently. They came by boat and the ambassador flattered me by saying that he had read *The Rise of Christian Europe*, and greatly admired it, on his way out. I was naturally pleased, and told him of my battle with 'the smallholders'.[117] He was very interested in Taiwan and I told him all about it. Both he and Scriveners took note of our immediate problem and I had two precise impressions, *viz*: (1) that Boyes' stock is low (I'm afraid we may have lowered it); (2) that some effort will be made to remedy the situation. We gossiped away till near midnight, when the ambassador sent us back to our hotel in his car.

---

113 King Chulalongkorn, otherwise Rama V (1853–1910), King of Siam from 1868, was a reformer who abolished slavery, the corvée system and prostration in his realm. The Marble Temple, Wat Benjamabopit, was the last wat built in Bangkok.

114 Ronald Scrivener (1919–2001) served in Bangkok, 1965–69. He was ambassador in Panama City, 1969–71, and in Prague, 1971–74.

115 Mary Lane (1919–2014) was married (1939–61) to Christopher Hohler (1917–1997), an art historian at the Courtauld Institute, who had served in military intelligence in Baghdad.

116 This is a slip of T-R's pen. David Cardiff (1944–2003) was an Etonian who read PPE at New College, Oxford. In 1975 he started the earliest honours-degree course in media studies in England at the Regent Street Polytechnic (later the University of Westminster). It was his father Maurice Cardiff (1915–2006) who worked for the British Council, 1946–73. 'In France cultural relations with foreign countries are fully a part of the Ministry of Foreign Affairs, while in England they are entrusted to the British Council, which we pretend is independent,' Sir William Hayter had described in 1960. 'Every foreigner who is interested knows that the British Council is wholly Government-financed and assumes that it is wholly Government-directed. But the Foreign Office feels that the British Council is not a part of itself, and thus relegates it to a kind of inferior status where it is exposed, fairly defenceless, to all forms of attack, especially from the lowbrow Press' (*The Diplomacy of the Great Powers*, pp. 50–1).

117 T-R's *The Rise of Christian Europe* had been published by Thames & Hudson in 1965.

Monday, 11 December

At 7.30 the telephone rang. It was Ronald Scrivener. 'Do not cancel your air-ticket for today', he said. He had been at work, and there were two possibilities. First, it was possible that the Indonesian embassy would open up specially at 9.15 to give us visas. Secondly, if that failed, it was always possible to telephone the Embassy in Pnompenh [*sic*] and ask them to arrange that we be admitted without visas. In that case, there was a risk we might be sent back to Bangkok. But it was a risk worth taking; and anyway, work was in hand with the Indonesians. Boyes had a girl-friend in the Indonesian Embassy, and he has been told to fix her. I fear that Boyes has been hauled over the coals. We got up at once and began to pack; and while we were still having breakfast, the telephone rang again, and again it was Scrivener, to say that the Indonesians would open up: we were to go there at 9.15 and collect the visas, then straight on to the airport to catch the Burma Airway plane on which, providentially, we had failed in our efforts yesterday to cancel our places.

All worked according to plan. We flew to Pnompenh [Phnom Penh], and there transferred into a Cambodian plane: a little old freight plane, of date (we were told) 1940, very ramshackle looking, converted into a passenger-plane capable of carrying 20 passengers. We flew fairly low following a great river, through largely flat country of nice-fields and forests. Then we came to a region of lakes, and among them we landed at the airport of Siem Reap and were taken by bus to the *Auberge des Temples*.

It is a rambling one-storeyed hostel, built in the form of open quandrangles, and all the rooms are alike; double-bedded with bathrooms but – to Xandra's horror – no baths: only showers. However, apart from the usual tropical failings, it is comfortable and efficient. We rested for a time and then went out on foot to look at the immediately neighbouring temple of Angkor Wat.

We walked away from the hotel to the noise of cicadas. Their note was not intermittent and dry, as in the Mediterranean, but constant and shrill, like an electric bell. We went over the wide moat by a great stone bridge, flanked by stone *nagas* and then entered court after court of the huge temple.[118] The central part towered above the rest, and we reached it by stone steps so steep that on returning, I preferred to descend in a sitting posture. Everywhere, of course, guides followed us, and I thought of Pausanias and his complaints of them in Greece and Asia Minor.[119] The passages stank of bats, and great

---

118 A *naga* is a serpent deity, which can take the form of a human or a cobra.

119 Pausanias wrote a lengthy account of his travels in Greece in the second century AD.

russet beetles – scarabs, I suppose – settled over the flagstones. On the whole
the temple was depressing: its vastity, its grey monotony of design, its repeti-
tious luxury of detail battered the mind into insensitivity. Xandra said that
it reminded her of Vishnayagan, near Madras, and indeed it is described as
'Vishnuite' in cult. A touch of life was given to this inhuman lunar architecture
by a casual procession of Buddhist monks, in their saffron robes, walking away
southwards on the eastern edge of the temple-complex. We followed their path
on our own way back and came to a village of wooden houses raised above the
ground on stilts. The monks were sitting upstairs, in their rooms or on balco-
nies, and their yellow robes were dangling over parapets or hanging on pegs.
They seemed unwilling that we should penetrate their village, so we withdraw,
returned to the hotel, dined and went to bed early after a long, somewhat
hectic, and tiring day.

Xandra in particular was very tired, and used this as a reason for insisting
that we leave a day early in order to break our homeward journey by another
night in Bangkok. A more powerful reason impelling her in the same direction
is her passion for Thai silk. Robert Swann told us that a Thai lady whom I
knew when she was an undergraduate at Oxford (but I have forgotten her
name) now works in Johnson's Thai silk shop[120] and wants English currency
in order to educate her children in England. The point has not been lost on
Xandra, who tried desperately to see her on our way to Bangkok airport this
morning; but time was too short. Another night in Bangkok might yet serve
her turn …

Tuesday, 12 December

We got up at 7.0 and at 8.15 went out on an organised expedition round
some of the temples. The whole morning – that is till 11 o'clock – was spent
in the vast complex of Angkor Thom. We were spent delighted by it. Here was
none of the oppressive naked monotony of Angkor Wat, for the ruins were
everywhere intermingled with greenery: sometimes rising out of flat, peaceful water-meadows, sometimes appearing at the end of long vistas among the
trees, noisy with woodpeckers. We visited Bayon, the central temple of Angkor

---

120 *Sic.* James ('Jim') Thompson (b. 1906) was a Princeton graduate and fashionable
American architect. He organized the Bangkok office of the US Office of Strategic Services
in 1945, and was appointed military attaché in the embassy there in 1946. He co-founded
(1948) the Thai Silk Company, which made its fortune by supplying fabrics for the Rodgers and
Hammerstein musical *The King and I* in 1951. He disappeared in Malaysia in 1967.

Thom, a Buddhist temple; Baphuon, now being restored, a Shivaïte temple; Phimeanakas, an earlier brahminical temple; and splendid carved stone terraces which enclosed a kind of pastoral hippodrome. All these we enjoyed in spite of a dreadful, garrulous vulgar guide and some very tiresome fellow-tourists. There was a bossy American lady, for instance, with a small boy in tow: she laid down the law on all subjects, in long and strident tones; lectured every captive auditor whom she could entrap; and with her tape-recorder sought to preserve the vulgarities of our guide which more sensitive members of the party were seeking to avoid or forget. There was an elderly American couple, of indescribable dreariness, the pattern of the transatlantic common man to whom Vice-President Wallace has devoted this unfortunate century.[121] The husband followed the wife in mute docility, made bearable to him, but not to us, by incessant cigar-smoking. And there was a single French lady with a long nose, dyed, short, frizzy hair, a greenish complexion and crossed green eyes, who gave us the creeps. She wore close-fitting sponge-bag checked trousers clinging indecently to her ungainly bottom and a brief armless orange blouse clinging to her ungainly top, so that she looked like a naked biped with a discoloured skin moving, silent and sinister, among the ruins. But there was also a civilised American couple whom we liked, and who seemed to have spent the last two years, with their two children, in travel, sailing their own boat across the Pacific, exploring the Trobriand Islands and New Guinea, and now taking photographs of Angkor. They reminded us of the Eugene Sterns and at first – till I learned of their roving life – I suspected that he too was a doctor – doctors being, in our experience, the aristocracy of America.[122] Now I suspect that he is an author, slowly writing a travel book on private income and a publisher's advance.

---

121 Henry Wallace (1888–1965), agronomist and theosophist, developed the first commercial hybrid seed corn in 1924, and was vice-president of the United States 1941–45. In a speech of 8 May 1942, he had proclaimed that the twentieth century, 'the American century', 'must be the century of the common man'. The speech presented the United States as a liberty-loving, egalitarian theocracy. 'Democracy is the only true political expression of Christianity,' Wallace declared. Hitler was 'the Supreme Devil operating through a human form ... Satan now is trying to lead the common man of the whole world back into slavery and darkness ... Is there any hell hotter than that of being a Quisling, unless it is that of being a Laval or a Mussolini?'

122 Eugene Stern (1920–2017) was chief of neurological surgery in UCLA medical school, 1952–82, and president of the Society of Neurological Surgeons, 1976–77. He was also senior churchwarden of St Augustine-by-the-sea in Santa Monica. His wife was Elizabeth ('Libby') Naffziger.

After lunch at the hotel we went on another organised expedition. It was called the 'Petit Circuit' and took us to a group of buildings to the east of Angkor Thom: Chan Say Tevoda Thommanom, Takeo, Taprohm, Benteay-Kdei, SrasSang Prasat Koravan. The best of them all, in our view, was Taprohm, which had been invaded by the forest, so that its ruins were intermingled with green nature and almost smothered by its great trees – *fromagiers* they were called (*dipterocarpus alatus*) – sprang out of broken walls, with white trunks and huge wing-like bases; giant creepers, like octopuses, embraced the cracked and gaping stonework; every opening in the forest revealed the pink or grey relics of a Buddhist temple, and every cleft in the sinking masonry put forth a twisted stem. This symbiosis of stone and forest was not oppressive but gentle and restful. Woodpeckers, cicadas and parakeets kept up a natural chorus, and we contrived to overlook the French lady with her skin-tight trousers who constantly appeared before us, moving like a speckled spider over those ancient stones. Our other companions were few, female and silent: they did not trouble us, nor we them.

In the evening we dined with Pierre Groslier, the director of the Ecole Française de l'Extrême Orient,[123] who is in charge of the excavation and restoration of the temples. I had met him when he lectured on this subject at Oxford, a couple of years ago, and William Hayter[124] had written to him about our visit. He sent his car to collect us at 7.45. It took us to his house in Siem Reap. His other guests were Louis de Guiringaud, the French ambassador in Tokyo,[125] and his wife, who are here to inaugurate a new Air France service between Tokyo and Phnom Penh.

We had an excellent Cambodian meal. Course followed course and wine followed wine. The ambassador and his wife did not contribute much. He was a dried-up official, without life or charm, and with a tendency to lecture his host,

---

123 Bernard-Philippe Groslier (1926–1986), conservator of Saigon Museum 1950–54, director of archaeological research at l'École Française de l'Extrême-Orient and conservator of the monuments at Angkor Wat, 1960–72.

124 Sir William Hayter (1906–1995), ambassador to the Soviet Union 1953–57, had been dismayed by Anglo-French bungling of the Suez expedition, which he believed had eased the Soviet Union's occupation of Hungary in 1956. He left the diplomatic service to be warden of New College, Oxford 1958–76.

125 Louis de Guiringaud (1911–1982) had his first posting at Ankara in 1938. He was badly wounded while fighting the Germans in Alsace in 1945. He spoke good English after his posting as first secretary at the French Embassy in London 1948–49. Director of political affairs at the French High Commission in Germany, 1949–52; ambassador in Japan, 1966–72; France's representative on the United Nations Security Council, 1972–76; Minister of Foreign Affairs, in the government of Raymond Barre, 1976–78; shot himself.

and she who was elegant and young – she looked about 30 years younger than he – scarcely opened her month. Only on one occasion did she show any vitality, and that was when reference was made to the Beatles, of whom she appeared to be an admirer. She had been – with her husband – to hear them in Tokyo and knew all their songs.[126] Except on that subject she remained mute all the evening. Groslier did not give himself too much trouble about such irresponsive guests, and the conversation was mainly between us and him. He also kept us back after the de Guiringauds had gone and offered us his car in order to go on expeditions tomorrow and Thursday, and invited us to his museum in Siem Reap.

We had interesting conversation on Cambodia and South East Asia in general. Groslier told me that there is a total gap in Cambodian history between the end of the Angkor period, say 1250, and the coming of the Europeans. There are no written records and the stones no longer speak (the same is true, I believe, of Siam). I asked if Chinese sources did not help, but he said that the few students of Chinese history concentrated on China, not on outlying countries; besides sinologists stop with the coming of the Ming, or at least with Yung Lo.[127] However, he told me that there was a good young French historian – a son of Maurice Lombard – who is working on Indonesia.[128]

I longed to ask him about André Malraux, whom he must know and whose pretensions he can judge.[129] Presumably also he knows the facts about Malraux's

---

126 'The Beatles M.B.E.', as reported by Dudley Cheke, British minister in Tokyo, played five concerts in Tokyo's Nippon Budokan hall between 30 June and 3 July 1966. 'During the performance inside the Budokan, there was the clamour and the hysteria which the Beatles provoke wherever they go, and little or nothing could be heard of the music. Police had cordoned off the stage and were sitting, with a contingent of firemen, in every aisle. The greatest burden which they had to bear … was to comfort sobbing teenage girls who found that the physical presence of John, George, Paul and Ringo was more than they could take' (NA FO 371/187127, despatch 24 of 19 July 1966).

127 Yung Lo, the third Ming emperor, died in 1424.

128 Maurice Lombard (1904–1965), professor at l'École des Hautes Études en Sciences Sociales and l'École Normale Supérieure in Paris, specialized in medieval economic history and in the Islamic world from the eighth to the eleventh centuries. His son Denys Lombard (1938–1998), director of l'École Française d'Extrême-Orient, was a maritime historian who adapted Braudel's methods in studying the Mediterranean to his own work on the South China Sea.

129 The novelist André Malraux (1901–1976) was reared by a grandmother who kept a sweet shop in a small town. After visiting Angkor Wat in 1923, he was convicted of stealing a bas-relief from Banteay Srei and four *devatas*, which he planned to sell in London or New York. A mythomaniac, who pretended to friendships with Stalin and Mao, Malraux converted from communism to Gaullism after serving as Minister of Information in 1945–46. He was Minister of Cultural Affairs in the Fifth Republic, 1958–69.

misadventures in Cambodia, where he was imprisoned, I think, for seeking to carry off Khmer statues. I would like to know what real scholars think of Malraux, whom I regard as a mere Gaullist gasbag. I first met him in Paris in 1948, when he was the intellectual of de Gaulle's *Rassemblement du Peuple Français*. He then invited me to his flat and lectured me for an hour, largely about himself. He told me that all history was the history of secret societies, '*par exemple, en Angleterre du 17éme siècle, il y a avaient les Têtes-Rondes*'. When I began to demur, he realised that perhaps, on this subject, I was on home ground; so he quickly adjusted his position. With a wave of his hand he dismissed my objections and began again, '*Mais en Chine ...*' From that day on, I had always regarded the man with contempt; but with the passage of years I began to think that I might be mistaken, and I was prepared to give him another chance. The opportunity came three weeks ago, just before we left Oxford. Malraux had come to Oxford to open the new *Maison Française* and to receive an honorary degree from the university. He stayed with the Berlins (Isaiah, that great social cultivator, declaring himself publicly to be an admirer), delivered a public lecture in the Sheldonian, and dined with the Vice-Chancellor. Xandra and I went to the lecture, and the result of this, and of his visit in general, was to revive my old contempt for the man and confirm me in it.

First the lecture. The title was 'L'Art et le Temps' – a large subject, I thought, and one which might well occupy a philosopher for the full hour at least. But Malraux despatched it in half-an-hour and contrived to say nothing concrete or verifiable except the remarkable statement that the cult of beauty was unique in our Western civilisation. At dinner with the Vice-Chancellor he convulsed the arrangements by importing an uninvited, unnamed and unexpected guest for whom an extra place had to be set. This intruder was described as a personal secretary, but in fact he was not: the Oxford police had refused to allow him through the barrier until he had shown his identity card, which proved that he was a detective. Later the same night Xandra and I went to Headington House,[130] bringing the Duchess of Argyll[131] and Tony Quinton,[132] who had

---

130 The Oxford home of Aline and Isaiah Berlin.

131 Mathilda Mortimer (1925–1997) was married (1948–61) to Clemens Heller, professor of human sciences at Paris University, and secondly (1963–73) to the eleventh Duke of Argyll.

132 Anthony Quinton (1925–2010), Lord Quinton 1983, philosopher, one of the few survivors among the evacuated children after the torpedoing of *City of Benares* in mid-Atlantic, 1940; scholar of Christ Church (first-class honours in PPE); RAF navigator; Fellow of All Souls College, 1949–55, and of New College, 1955–78; a showman who drove a Cadillac in Oxford of the 1950s; FBA, 1977; President of Trinity College, 1978–87.

been dining with us, and I had my second personal meeting with Malraux, who spent the time dogmatising about the Vietnam war. I found him a pretentious, humourless bore, an uncivil egoist. However, today, although M. de Guiringaud showed himself to be strongly anti-Gaullist, I did not dare to raise the topic in his presence, and after he had gone, our conversation with Groslier was deeply involved in historical questions. We left his hospitable house about midnight, having arranged that his driver would call for us at the hotel at 9.0 a.m. tomorrow.

Wednesday, 13 December

Groslier's car duly picked us up and took us to the Roluos group of Shivaite temples, about 20 k.m. east of Siem Reap. First we visited Preah Ko, which consists of six stupas, equal in size, arranged in two lines of three, built of pink brick, with grey stone elephants and oxen in front of it. It was the most attractive of the three which we saw. The other were Bakong, a huge mass rising to a central point, and Lolei of which little is left, At both Bakong and Lolei there are modern buddhist temples and the monks were intoning their nasal chant. At Lolei I mounted the steps and looked into the hollow stone cave. It stank terribly. When my eyes had become used to the darkness, I saw that all the form walls were lined with pendulous bats, hanging upside-down in orderly rows, stuck to the wall like stamps in a well-filled album. At the bottom two peasant women were squatting engaged in some invisible operation I suppose they were collecting bat's dung for manure. The new Buddhist temple at Lolei was to the left of the old Shivaite temple, and the monkery – on stilts, as all Cambodian peasant houses seem to be –was opposite it, on the right, so that the three sets of buildings made a kind of village square.

After visiting these three temples, we went to Groslier's museum. He took us round and showed us the immense work of scientific reconstruction on which he is engaged, – and on which he had lectured at Oxford. Thanks to the exact stylisation and symmetry of the temples, it has been possible, from the surviving or recovered details, to create complete architectural models of them all and the scientific basis for repair and even reconstitution. We could not but admire the vast enterprise that has rescued the temples from further decay, and yet, having a romantic love of ruins, I cannot relish the thought of more positive restoration. The Greeks, or their American experts, threaten to recreate the Parthenon and present it again, bran-new, as it was in the 5th century BC; but I prefer the broken columns and cracked pediments that show the passage of time and the erosion of history; and would not a series of gigantic brahminical and buddhist temples, rising perfect and polished above the flats of 20th century Cambodia, be something of an anachronism? Of all the temples we have seen so far, it is Taprohm that has pleased us most; and it has pleased us precisely because it has settled into its historical perspective, its ruins enveloped by the forest around it. Naturally I reserved the expression of these thoughts as we admired the detailed architectural drawings unrolled by M. Groslier, revealing the whole structure of the temples as they were in the 9th–12th centuries, and as they may be again – but I hope they will not – in the 21st.

We had lunch in the hotel, and then we slept: slept for three hours, till it was too late to do anything outside, which, in a way, was a relief. I wrote my diary and read *Middlemarch*. What a good book it is! Why have I never read it before? I suppose because I read *The Mill on the Floss* at Belhaven,[133] when I was too young, and was put off George Eliot; and anyway I seldom read novels. But it is a wonderful book, worthy of Tolstoy: what a marvellous picture of provincial life in 1830, of the submerged tensions of converging but still distant social classes! I fear that Mr. Casaubon must be Mark Pattison: the name, the young wife, the mental dryness; and yet there are notable departures from the original.[134] For instance, Mr. Casaubon owns a trout-stream but does not fish (p. 95): indeed, when Mr. Brooke recommended fishing to relax his mind after his first heart attack, Mr Casaubon indignantly refused 'to anticipate the arrival of my second childhood' by adopting such puerile pastimes (p. 320). But Mark Pattison was a devoted fisherman and relaxed his mind, after his failure to be elected Rector of Lincoln College, by going on a prolonged fishing holiday.[135] Even more striking is another contrast. In Rome, Will Ladislaw remarks that Mr. Casaubon's learning, like so much English scholarship, is 'thrown away ... for want of knowing what is being done by the rest of the world. If Mr. Casaubon read German, he would save himself a great deal of

---

133 T-R attended this preparatory school in Dunbar, 1924–27.

134 Mark Pattison (1813–1884) wrote *Isaac Casaubon 1559–1614* (1875). T-R's comparisons were prompted by reading John Sparrow's recently published *Mark Pattison and the Idea of a University* (Cambridge, 1967).

135 These piscatorial thoughts arose from Eliot populating *Middlemarch* with a shoal of fishy-sounding scholars called Pike, Tench and Carp. In chapter 20, Eliot dilates on fishgods. See Colin Kidd, *The World of Mr Casaubon: Britain's wars of mythography, 1700–1870* (Cambridge, 2016), pp. 11, 176.

trouble'. Precisely the same remark, if I remember aright, is made (or perhaps quoted) by Mark Pattison about Newman: if only Newman read German, he says in his *Memoirs*, how different the religious and intellective history of early Victorian Oxford would have been ...[136]

We watched a film in the evening – a couple of Cambodian propaganda films – shown in the courtyard of the hotel, and then went to bed. Cambodian propaganda is discreet but pervasive, and it is linked pretty closely to a certain 'personality-cult' of the ruler. What surprises me most – indeed extorts some admiration from me – is the personal propagandist energy of Prince Sihanouk, who himself edits the periodical *Kambuja*, himself writes, or seems to write, all or most of the articles, himself replies, by public letter, to every supposed attack on his policy in the international press, as well as himself (apparently) directing the arts, the enterprises and the policy of the state. It would be natural to suppose that this is made possible, or is really done for him, by the bureaucracy. But what bureaucracy is there in Cambodia? Groslier told us at dinner yesterday that the Cambodian government had not copies even of its own recent treaties and that when a recent Franco-Cambodian treaty was to be revised, the minister appealed to him for a copy. Groslier obtained a copy and made a typed copy of it for the government, which used that copy as its text without even seeking to compare Groslier's typed copy with his original: '*j'aurais pu écrire ce que je voulais!*'[137] This makes me wonder whether Prince Sihanouk's skilful neutrality is solidly based or merely the result of inspired opportunism.

Thursday, 14 December

Groslier's driver appeared at the hotel at 9.0 a.m. and took us out on another tour of the temples. We went first to Prasat Kravan, which we had seen late on Tuesday afternoon; but Groslier afterwards advised us to see it in the morning, when the east light illuminated the surviving reliefs within the building. Then we visited Pre Rup, a big, imposing temple whose levels rise regularly towards

---

136 In chapter 6 of Pattison's memoirs he wrote: 'A. P. Stanley once said to me, "How different the fortunes of the Church of England might have been if Newman had been able to read German." That puts the matter in a nutshell; Newman assumed and adorned the narrow basis on which Laud had stood 200 years before. All the grand developments of human reason, from Aristotle down to Hegel, was a sealed book to him.'

137 French: I could have written what I wanted.

the centre: Shivaïte and early (961 A.D.); and from it went on, over a long, rough road, through a succession of villages, all identical on their wooden stilts, till we reached another 10th century temple, also Shivaïte: Banteary Srei. This was perfectly charming, the most delightful, I thought, of them all. Unlike every other temple so far, it was built on one level only, in the shape of a long rectangle, surrounded by water. The gate is at one end of the rectangle and leads into a long courtyard divided lengthwise by short stone-pillars, rounded at the top, like phalli which seem never to have been higher or to have supported anything. Then a gateway with a fine carved pediment leads into a series of smaller courts, and at the end are half-a-dozen *stupas*, marvellously decorated with flowing designs and crowded figures of wonderful vitality, perfectly preserved. The buildings are all of pink stone. Outside them are high trees. The sylvan setting, the relatively small scale, the simplicity of lay-out, the warm colour of stone, the brilliance and liveliness of the carving, all enhanced the character of the place. We delighted in it more than in any other, and lingered long, enjoying the solitude. What a relief it is to have escaped from those chattering guides and those fellow-tourists – particularly from the cigar-smoking American business-man and the tight-trousered French lady! We could have spent the whole morning there. But there was another temple still to see in that area, and so ultimately we forsook Banteay Srei and went on till the jeep stopped in front of a stream and our driver told us that, 500 metres ahead, we would discover the remains of Banteay Samre.

Banteay Samre is much later – mid 12th century – and is Vihnuïte, like Angkor Wat; but is small by comparison with that monstrous citadel. On our way we were joined by a man who recognised Grolier's jeep and introduced himself as M. Groslier's guardian of the temple. He took us round. There was one great court with double walls, and in the centre a raised system of *stupas* with carved pediments showing scenes from the Ramayana. There was noth-ing here to rival Banteay Srei, which was the great discovery of the morning, and after a brief visit, we followed our guide back through groups of peasant cottages and seething caldrons – for the peasants were all boiling sugar from sugar-palms outside their houses – till we regained the jeep and returned to the hotel for lunch. It had been a long, full morning, for Banteay Srei and Banteay Samre are a good way away from the hotel: much further, it seemed, than the Roluos group which we visited yesterday. Today was perfect morning, a little cooler than it has been hitherto, but bright and sunny: ideal for travel in an open jeep.

In the afternoon we rested, and then walked once more round Angkor Wat. It still oppresses me by its hugeness, its almost grim, prison-like symmetry. It is the Versailles of Cambodia; I prefer the Petit Trianon of Banteay Srei. But after dinner I warmed a little to it, for then we attended a performance of Cambodian classical dances in Angkor Wat. The dancing, to me, being no balletomane, was not very exciting; but floodlit, and moonlit, the Wat shed some of its formidable quality. The audience included, inevitably, a lot of Americans, who behaved abominably: when they were not darting forward and flashing camera-bulbs, they were leaning back and emitting sterterous yawns which re-echoed round the vast stone amphitheatre. The best of the dances was *L'Histoire de Preah Samut*, in two acts: '*la rêve de la Princesse Boutsomaly*' and '*Rencontre de la Princesse Boutsomaly avec le Prince Preah Samut*'.[138]

---

138 On 16 December the T-Rs left Cambodia, and the following day, after lunching at the British Embassy in Bangkok with the Scriveners, flew to London.

APPENDIX A

IN OTHERS' WORDS
Peking and London

This book has presented Trevor-Roper's experiences in communist China, and his relations with its English admirers, in his own words. Sometimes other participants have left accounts of the same episodes.

In Peking

Michael Wilford

Trevor-Roper describes the 'very pleasant lunch party' given for the SACU delegates on 21 September 1965 by the Counsellor and Consul General of Peking, Michael Wilford, soon to be Visiting Fellow at All Souls College, Oxford. Wilford sent a report of the occasion to the Foreign Office:

> I invited the party to lunch on 20 September, and they gave us their first thoughts on China and asked for our advice about tours, meetings, etc. Trevor-Roper was horrified (and still is) at the total lack of ability on the part of his various guides to see anything but the pure party line, and at their unwillingness to admit that there is any other way of doing things than that dictated by the party. Robert Bolt is clearly fascinated with Peking. To the amazement of a member of the Ministry of Higher Education to whom we introduced him at a farewell party for the last group of Chinese students who left on 25 September, he said that he had never seen anything so beautiful as the Forbidden City and that he wouldn't have minded being the Emperor and living there! These two have paired together. Both are

angry at the stubbornness of their Chinese guides in refusing to let them see what they ask for and are interested in individually, and they object to being trailed round as a group the whole time. They despise their interpreters for ignorance and incompetence. I think, nevertheless, that Trevor-Roper's and Robert Bolt's views are a little exaggerated ... Mrs. Adams and Mr. Roberts likewise appear to have teamed up. The former seemed quite reasonable at our lunch, and did not seem too "frontish",[1] but I imagine that she is only too susceptible to flattery and generally starry eyed ... Roberts ... is, I think, the happiest of the party and most uncritical. Trevor-Roper said that at a banquet in their honour the other day he was somewhat surprised to hear Roberts unctuously congratulating the Chinese on their liberal policy in Tibet![2]

Alan Donald

Trevor-Roper's diary records the presence at the same lunch of the First Secretary at the legation, Alan Donald, the 'highly intelligent' authority on China with whom he enjoyed other contacts during the visit to Peking. Donald reported to the Foreign Office's Information Research Department on his dealings with Trevor-Roper and Bolt:

They made no bones about how appalled they had been by the treatment accorded to them. Their chief grievance continued to be the stupidity and lack of imagination on the part of their interpreters and guides. Both were angered by the fact that though they had asked to see representatives of their own professions, in order to exchange meaningful views, they had been palmed off with stuffed dummies who handed out platitudes and never got down to any meaty discussion. (As an example of the state of frustration they seemed to be in, you might be amused to hear that their chief pastime when being entertained by members of this office was to retail

---

1 That is, similar in opinions to France's leftist Front Populaire (1936–38) and to Spain's Frente Popular (1936–39). In England, a smaller Popular Front movement was started in 1936 by Sir Richard Acland, Robert Boothby, G. D. H. Cole and John Strachey. It ran 'Sandie' Lindsay, Master of Balliol, as its parliamentary candidate in the Oxford by-election of 1938. Another of its candidates was successful in the Bridgwater by-election later in 1938.

2 NA FO 1110/1994, 1044/65, Michael Wilford to Edwin Bolland, 29 September 1965.

endless anecdotes about their mentors whom they had christened 'Goosebottom', 'Cement Head', 'The Presbyterian' and other such colourful nicknames.)

To mitigate Trevor-Roper's annoyance at being kept from meeting real Chinese historians, such as had heard of Balázs, Donald introduced him to a contact who taught Western history at Peking University. 'Though Trevor-Roper described him to me afterwards as being intellectually a "light-weight" with only superficial knowledge of Western history (this may only be his normal way of writing off someone with whom he disagrees), I think that the meeting was of some value,' Donald recorded. 'I have no doubt that it did the Chinese professor a lot of good to be exposed to the critical brain of a Western historian.' Donald supplied a lengthy account of the conversation:

Professor Trevor-Roper came to my house on 29 September in order to meet Professor Chang Chih-lien. In all we were a party of five, the two professors, Mrs. Chang, my wife and I.

I was able before dinner to give Trevor-Roper some briefing on the nature of my relationship with the Chinese Professor. I had suggested to him that provided he bore in mind the risk that everything he said would be communicated to the Chinese authorities and that he should avoid saying anything which might ultimately be distorted ... there was no reason why he should not speak frankly and fairly freely with Chang.

Trevor-Roper took this almost too literally, however, in his opening remarks. In answer to questions by our Chinese friend about how he was enjoying his programme in Peking, he delivered himself of a pretty powerful broadside of criticisms directed at the low quality of his guides and interpreters. He also expressed dissatisfaction at being 'pushed around' and not being allowed to see things that interested him. He complained, for example, that he would have been to Peking and never have seen the Temple of Heaven if he had not himself discovered of its existence from other sources. He implied that his visit to the Institute of History and to Peking University had been a complete waste of time. At the Institute, he had met four professors, one of whom had done all the talking while the other three remained silent, and that he had been totally unable to engage in any satisfactory exchange of ideas or discover anything about the kind of historical research on which they were engaged. At Peking University he said that he had been introduced to a History professor who turned out to have spent most of his earlier years as a local government official.

Chang received this initial tirade with politeness, but refrained from comment … Thereafter … the conversation was mainly confined to academic or professional topics. During dinner Trevor-Roper gave a fascinating account of his researches into the last days of Hitler, touching upon the discreditable part played by the Russians in trying to suppress evidence of the circumstances surrounding Hitler's death. We spent some time discussing characters in English and Chinese history, e.g. Richard III, Judge Jeffries, Tsao-Tsao and the first Ch'in Emperor (who burned the books). Trevor-Roper asked a lot of questions about the ex-Emperor, Pu-Yi, at the end of which Chang asked whether or not it was remarkable that an ex-Emperor had been allowed after his 'crimes' to live peaceably in his own country. This led on to Richard Cromwell (the parallel in English history which Trevor-Roper produced) and on to a general discussion of 17th century England.

After dinner the conversation settled down to the question of how to interpret the English Revolution (1640–60), with Chang advancing theories which he attributed to his students at Peking University, but which I think either reflected his own views or the views which he was compelled to teach. His basic analysis of the English Revolution was couched in Marxist terms (struggle between classes with the Restoration being represented as a kind of counter-revolution). Trevor-Roper, with great skill and a wealth of evidence, gave an analysis of the social structure of England during the Civil War and crushingly demolished the Chang analysis. Trevor-Roper pointed out the general failure of Marxist theorists to back up their generalisations with detailed evidence ('theories killed by facts'). The conversation at this point also involved a comparison of the English and French Revolutions, with Trevor-Roper arguing with examples that it was naughty of Marxist historians to select only the evidence which suited their theories in either country, and to ignore the rest. One other topic of some interest was the question of the history of peasant revolutions in China. Chang was arguing that it was significant that in the majority of cases before any change of dynasty in China there had been a peasant revolt, and seemed inclined to a Maoist interpretation of Chinese history i.e. repeated attempts by an oppressed peasantry to overthrow their oppressors until final success in 1949. Trevor-Roper argued on the other hand, that peasant revolutions were usually a symptom (as opposed to the cause) of disorder and political weakness and that, as European history had shown, a peasant revolt in itself was rarely a threat to a stable political power.[3]

Roland Berger

On 8 October, his last night in China, Trevor-Roper describes a meeting with Roland Berger, whom he had already learned to mistrust, and to whom he and Bolt lamented the inadequacies of the tour. Berger reported on this evening to his SACU ally Jack Perry in a letter from Peking dated 11 October:

I'm afraid the Delegation has been a pretty sizable failure. When I arrived I heard at second-hand of T-R's objectionable behaviour but also of some ham-handling on the part of the Association.

When I saw the Association people on Friday they seemed quite satisfied with the reactions of the four members and with the programme they had arranged for them. But I could tell that all this was very general and it seemed that the itinerary had followed a stereotyped formula.

T.R. and Bolt returned from Loyang and Sian late on Saturday and left early on Sunday morning. I met them at the station and went back to the Hotel with them for a chat. Despite reports of T-R's boorishness and bad manners, I found him quite friendly and affable.

Although T.R. goes a lot further than Bolt in criticising the programme and attributing political motives to what is obviously inefficiency and lack of thought on the part of the Association, they both agree on the inadequacy of the programme provided for them.

If their report is a correct one, and I believe that with the exception of a few exaggerations here and there it is, they have been given

3 NA FO 1110/1994, Alan Donald to John Edmonds, 7 October 1965. As head of the IRD's International Section, Edmonds had close contacts with the Security Service.

a general sight-seeing run-around. Both complain that they have had only one real discussion that went any deeper than pamphlet material and this was with a Professor of Biology at the Peking University. Bolt met one critic – no writers. T.R. was given after much pressure a meeting with four members of the Historical Association, three of whom remained completely silent … Both complain that they have never been able to get through the crust of a not-too-good interpreter and a sloganising guide … I think they have been seriously mishandled …

I am afraid that we shall be getting pretty dirty stuff from T.R. maybe in the Sunday Times. Despite his affability to me, it is clear that as a not-so-brilliant intellectual, he expects to be treated as an intelligent person and not given what Bolt referred to as 'fourth form Marxism'.[4]

In England

Richard Clift

Trevor-Roper's account of the open meeting for the SACU membership at Church House, Westminster on 16 November 1965 is complemented by an account by Richard Clift,[5] a young Foreign Office specialist in the PRC, who attended the meeting with Julian Walker[6] of the Foreign Office's Information Research Department. 'There was quite a large audience, perhaps 300, including some members of the Chinese Chargé d'Affaires Office, who sat apart and remained deadpan throughout,' reported Clift. Clift's report is a key document in SACU's history:

Interest at the meeting naturally centred on the report by Professor Trevor-Roper, because of the article 'The Sick Mind of China' which had already appeared over his signature in the *Sunday*

---

4 SOAS, papers of Derek Bryan, 99/1/5/4, Roland Berger to Jack Perry, 11 October 1965.

5 Richard Clift (b. 1933) worked, among other posts, in the office of the *chargé d'affaires* in Peking, 1958–60, in the FO 1964–68, as Commercial Counsellor in Peking 1974–76, and as head of the Hong Kong department of the FCO, 1979–84.

6 Julian Walker (b. 1929), the Foreign Office's News Department spokesman, 1963–67, was afterwards ambassador to the Yemen 1979–84 and to Qatar 1984–87.

Times. The Professor spoke second, after Mrs. Adams, the leader
of the Delegation. He did not pull any punches. After agreeing
briefly that the Chinese were a dynamic people, healthy and well-
fed, he suggested that contacts of the type promoted by SACU
were pretty meaningless because the Chinese were not interested
in any way in Britain. Only the most formal contacts with the host
body, the Chinese People's Association for Cultural Relations with
Foreign Countries, had been allowed to the Delegation. He had
been able to meet nobody with whom he could talk sensibly about
history. He considered that China was going through a Stalinist
phase and their dreary propaganda made it impossible necessarily to believe what the Chinese said. Anyone considering joining
SACU should realise that there was no opportunity to make the
Chinese understand us and precious little to understand China.
In any Society of this sort a dialogue was necessary, not a monologue: if SACU could provide it then it was worth supporting,
and if not, not … Mrs Mary Adams was at pains to paint as rosy a
picture as possible – beautiful flowers, quality of consumer goods,
university of the air on T.V., etc. – but she could not help pointing
out what a bad impression the continuous propaganda had made
on her, particularly as she saw it applied to children in the form
of songs about hating U.S. imperialism. Mr. Ernie Roberts gave
the impression of speaking from a rather old-fashioned Chinese
brief. He did acknowledge that the Chinese had a long way to go,
but spoke enthusiastically of leaps forward and the possibility of
overtaking Britain by 1970 in the production of certain commodi-
ties. He got launched on a long dissertation on Chinese foreign
policy in which he was able to bring in Vietnam. This got a round
of applause as did his remark that in nuclear disarmament the
important thing was not banning tests, but stopping production.
It was noticeable that he was given nearly twice as long to speak
as the others.

Mr Robert Bolt did his best to keep away from controversy, stick-
ing to education and the theatre. He thought the former first-class
except for the propaganda, although he thought the latter mainly went
in one ear and out the other. He was generally in favour of the new
trend towards modern Peking Opera, although he considered that the
Chinese were being dishonest in claiming that they were preserving

the old medium. But he thought that the Chinese had no love of beauty – their modern architecture was drably totalitarian – and he supported Professor Trevor-Roper in saying that he was unable to meet the people, such as writers and directors, whom he wanted to see.

Before the questions, Professor Robinson, who had looked as black as thunder during Professor Trevor-Roper's talk, read out a message from Dr Needham. This referred to the need for objective discussion on China and for constructive criticism and expressed regret that the Professor had published an article under a sensational headline in advance of the meeting (applause).

The questions took some time to warm up. There were a number of remarks about Vietnam which earned applause and a question on India gave Mr. Roberts a chance to enthuse about a film showing the conversion to the Chinese point of view of Indian soldiers captured in 1962. However, at the end, a questioner asked whether Professor Trevor-Roper's statement was not inconsistent with the aims of the Society. Professor Robinson replied that she thought it was inconsistent for visitors to China to be discourteous. This was loudly applauded. The M.C. gave Professor Trevor-Roper a chance to reply and he repeated what he had said about the need for two-way discussion rather than allowing the Society to be a sounding-board for a one-sided monologue. If it was to be the latter he could not continue to act as a sponsor. This was booed by some people, but the Professor also got some applause.

On the whole, I think that, while Professor Trevor-Roper's article in the *Sunday Times* has done a good deal to make people think twice about China, his presentation to SACU, although forthright, courageous and stimulating, may have been counter-productive. I was impressed by the number of people in the audience who were quite obviously determined to shut their ears to criticism of China and to regard it as in the worst possible taste. This impression may have been increased by the presence of a very obvious claque, who applauded and booed in all the right places, but even they show, I think, that the Communist organisers of SACU have got it quite well buttoned up.[7]

---

7 NA FO 1110/1994, Richard D. Clift, 'Society for Anglo-Chinese Understanding (SACU): Meeting at Church House on 16 November, 1965'.

Joseph Needham

Thirteen days after the SACU open meeting at Church House (described above by Richard Clift), Joseph Needham put his views in a letter to Trevor-Roper:

> I gather that frustration seems to have been the keynote to your reaction to China. For this I am extremely sorry. But I cannot help feeling that the fault can hardly have been all on one side. One must remember that one is dealing not only with a country with a different social system, but with a civilisation with traditions totally different from our own. One of these traditions was a profound and unfailing tact and courtesy – the old 'face-saving' politeness was a real desire to save people being put 'out of countenance' – and though the Chinese now deprecate the extremes of this, their natural courtesy is great. They react very markedly to friendliness; and to start with an openly unfriendly, unsympathetic, provocative or merely destructively critical attitude is to be sure of not getting anywhere. I speak from long personal experience. Understanding (the word in our title) implies a certain friendliness, and this in turn implies a measure of humility, that quality without which intellectuals like ourselves can never get to apprehend the merits of relatively simple people, whether peasant-farmers or factory-workers or even semi-educated guide-interpreters ... Looking back now, I feel that you never ought to have gone on this particular expedition. It was the fault of our SACU organisation for inviting you on an occasion when, as at the annual Anniversary Celebrations, all the Chinese are overwhelmed with social duties and have no time to relax to talk with visiting scholars ... It is now agreed that parties of scholars and specialists should not make visits at Festival times henceforward.[8]

Ernie Roberts

Trevor-Roper's article in *The Sunday Times* on 31 October 1965 troubled Roberts. On 8 November he tried to make amends to his hosts by a letter addressed to the Chinese People's Association for Cultural Relations with Foreign Countries:

---

8 Dacre 6/14, Needham to Trevor-Roper, 29 November 1965.

The opportunity to see for myself the very great problems that you inherited from past destruction by imperial powers, restrained by the centuries of neglect from your own feudal lords and capitalists and other reactionary elements in your country prior to 1949 was greatly appreciated.

It was also a good opportunity for me to see the considerable progress your country has made since liberation day in spite of the considerable difficulties of the past. There is ample evidence of the better, more secure and happier life of the people of China. They are now both well-fed and well-clothed. The problem of education, housing, health and cultural development is being tackled by your Government in a most energetic and successful way. I was pleased that every opportunity was given to me to visit any place that I was interested in. Information I asked for was made readily available by the guides and interpreters that you so kindly arranged for me to have.[9]

In the last months of his life, as he lay dying, Roberts reverted to the inaugural SACU delegation of 1965:

This was the first such visit to China by Britons in many years [*sic*], and it marked the beginning of a new era in Anglo-Chinese relations. Hugh Trevor-Roper repaid the hospitality of the Chinese by contributing on his return to England a two-page article to the 'Sunday Times' headlined 'The Sick Mind of China'. I myself had seen, not a sick mind, but the healthy bodies of millions who had formerly been starving, and the steady development of industries and services in a politically-conscious community.[10]

---

9 Working Class Movement Library, Salford, Roberts papers, Ernie Roberts to General Secretary of Chinese People's Association for Cultural Relations with Foreign Countries, 8 November 1965.

10 Ernie Roberts, *Strike Back* (Orpington: Ernie Roberts, 1994), p. 180.

APPENDIX B

TREVOR-ROPER'S COMPANIONS IN CHINA

Mary Adams (1898–1984)

Mary Adams was the daughter of a Berkshire farmer.[1] After her father's death of tuberculosis in 1910, she was reared by her mother, under conditions of hardship, in a seaside resort in Glamorganshire. She won a scholarship to Godolphin School, Salisbury, which was then flourishing under a formidable headmistress, Miss Douglas. 'Climb the Hill of Difficulty! Never say die! Never despair! Peg away at your work and games!' Lucy Douglas urged her pupils. The school ethos of striving activity and social responsibility was ineffaceably stamped on Adams, who proceeded to University College, Cardiff, where she gained first-class honours in botany. In 1921 she became a research scholar at Newnham College, Cambridge, and from 1925 (the year of her marriage) she held extramural tutorial and lectureship posts in Cambridge. Her husband, Vyvyan Adams, was elected as a Conservative MP in 1931. There was one daughter from what proved a discontented marriage: at the age of fourteen she saved her mother's life in Gunwalloe cove in Cornwall in the accident that drowned Vyvyan Adams.[2]

Cambridge in the 1920s became Adams's 'enchanted town', she recalled in 1959. 'I worked there, bicycled there. I looked at clocks and they were stopped at ten to three. I ate bread and cheese for lunch, and would consider

---

1 The chief source for the following section is the account of Adams in the *Oxford Dictionary of National Biography*.

2 'Ex-M.P. Drowned While Bathing: Daughter's Bravery', *Manchester Guardian*, 14 August 1951.

an evening well spent with a good book. I went walking in the afternoons, not for therapeutic reasons, but for pleasure.' In the laboratory she experimented with aceto-carmine dye, and used jargon like vascular bundles, semi-permeable membranes, and genetic cytology. 'I took sides in conversation, made passionate protests in public, and was disdainful, dissatisfied and disloyal.' Her Cambridge set included Joan Robinson, who enlisted her in SACU over thirty years later. The experience in 1928 of giving six BBC radio talks on heredity alerted her to the educational possibilities of broadcasting. She joined the BBC's staff as adult education officer in 1930. Her more idealistic colleagues hoped that radio, properly handled by a public corporation, would discredit the corrupting stunts of the press barons, and hammer 'a new nail for the coffin of class-conscious snobbery and ignorance,' she wrote. 'Personally I just imagined the microphone was a new technique in the diffusion of culture.'[3]

In 1936 Adams was appointed to the newly established television service, based at Alexandra Palace, and thus became the first woman television producer. She was charged with responsibility for educational, cultural and political talks, and recruited such future stars as John Betjeman and Julian Huxley to the new medium. After the outbreak of war in 1939, when television was suspended, Adams became director of home intelligence in the Ministry of Information. In 1942 she was transferred to North American service broadcasting, where she produced programmes, such as *Transatlantic Quiz*, which were intended to improve Anglo-American affinities.

After the war Adams returned to television as head of BBC television talks (1948–54) and as assistant to the controller of television programmes (1954–58). She preferred the programmes for which she was responsible to be purposive or mind-improving: television quizzes, notably *Animal, Vegetable, Mineral?* (1952), and science programmes such as *Eye on Research* (1957) were her specialty. She also oversaw the children's programmes *Muffin the Mule* (1946) and *Andy Pandy* (1950). In an era when the legal and medical professions had strict restrictions on personal publicity, and sought to preserve a secretive mystique, she launched several medical series, including *A Matter of Life and Death* (1949) and *Your Life in their Hands* (1958).

Adams left the BBC in 1958 to be deputy chairman of the newly formed Consumers' Association. She induced an apprehensive *Which?* magazine to produce the first comparative tests of contraceptives and coaxed a chary BBC to produce the first consumer programmes giving brand ratings. Above all

---

3 Mary Adams, 'Microscope to Microphone', *Punch*, 18 November 1959, p. 468.

she became an inveterate committee woman. At the committee table, she had an air of knowing confidence and liked what Humpty-Dumpty called a nice knock-down argument; she pushed her opinions in a quick and lively way; if brooked, she took her stand by appealing to common sense, as defined by her. But her manner was a little too sensible to be true. She suffered the strains of being a married woman with a full working life at a time when this was rare. In the office she managed people well, had good ideas, took brisk decisions and made people laugh. At home she was ambivalent, indecisive and felt unsuccessful. She dreaded, but also courted, loneliness. With age she increasingly misjudged the fine line between being winningly provocative and just tactless. She professed herself a socialist, a seeker of universal progressive harmony, 'a romantic communist' and a fervent atheist. Mrs Jellyby was her prototype: despite her altruistic attitude to the wider world, she failed to support her intimates when they needed help.

Maoist propaganda was wearisome, said Adams after returning from the PRC.

> But after all, one must be mature about this. The Chinese have a consistent philosophy and are very anxious … that we should understand it. The intelligentsia see its expression as their mission, while to the peasants and workers, it is part of their expression of happiness and satisfaction in their way of life, for people not only looked happy, well-fed and well-clothed, but were.

She was, however, 'irritated by the self-righteousness of the Chinese', and by their insularity. 'They are not interested in Britain, not curious about our habits of thought or culture.'[4]

Robert Bolt (1924–1995)

Robert Bolt had been born in Cheshire.[5] His father ran a glassware and furniture shop, and his mother was a socialist schoolteacher. They kept a typical northern Methodist household, imbued with a sense of right and wrong, thoughtful in its ethos, and wedded to social justice. He won a place

---

4 'China – a Consumer's View', *SACU News*, December 1965, pp. 1–2; Bodleian, Kurti papers H943.

5 This section follows Adrian Turner, *Robert Bolt: scenes from two lives* (London: Hutchinson, 1998).

at Manchester grammar school, where he disappointed his teachers and parents. He left school aged sixteen, after being caught shoplifting, and was set to work in an insurance office, which he detested. In 1943 he began reading economics at Manchester University, and joined the CPGB. This was not an extreme act at a time when Britain and the Soviet Union were allies in the war against Germany and Japan: as the Conservative cabinet minister Leo Amery had recently told the Chinese ambassador in London, 'once Russia was in the war on our side we had dismissed from our minds any possible criticism of the Bolshevist system'.[6] Bolt's studies were interrupted by wartime conscription (he served with the Royal West African Frontier Force), but he returned to Manchester University in 1946, switched from economics to history, left the CPGB in 1947 and graduated in 1949.

After a teacher training course at Exeter University, Bolt taught at a primary school in the Devon village of Bishopsteignton and then as an English master at Millfield public school in Somerset. David Cornwell, alias John le Carré, mentioned in the Trevor-Roper journals, was teaching at Millfield's preparatory school for part of the same period. Bolt's success in writing a nativity play for his Bishopsteignton pupils led him to write radio plays and children's stories for television. His first stage play, *The Critic and the Heart*, which he modelled on Somerset Maugham's *The Circle*, was performed at the Oxford Playhouse. His next and more imaginative play, *Flowering Cherry*, showed him as 'plainly destined to become a distinguished dramatist,' wrote Harold Hobson of *The Sunday Times*. The central character is a failed but boastful insurance salesman, who deludes himself with dreams of owning orchards in Somerset. 'Mr Bolt looks on the writhing misery, the complete self-contempt, the unescapable weakness of this unfortunate man with the analytical, relentless perceptiveness of a Proust,' wrote Hobson.[7] Bolt won the 1957 *Evening Standard* award for most promising playwright, and left Millfield to write plays.

Bolt's greatest triumph in the theatre was *A Man for all Seasons*, which opened in 1960. It established him as a pre-eminent anti-naturalistic playwright of Brechtian type. On the strength of *A Man for all Seasons*, Bolt was hired to rewrite a screenplay about T. E. Lawrence, which was being directed by David Lean. *Lawrence of Arabia* won seven Oscars. 'Lean's attitude to Lawrence was more than somewhat suited to Bolt's style of careful embalming,' in the view

---

6 Leo Amery, *The Empire at Bay: the Leo Amery diaries 1929–1945*, ed. John Barnes and David Nicholson (London: Hutchinson, 1988), p. 829.

7 Harold Hobson, 'Playwright to Watch', *Sunday Times*, 24 November 1957.

of another Oscar-winning scriptwriter Frederic Raphael. 'Bob was a somewhat middle-aged young man, slow spoken and, in the nicest sense, calculating. His services to Lean made him rich and perhaps a little complacent. He was a careful writer, never a wit; took pains, never risks, except in his private life, when his passion for Sarah Miles (wasn't it?) led him into passion for which he was, physically, not good casting.' Raphael saw a similarity between Bolt and John Fowles: 'Each affected a certain lofty daring, but made no decisive break with propriety. Success gave them the illusion that they had said something interesting.'[8]

Lean, who seemed in Hollywood to ape the style of Field Marshal Lord Alexander of Tunis, was distressed when production of *Lawrence of Arabia* was threatened by Bolt's political activism. Bolt's fear of a nuclear holocaust had motivated his writing of his radio play, *The Last of the Wine*, broadcast in 1955: a satirical depiction of an English middle-class family on the evening that an atomic bomb was dropped on them. In his stage play *The Tiger and the Horse* (1960), in which Michael Redgrave played the master of an Oxbridge college and his daughter Vanessa was cast as his unmarried pregnant daughter, nuclear weaponry is described as 'the high peak, the show place, of the wickedness that's in us'.[9] In 1960 Bolt joined the Committee of 100, an organization 'formed to promote a campaign of civil disobedience against the present nuclear policy of H. M. Government' (in the words of Special Branch).[10] 'The human situation today is … uniquely perilous,' Bolt wrote in 1961. 'If, as seems probable, Man destroys himself, it will be because … his hatred of life is stronger than his love of life, because his greed, aggression and fear are stronger than his self-denial, charity and courage.' Atomic weaponry, Bolt continued, 'enables Man for the first time to realise irreversibly whatever fantasies of evil he may have'.[11]

In September 1961 Bolt was arrested at a Trafalgar Square sit-down demonstration, in company with his fellow playwrights John Arden, John Osborne and Arnold Wesker. He refused to be bound over to keep the peace, and was sent to an open prison in Staffordshire where he shared a cell with the poet Christopher Logue. Shortly after the group arrest, Noël Coward warned his friend Wesker against wasting his 'energy and creative talent in coping with

---

8 Email from Frederic Raphael, 11 September 2018.

9 Robert Bolt, *Three Plays* (London: Mercury Books, 1963), p. 227.

10 NA KV 2/4058, serial 211a, 'Special Branch re The Committee of 100', 26 October 1960.

11 Robert Bolt, 'Mr Coward had the last of the wine', *Sunday Times*, 29 January 1961.

mediocre little Bureaucrats and organizing a "Cultural Revolution" ... Nor will it avail the world situation one iota for you and Robert Bolt to spend occasional weeks in the clink in protest against humanity's yearning for self-destruction.'[12]

Bolt emerged from his years of CPGB group discipline as a militant individualist who wanted to muster a resistance movement against the mass conformity of his times. 'Socially, we fly from the idea of an individual to the professional describers, the classifiers, the men with the categories and the quick ear for the latest sub-division, who flourish among us like priests,' Bolt wrote in 1963. 'Individually, we do what we can to describe and classify ourselves and so assure ourselves that from the outside at least we do have a definite outline.' He professed rationalism, not Christianity. 'The paramount gift our thinkers, artists, and for all I know our men of science, should labour to get for us is a sense of selfhood without resort to magic.'[13] Such beliefs made him antipathetic to the group faith and quasi-religious incantations that he encountered in the PRC. The officials whom he met there were 'immaculately self-righteous, yes, but not aggressive,' so he told *SACU News* in November 1965. 'They are, naturally enough, bedazzled and enchanted by what they have done.'

Ernie Roberts (1912–1994)

Ernie Roberts was the eldest of eleven children.[14] His father was then an ostler, and his mother (a blacksmith's daughter) had worked before her marriage in domestic service. The family lived in a garret in a sixteenth-century slum at Frankwell near Shrewsbury. The downstairs floors of the hovel were occupied by the local mole-catcher. His father was a drunkard, who often fell insensate in the gutter where neighbouring children jeered at him. He hit his womenfolk, and beat his sons with a bicycle chain. Ernie was sent scavenging for fag-ends, and spent his evenings reconstituting old cigarette papers and tobacco fragments into cigarettes for his father. He felt humiliated when his school-friends saw him pushing a broken pram through the streets

---

12 Barry Day, ed., *The Letters of Noël Coward* (London: Methuen, 2007), p. 238.

13 Bolt, *Three Plays*, pp. 93, 96.

14 The following section is based on the Roberts paper at the Working Class Movement Library at Salford and on Ernie Roberts, *Strike Back* (Orpington: Ernie Roberts, 1994). These memoirs, written when Roberts (a lifelong non-smoker) knew that he was dying of lung cancer acquired passively from decades of tobacco-filled meetings, were prefixed by tributes from Tony Benn, Fenner Brockway and Arthur Scargill.

shouting 'rag-bone'. He also hawked tie-pins, collar-studs, pegs and shoe-laces door to door. Sometimes he stole a potato or carrot from a market stall to eat by himself. In adolescence, he learnt palmistry, and sometimes made pennies by reading hands at travelling fairs. He slept rough under a hedge until the showmen took him into their caravan.

At the age of fourteen he went to work in Binley colliery. His next jobs were in the Terry Road Valve Company in Coventry, the back-axle section of Armstrong-Siddeley Motors, the small parts production line at Humber Motors and in the finishing-shop on the Triumph Super Seven. In 1929, at the age of seventeen, he cycled to Oxford, where he got work as a paint-sprayer in the Pressed Steel works at Cowley. He moved into lodgings in Rose Place, close to the house in St Aldate's to which Trevor-Roper moved in 1955. Two unmarried daughters of the Reverend William Spooner, late Warden of New College, gave him lessons in musical appreciation, which left him with a lingering pleasure in oboe and violin music. He attended lectures given by Oxford professors whom he found absurd in their abstractions.

Returning to Coventry in 1931, Roberts served a month in Winson Green prison, breaking stones and sewing mailbags, after taking the blame for a motoring offence committed by his father. After a spell of unemployment, he joined the Young Communist League in 1932. Two years later he became a full member of the CPGB. In 1935 he founded the Coventry Young Workers' Social Club, which was raided one evening by policemen, who either hoped to find a thieves' den or were making a spot-check for Special Branch. He made the most of his opportunities as a factory agitator at a time when the communists were gaining tactical strength in the Amalgamated Engineering Union (AEU): a penetration which was helped by the Union then possessing 'the most unworkable constitution since that of the Polish monarchy'.[15] On 28 August 1939 Roberts organized an unofficial walk-out and protest march by 2,000 workers from Armstrong-Whitworth's aircraft factory at Baginton, three days after the detonation of an Irish Republican Army bomb in Coventry's main shopping street had killed five passers-by and wounded seventy. The marchers threatened that unless all Irish workmen in Coventry were immediately discharged, they would strike.[16] As the Russo-German Non-Aggression Pact had been signed as recently as 23 August, and Europe was to go to war on 1 September, with Germany invading Poland and Russia turning on Finland,

15 Sir Ian Gilmour, *The Body Politic* (London: Hutchinson, 1969), p. 110.
16 'Anti-Irish Demonstration in Coventry', *Manchester Guardian*, 29 August 1939.

this threat to aircraft production suited communist aims; but it was quashed by trade union officials.

Armstrong-Siddeley Motors sacked Roberts in 1940 because of his trade union activities. Despite his notoriety as 'Roberts the Red', he was soon taken on as a fitting inspector of aero-engine parts in Rootes Motors' assembly plant at Ryton-on-Dunsmore. When King George VI visited the factory in 1940, two Special Branch men kept Roberts under watch. After the German air-raids on Coventry began in August 1940, he organized discussion groups among the night-time fire-watchers with the causes and aims of the war, fascism, capitalism and socialism as their topics. He worked at a Rover factory making aero-engines and airframes for Lancaster bombers, became a shop steward at the Jaguar plant, then at Alvis, and finally at Humber. His statements at CPGB meetings that, contrary to the party's wartime policy, the class war should continue to be waged in wartime led to his expulsion from the CPGB in August 1941: the indictment against him was that he was 'individualistic, disruptive, egotistical'.[17] His accusers claimed that he had collaborated with Trotskyites, although it is hard to imagine where he found Trotskyites in the Midlands of 1941. Roberts joined the Labour Party in 1942.

Wal Hannington, a founder member of the CPGB and national organizer of the Amalgamated Engineering Union (AEU), had meanwhile become Roberts' mentor. Hannington's support enabled Roberts' election as a contentious District President of the AEU in 1944–48. The belief that he was a communist Trojan Horse within AEU and Labour party prevented his adoption as a Labour parliamentary candidate for Coventry in 1945. Instead Roberts served as councillor for the Holbrook ward of Coventry in 1949–58. He always wore a red tie when forced to wear a suit, disliked flummery, and opposed the priority over house-building given to the reconstruction of the cathedral (well into the 1950s he and his wife had to live in a caravan as they could not get other accommodation). He decried Civil Defence publicity in the 1950s as a cruel deception, and made fun of the Central Office of Information booklet, *Civil Defence is Common Sense*, which was based on an absurd premise: 'a fire, whether caused by a careless match or the heat from a H-bomb, is still fought in the same way.'[18] He led a campaign against pubs which operated a 'colour-bar'.

---

17 Roberts, *Strike Back*, p. 50.
18 Roberts, *Strike Back*, p. 83.

In 1957 Roberts became assistant general secretary of the AEU, which had its headquarters in Peckham, and was enabled by his salary to buy 43 Copers Cope Road in New Beckenham. As an ex-communist, he was marginalized by other senior officials in the union. He and the union's president, Bill Carron, hated one another. Carron became set on ruining him, and once obtained Roberts' suspension from his post; but Roberts was reinstated after litigation. Injustices in capitalist but not in communist countries concerned Roberts. In 1960, for example, he joined Bertrand Russell and Fenner Brockway in the Campaign for the Release of Untried Prisoners in Belfast. In 1962 he campaigned for the release of Morton Sobell, an American electronics engineer who had begun spying for the Soviet Union in 1944 and spent thirteen years in Alcatraz.

Roberts joined every Campaign for Nuclear Disarmament (CND) march to Aldermaston from the first in 1958, and spoke across England on behalf of CND (once alongside Bertrand Russell at a rally in Trafalgar Square). He declined, however, Russell's invitation to join the Committee of 100 because he feared that his involvement in civil disobedience would enable Carron to weaken him in the AEU. On a Saturday in September 1960 he formed a picket, together with the artist Michael Ayrton, the actress Constance Cummings, the novelist Doris Lessing and Arnold Wesker, which patrolled Whitehall on behalf of CND. At that time Roberts sat on the executive council of a body called Victory for Socialism, alongside such MPs as Michael Foot, Ian Mikardo, Sydney Silverman and Konni Zilliacus. 'In the last few years the Right has had its own way,' declared a Victory for Socialism manifesto of 1960 seeking the overthrow as Labour Party leader of Hugh Gaitskell, who had, complained the rebels, 'induced the party to muffle the attack on capitalism, play down the radical aims of the party, and chose bi-partisanship with the Conservatives on vital issues such as the bomb'.[19]

Roberts' later career deserves recording. After retiring from the AEU, he was elected as Labour MP for Hackney North and Stoke Newington in 1979. He advocated workers' control in nationalized industries by the installation of worker-directors elected directly by employees. He opposed worker representation in the management of private industry as 'class collaboration'. Instead, he wanted the workers to demand 'socialization' of their capitalist employers. He supported the state takeover of financial institutions, 'abortion-on-demand', withdrawal from NATO, repeal of 'racist laws' and recalling

---

19 'War Declared on Mr Gaitskell', *Guardian*, 20 June 1960.

troops from Ireland. He was one of the parliamentary leaders of Don't Let Irish Prisoners Die campaign launched a month before Bobby Sands starved himself to death in 1981. When Hackney North Constituency Labour Party held 'a fun-packed, star-studded election school' in April 1987, its keynote speakers were Diane Abbott, Tony Benn, Jeremy Corbyn and Roberts.[20]

Roberts was a genuine internationalist, who helped all the different nationalities in his constituency. These included the members of a small bakers' union who all belonged to a strict orthodox Jewish sect. After cheerful photographs of him with Jewish loaves and bakers in distinctive black clothes were published in the local press, he was denounced as a philo-Semite, a closet Jew and as a toady to Israel. He received hate-mail addressed to 'Rabbi E. Roberts', inscribed with swastikas and obscenities, and was reviled as a Zionist agent of influence. There were systematic malpractices when the time came to select Hackney North's Labour candidate for the 1987 general election: voting in some wards was held at times when Roberts' Moslem supporters were at prayer; some of his stalwart constituency friends were kept uninformed of the time and place of the ballot; trade unionists who had been mandated by their members to vote for Roberts instead backed his rival on the day. The successful candidate, who benefited (doubtless unknowingly) by these tricks, was Diane Abbott.

---

20 Working-Class Movement Library, Salford, Roberts papers.

Bibliography

Archives

Bodleian Library, Oxford. Papers of Sir Isaiah Berlin, Dorothy Hodgkin, Nicholas Kurti, Kurt Mendelssohn, Sir Patrick Reilly, Sir Stephen Spender and Harold Wilson.
Cambridge University Library. Papers of Joseph Needham.
Christ Church, Oxford. Papers of Lord Dacre of Glanton.
Churchill College, Cambridge. Papers of Patrick Gordon Walker.
Hoover Institution, Stanford University. Diaries of Jimmie Wei.
I Tatti, Settignano. Papers of Nicky Mariano.
King's College, Cambridge. Papers of Lord Annan and Joan Robinson.
Mitchell Library, Sydney. Papers of G. E. Morrison.
National Archives, Kew. Papers of Foreign Office, Foreign & Commonwealth Office and of the Security Service.
School of Oriental and African Studies, London. Papers of Derek Bryan.
Worcester College, Oxford. Papers of J. C. Masterman.
Working Class Movement Library, Salford. Papers of Ernie Roberts.

The following secondary sources were written by members of SACU.

Ash, William. *Morals and Politics: the ethics of revolution*. London: Routledge & Kegan Paul, 1977.
Ash, William. *Red Square: the autobiography of an unconventional revolutionary*. London: Howard Baker, 1978.
Ash, William. *Marxist Morality*. Delhi: Ajanta Publications, 1998.
Ayer, A. J. 'Impressions of Communist China', *The Listener*, 2 December 1954.
Ayer, A. J. *More of My Life*. London: Collins, 1984.
Beatson, Peter and Dianne, eds. *Dear Peggy: letters to Margaret Garland from her New Zealand friends*. Palmerston North: Massey University Sociology Department, 1997.

Bryan, Derek. *China's Taiwan*. London: British-China Friendship Association, 1959.

Bryan, Derek. *The Land and People of China*. London: A. & C. Black, 1964.

Collier, John and Elsie. *China's Socialist Revolution*. London: stage 1, 1973.

Dawson, Raymond. *The Chinese Chameleon: an analysis of European conceptions of Chinese civilization*. London: Oxford University Press, 1967.

Dawson, Raymond. *The Chinese Experience*. London: Weidenfeld & Nicolson, 1978.

Gelder, Stuart and Roma. *The Long March to Freedom*. London: Hutchinson, 1962.

Gelder, Stuart and Roma. *The Timely Rain: travels in new Tibet*. London: Hutchinson, 1964.

Gelder, Stuart and Roma. *Memories for a Chinese Grand-daughter*. London: Hutchinson, 1967.

Luard, Evan. *Britain and China*. London: Chatto & Windus, 1962.

Mendelssohn, Kurt. *In China Now*. London: Hamlyn, 1969.

Needham, Joseph. *Time: the Refreshing River (Essays and Addresses 1932–1942)*. London: George Allen & Unwin, 1943.

Needham, Joseph. *History is on our Side*. London: George Allen & Unwin, 1946.

Needham, Joseph. *Science and Society in Ancient China: Conway memorial lecture delivered at Conway Hall, Red Lion Square, WC1 on May 12th, 1947*. London: Watts & Co., 1947.

Pulleyblank, Edwin G. *Chinese History and World History: an inaugural lecture*. Cambridge: Cambridge University Press, 1955.

Roberts, Ernie. *Strike Back*. Orpington: Ernie Roberts, 1994.

Robinson, Joan. *Letters from a Visitor to China*. Cambridge: Students' Bookshops, 1954.

Robinson, Joan. *The Cultural Revolution in China*. London: Penguin, 1969.

Timberlake, Percy. *The 48 Group: the story of the Icebreakers in China*. London: the 48 Group Club, 1994.

The making of books and articles about Mao's China is illimitable. The following list gives those that were notably helpful in providing either general background information or specific details.

Acton, Sir Harold. *Memoirs of an Aesthete*. London: Methuen, 1948.

Ashton, Stephen and Bennett, Gill, eds. *Documents on British Policy Overseas*. Series 1, volume 8. London: Whitehall History Publishing, 2002.

Balázs, Étienne [Istvan]. *Chinese Civilization and Bureaucracy: variations on a theme*. New Haven: Yale University Press, 1964.

Barthes, Roland. *Travels in China*. Cambridge, Mass: Polity, 2012.

Bodard, Lucien. *La Chine de la douceur*. Paris: Gallimard, 1957.

Bodard, Lucien. *La Chine de cauchemar*. Paris: Gallimard, 1961.

Boyd-Orr, Lord. *What's Happening in China?* London: Macdonald, 1959.

Brady, Anne-Marie. *Making the Foreign Serve China: managing foreigners in the People's Republic*. Lanham, MD: Rowman & Littlefield, 2003.

Buchanan, Tom. *East Wind: China and the British Left, 1925–1976*. Oxford: Oxford University Press, 2012.

Caute, David. *Isaac & Isaiah: the covert punishment of a Cold War heretic*. London: Yale University Press, 2013.

Clayre, Alasdair. *The Heart of the Dragon*. London: Collins, 1984.

Crossman, Richard. 'Chinese Notebook', *Encounter*, March 1959, pp. 11–22.

Cormac, Rory. *Disrupt and Deny: spies, Special Forces, and the secret pursuit of British foreign policy*. Oxford: Oxford University Press, 2018.

Croft, Michael. *Red Carpet to China*. London: Longmans, Green, 1958.

Dikötter, Frank. *Mao's Great Famine: the history of China's most devastating catastrophe, 1958–62*. London: Bloomsbury, 2010.

Dylan, Huw. *Defence Intelligence and the Cold War: Britain's Joint Intelligence Bureau 1945–1964*. Oxford: Oxford University Press, 2014.

Fabre-Luce, Alfred. 'Chinese Journey', *Encounter*, August 1959, pp. 17–26.

Feuerwerker, Albert, ed. *History in Communist China*. Cambridge, MA: MIT Press, 1968.

Goldman, Merle. *Literary Dissent in Communist China*. Cambridge, MA: Harvard University Press, 1967.

Guillain, Robert. *The Blue Ants: 600 million Chinese under the red flag*. London: Secker & Warburg, 1956.

Hollander, Paul. *Political Pilgrims: travels of Western intellectuals to the Soviet Union, China and Cuba, 1928–1978*. New York: Oxford University Press, 1981.

Hollander, Paul. *From Benito Mussolini to Hugo Chavez: intellectuals and a century of political hero worship*. Cambridge: Cambridge University Press, 2016.

Hudson, Geoffrey. *Europe and China: a survey of their relations from the earliest times to 1800*. London: Edwin Arnold, 1931.

Hudson, Geoffrey. *Questions of East and West: studies in current history*. London: Odhams, 1953.

Hudson, Geoffrey. 'Mme de Beauvoir in China', *Encounter*, February 1959, pp. 64–7.

Koningsberger, Hans. *Love and Hate in China*. London: Jonathan Cape, 1967.

Leys, Simon. *Les Habits Neufs du Président Mao*. Paris: Champs Libre, 1971.

Leys, Simon. *Chinese Shadows*. New York: Viking, 1977.

Leys, Simon. *The Burning Forest: essays on Chinese culture and politics*. New York: Holt, Rinehart and Winston, 1986.

Leys, Simon. *The Halls of Uselessness: collected essays*. New York: New York Review Books, 2013.

Lovell, Julia. *Maoism: A Global History*. London: Bodley Head, 2019.

Lowenthal, Richard. 'Mao's Revolution: The Chinese Handwriting on the Wall', *Encounter*, April 1967, pp. 3–9.

Mitter, Rana. *A Bitter Revolution: China's struggle with the modern world*. Oxford: Oxford University Press, 2004.

Passin, Herbert. *China's Cultural Diplomacy*. New York: Frederick Praeger, 1962.

Peyrefitte, Alain. *La Chine s'est éveillée: carnets de route d l'ère Deng Xiaoping*. Paris: Fayard, 1996.

Pike, Francis. *Empires at War: a short history of modern Asia since World War II*. London: I.B.Tauris, 2010.

Robinson, Geoffrey R. *The Killing Season: a history of the Indonesian massacres, 1965–66*. Princeton: Princeton University Press, 2018.

Roy, Jules. *Le voyage en Chine*. Paris: Juillard, 1965.

Smith, Stephen A. *Revolution and the People in Russia and China: a comparative history*. Cambridge: Cambridge University Press, 2008.

Smith, Stephen A., ed. *The Oxford Handbook of the History of Communism*. Oxford: Oxford University Press, 2014.

Schoenhals, Michael. *Spying for the People: Mao's secret agents, 1949–1967*. Cambridge: Cambridge University Press, 2013.

Sisman, Adam. *Hugh Trevor-Roper: the biography*. London: Weidenfeld & Nicolson, 2010.

Thomas, Donald. 'East Wind, West Wind: Chinese Students in Cardiff', *Encounter*, July 1967, pp. 56–60.

Trevelyan, Humphrey. *Worlds Apart: China 1953–5: Soviet Union 1962–5*. London: Macmillan, 1971.

Trevelyan, Humphrey. *Diplomatic Channels*. London: Macmillan, 1973.

Tsang, Steve. *The Cold War's Odd Couple: the unintended partnership between the Republic of China and the UK, 1950–1958*. London: I.B. Tauris, 2006.

Tuohy, Frank. 'From a Chinese Diary', *Encounter*, December 1966, pp. 7–13.

Welch, Holmes. 'The Chinese Art of Make-Believe', *Encounter*, May 1968, pp. 8–13.

Will, Pierre-Étienne and Ang, Isabelle. *Actualité d'Étienne Balázs (1905–1963): témoignages et réflexions pour un centenaire*. Paris: Collège de France, Institut de Hautes Études Chinoises, 2010.

Wootton, Barbara. 'Journey to China', *Encounter*, June 1973, pp. 21–7.

Wright, Patrick. *Passport to Peking: a very British mission to Mao's China*. Oxford: Oxford University Press, 2010.

Index

Abbott, Diane 252
Abse, Leo 34
Academia Sinica (ROC) 44, 191–2, 196, 201, 215
Academy of Sciences (PRC; *formerly* Academia Sinica) 79, 81, 89, 191 n.49
Acland, Sir Richard 234 n.1
Acton, Sir Harold 10 n.28, 195 n.56
Adams, Mary: background, life and career 6, 60, 154, 243–5; character and characteristics 60–61, 67–8, 69, 73–4, 77, 82, 94, 115, 118–19, 127, 154, 234, 245; political views 43, 60, 62, 68, 123, 245; committee memberships 60–61, 80, 154, 245; role in SACU 43, 105, 114, 137, 146, 154, 163, 244; during 1965 China trip 6–7, 77, 94, 95, 105, 158; as designated group leader 79–80, 82, 94, 155; at lunch at British Legation 234; at CPA banquet 67–8; tour of Imperial Palace 70; primary school visit 73–4; Peking University visit 80–81; excursion to Summer Palace 86–7, 94; at rally for state visit of King Sihanouk 101; tour of Ming tombs 102; at Great Hall of the People banquet 106; at National Day celebrations 110; at presentation to 'Heads of State' 111; visits Chinese Medical Association 115; trips to Loyang and Sian 114–15, 118–19, 121, 123, 124, 125, 126; travels on to Shanghai with Ernie Roberts 127; lectures on design in Prague 108, 125, 154; at open meeting of

SACU (16 November 1965) 135, 141, 160, 239; at SACU council of management meeting (13 December 1965) 147, 149; response to *Sunday Times* article on SACU 35, 46–7, 171, 172; at SACU annual general meeting (21 May 1966) 171, 172–3
Adams, Vyvyan 60, 243
AEU *see* Amalgamated Engineering Union
Air France (airline) 224
air travel 57–8, 126, 128–9, 177, 182, 193–4, 203–4, 211, 212–13, 221, 224
Albania 66
Aldermaston marches 251
Alexander of Tunis, Harold Alexander, 1st Earl 247
Ali, Tariq 44; *Street Fighting Years* 30, 35 n.94
Alley, Rewi 5, 10 n.28
Amalgamated Engineering Union (AEU) 61, 65, 155, 158, 170 n.28, 249–51
Amery, Leo 60 n.12, 246
Amoy (Xiamen) 9, 186, 187
Amsterdam 131, 173
Amulree, Basil Mackenzie, 2nd Baron 33
An-yang 192, 196
Angkor ruins (Cambodia) 199, 221–4, 227–8, 229–31
Annales d'histoire économique et sociale (journal) 90, 91
Annan, Noël Annan, Baron, on Joan Robinson 22–3, 48 n.132
Anping 207
anti-Semitism 252
Arden, John 247

Argyll, Mathilda, Duchess of 226
Ariel Hotel (Heathrow airport) 131
Aristotle 229 n.136
Armstrong-Siddeley (engineering
    company) 249, 250
army, Chinese, abolition of officers' ranks
    125
Arts and Sciences in China (BCFA
    magazine) 30
Ash, William ('Bill'): background, life
    and career 137 n.15, 163 n.14;
    role in formation of SACU 18, 32;
    member of SACU General Purposes
    Committee 32, 43, 45, 137, 163-4,
    166 n.17; calls for expulsion of T-R
    from SACU 143, 146, 163; election to
    SACU council of management 47-8,
    52, 170; formation of CPGBML 45,
    137 n.15, 170 n.28; *Marxism and
    Moral Concepts* 163; *Red Square: the
    autobiography of an unconventional
    revolutionary* 18
Ashby, Sir Eric (*later* Baron Ashby) 33
Asquith, Conrad 171 n.30
Asquith of Yarnbury, Violet Bonham Carter,
    Baroness 177
Astor, David 180
Athenaeum (club) 40, 134 n.3
Athens, Parthenon, proposed recreation
    227
atomic weapons *see* nuclear and atomic
    weapons
Attlee, Clement (*later* 1st Earl Attlee) 16,
    20
Austin Motors 26
Ayer, Sir Alfred Jules ('Freddie') 31, 33, 35,
    42, 48, 58 n.4, 65 n.29, 79 n.66
Ayrton, Michael 34, 251

Backhouse, Sir Edmund 2, 10 n.28, 38
Baikal, Lake 57 n.3, 59, 128
Balazs, Étienne 2, 90, 235; *Chinese
    Civilisation and Bureaucracy* 8-9,
    10, 17
Balogh, Thomas Balogh, Baron 39
Bangkok 177, 182, 218-20, 222, 231 n.138
Bao Zheng 112
Barebones' Parliament (1653) 151 n.1

Barry, John 169 n.23; 'All-party group for
    Anglo-Chinese understanding' 29,
    32, 46; 'Battle to Control China
    Society' 46, 169, 170-71
Barthes, Roland 7
Bartók, Béla 39
Basic English (international auxiliary
    language) 60, 69, 74, 123
Bateson, Frederick Wilse 168 n.21
Bateson, Nicholas: background, life and
    career 44-5, 168 n.21; membership
    of SACU Oxford branch 44; reports
    to SACU management on T-R 46, 49,
    168, 169-70, 173; at SACU annual
    general meeting (1966)49, 50
BBC (British Broadcasting Corporation) 60,
    137 n.15, 244
BCFA *see* British-China Friendship
    Association
BCPIT *see* British Council for the
    Promotion of International Trade
BEA (British European Airways) 129
Beatles (band) 171 n.30, 225
Beauvoir, Simone de 7
Beckenham (Kent) 251; Langley Park
    Garage ('Chinese Garage') 70
Beefsteak Club 140 n.22, 149
Beijing *see* Peking
Beirut 180
Belhaven Hill preparatory school (Dunbar)
    228
Beloff, Michael, 'The L.S.E. Story' 45
Benn, Anthony Wedgwood 82, 248 n.14,
    252
Berger, Nancy ('Nan') 27, 43, 138, 163;
    editorship of *SACU News* 138, 139,
    143, 175
Berger, Roland ('Ro'): background, life and
    career 26-7, 128 n.193; character and
    characteristics 155; political views
    26, 31, 43, 127-8; secretary of BCPIT
    26, 27, 137-8, 174-5; visits China
    27, 127; member of SACU General
    Purposes Committee 32, 43, 47,
    137-8, 155, 163-4, 166; meets T-R
    during 1965 China trip 127-8, 137,
    158, 237; reports on China trip to
    Jack Perry 237-8; attempts to cancel

November 1965 SACU open meeting 137, 139, 158, 160; attends November open meeting 141, 160; criticisms of SACU Oxford branch and T-R 44, 167–8; at SACU annual general meeting (21 May 1966) 172; and removal of T-R from SACU council of management 46; election to SACU council of management 47–8, 52, 170; and financing of SACU 174–5; views on Maoist China 27; views on Soviet Communism 31

Berlin: Congress for Cultural Freedom (1950) 35, 184; Frederick William University 183 n.22; Free University 183

Berlin, Aline, Lady 226

Berlin, Sir Isaiah 11 n.32, 39, 184, 226; on Lady Alexandra Trevor-Roper 92 n.114; on Sir Noel Hall 44 n.121

Berlin Wall 68–9, 155

Bernadotte, Count Folke 100

Betjeman, Sir John 244

Bevan, Robert and Natalie 75–6, 98

Bing, Geoffrey 25–6

Binning, John Baillie-Hamilton, Lord (*later* 13th Earl of Haddington) 172

Birch, Reg 45, 137 n.15, 163 n.14, 170

Birmingham University 71

Bishopsteignton (Devon) 246

Blackett, Patrick Blackett, Baron 82

Blackshirts (British Union of Fascists) 23–4

Blake, George 181

Blake, Robert Blake, Baron 36, 42

Blanc, Raymond 39

Bloodworth, Dennis, *Chinese Looking Glass* 54

Blue, Gregory, 'Joseph Needham' 27 n.75

Blumenthal, Heston 39

Blunden, Edmund 48

Bodard, Lucien 7, 13–14, 93 n.117

Bolland, Edwin 234 n.2

Bolshevism 3, 97, 246

Bolt, Robert: background, life and career 6, 83, 95, 245–8; character and characteristics 61–2, 95, 101, 105, 120; political views 62, 65, 83, 95, 98, 246, 247, 248; relations with T-R 6, 62, 155; during 1965 China trip 6, 58, 64, 65, 72, 77, 80, 85, 95–6, 105, 108, 155, 158; at lunch at British Legation 233–5; at CPA banquet 67, 68; tour of Imperial Palace 70; at reception for Chinese students 71, 233–4; primary school visit 73–5; arts-and-crafts factory visit 75; tour of market-gardening commune 78; at Museum of Chinese History 79; Peking University visit 80–81, 238; returns to Imperial Palace with T-R 82–3; dines with Timothy George 84; excursion to Summer Palace 86; at Peking opera 87–8, 101, 103, 112–13; visits Lama Temple, Hall of the Classics and Northern Lake 91; at the theatre 92–3; visits Temple of Heaven 98; appointments at Russian Embassy to obtain visas 98–9, 111; at rally for state visit of King Sihanouk 99–100, 101, 166; tour of Great Wall and Ming tombs 101, 102; questions Chinese drama critic 103–4; at Great Hall of the People banquet 106; at presentation to 'Heads of State' 111; visits National Art Museum 111–12; discusses future of SACU with T-R 113–14; trips to Loyang and Sian 115, 117, 119, 120, 121, 124, 125, 126; returns to Peking 126–7, 158; Roland Berger reports on 237–8; leaves China 126 n.189, 158; returns to London via Moscow and Amsterdam 130–32, 173; and T-R's further investigations of SACU 139, 140; at open meeting of SACU (16 November 1965) 135, 141, 160, 239–40; dines with T-R after meeting 143, 161; decides to sever relations with SACU 161; *The Critic and the Heart* 246; *The Last of the Wine* 247; *A Man for All Seasons* 6, 61 n.21, 246; *The Tiger and the Horse* 247

Bolton (Lancashire) 117, 120

Bonham Carter, Lady Violet (*later* Baroness Asquith of Yarnbury) 177

Boothby, Robert Boothby, Baron 234 n.1
Borkenau, Franz 35
Bossuet, Jacques-Bénigne, *Universal History* 198
Boulder (Colorado) 2
Bowra, Sir Maurice 6, 33, 62, 75, 146 n.38
Boxer, Charles 215
Boxer rebellion (1900–1) 10, 72 n.53, 73 n.54, 76 n.60
Boyd-Orr, John Boyd Orr, 1st Baron 22, 23, 24, 25, 30
Boyes, William 219, 220, 221
Brahmaputra river 182
Braithwaite, Sir Rodric 130–31
Braudel, Fernand 225 n.128
Bray, Raymond 185–6
Bredon, Juliet 86 n.87; *Peking* 86, 91, 102 n.135
Bridge, Ann, *Peking Picnic* 76 n.60
British-China Friendship Association (BCFA) 27, 28, 30–31, 135, 152
British Council 220 n.116
British Council for the Promotion of International Trade (BCPIT) 25–7, 32, 138, 139, 174
British European Airways (BEA) 129
British Union of Fascists 23–4
Britten, Benjamin Britten, Baron 34, 48
Brockway, Fenner Brockway, Baron 248 n.14, 251
Brontë, Emily, *Wuthering Heights* 58, 208
Brown, George (*later* Baron George-Brown) 85
Bryan, Derek: background and early life 30, 146; character and characteristics 30, 144, 155; career 30; marriage 30; political beliefs and views on Maoist China 19, 105, 135–6; BCFA activities 30; Secretary of SACU 6, 32, 105, 135–6, 136 n.11, 155–6; editor of *The China Broadsheet* (China Policy Group pamphlet) 135; invites T-R to join China trip 6, 12, 93, 153–4; T-R reports to on return from China trip 134–5; and T-R's further investigation of SACU 42, 135–6, 139–40, 145–7, 163, 164; monitoring of Oxford branch of

SACU 167; at open meeting of SACU (16 November 1965) 140–41, 143; reaction after T-R's speech at open meeting 143, 144, 145; at SACU council of management meeting (13 December 1965) 144, 147, 149; response to meeting's decisions 165–6; and T-R's removal from council of management 45–6, 168 n.22, 169–70, 173; supplies material for Joan Robinson's *The Cultural Revolution in China* 20
Buchanan, Tom 25 n.65
Buck, Pearl S. 112
Buckman, Bernard 23, 25, 32
Buddhism 117, 118, 121, 207
Bulgaria, T-R visits 4
Burchett, Wilfred 5
bureaucracy, in Maoist China 98–9, 103–4
Burma 100
Burma Air Lines 219, 221
by-elections: Bridgwater (1938) 234 n.1; Oxford (1938) 234 n.1
Byronism 97

Cable Street, Battle of (1936) 24
Cairncross, Sir Alexander ('Alec') 23
Calvin, John 3
Cambodia: rule of Prince Sihanouk 229; T-R visits 54, 56, 221–31
Cambridge 243–4
Campaign for Nuclear Disarmament (CND) 61, 62, 95, 251
Campaign for the Release of Untried Prisoners in Belfast 251
Canton 9
Cardiff, David 220 n.116
Cardiff, Maurice 220
Carron, Bill 251
Carter-Ruck, Peter 35 n.94
Casson, Sir Hugh 31
Castro, Fidel 2, 44, 168 n.21
'Cement-face' *see* To Chi-lou (guide in Peking)
Chain, Sir Ernst 33
Chairman Mao is the Red Sun in our Hearts (film) 45
Chamberlain, Neville 152

champagne-drinking 130, 131, 140, 142, 160, 161
Chance, Patrick 9
Chang Chaow 78 n.63
Chang Cheng-lang 89
Chang Chi-yun 200–201, 214, 215
Chang Chih-lien 66, 103, 235–7
Chang Kia-ngau 195, 196
Chaplin, Sir Charlie 136 n.11
Chatham House (Royal Institute of International Affairs) 183; T-R's 'China Today' talk 140
Cheke, Dudley 225 n.126
Chen Ching-men 195, 196
Chen Szu-chun 67
Chen Yi 20
Cheng Yao-wen 67
Cherwell, Frederick Lindemann, 1st Viscount 12, 39
Chiang Ch'ing 81 n.69
Chiang Fu-ts'ung 187
Chiang Kai-shek 13, 15, 19, 55, 82, 88–9, 187 n.34, 190, 201
Chiefswood (Melrose) 149
Chien Po-tsan 12, 153 n.3
China Broadsheet, The (China Policy Group pamphlet) 135
China National Import and Export Corporation 25
China Policy Study Group 71 n.48, 135
Chinese Civil War (1927–49) 15–16, 183 n.18, 187 n.34
Chinese Communist Revolution (1949) 3–4, 16, 84
Chinese Culture (journal) 201
'Chinese Garage' (Beckenham) 70
Chinese Medical Association 115
Chinese People's Association for Cultural Relations with Foreign Countries (CPA) 13, 30–31, 53, 59, 67, 139, 154, 239
Chinese Revolution (1911–12) 4
Chou En-lai 12, 93, 99, 106 n.141, 107, 110, 126
Chou Tien-kou 210
Christ Church (Oxford) 184
Chuang Shuang-yen 187
Chulalongkorn (Rama V), King of Siam 220

Church House (Westminster) 135, 140
Churchill, Randolph 75
Churchill, Sir Winston 136 n.8
CIA (US Central Intelligence Agency): funding of Congress for Cultural Freedom 35; funding of *Encounter* magazine 184; and Indonesian *coup d'état* 116, 124; Project WIZARD (Congo) 92 n.112; and ROC Institute of International Relations 184
circuses, Chinese 79
Civil Defence is Common Sense (COI booklet) 250
civil wars, English 37, 51, 103, 236
Clark Kerr, Sir Archibald (*later* 1st Baron Inverchapel) 30
Cleave, Maureen 171 n.30
Clift, Richard 238–40
Clutton-Brock, Alan 112 n.153
CND *see* Campaign for Nuclear Disarmament
Cockcroft, Sir John 48
Cohen, Ruth 33
Cole, George Douglas Howard 234 n.1
Colefax, Sibyl, Lady 140 n.23
Collier, Elsie and Johnny 149
Collins, John 33
Committee of 100 62 n.22, 148 n.41, 247, 251
Committee to Defeat Revisionism for Communist Unity 144 n.31
Commonwealth of England 51, 103, 236
Communist Party of Great Britain (CPGB): and Battle of Cable Street (1936) 24; Security Service surveillance of members 24, 25, 26, 27; Historians Group 91 n.105; Chinese views on 157–8; and trade union movement 249, 250
Communist Party of Great Britain (Marxist-Leninist) (CPGBML) 45, 137 n.15, 170 n.28
Confucianism 83, 186, 193, 207; Forest of Stone Tablets 122
Congo Crisis (1960–65) 92–3
Congress for Cultural Freedom (Berlin; 1950) 35, 184
Consumers' Association 80, 154, 244

contraception 119, 125, 154, 244; stainless-steel contraceptives 115
Coocoola, Princess *see* Pema Tsedeun, Princess of Sikkim
Copenhagen 133, 156, 177, 182
Corbyn, Jeremy 252
Cornwell, David (John le Carré) 178, 246
Coulson, Charles 44, 167 n.19
Council for Industrial Design 60, 70, 73, 108, 121, 154
Coventry 249, 250
Coward, Sir Noël 247–8
CPA *see* Chinese People's Association for Cultural Relations with Foreign Countries
CPGB *see* Communist Party of Great Britain
CPGBML *see* Communist Party of Great Britain (Marxist-Leninist)
Cranbrook, Caroline, Countess of (*née* Jarvis) 76, 79
Croft, Michael 8
Cromwell, Oliver 198; Chiang Kai-shek as Chinese counterpart 82 n.74; his weakness and folly 151
Cromwell, Richard 236
Crook, David 5, 51
Cuba, under Castro 2, 44, 168 n.21
Cuban missile crisis (1962) 181 n.14
Cuckney, John Cuckney, Baron 138 n.20
Cultural Revolution (PRC; 1966–76) 4, 17, 20, 43, 51–3, 153 n.3, 185
Cummings, Constance 251

D-Notices affair (1967) 179
Daily Worker (newspaper) 156
Davies, Harold (*later* Baron Davies of Leek) 23, 138 n.18
Davis, Stanley Clinton (*later* Baron Clinton-Davis) 107 n.144
Dawson, Raymond 43, 49, 50, 145–6, 147, 173; *The Chinese Chameleon* 11, 114 n.159
de Haas, Jacob Hendrik ('Joep') 145, 146, 167
de Haas-Posthuma, Hermana 145, 146
Dean, David 189–90; *Unofficial Diplomacy* 55
Dean, Mary Alice 189–91, 193, 197

Dell, Edmund 41
Deng Xiaoping 137 n.14
Descartes, René 198
Destenay, Anne (*née* Hawtrey) 84, 99; *Nagel's Encyclopedia-Guide: China* 84 n.80, 117 n.168
Destenay, Patrick 84, 99
détente: Sino-American 18 n.48, 23, 24, 106 n.141; Sino-French 84 n.80
determinism 37
Deutsch, André 178
Deutscher, Isaac 142–3, 161
dialectical materialism 37
Dinner Party (television programme) 6
disarmament campaigns, nuclear 61, 62, 95, 239, 247, 251
Disraeli, Benjamin (*later* 1st Earl of Beaconsfield) 161
Dobb, Maurice 23, 134 n.5
Dodds, Annie ('Bet') 44
Dodds, Eric Robertson 44
dogs: eating of 79; performing 79
Doll, Sir Richard 33
Donald, Sir Alan 66, 71, 86, 92, 103, 108, 112, 113, 120, 234–7
Don't Let Irish Prisoners Die campaign 252
Douglas, Lucy 243
Doyle, Sir Arthur Conan 15
Driberg, Tom (*later* Baron Bradwell) 25
Driver, Sir Godfrey 42
Dufferin and Ava, Serena ('Lindy'), Marchioness of 172
Dufferin and Ava, Sheridan Hamilton-Temple-Blackwood, 5th Marquess of 171
Dunbar, Belhaven Hill preparatory school 228
Dunhuang caves *see* Tun-hwan caves
Dutt, Rajani Palme 30

Eden, Anthony (*later* 1st Earl of Avon) 26, 106 n.141, 138 n.18
Edinburgh, Prince Philip, Duke of 60, 68, 115 n.162
Edmonds, John 237 n.3
Eisenhower, Dwight D. 92 n.112
Ekaterinburg (Sverdlovsk) 57
elections *see* by-elections; general elections
Elgin, James Bruce, 8th Earl of 199 n.71

Eliot, George: *Middlemarch* 56, 207–8, 228–9; *The Mill on the Floss* 228
Elizabeth I, Queen 197
Elizabeth II, Queen, coronation 76 n.58, 115 n.162
Elliott, Nicholas 180
Ely Cathedral, desecration of statues 51
Empson, Sir William 10
Encounter (magazine): 'Arnold Toynbee's Millennium' (T-R; 1957) 215 n.107; 'E.H. Carr's Success Story' (T-R; 1962) 37; 'Ghana's February Revolution' (Hinden; 1967) 26 n.68; 'The L.S.E. Story' (Beloff; 1969) 45; 'Cambridge in the 1950s' (Johnson; 1974) 11 n.32; funding 184; T-R's suppressed article on SACU 34–5, 41, 52, 151–76
English Historical Review (journal) 91
English-language teaching: Basic English 60, 69, 74, 123; in China 120–21, 125
Epstein, Israel 5, 51
Epstein, Sir Jacob 122
European-China Association 136 n.8
Evans-Pritchard, Sir Edward, *Witchcraft, Oracles and Magic among the Azande* 1
Evergreen Commune 78
examinations, university: Chairman Mao's views on 20; Ernie Roberts' views on 20

factories, Chinese, Westerners' visits to: PRC 7, 75, 119, 125; ROC 197, 205–6
Fairfax-Cholmeley, Elsie 51
famine (PRC; 1958–61) 19, 79
Far Eastern Air Transport 203–4
Faringdon, Gavin Henderson, 2nd Baron 33
farms, Chinese, Westerners' visits to: PRC 7, 78; ROC 192–3
Faure, Edgar 112 n.152
Femina (magazine) 100
Finchley, Holden Road 135
Finley, Sir Moses 36
Five Year Plans (PRC) 120 n.175
Florence, under Savonarola 2
Fontainebleau Restaurant (London) 178
food and drink, in Cambodia and Thailand 220, 224–5

food and drink, in China, Hong Kong and Taiwan 210, 211, 217; American-style 190, 205; best restaurant in Taipei 195, 196; bull's penis soup 201; international-style 208, 210; Kinmen wine 212; orangeade 65; Peking duck 67; sea-slugs 115, 215; Shansi-style 216; Szechuan-style 75, 201–2; thrown on floor 63, 157
food and drink, in England: bread and cheese in Cambridge 243; dining in London clubs 134, 149, 178; Jewish bakers 252; molecular gastronomy 39; at Savoy Grill 25, 143, 161; in Soho 25, 147; stolen from market stalls 249; tea at Heathrow 131; *see also* champagne-drinking
Foot, Michael 136 n.8, 251
Football Association 53
Formosa *see* Taiwan
Forster, Edward Morgan, *A Passage to India* 191
Fort Zeelandia 204 n.79, 207
48 Group Club 137 n.16
Fowles, John 247
Franklin, Albert 10
Frederick the Great, King of Prussia 97
Frente Popular (Spain) 234 n.1
Freud, Lucian, 'Woman in a fur-coat' 76 n.58
Frink, Dame Elisabeth 48
Front Populaire (France) 234 n.1
Fuchow (Fuzhou) 9

Gaitskell, Hugh 251
Galileo Galilei 198
Galton Foundation 154 n.5
Gandhi, Indira 113 n.157
Gandhi, Rajiv 113 n.158
Ganges river 182
Garland, Margaret ('Peggy') 29, 44, 45–6, 49, 145 n.35, 169–70
Garrick Club 140, 178
gastronomy, molecular 39
Gaulle, Charles de 10, 226
Gelder, Stuart and Roma 20–21, 43, 51; *The Long March to Freedom* 20; *Memories for a Chinese Grand-daughter* 51, 154 n.4; *The Timely Rain* 20–21

general elections: (1945) 26, 30; (1964) 85; (1966) 166; (1979) 251; (1987) 252
Geneva, Calvinist 3
Genius of China exhibition (1973–74) 53
George VI, King, death 92
George, Timothy 66, 84, 86, 99, 100–101, 111, 125
Gibbon, Edward 122
Gilchrist, Sir Andrew 116 n.163, 124 n.186
Giles, Frank 134, 135
Gilmour, Sir Ian (later Baron Gilmour of Craigmillar), *The Body Politic* 249
Gobi desert 59, 128
Goddard, Jesse 214
Goddard, William George 214, 215; *Formosa: a study in Chinese history* 214
Gollan, John 24
Gollancz, Sir Victor 34
Gordievsky, Oleg 25
Gordon, Eric and Marie 51
Great Britain–China Committee/Centre 53
'Great Leap Forward' (PRC; 1958–62) 2, 17, 19, 21
Great Proletarian Cultural Revolution *see* Cultural Revolution
Great Wall of China 101–2, 128
Greene, Graham 117 n.166
Grey, Anthony 51
Groslier, Bernard-Philippe 224, 225–6, 227–30
Guan Yu 118
Guardian (newspaper) *see Manchester Guardian*
Guiringaud, Louis de 224–5

Hackney North and Stoke Newington (parliamentary constituency) 251, 252
Haddington, John Baillie-Hamilton, 13th Earl of 172
Haig, Douglas Haig, 1st Earl 202 n.75
Hailsham, Quintin Hogg, 2nd Viscount 136 n.8
Hale, Leslie (*later* Baron Hale) 25
Hall, Sir Noel 44, 167 n.19
Hampshire, Sir Stuart 42, 136 n.10, 181 n.15, 184
Hannington, Wal 250

Harrington, Illtyd 85 n.82
Harrison, Edward 180 n.11; *The Secret World* (ed.) 38
Hart, Sir Robert 86 n.87
Harvard University, John F. Kennedy Memorial Library 209
Hassan II, King of Morocco 154 n.6
Hawkes, Jacquetta 28
Hawkes, Leonard 31
Hayter, Sir William 67 n.40, 220 n.116, 224
He Wei 71
Heath, Sir Edward 26
Heathrow airport 131
Hegel, Georg Wilhelm Friedrich 229 n.136
Hepworth, Dame Barbara 34
Herodotus 2
Hilaly, Agha 106
Hill, Bridget 61
Hill, Christopher 61, 135 n.6, 179
Hinden, Rita, 'Ghana's February Revolution' 26, 26 n.68
Hiroshima, nuclear bombing 40, 147 n.40
Hitler, Adolf 3, 37, 97, 181 n.15, 223 n.121; *The Last Days of Hitler* (T-R) 38, 40, 90, 100, 236
Hiuan-tsang 121, 123
Ho Ch'ang Ch'ün 89
Ho Chi-minh 78
Hobbes, Thomas 197
Hobsbawm, Eric 36, 91 n.105
Hobson, Harold 246
Hodgkin, Dorothy 22, 33, 44, 167 n.19
Hodgkin, Thomas 61
Hohler, Christopher 220
Hohler, Frederick 220
Hollis, Sir Roger 26
Homer, *Odyssey* 91, 189
homosexuality 10
Hong Kong: cession to Britain 9, 80; T-R visits 54, 182, 213, 216–18
Hoover, Herbert 183 n.24
Hoover Institution (Stanford University) 183
Hopkins, Sir Frederick Gowland 28
Horace 95
Horsham (parliamentary constituency) 85
Horsley, Alec 23, 148
Hou Wai-lu 12, 89–90, 153 n.3

House Unamerican Activities Committee 44

Howard-Johnston, Lady Alexandra *see* Trevor-Roper, Lady Alexandra

Howard-Johnston, Clarence ('Johnny') 187 n.33

Howard-Johnston, James 144 n.31, 207–8

Hoxha, Enver 66 n.30

Hsia, Eddy Ti-Chiang (guide in Taiwan) 183, 184, 185, 186, 187, 191, 192, 197, 199, 200, 201, 203, 205, 206, 216

Hsinhua News Agency 175

Hsiung Hsiang-hui 106

Hsu, Edward 216

Hu Chi Chung 195, 196, 199

Hu, Moses 188

Hua-Lien 194, 203

Huc, Fr. Evariste Régis 2

Hudson, Geoffrey 16–17, 88 n.90, 167

Hué (Vietnam) 182

Hughes, Emrys 23

Hume, David, *Essays* 119

Hurd, Douglas (*later* Baron Hurd of Westwell), *The Arrow War* 199

Huxley, Sir Julian 82, 105 n.140, 244

I.C.I. (Imperial Chemical Industries) 58

Independent Television Authority 60, 154

Indo-China War (1962) 74, 76, 113

Indo-Pakistani War (1965) 63–4, 65, 67, 74, 157

Indonesia: *coup d'état* (1965) 116, 124, 128; mass killings (1965–66) 124

Information Research Department (Foreign Office; IRD) 32, 53, 237 n.3, 238

International Red Cross 90

Inverchapel, Archibald Clark Kerr, 1st Baron 30

IRD *see* Information Research Department (Foreign Office)

Irish Republican Army, Coventry bombing (1939) 249

Irkutsk 57–8, 128–9

Irrawaddy river 182

James, Henry, *The Golden Bowl* 137 n.15

Jao Tsung-i 214

Jarvis, Caroline (*later* Countess of Cranbrook) 76, 79

Jeffreys, George Jeffreys, 1st Baron 236

Jen Ying-lun 59, 67

Johnson, Harry, 'Cambridge in the 1950s' 11 n.32

Johnson, Hewlett 30, 33, 58 n.4

Johnson, Lyndon Baines 90, 116 n.164

Jones Soong, Charles 88 n.93

Joshi, Heather (*née* Spooner) 49

Kahn, Richard Kahn, Baron 23, 34

Kaldor, Nicholas Kaldor, Baron 39

Kambuja (periodical) 229

K'ang Hsi, Emperor 207

Kaohsiung 203–6; Export Processing Zone 205–6; Grand Hotel 204, 208

Kashmir 63–4, 65, 67, 74, 157

Kell, Sir Vernon 62 n.23

Kendall, Bridget, *The Cold War* 183 n.18

Kennet, Wayland Young, 2nd Baron 33

Kermode, Sir Frank 184 n.25, 184 n.27

Keynes, John Maynard Keynes, 1st Baron 23, 105 n.140

Khachaturian, Aram, *Spartacus* 92

Khrushchev, Nikita 105; denunciation of Stalin 31; jibes against Chinese 66 n.30

Kim Il Sung 35 n.94

King, Cecil 184 n.25

King-Hall, Stephen King-Hall, Baron 142–3, 161

Kinmen (Quemoy) islands: PRC bombardment (1958) 55, 210 n.93; T-R visits 210–213

Kirwan, Lawrence 146

Kissinger, Henry 18 n.48, 106 n.141

KLM (Dutch airline) 131

Koestler, Arthur 35

Koningsberger, Hans 11, 125 n.188

Korean War 55, 151

Kuan, Thomas 205

Kublai Khan 91 n.111

Kung Yung Ho 78 n.63

Kuo Mo-Jo 89

Kuomintang (KMT; Chinese nationalist party): under Sun Yat-sen 88 n.90; civil war 15–16, 19;

in Taiwan 54–5, 82 n.74, 186, 190, 201
Kurti, Nicholas: background, life and career 39–40, 137 n.13; member of SACU council of management 44, 137, 145, 147, 173; alliance with T-R 12, 38, 42–3, 46, 47–8, 49, 139, 144, 146, 148; joint-treasurer of SACU 42, 49, 148; resignation from SACU 50
Kwang-Yü 118

Lalla Aicha, Princess of Morocco 154
Lao She 67
Laud, William, Archbishop of Canterbury 229 n.136
Lauru, Charles 86 n.87
Laval, Pierre 223 n.121
Lawrence, Thomas Edward 246
Lawrence of Arabia (film) 246–7
le Carré, John *see* Cornwell, David
Lean, Sir David 246–7
Lee, Orient *see* Li Dong-fang
Lee, Yih-Shou 206
Lenin, Vladimir, mausoleum 88
Leningrad 92
Lennon, John 171 n.30, 225 n.126
Lessing, Doris 251
Levellers 51
Leys, Simon (Pierre Ryckmans) 7–8, 60 n.10, 110 n.148
Li Da Zhao 77 n.61
Li Dong-fang (Orient Li) 195, 196, 214, 215
Li Ji 195, 196
Li Tien-min 184–5
Liao Hong-ying 30
Lin Chiao-chih 115 n.160
Lin Yutang 9–10, 195, 200, 215
Lin Zhao 21
Lindemann, Frederick *see* Cherwell, Frederick Lindemann, 1st Viscount
Lindsay, Michael (*later* 2nd Baron Lindsay of Birker) 5, 8
Lindsay of Birker, Alexander 'Sandie', 1st Baron 8, 234 n.1
Liu Chin Mao 78 n.63
Liu Ning-i 67
Liu Shao-chi 99, 107, 185

Liu Ye Yuan 101, 103–4
Lloyd, Selwyn (*later* Baron Selwyn-Lloyd) 180 n.9
Lloyd-Jones, Sir Hugh 42
Logue, Christopher 247
Lombard, Denys 225
Lombard, Maurice 225
London Export Corporation 25
London School of Economics (LSE): student protests 18, 44–5; T-R speaks at (1968) 18
Longmen caves *see* Lungmen caves
Loyang (Luoyang) 114–20, 213; Bai ma si (White Horse Temple) 118; Kwang-ling museum 118; tractor and bull-dozer factories 117
LSE *see* London School of Economics
Lu Ting-i 101
Luard, Evan 167
Luce, Henry Robinson 209
Luce, Henry Winters 209
Lumumba, Patrice 35 n.94, 92
Lumumba, Pauline 92
Lungmen caves 117–18
Luoyang *see* Loyang

McCarthyism 35–6, 113; T-R accused of 35, 47, 48, 52, 171, 172
McCreery, Charles 144 n.31
McCreery, Michael 144
McCrystal, Cal, 'All-party group for Anglo-Chinese understanding' 29, 32, 46
MacFarquhar, Roderick 147
Machiavelli, Niccolò 197
Macintosh, Sir Robert 33
Mackay, George 188, 189
McLachlan, Donald 41
Maclean, Donald 215 n.107
Macmillan, Harold (*later* 1st Earl of Stockton) 92 n.112, 180; election as Oxford University chancellor 62 n.24
Madge, Charles 23
Malloch, Simon 189 n.40
Malraux, André 225–7
Manchester Guardian (newspaper) 143, 249, 251; 'Ex-Communist v. Communist' (T-R; 1950) 35

Manchester University 83, 246
Mao Tse-tung: birthplace and early life 69;
    in later life 100, 185; at National Day
    celebrations 109, 157; personality-
    cult of 100, 107, 109, 185; and
    Cultural Revolution 185; on mass
    extermination 18–19; on necessity of
    physical culture 87; on self-criticism
    104; on university examinations 20;
    Little Red Book 18, 43
Margate (Kent) 154 n.4
Marlowe, Christopher, *Doctor Faustus* 91
Martin, Kingsley 36
Marxist history and theory 36–7, 89–90, 91
    n.105, 103, 153 n.3, 163, 236
Masterman, Sir John Cecil 178 n.3
Masters, William 58
Matsu islands 55
Maugham, W. Somerset, *The Circle* 246
Maurice, Sir Frederick 143, 160
Maxwell, Robert 41
Medalla, David 196
Mehta, Jagat Singh 113
Mendelssohn, Kurt 11–12, 30, 39, 44, 46,
    49, 169 n.26
Menon, K.P.S. junior 113 n.158
Menon, K.P.S. senior 113
Meyer, Michael 117
MI5 *see* Security Service
MI6 *see* SIS
Mikardo, Ian 25, 251
Miles, Sarah 247
Millfield School 246
Milligan, Spike 136 n.11
Ming tombs 102–3
molecular gastronomy 39
Molesworth, Beatrix 75
Mongolia 58, 59
Monkey King, The (opera) 101, 103, 112
Montgomery of Alamein, Bernard
    Montgomery, 1st Viscount 106 n.141
Moon, Sun Myung 40
Morning Star (newspaper) 78 n.63, 156 n.8
Morris, Ivan 147
Moscow 129–31, 156; British Embassy
    129–30; GUM department store 66;
    Leningradskii Prospekt 129; Patrice
    Lumumba University 92 n.112;

Tretiakov Gallery 111; World Trade
    Conference (1952) 22–5
Mosley, Sir Oswald 23–4
motor cars, manufacture of 249, 250
Mott, Sir Nevill 48
Movement for Colonial Freedom 28 n.79,
    115 n.161
Muggeridge, Malcolm 6
Mullins, David 208
Munich, Forschungsinstitut 183
Munich Agreement (1938) 152
Mussolini, Benito 37, 223 n.121

Nanking (Nanjing) 13, 88, 102 n.137; Cen-
    tral School of Party Affairs 183 n.21
Nanking, Treaty of (1842) 9
National Council for the Unmarried
    Mother and her Child 154 n.5
National Day celebrations (PRC; 1 October)
    108–111, 157, 162
National Union of Teachers 98
Nature (magazine) 39–40
Nazism 3, 12, 97, 101, 166, 181 n.15; Nazi-
    Soviet Pact (1939) 249
Needham, Joseph: life, career and
    reputation 27–8, 29, 51, 62 n.23, 95,
    151; character and characteristics
    27–8, 29, 62 n.23, 151; political views
    28, 136, 151; BCFA chairman 27, 30;
    visits China 27, 28; SACU founder
    and chairman 32–3, 151–3, 174;
    membership of China Policy Study
    Group 71 n.48; invites T-R to become
    sponsor of SACU and join council
    of management 28–9, 33, 62, 151–3;
    T-R's relations with 29, 47, 62, 151;
    and T-R's further investigations of
    SACU 139; response to *Sunday Times*
    articles on SACU 35, 46–7, 142,
    170–71, 172, 240; correspondence
    with T-R following November 1965
    SACU open meeting 143, 144, 147,
    162, 241; at SACU annual general
    meeting (21 May 1966) 171, 172–3;
    and T-R's removal from council
    of management and resignation
    as sponsor 46–7, 49–50, 168 n.22,
    170–71, 172–3; on Rewi Alley 5 n.17;

on Maoist China 33, 50–52; *The Levellers and the English Revolution* 51; *Science and Civilisation in China* 1, 28, 29, 90 n.102, 152 n.2

New College (Oxford) 184

New Hungary (periodical) 146 n.37

New Statesman (magazine) 36, 145 n.33, 168 n.21; 'Europe and the Turk' (T-R; 1955) 35–6

Newman, John Henry 229

Nicholls, Robert ('Bob') 185–6, 188–91, 213, 216, 217

Nietzsche, Friedrich 83 n.75

Ningpo (Ningbo) 9

Nixon, Richard, détente with China 18 n.48, 23, 24, 106 n.141

Nkrumah, Kwame 26

NKVD (Soviet People's Commissariat for Internal Affairs) 5, 179 n.8

Noel, Conrad 62 n.23

Noel-Baker, Philip Noel-Baker, Baron 136

Notestein, Wallace 191

nuclear and atomic weapons: American 40; British 39; Chinese 17, 50; Civil Defence advice 250; *see also* disarmament campaigns

Observer (newspaper): 'British Trade with the Chinese' (Mikardo; 1956) 25 n.67; 'China from Inside' (Mendelssohn; 1971) 12 n.35; and Philby affair 178 n.3, 180; T-R as special correspondent 4, 54

Offord, Cyril 33

Ogden, Charles Kay 60 n.15

Omsk 129

'100 Flowers' movement (PRC; 1956–57) 4, 17, 84

O'Neill, Sir Con 199 n.71

Opangu, Pauline (Mme Lumumba) 92

opera: China 81, 87–8, 92, 100–101, 112–13, 119, 124, 125, 186–7, 202, 239–40; Taiwan 186–7, 188, 197, 202–3

Opium War (1839–42) 9, 63, 77 n.61, 78, 80

Oppenheimer, Robert 82 n.71

orchid-growing 206

Osborne, John 247

Owen, David Owen, Baron 136 n.8

Owen, Will 34

Oxford: Ashmolean Museum 136, 146; Clarendon Laboratory 39; Cowley 249; Headington House 226; Magdalen bridge 39; Maison Française 226; Nuffield College 145; Parks Road 39; Rose Place 249; St Aldate's 249; Sheldonian Theatre 226

Pakistan: Indo-Pakistani War (1965) 63–4, 65, 67, 74, 157; T-R visits 4

paper, invention of 103

Parthenon, proposed recreation 227

Partridge, Benjamin Waring II 189–90

Partridge, Cora (*née* Cheney) 189–91, 193, 197

Past & Present (journal) 91

Paterson, Betty 51

Pattison, Mark 228, 229

Pausanias 221

Pearl, Valerie 38, 43, 49, 135–6, 139, 143, 144, 147, 166 n.17, 171 n.30

peasant revolts, in China and Europe 236–7

Pei, Ieoh Ming 209

Peking (Beijing) 63, 72–3; Bei hai (Northern Lake) 91; Bi yun si (Monastery of the Azure Clouds) 85, 88; British Legation 17, 66, 154; Chien Men (Southern Gate) 72–3; Chien Men hotel 59, 65–6; Chuan Chu Te restaurant 66–7; Chung-shan Park 71; Great Hall of the People 69–70, 106, 111, 201; Hsin Chiao hotel 13, 27; Imperial College (Guo zi jian) 91 n.110; Imperial Palace 70, 73, 82–4; Jin Yang restaurant 99, 105; Kuo Tzŭ Chien (Hall of the Classics) 91; Lama Temple (Yong he gong) 91; Monument to the People's Heroes 63; Museum of Chinese History 77–8, 79; Museum of the Chinese Revolution 77; National Art Museum of China 111–12, 125; Old Summer Palace 81; Park of the Temple of Heaven 79; Russian Embassy 98–9, 111; Sports stadium 98 n.127, 99–100; Summer Palace

85–6, 94; Sun Yat-sen Theatre 71–2; Temple of Confucius 91, 122; Tiananmen (Gate of Heavenly Peace) 16; Tiananmen Square 63, 69 n.44, 73, 108–9, 110; Tien Tan (Temple of Heaven) 76–7, 79, 98, 102, 235; Wang Fu-chin department store 66; Wo fo si (Temple of the Sleeping Buddha) 85; Xian nong tan (Temples of Agriculture) 98

Peking Daily News 26, 175

Peking opera 81, 87–8, 100–101, 112–13, 239–40

Peking University 14–15, 80–81, 84, 153 n.3, 235–6, 238; Institute of History 89–91, 153 n.3, 235–6, 238; Library 81

Pema Tsedeun, Princess of Sikkim ('Coocoola') 140

Peng Zhen 109

Penghu islands *see* Pescadores islands

Penkovsky, Oleg 181

People's Daily (Chinese Communist Party newpaper) 175 n.36

Perry, Graham 43, 107–8, 161 n.12

Perry, Jack: background, early life and career 23–4, 137 n.14; character and characteristics 24, 137 n.14; political views 24; Security Service surveillance 24; visits China 24; delegate at 1952 Moscow Trade Conference 24–5; member of BCPIT executive committee 25, 26, 138; role in SACU 32, 137, 163–4, 237

Perry, Jillian (*later* Tallon) 164

Pescadores (Penghu) islands 211, 213

Pestalozzi, Johann 178

Peters, Robert 38

Peyrefitte, Alain 10–11, 18

Philby, John 180–81

Philby, Kim 56, 178–82

Philby: the spy who betrayed a generation (1968), David Cornwell's introduction 178

Philco-Ford (manufacturing company) 205

Philip, Prince, Duke of Edinburgh 60, 68, 115 n.162

Phnom Penh 221

Pincher, Chapman 179 n.7

Piratin, Phil 24

PKI (Indonesian Communist Party) 116 n.163, 124

Pollitt, Harry 24

Popular Front movement (Britain) 234 n.1

Powell, Frederick York 9 n.24

Price, Ronald, *Education in Communist China* 120 n.176

Pritchard, Sir Neil 216, 218, 220

Pritt, Denis Nowell 30

Progressive Businessmen's Forum 24–5, 27

Pu-Yi, Emperor 236

Pulleyblank, Edwin 136–7, 146, 147, 148, 149

Queensberry, David Douglas, 12th Marquess of 60 n.16

Quemoy islands *see* Kinmen islands

Quinton, Anthony Quinton, Baron 226–7

Quisling, Vidkun 223 n.121

Radcliffe, Cyril Radcliffe, 1st Viscount 179 n.7

Radio Analysis Bureau (*later* Radio Intelligence Service) 181 n.15, 184 n.27

Rama V (Chulalongkorn), King of Siam 220

Rambert, Dame Marie 34

Raphael, Frederic 247

Read, Sir Herbert 48

'Rectification' campaign (PRC; 1957–59) 84

Red Cross, International 90

Red Gang (triad) 88 n.93

Red Lantern, The (opera) 87–8, 93, 100

Redgrave, Sir Michael 247

Redgrave, Vanessa 62, 75, 96, 247

Reilly, Sir Patrick 27, 54, 66 n.32, 85 n.81, 213 n.99

Republic of China *see* Taiwan

Reunion in an Old City (opera) 202

Ricci, Matteo 2, 112

Richard III, King 236

Richards, Ivor Armstrong 60 n.15

Richardson, Tony 62 n.22

Roberts, Ernie: background, life and career 6, 71, 85, 94–5, 155, 248–52; appearance, character and characteristics 61, 69, 71, 84–5, 94–5, 98, 102, 115, 127, 155, 250; political views 43, 61, 62, 68–9, 79, 98, 115, 136, 155, 234, 239, 249, 250–52; role in SACU 43, 105, 137, 139, 146, 163; during 1965 China trip 6–7, 65, 76, 79, 84–5, 94–5, 98, 105, 155–6, 158; at CPA banquet 67, 68–9, 234; meets Chinese trade unionists 67, 78; tour of Imperial Palace 70; at Museum of Chinese History 79; excursion to Summer Palace 87–8; at Peking opera 87, 93; at the theatre 92, 93; tour of Ming tombs 102; at Great Hall of the People banquet 106; at National Day celebrations 110; at presentation to 'Heads of State' 111; trips to Loyang and Sian 114–15, 116, 118, 124, 126; travels on to Shanghai with Mary Adams 127; reaction to T-R's *Sunday Times* article on China trip 159 n.11, 241–2; and attempts to found Oxford branch of SACU 167; at open meeting of SACU (16 November 1965) 135, 140, 141, 144, 160, 239, 240; at SACU council of management meeting (13 December 1965) 148–9, 165; at SACU annual general meeting (21 May 1966) 171, 172; last months of life 242, 248 n.14; *Strike Back* (memoirs) 95 n.123, 115 n.161, 159 n.11, 242, 248 n.14

Robinson, Joan: background, career and reputation 22–3, 134 n.5, 143; character and characteristics 22–3, 47–8, 143–4; political views 23, 43, 105 n.139; delegate at 1952 Moscow Trade Conference 22–3; speaks at Progressive Businessmen's Forum lunches 25; deputy at BCPIT 25, 138; visits China 20; views on Maoist China 11, 20, 43, 81 n.69; role in SACU 11, 32, 43, 136, 138, 139, 163, 244; membership of China Policy Study 71 n.48, 135; T-R reports to on return from China trip 134–5; at open meeting of SACU (16 November 1965) 140–42, 160, 161, 240; writes to T-R after meeting 143; and T-R's further investigations of SACU 164; at SACU council of managment meeting (13 December 1965) 165; response to May 1966 *Sunday Times* article on SACU 35, 46–8, 171, 172; at SACU annual general meeting (21 May 1966) 171, 172–3; and removal of T-R from SACU council of management 46–8, 171, 172–3; *The Cultural Revolution in China* 20, 81 n.69, 105 n.139; *Letters from a Visitor to China* 20, 66 n.34

Romania, T-R visits 4, 207–8

Rosenthal, Albrecht ('Albi') 214

Roy, Jules, *Le voyage en Chine* 14–15

Royal Institute of International Affairs (Chatham House) 183; T-R's 'China Today' talk 140

Royal Society 39; delegations to China 28, 44, 136 n.11

Rubery Owen (engineering company) 26

Rumbold, Sir Anthony 213, 216

Russell, Bertrand Russell, 3rd Earl 33, 64, 85, 95, 105 n.140, 251; nearly dies in China 72

Russian Revolution (1917) 3, 175; *see also* Bolshevism

Russo-German Non-Aggression Pact (1939) 249

Russo-Japanese War (1904–5) 73 n.54

Ryckmans, Pierre *see* Leys, Simon

Ryle, Gilbert 42

SACU *see* Society for Anglo-Chinese Understanding

SACU News (periodical) 68 n.42, 138, 139, 143, 160, 167, 175, 245 n.4; editorship 138; Robert Bolt interview (November 1965) 72 n.51, 88 n.89, 93 n.116, 119 n.173, 248

Salisbury, Godolphin School 243

Salisbury, Robert Gascoyne-Cecil, 3rd Marquess of 161

Salter, Arthur Salter, 1st Baron, on Chiang Kai-shek 82 n.74

Sanders, J.H., 'Nicholas Kurti CBE' 39 n.107

Sands, Bobby 252
SAS (airline), Trans-Asiatic express 177, 182
Savile Club 134, 196
Savonarola, Girolamo 2
Savoy Grill (London) 25, 143, 161
Scargill, Arthur 248 n.14
schools (British), teachers' strikes 98
schools (Chinese): teaching 121; Western
    tourists' visits to 73–4
Schrödinger, Erwin 39
Scotland-China Association 149
Scrivener, Mary 220, 231 n.138
Scrivener, Ronald 220, 221, 231 n.138
Scurlock, Ralph, 'Nicholas Kurti' 39 n.107
Seale, Patrick 178 n.3
Second World War: outbreak 249–50;
    wartime intelligence work 41–2, 181
Secret Intelligence Service *see* SIS
secret police: Chinese 15, 185; Soviet 5, 179
    n.8
Security Service (MI5): monitoring
    of Society for Anglo-Chinese
    Understanding 32, 40–41;
    surveillance of CPGB members
    24, 25, 26, 27, 137 n.16; wartime
    intelligence work 41–2
self-righteousness, of Chinese 64–5, 96, 97,
    104, 113, 126, 245, 248
Semedo, Álavaro de 122
Sen, Amartya 134 n.5
Shakespeare, William: *Hamlet* 110; *Henry
    IV Part I* 109
Shanghai 5, 9, 127, 187, 199 n.71
Shapiro, Michael 51
Sherwood, James 94 n.122
Sian (Xi'an) 120–26; Da Yan Ta (Big Goose
    Pagoda) 121, 123; factories 125;
    Historical Museum 122–3; Nestorian
    Stele 122, 123; Zhong lou (Bell
    Tower) 121
Siem Reap 221, 224; museum 227–8; *see
    also* Angkor ruins
Sihanouk, Norodom, King of Cambodia
    229; state visit to Peking 99–100, 101,
    107 n.143, 109
Sikkim 113, 140 n.23
Silver, Adolphe 23, 128
Silverman, Sydney 23, 251

Simon, Sir Francis (Franz) 39
Simpson, Alexander 94 n.121
Sino-British Scientific Cooperation Office
    28
Sino-Indian War (1962) 74, 76, 113
Sino-Japanese War (1894–95) 73 n.54
Sino-Japanese War (1937–42) 4, 28
Sino-Soviet split (1956–66) 31, 143 n.28
SIS (Secret Intelligence Service; MI6) 40,
    92 n.112, 116 n.164, 117 n.166;
    Philby affair 178–82; wartime
    intelligence work 41–2, 181
Smith, Adam 206
Smith, Alfred Lionel 61 n.20
Society for Anglo-Chinese Understanding
    (SACU): origins and formation 6, 22,
    27, 31–4, 135, 152–3; as communist
    front organization 6, 29, 32, 35,
    40, 45–6, 105, 133, 135–6, 173–6;
    sponsors 32–4, 48, 136 n.11; council
    of management 136–7, 148–9,
    163–4; budgets and finances 42,
    138, 139, 148, 162–3, 165–6, 174–5;
    organization of trips to China for
    British tourists 6, 53; Barnet branch
    21, 43, 166, 170; Cambridge branch
    43; Oxford branch 43–6, 49–50,
    144–5, 166–8, 169; T-R's membership
    and investigation of 6, 28–9,
    33–43, 133–49, 151–68, 173–6; open
    meeting (16 November 1965) 42–3,
    135, 140–43, 158, 160–61, 238–40;
    council of management meeting (13
    December 1965) 42–3, 144, 148–9,
    164–6; annual general meeting (21
    May 1966) 46, 168, 169, 171–3; T-R's
    resignation from 45–50, 52, 168–73,
    176; during Cultural Revolution
    50–53; *see also SACU News*
Society for Cultural Relations between
    the Peoples of the British
    Commonwealth and the USSR 105
Soong, T.V. 88 n.93, 191 n.50
Spanish Civil War 5
Sparrow, John, *Mark Pattison and the Idea
    of a University* 228 n.134
Spear, Ruskin 34
Spence, Sir Basil 34

Spencer, Sir Stanley 31
Spooner, Heather (*later* Joshi) 49–50
Spooner, William 249
Stalin, Joseph, Khrushchev's denunciation 31
Stanford University, Hoover Institution 183
Stern, Elizabeth ('Libby') 223
Stern, Eugene 223
Stiglitz, Joseph 134 n.5
Stockwood, Mervyn, Bishop of Southwark 33
'Stone-face' *see* To Chi-lou (guide in Peking)
Strachey, John 234 n.1
Stuart, Charles 36, 42
student protests (1960s) 18, 44–5
Suharto, Muhammad 35 n.94, 124 n.187
Sukarno (Kusno Sosrodihardjo) 116, 124
Sun Yat-sen 71 n.50; mausoleum 88
Sunday Times: 'Playwright to Watch' (Hobson; 1957) 246; 'Mr Coward had the last of the wine' (Bolt; 1961) 247; 'An Old Religion's Fire Burns Low' (T-R; 1961) 1; 'All-party group for Anglo-Chinese understanding' (Barry/McCrystal; 1965) 29, 32, 46; 'The Sick Mind of China' (T-R; 1965) 3, 6, 9, 34, 52, 132, 133–4, 135, 142, 156, 158–60, 161, 238–9, 240, 241–2; 'Battle to Control China Society' (Barry; 1966) 46, 169, 170–71; 'The essential heretic' (T-R; 1966) 36; 'The scholar's private world' (T-R; 1977) 44; 'The bitter lessons of the great McCarthy terror' (T-R; 1978) 35; 'Insight' team 169 n.23, 178; letters page 139; and Philby affair 178–9; T-R as special correspondent 4
Sutherland, Sir Gordon 33, 42, 136, 139, 140, 144, 148, 162–3
Sverdlovsk (Ekaterinburg) 57
Swann, Peter 136, 137, 145, 146
Swann, Robert 218, 219–20, 222

Taichung 207–210, 211; Provincial Assembly and Government 209–210; Tunghai University 208–9
Tainan 204–5, 206–7; Fort Zeelandia 204 n.79, 207; Koxinga's temple 204, 206–7

Taipei: Agricultural Exhibition Hall 187; Ambassadors hotel 183; Confucian temple 186; Historical Museum 213–14; National Palace Museum 187, 202, 213, 216; Taoist temple 186
Taiwan (Formosa; ROC): Kuomintang rule 54–5, 82 n.74, 186, 190, 201, 217; T-R visits 9, 54, 55–6, 177, 182–216
Taiwan (institutions): Academia Sinica 44, 191–2, 196, 201, 215; China Academy 201, 214; Chinese Culture University 197, 200, 214 n.102; Council for International Economic Co-operation and Development 188; Fu Sheng opera school 197; Government Information Office 183; Institute of International Relations 183–4; Institute of Pacific Relations 214; National Chengchi University (National University of Governance) 183 n.21, 187; National Taiwan University 197–200; Sino-American Joint Commission on Rural Reconstruction 188; Tunghai University 208–9; War Academy 200–201, 214–15
Taiwan (landmarks & places): An-ping 207; Hua-Lien 194, 203; Kaohsiung 203–6, 208; Kinmen islands 55, 210–213; Pescadores islands 211, 213; Taichung 207–210; Tainan 204–5, 206–7; Tamsui 188–9; Tamsui river 188; Taoyuang 192–3; Taroko Gorge 193–4, 203; Yang Ming Shan 197 n.68, 214; *see also* Taipei
Taiwan Ribao (*Taiwan Daily News*) 216
Tallon, Claude 164 n.15
Tallon, David 164
Tallon, Jillian (*née* Perry) 164
Tam-Tam de Combat sur l'Equateur (play) 92–3
Taoism 83, 186
Taoyuang 192–3
Taroko Gorge 193–4, 203
Tashkent 177, 182
Tawney, Richard Henry, *The Attack*, T-R's review 1
Telephone Users' Association 80, 154
Teller, Edward 39

Teng, O.I. 87

Tennant, Peter 25

Thailand: T-R visits 54, 56, 182, 218–21, 222, 231 n.138; *see also* Bangkok

theatres, Chinese: Western tourists' visits to 71–2, 92–3; *see also* opera

Thistlethwaite, Richard ('Dick') 40–41, 47, 134, 148 n.41, 165 n.16

Thompson, Sir Harold 44, 53, 167 n.19

Thompson, James ('Jim') 222

Thomson, George 71, 137 n.15, 163 n.14

Thorpe, Jeremy 136, 144, 170

Tibet 21, 68, 155, 234

Timberlake, Percy 32, 43, 137–8, 139; *The 48 Group: the story of the Icebreakers in China* 26

Ting hsi-lin 66–7

To Chi-lou (guide in Peking; 'Stone-face'/'Cement-head') 59–60, 63–4, 70, 79, 84, 86, 96, 101, 126, 157

To Tiu Feng 87

Tolstoy, Leo 228

Topolski, Feliks 115

Toynbee, Arnold 205, 215

Toynbee, Philip 215 n.107

tractors: manufacture of 117; replace water-buffaloes 192

trade unions: British 61, 98, 155, 158, 170 n.28, 249–51; Chinese 67 n.38, 78 n.63, 117

train travel, in China 114, 119, 120, 126–7

Trevelyan, Sir Humphrey (*later* Baron Trevelyan) 53, 99 n.129, 106 n.141, 129, 199 n.71

Trevor-Roper, Lady Alexandra (*earlier* Howard-Johnston; 'Xandra'): family background 202 n.74; character and characteristics 92 n.114, 146 n.38; first marriage 187; marriage to T-R 92 n.114; visits Leningrad with T-R (1957) 92; meets T-R on return from China trip 129, 131; attends November 1965 open meeting of SACU 141, 143, 160–61; at Malraux lecture in Oxford 226; joins T-R on trip to Taiwan, Hong Kong and Cambodia (1967) 55, 177; the journey to Taiwan 182; arrival in Taipei 182–3; at Institute

of International Relations 184; at lectures on land reform and rural reconstruction 188; at dinner with Bob Nicholls 189; shopping trips 191, 199, 210, 217, 219, 222; at dinner with James Wei 196; falls ill 199, 200, 201, 203, 208; at the opera 202–3; tour of Kaohsiung, Tainan and Taichung 203–5, 206, 208; trip to Kinmen islands 210–213; last day in Taiwan 216; in Hong Kong on route to Thailand 216–18; in Bangkok 218, 219, 220; in Cambodia 221, 222; returns to England via Bangkok 222, 231 n.138

Trevor-Roper, Hugh (*later* Baron Dacre of Glanton): All Souls fellowship examination 62 n.24; wartime intelligence work 41–2, 181; research for *The Last Days of Hitler* 40, 236; special correspondent for *Observer* and *Sunday Times* 4, 54; post-war intelligence work in Oxford 41; meets Malraux in Paris 226; delegate at Berlin Congress for Cultural Freedom 35, 184; marriage 92 n.114; visits Soviet Union (1957) 92, 116 n.165; role in 1960 Oxford University chancellorship election 62 n.24; becomes sponsor of Society for Anglo-Chinese Understanding 6, 28, 33, 62, 151–3; nominated to SACU council of management 6, 28–9, 153; invited to join group trip to People's Republic of China 6, 12, 29, 93, 153–4; travelling companions 6–7, 60–62, 154–5; the journey to China 57–9, 156; arrival in Peking 59–60; in China (September–October 1965) 2, 3, 12–13, 63–128, 156–8, 233–4; initial tour of Peking 63, 157; first night's dinner 63–4, 157; lunch at British Legation 66, 233–5; CPA banquet 66–9; tour of Great Hall of the People and Imperial Palace 69–70, 73, 201; *chargé d'affaires'* reception for Chinese students 71, 75, 233–4; student acrobats' performance 71–2; explores Peking on foot 72–3; arts-and-crafts factory visit 75; dines with Robert and Natalie Bevan 75–6; visits Temple of Heaven and Museum of Chinese History 76–8, 79; tour of market-gardening commune 78; at the circus 79; visits Peking University 80–81, 235–6; returns to Imperial Palace 82–3; dines with Timothy George 84; excursion to Wo fo si, Bi yun si and Summer Palace 85–7, 88, 94; first visit to Peking opera 87–8; meets historians at Institute of History 2, 12, 89–91, 235–6, 238; visits Lama Temple, Hall of the Classics and Northern Lake 91; at the theatre 92–3; assessment of first week in China 93–8; returns to Temple of Heaven 98; at rally for state visit of King Sihanouk 99–100, 101, 166; returns to Peking opera 100–101, 202; tour of Great Wall and Ming tombs 101–3; dines with Alan Donald 103, 112, 235–7; questions Chinese drama critic 103–4; trip to 'art' shop 104; tea with *chargé d'affaires* followed by banquet in Great Hall of the People 106–8; at National Day celebrations 108–111; presentation to 'Heads of State' 111; visits National Art Museum 111–12, 125; third visit to Peking opera 103, 108, 112–13, 202; discusses future of SACU with Robert Bolt 113–14; trips to Loyang and Sian 114–26; returns to Peking 126–8, 158; leaves China 126 n.189, 158; returns to London via Moscow and Amsterdam 128–32, 173; writes article on China trip for *Sunday Times* 34, 52, 132, 133–4, 156, 158–9; reports to SACU London office on China trip 134–5; reaction to publication of *Sunday Times* article 135, 142, 159–60, 161, 238–9, 240, 241–2; further investigation of SACU 34–40, 45–50, 135–40, 144–8, 162–4, 173–6; 'China Today' talk at Chatham House 140;

meets Princess Coocoola of Sikkim 140; at open meeting of SACU (16 November 1965) 42–3, 135, 140–43, 160–61, 238–40; aftermath of the meeting 143–4, 161–2; lunches with Roderick MacFarquhar and Ivan Morris 147–8; at SACU council of management meeting (13 December 1965) 42–3, 144, 148–9, 164–5; removal from SACU council of management and resignation as sponsor 45–50, 168–73, 176; visits Romania (March 1967) 4, 207–8; attends Malraux lecture in Oxford 226–7; discusses Philby affair over lunch with Dick White in London 177–82; visits Taiwan (November–December 1967) 9, 54, 55–6, 177, 182–216; the journey to Taiwan 182; arrival in Taipei 182–3; at Institute of International Relations 183–6; visits Confucian and Taoist temples in Taipei 186; witnesses open-air opera 186–7; at exhibition of agriculture and land reform 187; first visit to National Museum 187; at lectures on land reform and rural reconstruction 188, 190; dines with Bob Nicholls 188–91, 217; visits Academia Sinica 191–2; trip to Taoyang farm area 192–3; expedition to Taroko Gorge 193–4, 203; dines with James Wei 195–7; visits Fu Sheng opera school 197; lectures to students at National Taiwan University and Chinese Culture University 197–200; falls ill 199; visits War Academy 200–201; returns to National Museum 202; at the opera 202–3; tour of Kaohsiung, Tainan and Taichung 203–210; trip to Kinmen islands 210–213; visits Historical Museum in Taipei 213–14; interviewed by journalist from *Taiwan Daily News* 216; final visit to National Museum 216; speech to War Academy 213, 214–15; last evening in Taiwan 216; in Hong Kong on route to Thailand 216–18;

in Bangkok 218–21; dines with Ambassador Pritchard 216, 220; the flight to Cambodia 219, 221; visits Angkor ruins 199, 210, 213, 221–4, 227–8, 229–31; dines with Bernard-Philippe Groslier 224–7; attends performance of Cambodian classical dance 231; returns to England via Bangkok 222, 231 n.138

Character & characteristics: analytical rigour 41; clubs 40, 134, 140 n.22; ebullience 7; fear of flying 177, 182; ill health 114, 119, 125, 199; lack of small talk 7; language skills 1; love of ruins 227–8; not 'a joiner' 153; social skills 7

Views and ideas on: American behaviour and manners 189–90, 191, 193, 200, 217, 223, 231; American doctors 223; American university students 198; British Empire 217; Chinese art, architecture and literature 3, 83, 97, 102, 104, 201, 202; Chinese national character traits 64–5, 79, 83, 104, 115–16; communism 37–8, 83, 96–7, 115, 175; comparative religion 1; cross-cultural understanding 152, 175; Czechs 58; determinism 37; dialectical materialism 37; European history 1; funding of *Encounter* magazine 184; historical continuities 3, 97; McCarthyism 35–6; Maoist revolution 3–4, 83, 96–7; Marxist history and theory 36–7, 89–90, 103, 236; meritocracy 115; Nazism 3, 97, 101; non-European civilizations 1; peasant revolts 236–7; political power 38; pre-revolutionary China 9, 97; restoration of ruins 227–8; role of historians 2; ruling classes 115; Scotland 149; spies 179; water-buffaloes 192 n.52, 193, 202

Works (articles & reviews): 'Ex-Communist v. Communist' (1950) 35; 'Fifty Years of Change' (1953) 1; 'Kersten, Himmler and Count Bernadotte' (1953) 100; 'Europe and the Turk' (1955) 35–6; 'Arnold Toynbee's Millennium' (1957) 215 n.107; 'Through Eastern Eyes' (1959) 1, 9; 'Puritans – from Calvin to Castro' (1960) 2–3, 4; 'An Old Religion's Fire Burns Low' (1961) 1; 'E.H. Carr's Success Story' (1962) 37; 'Religion, the Reformation and Social Change' (1963) 29; 'The Sick Mind of China' (1965) 3, 6, 9, 34, 52, 132, 133–4, 135, 142, 156, 158–60, 161, 238–9, 240, 241–2; 'The essential heretic' (1966) 36; 'China, The Revolution Devours its Children' (1967) 3; 'Understanding Mao; or, Look Back to Stalin' (1967) 3; 'The Customs of the Country' (1976) 2; 'An Imperialist's Progress' (1976) 2; 'The scholar's private world' (1977) 44; 'The bitter lessons of the great McCarthy terror' (1978) 35; 'History and Imagination' (1980) 37; 'A Spiritual Conquest?' (1985) 2

Works (books): *The Balkan Journals* (forthcoming) 4; *From Counter-Reformation to Glorious Revolution* (1992); *A Hidden Life: the enigma of Sir Edmund Backhouse* (1976) 2, 38; *Historical Essays* (1957) 36 n.97; *The Last Days of Hitler* (1947) 38, 40, 90, 100, 236; *One Hundred Letters* (2014) 1, 2, 192 n.52; *The Philby Affair* (1969) 56; *Religion, The Reformation and Social Change* (1967) 38; *The Rise of Christian Europe* (1965) 2, 220; *The Secret World: behind the curtain of British Intelligence in World War II and the Cold War* (2014) 38; *Why I Oppose Communism* (introduction; 1956) 38

Tsao Kue-bing (guide in Peking) 59–60, 64, 111

Tsao Yü 67

Tsao-Tsao 236

Tun-hwan (Dunhuang) caves 214

Tupolev (aircraft) 57 n.3

Turfan (Turpan) 192, 214

Turner, Adrian, *Robert Bolt* 245 n.5

Tz'u Hsi, Empress Dowager 85 n.85, 86

Ulaan Baattor 58
Unification Church ('Moonies') 40
United Nations 93; Security Council 55
United Nations Relief and Rehabilitation
    Administration (UNRRA)
    26
Untung bin Syamsuri 116, 124
Usborne, Henry 23

Vanguard (magazine) 144 n.31
Vansittart, Robert Vansittart, 1st Baron, on
    Chiang Kai-shek 82 n.74
Vauban, Sébastien Le Prestre, Marquis de
    212
Vaughan, Dorothy, *Europe and the Turk*
    35
Vaughan, Dame Janet 33, 48
Vickers, Dame Joan (*later* Baroness Vickers)
    136, 144, 170
Victory for Socialism group 251
Vietnam War 17, 43, 52, 107 n.143, 182,
    218, 227, 239
Vishnayagan 222
Vladimir (Russia) 116
Voice of America (radio station) 124
Volkov, Konstantin 179
Voltaire 122; description of Chinese visitor
    to Holland 198
Voluntary Service Overseas (VSO) 219

Waley, Arthur, *The Opium War through Chi-
    nese Eyes*, T-R's review 1
Walker, Julian 238
Wallace, Henry 223
Wallace-Hadrill, John Michael 91 n.104
Wan Li, Emperor 118; tomb 102
Wang Chia Ching 78 n.63
Wang Ling 90
Wang Sheng 202
Wang Shih-chieh 191–2
Warner, Rex 31
Warsaw 131
water-buffaloes, Asiatic 192, 193, 202
Waugh, Evelyn 62 n.24
Wedderburn, Kenneth William ('Bill'; *later*
    Baron Wedderburn of Charlton) 141,
    142, 160

Wei, James ('Jimmie'; Wei Ching Meng)
    183, 195, 196–7
Wellby, Peter 219–20
Wells, Herbert George 196
Wesker, Sir Arnold 247, 251
West, Mae 211 n.95
Wheare, Joan, Lady (*née* Randell) 82 n.70
Wheare, Sir Kenneth 82 n.70
Which? (magazine) 244
White, Sir Dick 40, 56, 61 n.20, 62 n.22,
    134, 177–82, 184
White, Patrick 170 n.27
White Serpent, The (opera) 112, 202
White Terror (Taiwan) 55
Widgery, John Widgery, Baron 169 n.23
Wigg, George Wigg, Baron 182
Wiles, Peter 23
Wilford, Sir Michael 66, 123, 233–4
William II, German Emperor 73 n.54
Willoughby de Eresby, Jane Heathcote-
    Drummond-Willoughby, 27th
    Baroness 76, 79
Wilson, Harold (*later* Baron Wilson of
    Rievaulx) 17, 23, 116 n.164, 179,
    182
Winkleman, Leonard 24
Winnington, Alan 5
Woddis, Hillel Chayim ('Jack') 28
Woman General of the Yang Family (opera)
    100, 202
Women's Group on Public Welfare
    154 n.5
Wood, Sir Andrew 129–31
Woolf, Leonard 48
Woolf, Virginia 105 n.140
World Peace Council 138 n.17
World Trade Conference (Moscow;
    1952) 22–5
Wu Nanru 214, 215
Wu The Yao 209
Wynne, Greville 181 n.14

Xiamen *see* Amoy
Xi'an *see* Sian

Yang Chin 202
Yangtze River 114 n.159

Yao Chia-chi 89
Yeh, George Kung-chao 195, 196
Yellow River 114; flooding 19, 114; Three
    Gate Gorge dam 19
Yen Chia-kan 190, 196
Yeo, Charles Z. 188, 190
Yuan Chin-shen 199

Yung Cheng 91
Yung Lo, Emperor 225; tomb 102–3

Zaehner, R.C. ('Robin'), *The Dawn and
    Twilight of Zoroastrianism* 1
Zilliacus, Konni 251